PROGRESS AGAINST GROWTH

PROGRESS
AGAINST GROWTH

Daniel B. Luten on the American Landscape

Edited by
THOMAS R. VALE
University of Wisconsin—Madison

INTRODUCTION BY GARRETT HARDIN

Drawings by Faye Field   *Figures by Adrienne Morgan*

THE GUILFORD PRESS
New York   London

© 1986 The Guilford Press
A Division of Guilford Publications, Inc.
200 Park Avenue South, New York, N.Y. 10003

Printed in the United States of America

Art on part opening pages © 1986 Faye Field

LIBRARY OF CONGRESS CATALOGING IN PUBLICATION DATA

Luten, Daniel B.
  Progress against growth.

  Bibliography: p.
  Includes index.
  1. Environmental policy—United States.
  2. Conservation of natural resources—United States.
  3. Economic development—Environmental aspects.
  I. Vale, Thomas R., 1943–   . II. Title.
  HC110.E5L88   1986   333.7′2′0973   86–14296
  ISBN 0-89862-665-X

FOR LOIS LUTEN

ACKNOWLEDGMENT

My special thanks go to my wife, Geraldine, whose skill with the language I have depended on once again.

T. R. V.

PREFACE

During the 1960s and 1970s, no natural resource geographer on the West Coast influenced people more than Daniel B. Luten. His work revealed an unusual blending of technological expertise and humanistic competence. As a professor at the University of California at Berkeley, he stirred students' awareness of environmental concerns with his broad, exceptionally perceptive insights. He typically prodded his peers into reevaluating their positions. As a conservation activist, notably with the Sierra Club, he helped to guide the course of the American environmental movement.

Yet his articles and papers have been scattered, often appearing in narrowly circulated journals or as unpublished talks. This book gathers together some of Luten's best and most important papers and makes them readily available. The papers are arranged into seven topical sections. Within each group, the papers are generally presented chronologically, from least to most recent. Each section and each paper is prefaced by editorial comments that put the material in perspective.

The selections can be read for different reasons. First, they present basic factual material, such as the importance of different crops in American agriculture, the ways in which we use energy resources, or a description of the physical environment of the Colorado River. Their utility as a source of bald facts is mixed: Most of the facts in this collection continue "true" through time, but a few are time-specific and thus less valid today than when Luten wrote them. This reason for reading the book is the least important, and it certainly would not have been sufficient motivation for creating this volume.

Second, the papers may be read as history. Because each section is arranged chronologically, the reader can trace changing attitudes and perspectives on resource issues, not only within the mind of an astute observer but also within American society.

Third, and most importantly, the papers reveal the guiding philosophies of a remarkable student of natural resource controversies.

The reader can see the logic of a probing, even a skeptical, conservationist who tries to understand the nature of resource problems and conservation traditions. He has shown us the importance of considering the magnitudes of phenomena, looking at the implications of stances, and questioning assumptions. How he has approached his subjects and what he has done with them makes his papers valuable, independent of the time in which they were written. It is for this reason that this book has been compiled.

THOMAS R. VALE

INTRODUCTION

Some of those who claim the intellectual world as their territory are apt to think that appearances have no bearing on a man's role and effectiveness in life. This is not so, as is well known to every actor and politician. With statistical significance, the character and influence of a person are *not* independent of his or her appearance—though we can argue about which is cause and which effect until the end of time.

Physically, Daniel B. Luten is the very picture of a reasonable man. Here is no Cassius with a lean and hungry look, but one of the sleek-headed, such as sleep o'nights. We are not surprised to learn of his years of service to industry and to the military during the occupation of Japan. People recognize him as a man to be trusted, and this has been one of the reasons for his effectiveness. As a cherished advisor of David Brower, long-time executive director of the Sierra Club and later of Friends of the Earth, Luten's influence has extended to millions who may be no more than vaguely aware of his name.

A most admirable feature of Dan's life is the way his years of service to special interests have failed to bind his mind to their unexamined goals. His steadfast aim has been to further community goals, to which special interests must be subservient. Not many with his occupational background would say, as he did in 1972, that "moving water is more to be admired than used . . . the primary purpose of water is to beautify the earth."

To appreciate the revolutionary implications of this statement, we need to contrast it with one made by Winston Churchill in 1907. Standing on the brink of one of the natural falls of the Nile in East Africa, he wrote: "At your feet, literally a yard away, a vast green slope of water races downward. Below are foaming rapids, fringed with splendid trees, and pools from which great fish leap continually in the sunlight. . . . So much power running to waste, such a coign of vantage unoccupied, such a lever to control the natural forces of Africa ungripped, but vex and stimulate the imagination. And what fun to make the immemorial Nile begin its journey by diving through a turbine!''

The 33-year-old man who wrote these words was not insensitive to beauty, but he was thoughtlessly willing to destroy beauty to serve what most men of his time called "Progress" (as some still do). Churchill's was the orthodox attitude in 1907. It is so no longer, and Luten is one of a multitude of men and women who have persuaded the movers and shakers of this world to reexamine their concept of progress. The unhappy outcome of interventions like that of the High Aswan Dam (a remote consequence of Churchill's eloquent prose) have at last convinced many decision makers that they must take seriously the ecologist's nagging question, "And then what?"

Every deliberate intervention in the system of nature has had consequences we had not planned, and it is astonishing how our mastery of the art of generating new language is used to shield us from recognizing these consequences. The name "pesticides" focuses our attention on pests only, "herbicides" on weeds only, and "antibiotics" on human pathogens only. Each prejudicial term is a set of blinders to our mental eyes. Beyond the chosen rhetorical target a precipice opens up to more complete knowledge, but the skill with which we skirt this precipice would, in Luten's words, "amaze anyone but a rock climber."

"Reclamation" is one of these prejudicial words. When an estuary that has served as a nursery for marine life and a haven for migratory birds for a million years is filled in to serve as a site for factories, the resulting destruction is labeled "reclamation." If it were honestly named, the Bureau of Reclamation would be called the Bureau of Unprecedented and Unexamined Claims. Better yet, says Luten, this creature of the government should devote itself to the genuine reclamation of mine tailings, strip mine spoils, polluted streams, and the like. George Orwell had a name for words like "reclamation": "Newspeak." Exploiters of the environment perfected the art of "Newspeaking" long before 1984 was written.

"RVs"—"recreational vehicles"—is part of the vocabulary of Newspeak. For the sake of argument we can grant that driving a "totegoat" in the forest or a "dune buggy" over pristine sand dunes may recreate the impoverished spirit of the owner, but it certainly decreates the beauties of the natural environment. One of my favorite criticisms in this volume is Dan's demolition of Erle Stanley Gardner's eulogy of RVs.

Of immensely greater importance is Luten's devastating analysis of the outrageous proposal to bring Arctic waters to the southern United States and Mexico, a proposal going by the aptly ugly acronym NAWAPA (North American Water and Power Alliance). This concise analysis defies a briefer summary. Read it yourself; read and enjoy.

In fact, "read and enjoy" is a fit recommendation for this entire volume of critical analyses of environmental problems and their solutions. Few people in our time have had as much influence on people's thinking about the environment as Daniel B. Luten. To use an old but still good encomium, he has made the world a better place in which to live. There can be no warmer praise of a devoted environmentalist.

GARRETT HARDIN

CONTENTS

PROGRESS AGAINST GROWTH

PART ONE

BIOGRAPHICAL SKETCH

Walking home one afternoon, I hear a flock of Canada geese in the southern sky. At first, their song is all I sense, and I need 30 seconds of squinted searching before I can see the faint line of the birds. In fact, it is really two lines, one much larger than the other, and they are merging into one flock. They progress closer to me, winging their way northward, and I count easily the 27 geese jockeying for position in the line. As they pass overhead, I spot the bright white of their cheek patches, but cannot identify the individuals that are calling. Unceremoniously, three additional birds, rising from the lakeside beyond the hill and singing as they rise, join the flock by finding positions toward the front of the line.

A description of a person's life is a little like the description of that flight of geese. Even as we first see the birds in the sky, we know that they already have a history as a group. How far back should we go in order to understand the flock's origins? When they first grouped together? When they as individuals were hatched? When their ancestors moved northward to build nests and raise families? A person's life begins somewhere in the distant past, but just where is not clear. We usually start with the individual's birth, but recognize that even that notable date is arbitrary. A person coming into the world carries the past of a family, which, to complicate the linear chronology of a life, manifests itself more as the person develops than at the moment of birth. Moreover, just as the beginning of a life seems vague, so too are its "lateral boundaries"—the events and persons that influence someone living out an existence. How do we set boundaries around a life when it is connected to the lives of others? Is the flock of geese the same flock even after the last three birds join the group?

If the edges of a life are vague, the perspective from a particular place and time presents other complications. We think that we know a person best when he or she is close at hand, and we sense that our understanding is more clear for the immediate than for the distant past. But what constitutes "the present" itself varies. Someone standing in northern Illinois watching "my" gaggle of geese overhead would see the same flock—or would it be the same? The number in the group might be different. The individuals, in part, might have changed. The period of seeing them, including the view to the horizon from which they came and the other horizon to which they headed, certainly would be distinctive. The apparent clarity of the immediate is an illusion, a perspective that falsely simplifies the problem of the continuum of a life.

The life of an individual, then, is much like the life of a species— it is continuous with other lives in both space and time. Each of us, as with each species, is but part of an "immense journey," to use Loren Eiseley's apt words, through the corridors of time. I can try to describe a person's life, but I realize that my perspective is particular, perhaps unique, and that my decisions about what to include and what not are personal and arbitrary. How can it be otherwise?

Daniel Benjamin Luten, Jr., was born on March 15, 1908, in Indianapolis, Indiana. His grandfather, as a child, had immigrated with his parents from central Netherlands to Grand Rapids, Michigan, in the 1840s. He grew up, helped build bridges for Sherman's Civil War campaign as an enlisted man in the First Michigan Engineers, turned to farming, bore an eldest son who escaped the farm to study engineering at the University of Michigan. (Could a father's recollections of wartime adventures have stirred a son's ambitions? The geese are only faintly visible.) After teaching briefly at Ann Arbor, this son took a teaching position at Purdue University where he met and married a daughter of families (Hull, Heath) who had moved westward with the formation of the new states in the Ohio Valley. She, like her husband, was well educated, having earned her master's degree with a thesis on New England transcendentalism (another influence on Luten, no doubt, but the geese in this case are a long way off). Soon after marrying, Luten's father quit the faculty position, and started an independent engineering firm specializing in roadway bridges. More than 15,000 concrete arch bridges across the country attest to the success of the Luten engineering skill.

As a boy, young Luten's interests in nature were ambivalent, although they blossomed in his teenage years. His mother's concern for nature philosophy must have been a positive stimulus, as were his maternal (Hull) grandfather's hunting and fishing jaunts, suggested in this personal remembrance by Luten: "Wisconsin retains the romantic aura it had when I was a kid in Indiana. My grandfather used to take me with him fishing in the summer up at Lake Owen. He was 85 and still a great fisherman. I observed the lake, collected butterflies, and watched birds. (My first publication was about the blackthroated green warbler that I persuaded to take mayflies from my hand to feed her chick—all because I had the chick perched on my finger.) It was a pretty good symbiosis. I rowed the boat; he caught the fish, and I ate them." In his own opinion, the catalysts for Luten's serious interest in nature were his high school biology teachers, who conveyed not only knowledge about the natural world but also sensitivity to nature protection. Their influence was both immediate (Luten became an avid birdwatcher and an energetic collector of insects) and delayed (he traces the germ of the environmental concerns that have preoccupied his later life to these teachers).

Parental pressure dissuaded Luten from pursusing a college specialty that seemed logical—zoology at Cornell that would lead to an academic career. Instead, he followed his older brother's footsteps to Dartmouth, where a talent for chemistry stood in for a love of biology. Luten completed his bachelor's degree in chemistry in 1929.

Tired of New Hampshire winters, Luten looked to the West Coast for graduate schools. He considered Stanford, but his college professors at Darmouth recommended Berkeley's outstanding chemistry department. In his graduate research, Luten concentrated on organic chemistry generally and "reaction velocities" specifically, working with Gerald Branch. He earned his doctorate in 1933 with a dissertation titled *The Alkaline Hydrolyses of the Betaine Nitriles and Amides*. No jobs were available in that early Depression year, so Luten stayed on at Berkeley as a part-time instructor in chemistry. (He was one of the beneficiaries of Gilbert Lewis, dean of the College of Chemistry at Berkeley, who committed some of his funding to the temporary support of unemployed chemistry postdoctorates.)

In 1935, Luten was employed by Shell Oil Company at its nearby Martinez Refinery as a research chemist; a year later he transferred to Shell Development Company in the San Francisco East Bay and remained there for 25 years working on a variety of petroleum and petrochemical problems, was granted 50-odd patents, and acquired a local reputation for some independence of thought.

While working in Martinez, Luten met Lois Van Zile, who lived in the same boarding house in north Berkeley. Lois, working on her teaching credentials, was from Sacramento, California, but her roots were in New Amsterdam, French Canada, and the Deep South. Luten playfully speculates that his grandfather of the First Michigan Engineers might have helped burn the family plantation in Alabama that sent Lois's forebears west after the war, in one generation to Gainesville, Texas, in the next to Los Angeles—and thus Grandfather Luten might have been responsible for the subsequent meeting between Lois and her husband. She and Luten married in 1937, and they subsequently raised two sons and a daughter.

After World War II, a chance happening eventually led Luten into a second career as a population and natural resource specialist. Through a former roommate and fellow chemistry graduate student, Luten was offered a job as Technical Advisor to the Chief of the Natural Resources Section of the American Occupation Forces in Japan. As a result, the Lutens moved to Japan for two years, from 1948 to 1950.

Two experiences made the time in Japan a turning point for Luten. First, he was struck by the incongruity of trying to assess the natural resource base of Japan without paying attention to the growth of the Japanese population. How could the Americans fulfill their obligation to "conserve . . . Japan's natural resources" for their future development, and yet ignore the increase in the numbers of the Japanese? For Luten, natural resources and human population seemed inextricably tied together, although not all of his fellow advisors agreed. As discussed in a paper in this book (see "Why Does a Birth Rate Decline?"), the dispute within the Occupation Forces over the appropriateness of the Americans to influence Japanese childrearing patterns precipitated a national dialogue among the Japanese themselves; within a few years, the birth rate of Japan plummeted. Population growth would remain crucial in Luten's subsequent thinking about natural resources.

The second experience in Japan that propelled Luten into a career in natural resources was his reading in 1949 of a paper in *Science* by M. King Hubbert. The article, "Energy from Fossil Fuels," talked of limits to available supplies of petroleum and natural gas, and came at a time of optimism over the future production of fossil fuels. Moreover, Hubbert raised the question of population growth as a factor that would determine the availability of those resources in the future. (For decades, Hubbert, a distinguished Shell and U.S. Geological Survey petroleum geologist, would continue his soundly principled, pessimistic warnings in spite of rosy but baseless predictions by his fellow scientists; eventually Hubbert's views would become the conventional wisdom, and his early estimates of the years of peak production by the petroleum and gas industries of the United States would prove astute.)

Upon returning to the United States and Shell in 1950, Luten realized that his interests had changed. He began "poking around," as he describes it, on the campus at Berkeley, looking for places where population and natural resources were being talked about. Anthropologists proved uninterested; economists proved unsympathetic. Geographers, with their tradition of studying people–environment interaction, seemed logical, and the geographers at Berkeley, with their emphasis on such themes under Carl Sauer, were particularly inviting. Luten made contact with Sauer and James J. Parsons, biogeographer and cultural ecologist, and began attending graduate seminars that usually met in the evenings. In 1961, Luten was offered a one-third temporary appointment as a lecturer in geography. The following year, he retired early from Shell and inherited the responsibility for the department's basic course in natural resources. In the fall of 1962, he taught for the first time a course of his own creation on energy resources. Until his retirement from the university in 1974, Luten repeated these two courses and added several others: courses on open space as a resource, environmental contamination, water as a resource, and endangered species. His lecture courses and seminars were popular and well attended; in course evaluations, undergraduate students often used words like "rambling" to describe Luten's style, but almost always raved about his "insights" and "sympathetic mind." Graduate students who studied with Luten found him to have a wealth of ideas, even though their particular research topics varied from such matters as the historical geography of the petroleum fields of southern California, to the ecological interactions between people and nature in the Peruvian Amazon, to the turn-of-the-century concern over wild birds and early development of the Audubon Societies, to (my own) the sagebrush vegetation of western North America as a landscape element. Luten's visits to other universities, including Hawaii, Montana, Texas, and Louisiana State, were apparently similarly successful because he was consistently asked to return. Wherever he went, he combined the sharp analytical thinking of the organic chemist with the broad background of a humanist.

Luten's reputation as an academic geographer was equaled or exceeded by his reputation as an environmental activist. His involvement with environmental issues has been linked to a leading figure in

American conservation, David Brower. Luten had met Brower, then a director of the Sierra Club, as a neighbor in the 1940s. (Specifically, the Lutens had invited their new neighbor to come over "for a shower" when Brower was excavating a basement for his new house.) In spite of his long interest in nature and the out-of-doors, Luten had not joined the Sierra Club because one of the group's major activities was the organizing of outings for large numbers of people, an experience that did not appeal to the Luten family. During the 1950s, however, the purpose and image of the Sierra Club changed dramatically: Brower, focusing first on the proposal for Echo Park Dam in Dinosaur National Monument, transformed the group into the country's premier conservation organization. Luten, already a personal friend of Brower, became involved increasingly with the club's efforts.

That involvement allowed Luten's ideas to influence policies of the Sierra Club and consequently the course of environmental concern in the United States. Most prominently, Luten was probably responsible for the emergence of human population growth as a conservation issue. As Brower describes it, "Dan . . . was lecturing at Berkeley. . . . Meanwhile he was coaching me, and thus the club took the plunge. My contribution was a bit of editing and—best of all—dreaming up the title for Luten's [1963] article in the *Sierra Club Bulletin*, 'How Dense Can People Be?' As I remember it, 12 members resigned in protest. What was the club doing in the population business, which belonged elsewhere? We persevered. [Nearly] six years later I was able, with Ian Ballantine's notable help, to persuade Paul Ehrlich to write *The Population Bomb* [1968] . . . which sold 3 million copies in the U.S. and was translated into Swedish and Japanese." More generally, Luten's talks before public groups, statements to legislative bodies, addresses at symposia, and presentations on public radio earned him an identity as a provocative and insightful commentator on natural resource issues, and his participation as a lecturer, commentator, and author was much sought after. But even while arguing in behalf of conservationist positions, Luten remained thoughtful, even skeptical. In recent years, in fact, he has found himself disagreeing with Brower and the conventional wisdom in the conservation establishment over population policy and energy issues. Luten reveals astute self-understanding when he suggests that his major contribution to conservation seems to have been one of generating controversy rather than one of providing answers.

The dual roles of academic and environmental activist are not always smoothly complementary. In particular, academics often look with suspicion upon colleagues who are active in conservation causes, reasoning that it compromises scholarly objectivity. Luten himself did not ease the differing demands of his dual roles. He published and talked with academics, but often contributed his writing and discussion to groups in the nonacademic world. Luten believed that geography specifically and academe generally would help themselves if they focused on environmental issues, because such involvement would demonstrate the importance of the discipline and the university to a sometimes unsupportive public.

A complete assessment of Luten's impact as a student of natural resources and conservation is difficult to make. Specifically, he has been the catalyst responsible for issues taken up by the American conservation movement. More generally, he has prodded many an academic and environmentalist into thinking about a myriad of natural resource problems and positions. It is particularly difficult to know what seeds he may have planted as a teacher. Many of the thousands of undergraduates who heard him lecture and the hundreds of graduate students who participated in his seminars may be unaware of the extent of his contribution to their questioning minds. But Luten's legacy, already carried on by his students and colleagues both within the academic world and the conservation movement, is a lasting endowment. His words will long continue to provide direction to a world much in need of wisdom.

I watch the geese overhead as they effortlessly wing their way northward, calling down to me their beautiful March music. Individual birds continue to fall in and out of line, and eventually they rearrange themselves into the familiar V. The birds pull away, becoming smaller and smaller but still singing their song, before they are lost in the haze of the future. I can see them still, in my mind's eye, flying over the farms and forests for nearly a thousand miles before gradually breaking up into pairs and settling down onto faintly remembered pools on the muskeg beside James Bay. Clutches of eggs will become broods of goslings and then flocks of geese—a new generation, certainly, but also a continuation of those other geese that I watch flying north, bringing with them the light and warmth of spring.

THOMAS R. VALE
Madison, Wisconsin

PART TWO

POPULATION

For Luten, population is a critical factor, perhaps *the* critical factor, in natural resource matters. He came to appreciate the importance of population growth while serving as a natural resource expert in post-World War II Japan, and he began talking and writing about population long before it became commonplace in the national media of the United States. His contributions were, in fact, instrumental in prompting the country's dialogue over population in the 1960s and 1970s.

Concern for population growth seems to have waned during the late 1970s and early 1980s, perhaps as a result of more immediate crises posed by shortages of food and energy, and also as a result of complacency generated by declines in human fertility. But the nation's and the world's populations continue to grow at rates unprecedented in human history, and Luten's lessons remain appropriate.

The fundamental importance of population growth as a factor in natural resource issues does not mean that problems of resource availability will disappear once stability in human numbers is achieved. Rather, continued growth in human numbers means that no attempt to resolve such problems, whether by changes in economies, technologies, or political systems, can ever be permanently successful; population growth hampers progress and precludes solutions. Thoreau's words are among Luten's favorites: "There are a thousand hacking at the branches of evil to one who is striking at the root" (1854/1964, p. 330).

WHY DOES A BIRTH RATE DECLINE?

The year 1958 was notable in recent population history because it was within a year of the peak in the post-World War II baby boom in the United States. In the preceding year, 1957, the birth rate stood at 25.3/1000, culminating a climb from a low of 18.4/1000 in 1936. The country, euphorically dizzy on growth, looked optimistically to an apparently limitless future. The tone of this short article published by Luten in 1958, therefore, seems misplaced in time. In arguing that the growth of human numbers was a crucial problem not only to Japan but to the entire world, Luten expressed a sentiment that would not become commonplace until a decade later.

Does the history of the last 25 years support Luten's suggestion that the decline in the Japanese birth rate might be "the most important social event of this century"? It would only be so, he argued, if the rest of the world, like Japan, would perceive population growth as a hindrance to social progress. The answer to the question is equivocal. Birth rates in most of the world have declined since the 1950s (the Japanese birth rate continued to drop, reaching 13/1000 in 1983; the U.S. birth rate fell to 16/1000, and the world's decreased from about 35/1000 to about 29/1000); even many less developed countries have experienced declines. Perhaps the most notable example of a recent repetition of the Japanese experience is China, whose earlier pronatalist policies have been rejected and whose birth rate has plummeted from over 40/1000 in 1963 to less than 20/1000 today. Significantly for Luten's suggestion, moreover, the motivations for reduced fertility include recognition of the social advantages of fewer births. On the other hand, the declines have often been too small to stem the inertia of population growth. India, in spite of a drop in its birth rate, continues growing at more than 2% per year. More disquieting, birth rates in most African countries remain high (45–50/1000), with growth rates the highest in the world (2.5%–3.0% per year). Thus, Luten's admonition about the Japanese experience remains valid today: "The reward will be . . . the world's if it will only heed."

Reprinted by permission from *Resources* (Japan Resources Association, Tokyo, Japan), February 1958, pp. 18–19.

"Population is the common denominator of all resources problems." This is a broad statement and one that can be criticized in detail in many ways. But, broadly, it is almost above criticism. It justifies our talking about population in connection with resources. And it gives us a starting point for examining a most interesting phenomenon: Japan's birth rate.

Seven years ago, Japan's population was 83.2 million (October 1, 1950) and it was predicted then (calculations of March 1949, by Margaret Stone, published in *Japanese Economic Statistics*, June 1949) that it would most likely be 92.3 million in 1957 (October 1). Actually, on last October 1, it was only 91 million. This population, substantially less than predicted, was the result of a dramatic fall in the birth rate which, at 17.6/1000 in 1957, was little more than half as great as the 34.3/1000 it had been in 1947. The effect on population was no greater only because the death rate has also fallen, less dramatically, but still surprisingly, to one of the lowest values on earth.

The fall in the birth rate is uncontestably a social event of worldwide importance. Conceivably, the future may look back on it as the most important social event of this century. Whether it will turn out so, depends on its causes. Two alternative hypotheses seem worth arguing:

1. The first hypothesis is that the effort to educate in techniques and to liberalize and extend certain birth-limiting practices was an overwhelming success. Thus, Miss Stone . . . had envisioned a great fall in the birth rate and she had expected this to begin almost immediately and to reach an essentially constant lower value of 26/1000 in about three to five years. She did not explain why she expected the major part of it to occur so rapidly (within two years) but we must imagine that her reasons for such a postulate stemmed largely from the, then current, successful efforts of the Welfare Ministry to liberalize abortion and sterilization laws and to establish birth control clinics at the health centers.

However, there are some puzzling aspects to the drop in the birth rate.

a. Why, if Miss Stone had assurance that the diminution in birth rate was going to be precipitate, did she miss its inception by an entire year?

b. She postulated that it would approach a level defined in terms of American practices of family limitation in 1940. In fact, though, it has fallen well below them, to a value of 17.6/1000. Miss Stone, fully cognizant of the problems of prediction, actually projected three birth rate curves, the values of which in 1957 were: high 28.0/1000, medium 24.9/1000, low 21.8/1000. Assumptions basic to the lowest curve imply "that the practice of controlling family size will be about as prevalent in Japan in 1970 as in the United States thirty years earlier." Presumably, then, she felt she had no basis to believe that Japanese family limitation practice would be more restrictive than American practice. But it has become so.

c. If the predictions were based on the anticipated spread of education on contraception, how is the important, possibly major, role of illegal abortions (not abortions sanctioned by the liberalized laws) in diminution of live births to be explained?

2. The second hypothesis may seem only a hair-splitting to some, but to me the difference appears of the greatest importance. To provide a basis for it, one must recall that, nine years ago, there was controversy among the personnel of the Occupation concerning Japan's population. Some felt it a matter for the Japanese to handle in their own way and time; others felt it to be too urgent for toleration of the deliberate approaches to steady state conditions which, at best, have occurred elsewhere. Still others felt it to be simply an issue with great potential for trouble and one to be avoided when possible. Thus, Margaret Sanger was denied entrance to Japan in 1950 probably because it was felt by such people that her exclusion would lead to less trouble than her presence—and the Occupation's rules provided only two alternatives: to admit her or not [to] admit her. There was no way simply to ignore her.

Among those who felt urgency, there was certainly no clear view of the future or of what events might be expected to follow a given stimulus. However, more or less blindly, and in a dual effort to obtain enlightenment on the one hand regarding what might be coming in Japan and, on the other, to attract Japanese attention to the problem, certain experts, notably Warren S. Thompson, were invited to visit Japan and to advise. One result was not surprising: A controversy was provoked which was only terminated six months later by General MacArthur's statement (published July 2, 1949) that ". . . he is not engaged in any study or consideration of the problem of Japanese population control. Such matter does not fall within the prescribed scope of the Occupation and decisions thereon rest entirely with the Japanese themselves. . . ."

A second result was that long pent up questions among the Japanese, as to just what the Occupation *really* thought about birth control, burst out into the open and touched off a protracted press discussion of population problems. Probably nowhere has such a discussion been brought so universally to a people's attention. Many aspects were argued: population projections, birth control, abortions, emigration, relocation, industrialization, foreign commerce, resources potential, imperialism, family limitation laws, chronic unemployment, tax penalties and subsidies, and the national versus the family economic dilemma. The discussion was not notable for its erudition— the writing was by amateurs in this field. But the discussion was public and was brought to the people at all levels and presumably it was read. The birth rate, which had been falling by 2% per year, fell 15% the next year (1950) to 28.1/1000.

I submit that what has happened is that the Japanese nation has argued the issue with itself and has made up its mind. The Japanese have not been "taught" what they should do by anyone. Really, all the technological West could teach them was techniques. The basic question was not one of techniques but rather, "what of the future?" And, nowhere will a people submit willingly to being taught how to approach their own future. Rather, they will insist on arguing for themselves whither they should go. Arguing, admittedly, from facts brought by specialists, but with motives and ethics, hopes and fear from their own heritage.

This, the Japanese have done. And it appears they are now fairly on course in the most constructive program to be found on the face of the earth. The technique is still rough and, it is to be hoped, improvement will come. But the thinking is Japan's own. No one predicted it. The reward will be Japan's too, but also the world's if it will only heed.

UNEASY CHAIR: OSTRICHES, POPULATION GROWTH, AND WILDERNESS SENTIMENTALITY

Three years after he wrote "Why Does a Birth Rate Decline?," Luten repeated his question, "What of the numbers of mankind?" His focus, however, had shifted from the "foreign land" of Japan to "within our own shores."

This short article introduced population growth as a wilderness issue to the membership of the Sierra Club, leader of the American conservation movement in the middle decades of the century. The tone of the article is restrained; the words have been cautiously chosen. At the time, the notion of population limitation was still clouded by popular hesitation to discuss contraception, abortion, or the government's role in population matters. Moreover, the attention that population growth had received in the conservation movement had been restricted to utilitarian resources such as food. Here, Luten argued that population growth is an issue not only for people's physical well-being, but also for their need for a high-quality existence. Like the Japanese, Americans should "insist on arguing for themselves whither they should go." They will be "[a]rguing, admittedly, from facts brought by specialists, but with motives and ethics, hopes and fear from their own heritage," which, for Americans, includes a love of wilderness. He was asking his readers here directly to "heed" Japan's experience.

This article prodded a segment of American society to consider population issues. It and other writings and talks by Luten in the late 1950s and early 1960s were catalysts—perhaps critical ones—that awakened conservation leaders and groups to the importance of population growth, and that led to the entry of population as an issue in the American conservation movement. That entry reached a sort of zenith with the publication of Paul Ehrlich's *The Population Bomb* in 1968.

During the recent Wilderness Conference, it seemed to me at one stage that it was high time to come to grips with a question new to Wilder-

Reprinted by permission from *Sierra Club Bulletin*, 1961, 46(7): 2.

ness Conferences. However, no appropriate moment occurred and, indeed, such a feeling of success and accomplishment arose as the Conference proceeded that the question would probably not have been well received. Accordingly, I withheld my comments and now lay them in your lap in the hope you will see fit to publish them in the *Bulletin*. They follow:

"Repeatedly during this Conference we have come to the brink of a certain question. But it is a controversial question even within our own numbers and none of us has cared to attack it. (The skill with which we skirt this precipice would amaze anyone but a rock climber.) It is not merely a question for foreign lands; it is just as important within our shores. It pervades all human society, North American as well as South American, Asian, and African. This question is, of course, 'What of the numbers of mankind; whither go we?'

"We, all of us, must know one thing: The growth in numbers so familiar to us cannot continue; some day it must cease. None of us can say when it will cease, but in broad terms, we can say how. It will cease either by a decrease in birth rates or by an increase in death rates.

"If by the former, many of us can see hope for a human society which will still grant room on this earth for a fragment of the wild life with which God and Nature endowed it.

"If, however, the end of growth is by increase in deaths, no one with a concern for human welfare can look to the future with anything but dismay. For before we come to that vindication of C. G. Darwin and Thomas Malthus, we shall have crowded every other living thing off the face of the earth, except it bend its will to our demand. Alan Gregg [1955] looked forward to this with dread in an epoch-making address to the American Association for the Advancement of Science in 1954. This was the day when he made a most acute clinical analogy between unrestrained population growth and cancer. Paul Sears will remember that day. He was there. Many people, outside of that hall, were horrified. And put their heads back into the sand.

"I am not speaking of or for birth control. Human societies have always been able to restrain their numbers when they have had the incentive to do so. Perhaps, mostly, they have associated such restraints with religious practices. Let me repeat: I am not speaking of what we have come to call birth control, namely, contraception. I am speaking of limitation of growth.

"Eleven years ago when I left Japan, something was beginning to happen there. Within the ensuing period, Japan's birth rate has fallen in half, and Japan may well be headed toward the stable population it needs for its own survival and for the survival of the Nature which is so central to its society.

"It is popular to say this resulted from legalized abortion and birth control. This is a misrepresentation. In fact, most abortions performed in Japan then and since then are illegal. The Japanese government followed, it did not lead toward birth control. The essential truth is that the Japanese people, acting as individuals, decided that the time had come for an end to growth. They ended it by their own means and it is probably not for us to criticize their means.

"Now, in these Wilderness Conferences the time has come when we must examine this question. For if we do not, if we are afraid to examine it and to come to a decision, then the Wilderness Conference and the wilderness movement will end as other great romantic movements have ended—in obscure history books.

"We have the next two years to think. The next Wildnerness Conference should be prepared either to examine this issue in detail or to admit that concern for wildnerness is sentimentality.

"Now is the time! The wind is rising! During these next two years we, each of us, should be asking himself whether he is concerned for an enduring wilderness or merely for his own lifetime.

"It is time to ask the question: 'Does a wilderness program, a wilderness policy, without a population policy make any sense? Or is it only a sop to the outdoorsman?'"

PARKS AND PEOPLE: AN EXPLODING POPULATION NEEDS PLACES TO EXPLODE IN

The stirrings of concern over population growth gathered momentum during the early 1960s. As with the Japanese experience earlier, in the United States "the discussion was public and was brought to the people at all levels and presumably it was read." This article constituted part of that discussion.

The paper was based on a talk presented to the California Society of the American Institute of Park Executives in Monterey, California; this explains its title and its concern with open space and park personnel. It is included here, not as an example of the importance of population growth to a particular land use or profession, but as a general treatment of the exponential expansion of human numbers. Several matters presented characterize Luten's particular insights about that expansion: (1) Growth will not continue; (2) population forecasters typically are prisoners of their assumptions that constrain their insight; and (3) population forecasts are often self-fulfilling, in that they help create the future that they predict. In addition, the emphasis on California should not be dismissed as a provincial outlook by Luten; rather, it should be seen as a reflection of the importance of steady, high growth in that state over the last 130 years, growth that is so familiar that it seems innately to belong there. It is not surprising that the national dialogue over population growth was centered in California, the "vortex of growth in this age of growth."

We live in an age of growth. In California, we live in a vortex of growth in this age of growth.

Reprinted by permission from *Landscape*, 1962–1963, 12(2): 3–7.

[GROWTH OF METROPOLISES]

It is not growth itself which has caused metropolises. When the world's numbers were a third as great, in 1850, there were less than a third as many metropolises; neither did anywhere near a third as many people live in them. How many of your grandfathers were city boys? Even today, in continental China, with a fourth of the world's people, large cities are few. I would guess that less than 15% of the Chinese live in cities. In contrast, 80% of Californians do.

Why? Well, primarily because of technology. To mix some metaphors, a human technology, which grew imperceptibly for millennia, which got off the ground 10,000 years ago and took fire two centuries ago, has burst all bounds only in the last three decades. This technological society now, while enormously demanding of natural resources, is still so efficient in extracting raw materials from the earth that fewer and fewer of us are bound to the land.

In general, of course, the location of our raw materials dictates that the people who harvest them must live near them. In China, the location of probably 90% of the population is determined by the fact that they are engaged in extraction—mostly agricultural. Even in Japan, well industrialized, about half the people live on the land. In this country, only about a sixth of us have our residence determined in this fashion. In California, it is perhaps a little less, even though the state is not heavily industrialized.

The result of all this is that the great bulk of Americans do not have their location determined by any such dominant force as the need to get out into the fields at daybreak. In another sense, they are footloose, dispossessed even. Where, then, will they live? Labor seems to seek a place where there is lots of industry, and industry seeks a place where there is lots of labor. The decision where they should get together was not made chicken–egg-wise. Rather, in our best modern manner, no decision was made at all. Instead, for the most part the earlier decisions where cities should be were confirmed. These earlier decisions were mostly due to transportation costs, but there were political overtones and mineral deposits involved too. Else why Washington, D.C., or Indianapolis? . . .

The automobile, because of the mobility it gives, is a major factor in our living patterns. It provides the fluidity, the quicksilver aspect of our changes. The diffuse structure of the metropolis results from it. An average sort of man who is willing to travel 15 miles each way to work has a job-hunting area of 700 square miles. And, since he can bail out of the house he owns at virtually no expense ("nothing down, no closing costs"), he can shift his operations base if the job hunting is poor. His cruising radius does not limit the size of the metropolis at all. The overlapping of millions like him gives a sort of cohesiveness to a metropolis, even to a megalopolis, that can be 100 miles across. And just as the jobseeker has this vast area of prospects, so any industry located well within the metropolis can bid for any of the labor force living within a 700-square-mile area.

A compounding of all this agglomeration comes from the extent to which we live by taking in our own washing. Every person on a primary payroll coming from outside the community seems to support another 1.5 to 2.2 people: the grocer, the TV man, the plumber, the doctor, the lawyer. Defense contracts are the best examples. Only recently did I get an inkling of what Lockheed is doing to the San Francisco peninsula with a payroll of $130,000,000 per year for a labor force of 18,000. These employees and their families, 60,000 people, are directly supported, but another 130,000 live by taking in the laundry. The addition of 10,000 to the payroll each year seems to mean an annual increase of 100,000 people dependent on this government contract.

PREDICTIONS, TRUE AND FALSE

In 60 years the San Francisco Bay Area is expected to comprise 14 million and Los Angeles to be twice as large. The metropolis is in flood. How high will the waters rise? When will they perhaps recede? Forecasts now on record put California at about 60 million and the United States at 418 million in the year 2020. Rather than discuss these prospects of monumental growth, I am going to question them.

If we are willing to take a long view of things, we can come up with one firm conclusion: that the growth so familiar to us is transient and cannot continue [Figure 1]. The current three billion of us on the earth, increasing at the current 1.8% per year would, in about 800 years, come to [1000 trillion] people. This is the SRO, the standing-room-only, population, with two square feet per person, land and sea.

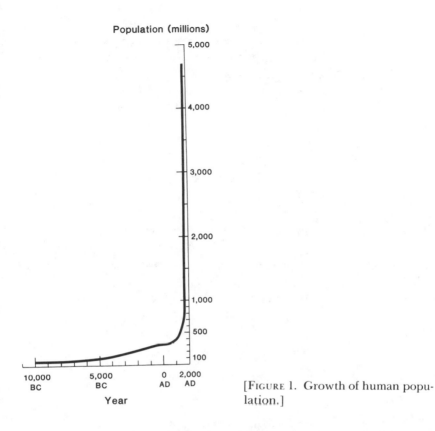

[FIGURE 1. Growth of human population.]

Picture a city of 300,000 where each of us now lives. There are lots of reasons why this cannot come to pass. If they are not convincing, extension for a few years further should be. Since such a thing *cannot* happen, then the 1.8% growth per year must dwindle. Somewhere it must end. But we can't extend our worries 800 years ahead. What will the next 60 years, or perhaps, the next 100 years, be like?

The next generality about growth prediction, after we concede the transience of growth, is that the more information we can put into our prediction, the better it is. It is easy to make predictions with a minimum of information. The easiest horrible example is to assume that what is happening now will *continue* to happen. All that we need is a population figure, a growth rate, and a slide rule—no common sense, no discretion, no background.

Let me give a few examples: California's population is 16 million, its growth rate 3.8% per year; the United States has 180 million people and a growth rate of 1.6% per year. California's population extrapolates to 72 million at the end of the century, to 100 million in the year 2010, and in about 115 years—that would be 2075—it overtakes the national population. That is, all Americans then would be living in California [Figure 2]!

We have already run the world's population forward for 800 years on the assumed 1.8% growth rate. Why not assume it has always grown at that rate, too, and run it backward? This leads to the conclusion that Adam and Eve should have been born in about 800 A.D. Beginning with one couple, a population growing from that time at such a rate would give rise to the present world population of three billion. This calculation demonstrates that the growth we find commonplace has not been common in history. It is new; our ancestors did not know it. . . .

The best example I can give of ignoring information was in a curiously whimsical article in *Science* entitled "Doomsday: Friday, 13 November, A.D. 2026" [von Foerster, Mora, & Amiot, 1960]. This article was written with tongue in cheek, but it's hard to know whose. The assumption was that as people live closer to each other and in

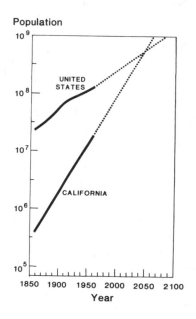

[FIGURE 2.] One kind of prediction: in A.D. 2075 all Americans will be living in California.

better communication, their ability to grow in numbers will increase. The mathematical relation set up to describe this growth seems inconsistent with our records for 2000 years. But it predicts an utterly infinite population on an autumn afternoon 66 years ahead. Shortly before that moment—earlier that same day—the SRO population would be reached. Now, let us bring one more piece of information into the picture. If the world's population is to increase from [three billion] to the SRO population in 66 years, how big will the average family have to be in those next three generations? Two hundred children each.

HOW TO FORECAST GROWTH

The only trouble with predictions such as these is that people jump to the wrong conclusion. Instead of seeing that the calculation illuminates the folly of an assumption, they accept the assumption. Then they jump from this conclusion to a more general conclusion that all forecasts are ridiculous. It is too bad that people who undertake such calculations are unable to make clear their real purpose.

Let me itemize some conclusions that even an amateur can reach: (1) Growth is transient. (2) How transient can be told better, the more information you can manage to use in your predictions. (3) Sometimes you can find physical limits [to growth]. (4) Sometimes you can use an old axiom: No part can be greater than the whole.

The professional forecasts of population are much more intricate. They stem from much solid vital statistics, but also from assumptions. Basically, all it takes is knowledge of the number of children the typical woman has in each of her child-bearing years, the age at which people die, and assumptions regarding the future trends in these quantities. These are the age-specific birth and death rates. The assumptions are made sounder (the forecaster hopes) by examining the age at which women have married and the age at which they have stopped adding to their families in the recent past, and guessing what they may do in the future. Also, the forecaster will note how these quantities vary for country compared to city women, for native-born compared to foreign-born women, for Negro compared to white women, for married women compared to unmarried women, for rich women compared to poor women, and will note how the relative numbers of all these statistical sorts of women have varied in the past. Then he will assume that the trends will or will not continue.

Projections of migration are on less secure ground. Sometimes, the problem is resolved simply by assuming that new cities will grow just as older ones have done.

Thus, every projection depends utterly on assumptions. And, in the last analysis, it is not given to most of us to know what the future will bring—whether disaster or prosperity, or whether the age-specific birth rate for the average, urban, native-born, white married American female of medial socio-economic status will wax or wane.

The population projections which concern us practically, the ones which predict 22 million people in California in 1970 and 45 million or so in 2000, are very sophisticated. If you don't like what they predict, don't bother checking the arithmetic; it's all right. But take a hard look at the assumptions.

Before leaving the population question, I want to put my fingers on two sensitive points. The first is that no serious projection, to my knowledge, has considered the impact of the tremendous growth of the literature on population. This literature didn't exist in popular form in 1945. The American housewife hasn't felt it. If this literature continues to grow, and I think it will, she and her husband are going to comprehend it one of these days. And on the day when they do, all the projections which now guide you will be knocked into a cocked hat.

THE SELF-FULFILLING FORECAST

The second sensitive point is a curious one. Current serious population projections for California pretty well agree on 22 million people in 1970 and 45 million for the year 2000. The first such projection was an act of boldness; the later ones are not. Taken together, though, they have a strong tendency to create the future they predict. Once it is really believed there will be 22 million people in California in 1970, the wheels will go into motion to provide the energy supply, the water supply, the sewers, the highway structure, the housing developments. And what does it take to build these? Well, it takes about another six million people—the workers, with their sisters and their cousins and their aunts, with their grocerymen, their cleaners, their schoolteachers, and so on.

GROWTH VERSUS PROGRESS

Let me say this again. The predictions of continued growth for California *are themselves generating that growth.* When the demographers confidently agree on growth, industry, with confidence, prepares for it. The preparations stimulate growth. If, after the capital is invested and the facilities are ready, the growth should then flag, all heaven and earth will be moved to get the people here. And, indeed, it must be conceded that once the money is spent, repayment will become burdensome unless the facilities are used to capacity.

But, somewhere, we must stand and say clearly that enough is enough. [We must say that] growth is no longer compatible with progress. Even though progress and growth have been compatible over most of our national history, nonetheless, they never were the same thing. Now, we have come close to a point where they are in utter opposition. We, all of us, and the whole American public as well, must and will some day soon come to distinguish between growth and progress.

I'm going to throw a first stone, sinful or no, and say that California population growth is going to fall short of official expectations. Termination of growth will bring painful adjustments. However, the longer it is postponed, the more painful they will be.

[GROWTH AND PARKS]

Now, to another question. Why should park executives be concerned [with growth, and] for the future? And how far into it?

Inherent in life itself is a concern for the future. This is the business of genetics. . . . Throughout the older phyla of the animal kingdom, especially in intricate detail in the insects, we find genetic patterns of conduct; these deal with concern for the future. With the emergence of recognizable consciousness in higher animals, concern for the future appears in a different light, not now as a pattern of life itself, not as a command always beyond the power of will, not always visible even, but always reappearing. Our very genetic make-up reflects eons of concern for the future. Man's success in dominating the earth reflects his preeminence as a worrier.

If, as I allege, a park executive is one of the highest forms of human life, it is because he has the most concern for the future, and spends the most time worrying—constructively—about it.

Let me give a concrete example: Do you remember Frederick Law Olmsted and John McLaren? Central Park and Golden Gate Park, which owe much to these two men, are now pushing the century mark. Would New York and San Francisco be better off if these parklands could have been kept on the tax rolls back in the last century? No! A hundred years of foresight is not too much for any park executive.

If you doubt the need to look so far ahead, ask yourself, where is the American city which is criticized for having too much parkland? Who dares to criticize any existing local, regional, state or National Park as unnecessary, a luxury? The only criticism is of *future parks*, and strangely, it comes from those who extol growth. Don't listen to them. Today we wait for hours behind an idling 100-horsepower engine to get into Bliss State Park on the west shore of Lake Tahoe. If you heed these critics, the symbol of the wonderful living standards of tomorrow will be a line waiting for days behind 1000-horsepower engines.

30 SQUARE FEET PER PERSON

In a recent report prepared by the Standard Research Institute for the East Bay Municipal Utility District, McElyea and Cone [1960] have suggested that 20 acres per 1000 people is a hopeful target for regional park lands in the San Francisco Bay Area. This sounds reasonably generous. How does it sound when put as 1/50 of an acre per person? Or 900 square feet? A plot of land 30 feet square for each of us? How close are we today to the Bay Area quota of 60,000 acres? How close will we be in 2020 when the parkland quota will be up to 280,000 acres? How close will Los Angeles be to its 600,000 acres?

These increasing demands for regional recreation land do not represent progress; they only represent at best a status quo, and maybe not even that. As our numbers and the stresses to which we are subjected grow, that 30-foot square plot may be less adequate than now. Today there are other escapes: open, private lands to be looked at, some even where you can still walk and picnic. Tomorrow, if not subdivided, they will be fenced to fend off the vandalism of the "traveling public," that brazen image worshipped by so many.

DO WE NEED SPACE?

McElyea and Cone only carry their projection 20 years ahead. I imagine this was because the research contract called for only that forecast. But the same Utility District has forecast its water needs for 30 years; the area's population has been forecast for 50 years; and the Department of Commerce [1960] has projected its economic development for 60 years. Is it that we won't need parks for more than another 20 years?

The moral here is to project our park needs just as far as others have projected population and economic development and then a good bit farther. If someone says we're being visionary, ask him whether his plans call for a society with a higher living standard or a lower living standard. I don't think anyone who is in this planning business for a living can afford to confess anticipating a lower living standard.

Don't hesitate either to suggest that if a man in the Bay Area needs a 30-by-30 foot piece of regional park today, he may even need a 50-foot square 60 years from now to get away from the 14 million people in the Bay Area.

If we predict a need for this space, we'll get the space. Or else the growth will never occur. . . .

ABORTION AND THE LAW:
RADIO COMMENTARY

Abortion, more than any other population issue and probably more than any other resource issue, remains clouded in controversy. In this commentary, in contrast to his cautious broaching of population growth as a conservation problem in 1961, Luten boldly confronted abortion. In both issues,

Commentary broadcast on radio station KPFA, Berkeley, CA, May 23, 1966.

however, he was acting as a catalyst for thinking about matters that were neither safe nor conventional.

Unresolved because unresolvable by objective standards, the morality of abortion lies clearly within the realm of personal feeling and judgment. Population and resource questions are typically based on subjective notions, but in the question of abortion the dichotomy and strength of people's views seem heightened. What Luten urged his listeners to do in this commentary was what he urged people to do in most matters of resources and population: to question the assumptions underlying our positions (e.g., that historically recent Western attitudes toward abortion are the most moral ones) and to consider the implications of extending our stances ("It is a minority doctrine that a life is created at the time of conception. . . . We do not count pregnant women twice in our censuses. . . . We do not count ages from date of conception. . . . We do not assign representation in Congress to the unborn").

Since 1966, the legal status of abortion has changed in many countries of the world, including the United States. More than 30 countries have liberalized formerly restrictive abortion laws; these countries include the world's most populous, China and India. On the other hand, limitations on abortions have been instituted in several countries, notably Bulgaria, Czechoslovakia, Hungary, and Romania. In the United States, the 1973 Supreme Court decision that reduced government constraints on abortions remains the law in 1985, but its future seems uncertain in view of the continuing intensity of attacks by antiabortion groups. Luten found it clear in the 1960s that we had "come to doubt the virtue of our 19th-century laws on abortion"; it seems equally clear in the 1980s that we are still far from a consensus on what are the most moral ones for the 20th. His observations are today as relevant to forming decisions on sincere moral principles as they were in 1966.

Tonight I want to direct your attention again toward one of the problems of population. But first, let me argue that this is appropriate in any discussion of natural resources, in any discussion of conservation.

Apparently, as our technology advances, the limits of our society's environment retreat—retreat more rapidly than our perception of depth increases. Today, two-thirds through the 20th century, it is quite impossible for us to say how many people this world might support. Each year, our estimates of the number it can support increase, and, generally, more rapidly than the world's population grows. And, recently, it has become popular to say that, because this has been going on for so long, there is no reason why it should not continue indefinitely.

In fact, though, no more palpable sophistry has ever been foisted off on a gullible public. The simple truth of the matter is that the earth can be shown to have limits, even though their magnitude cannot be estimated. In consequence, the problems of insufficiency and depletion of natural resources are compounded by population growth and cannot be resolved without a termination of population growth.

In general, it seems to have been easier for a primitive tribe, without the blessings of computers but also without the complexities of unbridled growth, to see the limits of its environment than it has been for a modern society to do so. Only within the last two decades have doubts about unlimited growth come to be voiced audibly. And yet it is in these same two decades that the worship of growth has become unbridled. The issue is still unresolved, but the opponents of growth do appear to be winning at least the concession that the world would be better off with [fewer] than with more people. No such concession has been granted on the parallel question of economic growth.

In stable primitive societies, change was slow; growth was so small as to be undetectable. The world an old man left was the same as the one he had entered decades earlier. Most such societies had developed a host of institutions to maintain the status quo, good or bad though it might seem to us. It seems reasonable to say of them that, seeing the limits of their environment, they managed their affairs so as to stay within those limits.

Almost universally, [portions] of these institutions were directed toward stabilization of their numbers. Among these were limitations on who might have families and who might not, on ages at which families could be formed; these are still familiar to us. But also, infanticide was perhaps more the rule than the exception, and the practice of abortion was common and has been reported from hundreds of primitive societies.

In recent centuries, perhaps because of an expanding environment, but certainly in association with the spread of Christian doctrine, abortion has come to be conceived improper and virtually all Western societies until quite recently considered it to be a crime. Nonetheless, as everyone knows, abortions go on.

In California, abortion is a felony, unless continued pregnancy would endanger the life of the pregnant woman. The situation is little different in most other states, although a few have quite recently liberalized their laws slightly. Abortion is illegal in Mexico, although apparently rarely and inconsistently punished. Abortion has become essentially entirely legal in Czechoslovakia and Hungary in recent years. In the latter of these Roman Catholic countries, legal abortions exceed live births in numbers, and it seems reasonable to believe that numerous Catholic women are resorting to abortion. Perhaps those who oppose such laws will blame the legislators who liberalized the laws rather than the women who chose to have pregnancies terminated. In Japan, I believe it is generally legal. Which of the United States will be the first to legalize abortion? Let us hope that, whichever it may be, the action is taken on the basis of principle and not for economic gain.

How common is abortion in the United States? If one searches in the *U.S. Statistical Abstract* under "Crimes Known to the Police," he must come away with the belief it is very rare—it is not specifically mentioned. However, estimates range from 200,000 to 1,200,000 and higher per year. The common belief is that the number is in the neighborhood of a million, virtually all of them illegal, or one for each four live births. Most of these abortions have terminated the unwanted pregnancies of married women, pregnancies which occurred because other means of avoiding them failed. At the same time, a higher fraction of pregnancies of unmarried women end in illegal induced abortion. A million each year seems, at first sight, incredible. Prorated, it comes to 4000 each year in San Francisco, or 11 per day. Expressed this way, it becomes easily credible.

It is common to vilify abortion as murder, and, necessarily, therefore, those women who seek and procure abortions must be regarded as the principals in murder and those who perform abortions as accessories to the crime. If, in fact this be the case, and if people who feel abortion is murder also believe in capital punishment, then it is hard to understand why such people are not demanding that a million American women be hanged each year for murder. This is the only kind of murder, if murder it be, where the principal goes free and the accessory goes to jail. In other sorts of murder, we do not grant immunity to the principal for turning state's evidence as an accessory. In fact, of course, we do not believe abortion to be murder, and it is only the vindictive and un-Christian among us who extol these laws.

It is a minority doctrine that a life is created at the time of conception. In all probability, no life has been created on this earth during the last three billion years. All life is a continuation of earlier life, and all that happens at conception is that two lives are joined. When this new organism becomes a person is another matter. Societies have held widely varying views on this matter. Not all of them have conceded this status even so early as the time of birth. Most of human practice has, however, been to this effect, that life begins at birth. In fact, this has been in large measure the U.S. practice. Thus, we do not count pregnant women twice in our censuses; if we were to do this, we should have to increase our population by three million at this moment. We do not count ages from date of conception; we do not assign representation in Congress to the unborn. Nowhere, except in this one matter, do we regard the unborn as people.

It seems unlikely that logic can be applied to the matter. The logical position, and a few societies have come closer to this than we, is to regard the organism as a person when it begins to act like a person. We, perhaps, would fear to apply this test to ourselves. We are on much safer ground if we take arbitrarily the moment of birth as the moment of creation of a new person.

To shift this date earlier and to argue that a person exists before birth exposes us to a new host of uncertainties and contradictions. If abortion is murder, who is it who has been murdered? Name him and tell us about him; let us establish by explicit testimony and presentation to the coroner of a corpse that a person has been killed, and not accede to this by presumption.

Nonetheless, we do feel a measure of uncertainty about the unborn, about the people who have never existed. In some doctrine, they may be envisioned as lined up, each waiting his turn to be born. To be frustrated after perhaps almost making it seems cruel indeed. But this partakes of an Oriental view of incarnation and reincarnation of a consciousness before birth, which we find strange. It is reminiscent of [the comic strip character] Pogo Possum, who noticed that "those folks who are for birth control all managed to get themselves borned first."

On the basis of another doctrine, that of genetics and human physiology, we can calculate that better than [one trillion trillion] different people are conceivable each year, and yet that only a minute fraction of them are born, [100 million]. Who is to say who makes it and who does not? Name those who do not. Their numbers are more than legion; there is not space on earth to write their names.

In recent years, it is quite clear that we have come to doubt the virtue of our 19th-century laws on abortion. These doubts have been recent, but they grow rapidly. The sad story of thalidomide was a great prompting; the equally sad story of German measles in pregnant women was another. Just in passing, "thalidomide" is a one-word answer to all who suggest [that] science is infallible and foresees all consequences of innovation.

Three years ago in the California Legislature, Assemblyman Anthony Beilenson introduced legislation legalizing abortion to terminate pregnancies resulting from certain criminal acts (rape, incest), or if the infant were likely to be deformed or the mother's health to be gravely impaired. This bill, I believe, got nowhere. Last year a similar bill might have received a favorable recommendation in committee, but for last-minute intervention by those who have so little faith in our moral sturdiness that they believe the state should intervene in what appears to be none of the state's business. However, perhaps I am old-fashioned in such matters; thus, [for example,] I have never understood how bribing basketball players could be any concern of the state, unless the state wants to protect the purity of gambling.

Early this year, a new organization, the Society for Humane Abortion, whose purpose is the elimination of legislation limiting abortions, held a one-day meeting in San Francisco. Not widely or long publicized, it nonetheless drew 500 participants, a remarkable showing for a subject which could hardly be discussed publicly five years ago. The Wilderness Conferences [of the Sierra Club] have required 18 years to reach attendance of 1000.

Early this year, a Gallup poll, nationwide, showed a four-to-one majority favoring legalization of abortion when the health of the mother is endangered. A five-to-three majority supported such action if the child might be born deformed. But a five-to-one majority opposed abortion where the family could not support more children. A similar questionnaire in San Francisco at about the same time showed substantially higher support for liberalization of abortion laws. Recently, the California Medical Association, after some controversy, [also] supported liberalization.

And earlier this spring, a committee was formed locally for the purpose of supporting a constitutional amendment which would eliminate the constraints on abortion. Its accessary first objective is to get 500,000 signatures to the initiative petition. If all of the California women who have had illegal abortions in the last five or ten years were to sign up, the task would be done. However, it is unlikely that many of them will step forward, so great is the stigma. Further, perhaps many will refuse to sign who privately are completely in support simply because to sign will be taken as an admission of complicity in abortion. While I find myself wholeheartedly in support of this committee's objectives, I anticipate rough sledding for them.

The last chapter in the chronology is the current press flurry over the local medical profession and its practice of approving and performing, as therapeutic abortions, terminations of pregnancy on the count that the pregnant woman had had German measles, and probably the infant would be deformed, defective, handicapped. These actions do seem, from a lay viewpoint, contrary to statute. They are in contrast to the other chief category of abortions, which are requested, approved, and performed therapeutically because the pregnant woman has threatened to commit suicide—certainly a threat to her life. How can the validity of such a threat be tested? What medical board will care to reject such a plea on the score that the woman is unlikely to carry out the threat? And if she does in fact kill herself, was the board which rejected her plea an accessory? Legally, probably, no. Morally, yes.

As the law stands today, the medical profession has been put in the position, and to a considerable degree has accepted it, of being [a] judge of morality. In other situations, it rejects the position. To my knowledge, medical training does not cover the field, and while medical practice certainly leads to a considerable degree of qualification in such matters, it has never been our deliberate intent that such decisions should be made by such people or in such fashion.

Where does all of this leave us, aside from in our usual posture of confusion? What should be [our] law and morals on the matter of abortion?

We are confused, always confused because, of course, we live in an age of revolution, unprecedented revolution. The world's population growth today is new; [it] was unknown to our ancestors; and yet it must be unknown to all but the closest of our descendants. The revolution in technology has been gaining momentum for centuries and still seems to accelerate without limit, but it, too, must become stabilized before long. For while only 5% of all men who have ever lived are alive today, it is said that 90% of all scientists still live. If the growth in number of scientists were to continue they would soon exceed the total population, and, as it has been phrased, "Jonah would swallow the whale."

Which is revolutionary—the growth so familiar to us but not to our ancestors, or the impending termination of growth, new to us, familiar to our ancestors?

Perhaps our moral code is the most traditional part of our lives. Even here, we are in trouble. Law-abiding, we are faced with so many laws that a typical Californian will protest lawlessness on the campus while driving 75 miles an hour on a California highway. Which laws are to be obeyed and which are merely to serve as guidelines? Do we wish a traditional society or a revolutionary society? Neither for its own sake; we wish a better society. If out of such a maze, we are to seek to be better by being traditional, which traditions will we choose and which reject?

Inescapably, we find ourselves seeking new guides. One of those which grows stronger and which seems thus far to have merit is the proposition that children should grow up in a world having a measure of security, should live in the confidence of being loved and wanted. From this stems the proposition that all children born should be wanted by their parents.

As another guide, we find ourselves looking ever more searchingly at the notions of human dignity and human rights. Only recently do we find the proposition coming up that abortion laws are a relic of a double-standard world, a world where women stood legally with children, idiots, and slaves. Read Garrett Hardin [1966] on "Abortion and Human Dignity."

As a third guide, we have the knowledge that the more crowded we become on this planet the more difficult our existence will be, and we have the probability that the more crowded we become the less human we will be.

All of these guides suggest that the sooner at least one of the 50 United States eliminates such statutory constraints, the better this society will be.

Opposition will arise, will be vilifying [and] splenetic. It will come from the insecure, from those who don't trust their way in this world, who feel unable to stand on their own moral feet and want the compulsion of conformity by others to reinforce their own instability.

THE DYNAMICS OF REPULSION

The issue of immigration invites emotional controversy. It requires consideration of individual freedoms, of governmental coercions, of people's unequal access to resources. In this article, Luten explored immigration—not between nations (which he did address in a letter that appears later in this book; see "The Immigration Bomb"), but between states. Just as he raised inflammatory matters with his previous discussions of population regulation and abortion, Luten was again breaching the limits of the conventional.

The history of California, the image of California, epitomizes the society dominated by growth. Adjustments to a condition of no growth (when it comes—and come it must) will be more traumatic in California than in most other areas of the country or the world; consequently, the bellwether character of the Golden State makes its adjustments ones to watch.

Since Luten wrote this article in 1967, however, California has not made such adjustments; its growth has continued. California's population has grown by more than five million, an increase of about 25%. Fertility rates have declined sharply, as they have throughout the country, and immigration from other states has continued to carry "the burden of growth," accounting for about one-half of the increase during the 1970s. Apparently the "repulsiveness" of California remains low relative to most other parts of the country, although another Western state, Arizona, seems to draw immigrants from a much larger portion of the United States than does California.

Edmund G. Brown [Sr.], when he was governor, would speak with enthusiasm in election years of the growth of California. In the alternate, budget, years, he spoke with concern of the numbers problem. Late in the evening of November 8, 1966, when he conceded the election to Ronald Reagan, his own feelings were not in evidence. But Mrs. Brown stood by his side with an undisguised grin on her face. One wonders if she was thinking about 1967, a budget year. One also

Reprinted by permission from *The Nation*, January 30, 1967, pp. 133–138.

wonders how other Americans, the one-tenth who are Californians and the nine-tenths who are not, should look at the problems of California and its growth.

Everyone knows that California grows, and it is common to think of this as a recent phenomenon. Thus, the increase of 3.5 million (from 15.7 million in April 1960, to 19.2 million in July 1966) is greater than that witnessed in any other six-year period for California or any other state. Again, between 1940 and 1950, the population grew by five million—surely a state record for a decade and as sure to be broken in 1970. . . .

It may be objected that California's growth is not all internally generated; the major part of it has always been by immigration, some from foreign countries, most from other states. Thus, while growth before 1849 was internally generated and small, with the gold rush it became enormous. Putting aside qualms on this score, how has the state grown?

The record is unexpected: Viewed broadly, the growth rate of California's population has been constant for a century. While it has grown more rapidly in one decade than another, ranging from least (2%) in the depression to greatest (5.2%) in the 1920s, if you look at the entire interval from 1860 to 1960, the tale is simple: The population, on the average, has grown at 3.8% per year, doubling each 18.5 years, over the century. The increase totals more than 40-fold. The slow decades and the fast decades were so closely associated that the overall trend is one of spectacular regularity. The 1890s were slow but were followed by the prosperous 1900s and the deficit in numbers was made up. The Depression was a period of low birth rates and, contrary to popular belief, also of low immigration. But it was preceded by the 1920s, with heavy immigration, so that by 1930 the population was "ahead of the curve." Then followed the war decade which made up the deficit, so that by 1950 the state was back on the curve. And it stayed there in 1960.

Natural increase has ranged eight-fold from a low of approximately 0.3% per year for the depression decade to a high of about 2% in the 1870s. The general trend has been one of slow decline, with a sharp drop in the 1930s, followed by a postwar upsurge almost to the level of a century ago. During most of these 100 years, Warren Thompson has calculated, families were too small to have maintained a constant population had immigration ceased.

Immigration, surprisingly, has varied less, ranging from a low of a little over 1% per year in the 1890s to a high of more than 4% in the 1920s. It has always carried the burden of growth, providing from 55% (1870s) to 85% (1930s).

When one looks at the state regionally, similar irregularities appear. In 1860, a third of all Californians lived in the San Francisco Bay Area and another third in the Sierra foothill gold country. Less than 5% were in the south coastal region. Today, the Bay Area has shrunk to a fifth, the mountain counties to less than 5%, while the south coast has grown to half.

So much for the past. Today, many of the trends persist. First, California's birth rate remains lower, but only a shade lower, than the nation's, and it has declined, as has the nation's, from a postwar peak in 1957. From this high of almost 25 infants annually per 1000 persons in California, and just over 25 for the nation, the rate dropped in 1964 to 20.6 for California and 21.7 for the United States. Whether it will rise again within the next few years, when the postwar babies marry, is still uncertain. Californians will probably continue to have slightly smaller families than Americans as a whole.

Second, distribution of growth within the state continues to deviate widely from the average. Between 1960 and 1965, Orange County on the fringe of Los Angeles grew at 10% per year, while five other counties had a very slight population loss. Four of these counties, in the northern Sierra Nevada, were small. The fifth is San Francisco, city and county, so urban that increasing metropolitan functions leave less and less room for living. Los Angeles County grows at about the rate for the entire state; the San Francisco Bay Area grows more slowly. Suburban counties grow more rapidly. All of these trends are plausible.

Although doubts may be voiced as to the urbanity of California's cities, statistically it is the least rural of the states. Close to 90% of its residents are classed as urban. Among the many causes which could be cited, the most obvious [are] the mechanization and low manpower requirement of its extractive industries. Do not, though, overlook the effect on the great cities of national publicity. With immigration providing the bulk of growth and immigrants educated by press and TV, growth gravitates to massive centers. Everyone in New York has heard of Los Angeles, but how many know of Placerville?

Third, age distribution in California is not as usually imagined: Compared to the United States as a whole, California is a little deficient in elderly folk and has a small surplus of young adults.

Fourth, it is commonly thought that migrants become more and more the disadvantaged, the deprived, the poor, who escape from a bad into what they hope will be a better environment. Whether this is so I cannot say. At one time it appeared that immigrants from the Southwest came to the agricultural land of the Central Valley, were only transiently employed, and had to return to the family farm for the winter. They commonly made the seasonal migration for summer farm work several times before developing a niche of stable employment in California. How many times might such an immigrant be counted? In contrast, immigrants from the Northeast were believed to be going to California's cities, already assured of jobs or confident of employment. For example, within a stone's throw of my home, three new families arrived from out of state within a year. But all of these were corporate transfers, and were replacing equal numbers of emigrants. How shall we count these migrants?

In fact, one must hedge today on the patterns of immigration. Assessment of immigrants by automobile has been undertaken, but did the poorest arrive by car? Was the state of previous registration the state of origin, or did the person or family reach California only after several stops along the way? Disregarding these substantial doubts, immigrants today seem to obey reasonable laws of diffusion: more from populous areas, fewer from remote areas. Net annual immigration per 100,000 persons in the area of origin amounts to about 200 for the 11 Western states, around 75 for the plains, 85 for the Southwest, 25 for the Southeast, 50 for the North Central, and 30 for the Northeastern states.

One pattern that emerges clearly is that the slightly younger California population is being made still younger by immigrants. Those entering the state are rarely elderly. The proportion of persons over 40 years of age is lower than in the state's population. The fraction of immigrants between 20 and 30 is almost twice the fraction of residents of the state in that age group. Children under five are also more frequent among immigrants than among residents, but older children, plausibly, are scarcer. The picture, then, is one of immigration of young adults with young children.

In recent years, approximately 60% of the state's growth has been due to immigration, 40% to natural increase. This comes to 1000 per day net migration, the difference between 2000 immigrants and 1000 emigrants. These numbers reflect the high mobility of the American population, the loss among many of them of traditional attitudes about where to live. Americans will go where they are attracted, will leave places which repel them. . . .

But one year does not make a decade, much less a century. What comes next? Early last year, a brief press flurry arose when the State Department of Finance, the reputable and competent source of most of my data, released a statement that immigration to the state had ceased. Stopped dead. The test, a neat one, was that the population of school children in the third to the eighth grades was no greater than the population the year before of children in the second to seventh grades. The test is good because no children are born into this group, very few die out of it, [and] very few drop out of school; the only change is due to migration. It assumes only that family patterns do not change rapidly, an assumption justified by experience. A week later the statement was retracted and it was explained that a change had taken place in the manner of assembling the data and that some reports had stuck in the new channels and had been overlooked. Immigration has not, in fact, ceased.

Enough of the present. What of the future? . . . Continuance at 3.8% per year leads to 72 million Californians in the year 2000, 100 million in 2020. But estimates have rarely been for more than 45 million in 2000 and no one cares to project to 2020. Recent projections suggest less growth by century's end, and the State Department of Finance's current projection is for 39 to 42 million.

If there are not to be 72 million Californians at the end of the century, then California's growth rate must diminish. What will cause this to occur? The answer can be given in the form of a truism, and it must be emphasized that this answer is only a truism. It was phrased a few years ago in these terms:

California will stop growing one day because it will have become just as repulsive as the rest of the country.

The phrasing is provocative because of the twofold implications of "repulsive" meaning simply to repel like a magnetic field, but also carrying the sense of "disgusting," "repugnant," "distasteful." Taken at its face value, it says Americans will go where they are attracted, will leave where they are repelled. Today, they are more attracted than repelled by California; the day must come when as many are repelled as attracted.

Chemistry has an analogous term, the "fugacity," the escaping tendency, the tendency to flee. A gas tends to flee from a region of high fugacity to a region of lower fugacity and, as a result, its escaping tendency approaches equality in the two places. All people have tended to escape unhappy environments, to seek better ones. This is one of the essences of humanity. What else is hope? In the past its expression was slow; migration reflected bitter unrest. Today, it is easier.

The analogy suggests only that migration will continue until the escaping tendency is equal everywhere; until, on the average, for each Easterner who sees greener pastures in the West, a Westerner will see them in the East. How fast the adjustment will occur, how fast reaction to a vision of withering pastures will take place, is another matter. Willingness to migrate has been increasing for centuries, but even in the 19th century, migration was not for the timid, the secure, the provident, the affluent; rather, it was for the bold, the disinherited, the wastrel, the indigent. Provincialism, ignorance of remote lands, myths of perils along the way, all of these limited equilibration. Today, most Americans see California daily on the TV screen; [they] know that its customs, its hostelries for the itinerant differ but little from those of Maine or South Carolina; and they have a pretty clear notion of job opportunities in Los Angeles and San Jose. "If you think California is the promised land, fly out this weekend and have a look. But be back for work Monday!" Or case the entire state next vacation.

By and large, it is inescapable that equilibration is more rapid today than yesterday. If the fugacity relative to the rest of the country has not changed, then migration should have increased. Since it has not, the attractive force of California must be dropping. . . .

If growth will end with nationally uniform repulsiveness (and attractiveness), what is the anatomy of repulsiveness and attractiveness? A host of visions comes to mind. On the one hand: roses and sunshine in December, cool fog in summer, picnicking without rain, sunny beaches, magnificent mountains, coast lines, forests, vast empty lands, all near at hand; action, the metropolis of glamour always in the very pupil of the public eye; the metropolis of beauty, ringed by sea, hills, and bay; great universities. But on the other: crowded, stinking, smarting air, crowded highways, whether at weekend's close or workday's end; crowded schools, crowded prisons, crowded sewers; exorbitant taxes, instability, cranks and extremism from wing to wing: dissension, incipient revolution, unrest, unrest, unrest! Did everyone who went to California go because he couldn't get along with his neighbors?

Visions and knowledge of nearer places also swing the balance. What makes the climate of the Northeast repulsive? Those midweek winter storms, when you must shovel the driveway and hit the road in the gloom! Our grandparents stayed in and read "Snowbound"; we must go to work. Where have the water shortages been close to home? In the East. . . .

The greatest determinant of immigration must be the assurance, the realistic prospect or the vision of employment. Unemployment is higher in California than nationally. One of Governor Reagan's first campaign promises was that he would do better at creating new jobs than had Governor Brown. But, transparently, if he does create new jobs, resident Californians will not have a prior right to them. New jobs will create new immigrants. The only thing proved by high unemployment in California is that the state is still more attractive, less repulsive, than the rest of the country. The mobile American will still take a greater chance on being unemployed in California than elsewhere. This, too, will change.

Three years ago, a conference entitled "Man in California, 1980's" spent two days on the almost insuperable problems facing California in the next two decades: polluted air with the prospect of [two] billion [dollars] a year to be spent merely to maintain the present distressing status, polluted water, growing imbalance in water supply; agriculture disappearing under suburbs, deteriorating urban transport, and an unremitting struggle to improve highway transport; overcrowded parks, littered beaches, vanishing wildlife; urban slums, a perennial focus of unemployment; increasing crime, disturbed minds. All of these typical American phenomena, the discussion made quite clear, were to be most severe in California because of California's unremitting growth. The last act of the conference was to present a most convincing outline of the enormous task involved in attracting new industry to California, burdened by high taxes, long hauls, restrictive legislation. And yet, by virtue of the extraordinary competence of those searching for new industry, complete success on this score was to be expected. So here we have it: entire agreement that the state's problems are associated with its growth, and yet growth must be maintained. Do we conclude that a fate worse than an environment in ruins is an economy in ruins?

Growth means new jobs and new jobs mean growth. On this merry-go-round, which is cart and which is horse? And what drives the merry-go-round? . . .

The forecasts of California's growth are self-fulfilling forecasts. As long as they are believed, growth will continue. When they become incredible, growth will end. The mistaken announcement last February that growth had ceased was a remarkable act of bureaucratic integrity. If the statisticians had, in fact, decided that growth was about to end, would growth have ended?

Look now at the record of housing starts, of savings and loans failures, of residential vacancies. In spite of this record, which is disturbing, if we may judge from the level of unemployment, which remains high, California is not yet repulsive.

Finally, it has also been said that when growth ends in California, the party out of power will be congratulating itself for a decade. So the final questions remain. What *was* Governor Brown thinking of when, after that dead political campaign, he conceded the election to Ronald Reagan? And how can California remain attractive without attracting its ruin?

PROGRESS AGAINST GROWTH

The public questioning of the benefits of continued growth, in human numbers and in the facilities to serve those numbers) was more apparent in 1972 than it would be ten years later. (To many people, economic recession and unemployment have made growth seem desirable.) Economic recovery, getting the economy "going again," is equated with expansion of industries, increases in production of goods, and acceleration of construction. This positive view of growth is shortsighted and serves immediate human needs. Such a "solution" only forestalls the inevitable adjustments of economies to a condition of no-growth, of steady state. Thus, Luten's distinction between "growth" and "progress," and his suggestions for how we might turn from "pathological growth to humanistic progress," are appropriate regardless of the condition of the national or world economy.

In a young land that has experienced development at an unprecedented pace, it is not surprising that we struggle with the confusion between growth and progress. Historically, growth and progress have been to us almost interchangeable, so much so that even though we may not buy the shopworn idea that bigger is better, we still do not act as though we understand a distinction that seriously affects our lives and will determine the quality of life that our children will live.

The dictionary on our desk—a modest monument to popular opinion and usage—has no more than clues as to the distinction between growth and progress. The Sierra Club itself has informally stated that it is "not blindly against progress, but against blind progress." Yet one thing that "progress" definitely means is betterment, the movement from one stage toward a more advanced level. Are we to be against betterment, even if blind[?] Logically it would be more appropriate to say, "not blindly against growth, but against blind growth."

Reprinted by permission from *Sierra Club Bulletin*, 1972, 57(6): 22–24.

Growth can be something other than progress. Our dictionary gives "augmentation" as a synonym for growth—but it also lists "excrescence." There is the rub: Growth can go quite beyond healthy increase into the realm of pathology, and here we find that growth is "an abnormal proliferation of tissue, as in a tumor." Here cells lose their stable relationship with the organism, multiply without control, and die for lack of system. Alan Gregg [1955] has spoken of such growths passionately reproducing their cells while necrosis works outward from the center and the signs of death are seen in the process of growth. "Our rivers run silt," he says, "although we could better think of them as running the telltale blood of cancer." . . .

(We are told that we must have growth because economists insist upon it. We have listened intently because economists have said what we wanted to hear) Yet John Stuart Mill, over a century ago, saw problems ahead. Today, many others, such as Kenneth Boulding, tell us that indeed we do not need growth—but no one has been able to tell us clearly how to achieve a steady-state economy that we will accept. They have, though, illuminated important issues.

Herman Daly [see Daly, 1980] has contrasted Adam Smith's "unseen hand" which leads private self-interest unwittingly to serve the general welfare, with the "unseen foot," which kicks to pieces our common interest in the environment. And Mason Gaffney [1967], focusing more narrowly on the growth of cities, has outlined three sorts of "urban containment." The first, ordinarily called "positive planning" and depending heavily on zoning, he calls "negative containment" because he thinks it cannot stand up under the pressures of developers. The second, "neutral containment," is to have the cities quit subsidizing the suburbs. The third, "positive containment," is close to Henry George's "single tax."

The reality of urban subsidy to suburban growth is clearly shown in a $250 million bond issue passed in 1958 to provide water for the growth of metropolitan San Francisco's East Bay area. Berkeley's burden was some $20 million. What did Berkeley get in return? Essentially nothing, because the growth was not in Berkeley, but in Walnut Creek, Upper Pinole, and Lower Slurbovia. But since it was promised that taxes would not increase, Berkeley citizens voted for the bonds four-to-one, without realizing that water rates could be half as high were it not for the need to support new suburban growth. How many cities have paid for their own schools, then chipped in to pay for the schools in successive suburban rings? Gaffney would have the suburbs pay the whole cost of the new services they demand.

It is not surprising that California, the focus of the growth mystique, should generate the strongest opposition to growth. Force begets counterforce. Where the fever of growth is hottest, the antibodies form fastest. The conservation movement grows best on the site of worst abuse. Today, many in California question burgeoning development and when they are told that growth is good, are prepared to look the developer in the eye and ask him how much of that good will end up in his pocket.

In California, as in other places, an aversion to needless growth waxes:

• Palo Alto, persuaded by a Livingston and Blayney report, has concluded that it is wiser, and more economical to boot, to buy its hills for parkland than to permit subdivision.

• Marin County has rejected a new water supply on the grounds that it will only stimulate growth. (The voters are unlikely to have considered the issue of subsidy for newcomers.)

• Bolinas and Stinson Beach have rejected an oversized sewer project because they believe it will lead to undesirable growth.

• Berkeley has steadily lost interest in developing its submerged waterfront.

• Petaluma has proposed to limit its growth to 500 new homes per year.

• Mendocino voters have rejected a proposal to subdivide much of Round Valley.

• The Association of Hawaiian Counties is reported to have memorialized the legislature to bring that state's population growth to an end.

• Boulder, Colorado, has almost decided to set an upper limit for its population based on a study which concluded that the optimum size for an American city, based on per capita cost of municipal functions, is between 50,000 and 100,000.

The Boulder study is less than convincing in detail, but clearly an optimum size must exist. While the optimum size for a metropolis obviously exceeds that for a provincial city, few people who live in the San Francisco metropolitan area could easily identify any progress of importance in the last three decades. Economically and culturally, it is still the same regional center, but the amenities that made it one of the most attractive of great cities are disappearing at an alarming rate.

New York, as almost everyone agrees, has become ungovernable, almost inoperable, neurotic, necrotic, perhaps cancerous.

(But those who extol growth keep saying, "growth means jobs." Yes, jobs for today and for immigrants, but none guaranteed to local unemployed) Growth looks good to small business—up to a point. For winners can become losers with frightening suddenness: the local grocery store in a growing neighborhood until the supermarket moves in; the frontage on an increasingly busy street until the freeway by-passes it; the easy drive to work, and then the traffic jam. (The longer you ride the tiger of growth, the more dangerous it becomes.) The walls of growth press in on the city, shrink room to maneuver, bleed bargains dry, bankrupt the central stores, drain support from schools and libraries. Then the loss of pride, the strife that succeeds sense of community, the rubbish in the streets all suggest a condition where "the mass of men lead lives of quiet desperation." Finally, only friction and litigation can grow.

The consequences of growth so pervade the society that even when we can agree that it should end, a quality of momentum, an inertia, carries it along. We are dismayed to find that we have geared school construction and teaching training to a baby boom now passed, while we never thought of jobs for the adults they have become. Did we not want them to grow up? Again, in California, we have a system of highway financing almost guaranteed to meet the needs of an exponentially growing population of automobiles, and sure to lead to highway construction after all reasonable need has ended.

How do we turn from pathological growth to humanistic progress?

1. We need more sophistication. When your mayor tells you that growth broadens the tax base, laugh in his face and ask him to count for you the growing cities with growing tax bases—and with declining tax rates. When your antagonist tells you that your love of beauty is emotional, reply that love of money is an emotion, and hunger, too.

2. We need to be more skeptical. When opponents of the Redwood National Park argued that it would destroy Humboldt County's tax base, they sought to play on the gullibility of a public that could not easily check for itself that the loss would be less than 5%. When the power industry warns us that energy needs for environmental protection and mass transit will require great expansion, common sense should tell us that the incremental needs in these areas will be trifling

in comparison with the other "growth needs" that the utilities have in mind to promote.

3. We can vote down bond issues, try to limit facilities, but I think this will do more to publicize our feelings than to end growth. Dasmann suggested denying water to Southern California; water control authorities have come close to denying sewers to San Francisco; the Sierra Club suggests denying electric power. Facetiously, it has been said that this won't work but will, instead, trade the present population for one which drinks only alcohol, doesn't wash, and uses outhouses and kerosene lamps. Yet such measures might help if we were to increase water rates to the point where per capita consumption would level off, and if we were to require new developments to pay for all of the services provided rather than only for their incremental costs.

4. Can migration to growing areas be restricted? Probably not. Proposals to exact a California immigration fee of $1000 would be judged unconstitutional. But what of a carefully measured fee reflective of the facilities available to new residents but paid for by prior residents? If it is a denial of the privileges and immunities clause of the Fourteenth Amendment to restrict interstate migration, is it not a denial of the due process clause to force prior residents to contribute their property to the support of immigrants? Today Hawaii is seeking to limit the numbers of people traveling to and from the mainland, and also to control the number of its automobiles.

5. We must modify our institutions. They were developed for a juvenile, growing society, a poor society in an empty land. We now have a rich society in a full land, a mature society past its era of growth. The Federal Constitution may require amendment and, if we can identify changes based on sound principle, not expediency, we should not shrink from undertaking them. Would it be a disaster to revise the due process clause of the Fourteenth Amendment to give a man no more than a fair return on investment in land destined for public use? Would it be a disservice to society to exact an almost confiscatory capital gains tax on unimproved land? Its value is generated by the growing society, not by the productivity of its owner. Above all, it is time that we abandon our treasure-hunt philosophy of economics and reward productivity, not opportunism.

6. If growth is to end, we must abandon the growth mystique. Planners, all of them, relish growth. The plan for the San Francisco Bay Area prepared by the Association of Bay Area Governments envi-

sions a persistence of population growth at what is probably a conventional rate for planners. No evidence of effort to restrain growth appears; no effort to suppress and reinforce what may be a current magnificent, intelligent, and abrupt decision by the American people to end population growth. Can our generation close its eyes to growth when we know that the next generation must face up to it? Shall we live our lives as addicts to growth and then, having addicted our children, tell them in our wills to kick the habit? Let us say instead, and say it in our plans, that we expect growth to end soon; let our plans cover the period until growth has ended. Let our planning schools begin to produce planners who do not themselves believe in growth.

In California the temper is becoming clear: Given a choice between competent plans for growth and competent plans for nongrowth, voters will choose the latter. Rarely do they get such a choice. Usually, if any choice is granted, it is plans for growth prepared by a competent planning staff against plans for nongrowth prepared by overworked amateurs with no experience, working at midnight, with little access to needed details. When voters choose the former over the latter type, it is not because they are for growth, but because they are realistic. Witness the recent rejection by the voters of a categorical six-story limit for San Francisco.

The real power of planners is in their resources and technical competence. Why don't we give the progress-against-growth concept a chance by creating publicly supported groups of technically competent people who are committed to the idea of progress without growth? The cost would be slight, the stakes are large, and the voter would have the chance to decide between workable alternatives.

PART THREE

FOOD AND AGRICULTURE

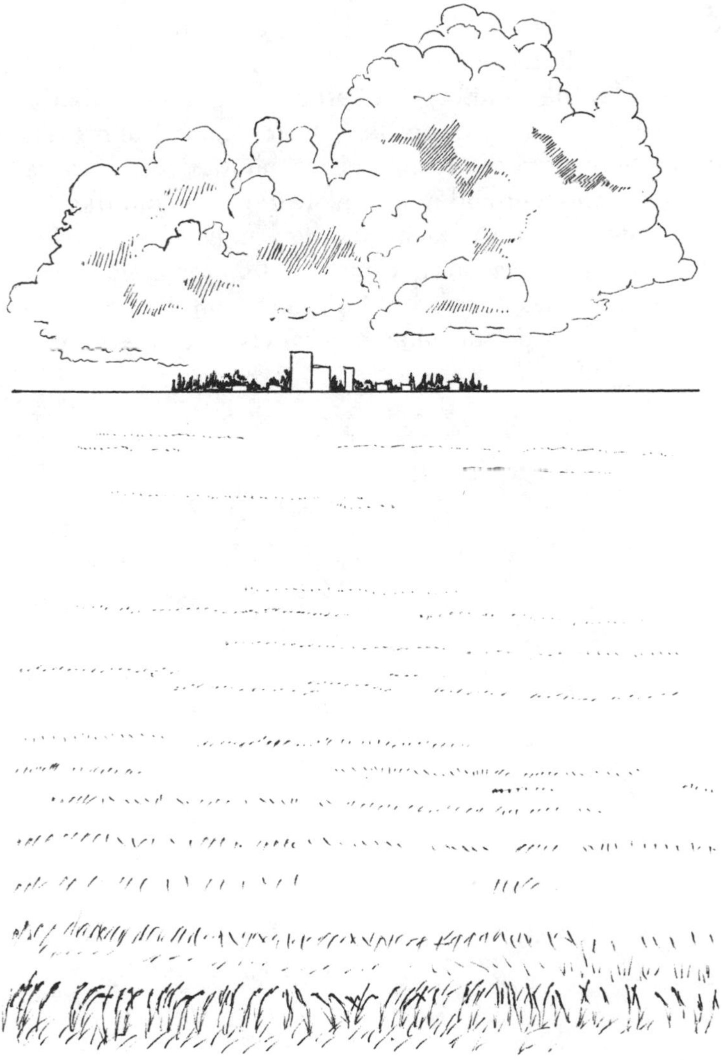

Luten's papers on food and agriculture are short essays on restricted topics; they lack the grand structure inherent in his discussions of energy resources ("The Economic Geography of Energy")
and the conservation movement ("Fading Away?"), or the synthesis that is so obvious in his work on water ("The Use and Misuse
of a River"), or the long and thoughtful penetration of rationales
that marks his defense of preserving wild nature ("Resource Quality and Value of the Landscape"). Perhaps questions of food have
been too far from his predisposition for technological matters or
his worry over wilderness. Nonetheless, the four papers in this section, more than longer and more involved papers in other sections, illustrate in their simplicity and directness Luten's style of
handling resource questions and his affection for them. Read
them for what he has done with the topics (and think what a similar approach might do for others), as much as for the information
that they present.

VANISHING FARMLAND

In a paper that appears in the preceding section (see "Progress Against Growth"), Luten suggested that those concerned with environmental matters must become more sophisticated in their understanding of the workings of society and more skeptical about the alleged benefits of development. In this paper on loss of farmland in the United States, Luten explored the importance of numbers in a highly visible environmental issue, and he illustrated the type of questioning that can result from increased sophistication and skepticism.

The article's tone may surprise many people who identify themselves as "environmentalists"; some could even see in its paragraphs a defense of the development that eliminates farmland. Luten did not intend that such an interpretation be made, but he did urge his readers to question conventional thinking, whether it is that of "developers" or "environmentalists." Although he expressed considerable doubt that the growing complexity of environmental issues in 1981 was within the grasp of individual minds, his admonition remains clear: It is just as important to *think* as simply to think *right*.

What is happening to our farmland? Twenty years ago it was conventional wisdom to say we were losing a million acres a year. Today I read, "Every year, in the United States, we lose not less than three million acres of cropland."

At first sight farmland is lost to suburbanization, but from 1970 to 1978, one-third of new housing was in multiunit structures that displaced little farmland. The single-family houses, averaging 1.2 million a year during that interval, could hardly have claimed 2.5 acres each. A common response is that they did indirectly, because the leapfrogging of new suburban developments removes much more land from farming than is actually occupied by house lots. This is a good

Reprinted by permission from *Landscape*, 1981, 25(2): 32.

rebuttal for the first year, but it wears out because the unused parcels do fill in. By now we should be close to a steady state; that is, for each new area, older areas should be filling in.

A more careful statement in the brochure, "Where Have the Farmlands Gone?," from the National Agricultural Land Study (NALS) [1980] reads, "One million acres of America's prime farmlands are urbanized each year. . . . We are losing another two million acres of less quality, nevertheless productive agricultural land, to nonagricultural conversion each year."

Taxed by me, Dr. Michael Brewer, the agricultural economist who directs research for NALS, responded in more detail. He explained that a high percentage of new, single-unit housing starts during the last decade was in nonsewered areas, and therefore likely to remove considerable land from farms. He also pointed out that annual conversion to urban and transportation uses is estimated at 675,000 acres of cropland, 400,000 acres of range and pasture, 550,000 acres of forest land, and 520,000 acres of other uses. Also, agricultural land converted to water uses, such as reservoirs, is 75,000 acres of cropland, 135,000 acres of range and pasture, 270,000 acres of forest, and 355,000 acres of other uses. The total land converted to urban, transportation, and water uses adds up to 2,980,000 acres—close to the three million commonly cited.

This leads to several lines of discussion. First, such numbers are terribly difficult to generate. Information must be assembled county by county. Even the agricultural censuses are unsatisfactory, because they do not interrogate ex-farmers who have sold out to developers; all the censuses show is how much cropland has changed use since the last census, without showing additions and losses. The study by NALS is trying to reach down to county levels via the Soil Conservation Service.

Second, most of the numbers cited on farmland loss are not intended to be used in arithmetic, but only to catch attention and to raise concern.

Third, communicating with this intensely urban society about agriculture is not easy. In despair an American agriculturist coined the ironic question, "What need have we of farms so long as we have supermarkets?" A primary problem of American environmentalism is that its self-assigned tasks are complex almost beyond the capacity of single minds to grasp. To demand synthesis, to demand holistic thought in a world of specialists is to demand superbrains. It is a testimony to failure that environmentalism has well nigh written off education in favor of indoctrination. Out of which comes another irony: "Holistic thought reminds one mostly of Swiss cheese, not from the odor but because it is just as full of holes."

Fourth, before we will get very far on the matter of land conversion, we must clarify our understanding of "cropland," "prime farmland," "farmland," and even "farm."

Fifth, we do have a problem in farmland conversion, but land conversion is not new. Much of New England has been converted from forest to garden and field and back via pasture. New York State is going through the same process. It is not beginning, neither is it about to end. Brewer's figure for annual conversion of cropland is 0.16%. It reflects that precious little of the corn belt is being converted. But some very special cropland is being converted and at an alarming rate.

Even these numbers are difficult to pin down. Everyone in California has been told so many times about paving over wonderful soil that they have no doubts about it. San Jose and its growth is a prime example. Yet Santa Clara County's agricultural production in 1978 was over $100 million and in 1974 the value of its agricultural production exceeded that of all but one of North Dakota's counties.

What can we do? If we become competent in this field, what other field will we have to abandon for lack of time? If we are to be educated rather than indoctrinated, whom can we trust to teach us? Can the environmental movement turn from indoctrination to education? Probably not. The universities? It is doubtful.

CENSUS OF AGRICULTURE

"Most of the numbers cited on farmland loss," Luten said in the preceding essay, "are not intended to be used in arithmetic, but only to catch attention and to raise concern." In other words, numbers are typically part of the

Reprinted by permission from *Landscape*, 1979, 32(2): 1–2.

rhetoric used by "developers" and "conservationists" to influence decisions. Few people pay close attention to numbers or understand them well enough to catch their misuse. In this essay, Luten urged his readers to learn to use numbers "in arithmetic" as part of the increased sophistication and skepticism necessary to be effective either as scholars or as defenders of the environment.

The U.S. Census of Agriculture is a valuable source of numbers relevant to these purposes. This essay thus provides a few facts about farms, but, more importantly, it reminds us to use such a source frequently and with thoughtfulness.

Farming, from feedlots to orchids, from corn to carrot seed, from Florida to Alaska, from mushroom cellar to the King Ranch, is diverse and complex almost beyond comprehension. Even defining a farm and farming can be vexing and must be arbitrary. The federal government over the years has tried to learn about farming just as it has tried to learn about the nation's population. From 1840 to 1920 a census of agriculture took place every ten years as part of the population census. The U.S. Bureau of the Census now interrogates American farmers every five years. These censuses are out of phase with the decennial population census—job leveling, I suppose—and are dated 1969, 1974, and so on. Interrogation for the 1979 census is under way now.

Since 1974 a "farm" is a "place" (not necessarily of contiguous land) under an "operator" that normally produces at least $1000 worth of agricultural products. No effort is made to define a farmer. Is it the person who plows, seeds, cultivates, and harvests; the person who decides when, where, and how to do these things; or the person who pays the bills and banks the proceeds? Rather than deal with such questions, the census directs its questions at "operators." The operator may or may not be the laborer, and may or may not be the owner. The census officials apparently have decided that these are too elusive to identify. The operator is commonly in residence on the land and can be found. More and more I think we agree that the operator is the farmer.

Publication of the results takes time: The 1974 principal reports, *State and County Data*, one for each state, came out in 1977. They fill a five-foot shelf. Their size stems from the detail, some of which is broken down to the county level. Texas, with 254 counties, is the thickest.

Census reports are not the place to look for details of agricultural production; try *Agricultural Statistics* and its state counterparts for that. Many of the census questions are "check appropriate box" type and, accordingly, reveal only ranges. For example, farm area may be 100 to 139 acres, or sales, $20,000 to $39,999.

But the census does sort out results in great detail. If you want to know how many of the farm operators in Aroostook County are between 45 and 54 years of age, it will be in the Aroostook County section of the volume for Maine. If you want to know how many of them are "black or other races," you will find the total in the county section, but the breakdown by age is reported only by entire states.

Farms with small sales, from $1000 to $2500, are set aside in a special class. In 1974, 77,000 such farms, 31% of the total number of 2.45 million, provided only one percent of the total value of farm products sold. Most of these farms are operated part-time or by farmers over 65. These farms tend to be small, although 67 farms in California are over 2000 acres. Many are avocational. Some reflect welfare problems.

Size of farms is also pertinent. Although half the nation outside of Alaska is in farms, most of it is in pasture and range. But if public land is leased for grazing with payment based on the number of animals grazing the land, it does not count as farmland. In contrast, if it is leased for a fee per acre, it *is* counted as farmland. As a result, a great deal of public land in the West that is used for grazing and looks like the private land beside it, is not counted as "farmland." Because of this limited definition of farmland and because grazing land is generally of low value and productivity, harvested cropland is a more useful category. Harvested cropland is a minor part of the area of farms: 307 million compared with 1017 million acres in 1974.

I pulled three volumes off the shelves to do some comparing. I chose California because it is most complex and is first in sales, Indiana because it is pure corn belt and is the smallest of the corn belt states, and North Dakota because it is large, simple, and poor.

I wanted to begin by snipping off those confusing fringes: farms without harvested cropland, farms with trivial sales, and, yes, why not, farms with less than ten acres. The lack of harvested cropland ordinarily identifies a farm as depending on pasture and range for livestock production, but a great many such farms also harvest crops. So all you can do is focus on harvested cropland and let pasture and range wait for another day. The small farms cannot be easily rejected, because

Number of Farms

	Total	Less than 10 acres	Less than $2500 sales	Without harvested cropland
California	67,674	13,480	18,587	15,920
Indiana	87,915	3,594	18,215	7,720
North Dakota	42,710	981	2,267	2,067

some have enormous sales. Forty-four in California sold over $500,000 each. The scarcity of small farms in North Dakota, where farming is for keeps, not for fun, suggests that in California and Indiana many of the small farms are avocational like the farms with small sales. The only fringe that can be snipped off is farms with small sales, and this the census has done. All that follows is limited to farms with sales over $2500.

Compare harvested cropland.

Farms with Harvested Cropland

	Number	Harvested cropland (million acres)
California	42,000	8.2
Indiana	68,000	11.0
North Dakota	40,000	19.2

California has less harvested cropland than Indiana, which is less than a quarter its size. North Dakota farms are largest, averaging 473 acres of harvested cropland. California at 157 acres and Indiana at 140 acres are almost the same. But the range from small to large is dramatic.

Size of Farms with Harvested Cropland (HC) as Percent of All Farms

	Farms with less than 100 acres HC	Farms with more than 2000 acres HC
California	72%	0.83%
Indiana	53%	0.05%
North Dakota	7%	1.00%

Now, how about the farmers, excuse me, the operators. They are said to be old and growing older. What does the census say?

Average Age of Operators

	1964	1974
California	51.9	53.2
Indiana	50.9	50.2
North Dakota	48.1	49.9

Why should California farmers be oldest, and Indiana farmers be growing younger? Perhaps something comes out of another pattern.

Modal Size in Acres of Harvested Cropland with Age of Operator

Age	California	Indiana	North Dakota
Under 25	1–49	100–199	200–499
25–34	1–49	200–499	200–499
35–44	1–49	200–499	500–999
45–54	1–49	200–499	200–499
55–64	1–49	100–199	200–499
65 and over	1–49	1–49	200–499

In California small farms so dominate that operations of 1 to 49 acres are the mode regardless of the age of the farmer. Indiana is an interesting case. Farmers seem to increase their operations into their 50s and then taper off. North Dakota exhibits this pattern, although it is less clear.

The examination could go on and on. The census is clearly a field ready for cultivation on many axes. My best answer to the question, "So what?" is that one must work a field to understand it.

WHAT AMERICA GROWS

In the preceding paper, Luten suggested that the U.S. Census of Agriculture is a valuable source of numbers and information on food and food growing in the United States. In this article, he used another source, *Agricultural Statistics*, in the creation of a single, graphic representation of "what America grows" on the "average American farm."

Americans from various parts of the country probably would have different images of such a farm. A Californian might envision vast areas in vegetables and fruit. Someone from Florida might picture a sizable area of citrus. A person from Ohio would see corn and soybeans. The view of the Midwesterner, as Luten pointed out, would be the most accurate.

The predominance of grains in U.S. agriculture is typical for the world as a whole. Probably two-thirds of the world's cropland is used to grow cereals (and much of the rest supports tubers). Yet the large proportion of the U.S. cropland devoted to feed grains makes American agriculture unusual, even unique. The large quantity of cropland in the United States, about 10% of the total for the world, is also distinctive.

The calculation of total world land area devoted to the raising of livestock for meat imports to the United States is particularly apropos today. Many people suggest that the clearing of tropical forests in Latin America is motivated by desires to market meat in the United States. Luten's number indicates that the land used for imported meat is equivalent to a square about 125 miles on a side. Such an area is a sizable portion of Central America (maybe 8%), but it is a trivial part of the huge Amazon basin (less than 1%). The image of American desires for cheap beef as responsible for deforestation in Latin America seems erroneous.

A lot of talk is heard these days about the evils of mechanized agriculture, and the criticism comes with recommendations that all of us grow our own food. Advice on diet reform is often included, together

Reprinted by permission from *Landscape*, 1981, 25(1): 18–19.

with hints on possible energy savings, and, almost always, promises of enormous production. Lacking competence on most of this but feeling a need to be helpful, I have done a bit of work to help you plan your own farm. This won't answer all the questions nor solve all the problems, but it will get you started.

In the diagram [Figure 1] you will see how to lay out your own "national average agricultural operation." You must be willing to imagine that the cropland you have in mind is typical of the nation's cropland—no better, but no worse, and just as diverse, climatically and edaphically. Also your land is to be more geometrically organized than the nation's, which has its worst cropland in the high plains and its best scattered from New Jersey to California.

Less facetiously, this is an exercise that may surprise you by revealing how the nation uses its cropland. The source is the 1979 edition of the government publication *Agricultural Statistics* [U.S. Department of Agriculture, 1979]. The numbers are for "area planted" to crops for 1978. Complications with the statistics abound; however, I think the resulting picture is fair and adequately representative.

The total "area planted" includes hayland (but not pasture or range) and permanent crops such as orchards. Some of the "area planted" results from double cropping, for example, soybeans follow-ing winter wheat. The diagram is not planned for double cropping; if you can manage some double cropping, the dimensions of your tract will be smaller. A few minor items, such as peppermint, have been ignored. Seed growing was also ignored. The total U.S. acreage in crops comes to 351,145,000 acres, or 1.607 acres for each of the 218,548,000 Americans that year. Accordingly, I laid out your plot as a rectangle, 208.71 feet (the side of a square acre) by 335.34 feet.

To show how this is used, I have indicated (a) what we use domestically for food, (b) what we use for livestock feed, (c) what we use in industry, in this case limited to tobacco and cotton, and (d) what we export.

Pasture has been ignored because it is not treated in my source. Range has been ignored on T. R. Vale's authority [Vale, 1979]. He finds that only about 2% of American beef can be traced back to the [federal] range. This is not the number of cattle born there, but the pounds of beef. I have suggested the land required for production of imported meat. Similarly, I have estimated land required for imported sugar.

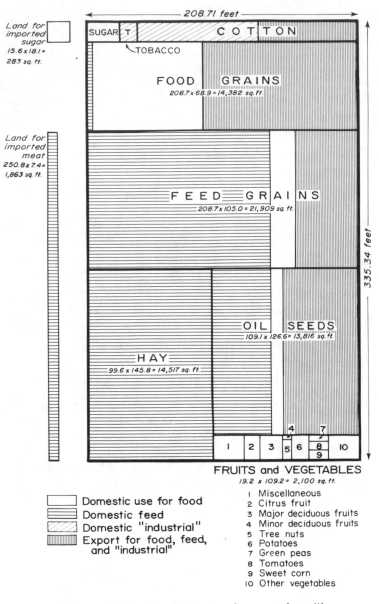

Land for imported sugar
15.6 × 18.1 =
283 sq. ft.

Land for imported meat
250.8 × 7.4 =
1,863 sq. ft.

208.71 feet

SUGAR T

TOBACCO

COTTON

FOOD GRAINS
208.7 × 68.9 = 14,382 sq. ft.

FEED GRAINS
208.7 × 105.0 = 21,909 sq. ft.

335.34 feet

OIL SEEDS
109.1 × 126.6 = 13,816 sq. ft.

HAY
99.6 × 145.8 = 14,517 sq. ft.

4 7
1 2 3 5 6 8 10
9

FRUITS and VEGETABLES
19.2 × 109.2 = 2,100 sq. ft.

Domestic use for food
Domestic feed
Domestic "industrial"
Export for food, feed, and "industrial"

1 Miscellaneous
2 Citrus fruit
3 Major deciduous fruits
4 Minor deciduous fruits
5 Tree nuts
6 Potatoes
7 Green peas
8 Tomatoes
9 Sweet corn
10 Other vegetables

[Figure 1. Plan for the "natural average farm."]

Coffee and tea have been left out, not because they are vicious drugs, but for lack of an easy way to deal with them. Fish also have been omitted; they are trivial in the American diet. Cottonseed oil has been ignored because I have no clear way to divide acreage between fiber and seed; fortunately it is not large. Oil seeds are divided between feed and food in proportion to the yield of soy meal and soy oil; most of the export is as soybeans.

Aside from telling you how to divide up your 1.607 acres, the diagram shows you that a spectacularly small part of America's planted cropland is devoted to the crops we have in mind when we think of gardening and growing our own food. In contrast, an enormous portion, nearly half, goes for feed, and a third for export. Only a sixth is planted directly for domestic food. And of that sixth, seven-eighths is for staples: wheat, rye, corn, soy oil, sugar, potatoes, and dry beans. (Included with dry edible beans in the miscellaneous category are items such as hops and popcorn.) The other eighth, 2.1% of the total cropland, includes amenity foods: citrus fruits, deciduous fruits, tree nuts, and most vegetables.

Here, in summary, is how your land might be used:

	Percent	Square feet
Domestic food	16.3	11,403
(Staples)	(14.2)	(9,964)
(Amenity food)	(2.1)	(1,439)
Domestic feed	49.5	34,647
Domestic industrial	2.3	1,637
Export	31.9	22,302
Total	100.0	69,989

Land outside of the United States used to provide your share of imported food:

Sugar	0.4	283
Meat	2.7	1,863

If when you think of agriculture you think of the orchards of the Sacramento Valley, the truck crops of New Jersey and the Salinas

Valley, and the cherry orchards of Michigan, then look out of the window if you fly across the continent on a clear day. Keep looking from the first time you see the squared fields of township and range in Ohio until they fade into the Rocky Mountains. Across Ohio, Indiana, Illinois, Iowa, and Nebraska, for two hours, on both sides of the plane, the section lines go north and south to a horizon three hundred miles away. Warren S. Thompson once said, "There is no other agricultural realm on the face of the earth that faintly compares to the Mississippi Valley." Five-sixths of our cropland is there. Five-sixths of your 1.607-acre personal plot represents the Mississippi Valley with its grain and feed crops.

With the diagram as a starting point, you could take off on many tangential crusades. Perhaps it is just as well that the page ends here.

HOW BIG IS AN ACRE?

Some agricultural topics, such as that discussed in "Vanishing Farmland," lie clearly in the arenas of policy and controversy. Other topics seem removed from contemporary crises. The dedicated activist or concerned student may be bored by the delving into matters that seem so lacking in obvious "relevance." But new perspectives often bring new insights, and the requirement that a study must have immediate application to particular problems only limits innovation. "One must work a field to understand it," Luten said in an article earlier in this section. That comment is equally apropos here.

On the northeast corner of Kauai, the most northwesterly of the larger islands of the Western state of Hawaii, the road comes down close to sea level before it ends at Kee Beach. On that coastal fringe we passed a house built up eight feet on stilts.

Reprinted by permission from *Landscape*, 1978, 22(3): 1–2.

"See," I said to my wife and son, in demonstration of my superior knowledge of these parts, "there's a smart man who's arranged to have the next tsunami sweep under his house rather than through it." We stopped to take a picture and to confirm my geographical competence by interrogating the owner. He assented, but grudgingly, to the tidal wave proposition and added that the real reason for the stilts was that the planning commission would only let him build a one-story house and, by doing it this way, he got a lot of free storage space beneath it. Besides, it improved his view. Set down a bit, I asked him how much land cost out there in that far corner of the United States.

"A dollar a foot."

"Not a front foot; it must be more than that!"

"No," he snorted. "A dollar a square foot."

"A dollar a square foot; that's $43,000 an acre!"

"No it isn't; it's $43,560 an acre."

And, of course, he was exactly right. (He owned 20 of those acres.) Buffeted by the jeers of wife and son, I retreated.

How big *is* an acre? When one tells urban college students, one thinks of squarish suburban acres. But it won't come out evenly: $208.71^2 = 43,559.86$. And yet a square mile is exactly 640 acres; and most homestead grants of 160 acres were certainly a half-mile square.

While the mile (1000 paces of two steps each) seems to have been pretty well standardized by Elizabethan times, diverse acres abounded all over western Europe, and in 1914, Frederick Seebohm was able to fill a sizable book, *Customary Acres*, with descriptions and speculations on interrelations among scores of variously defined acres. No *a priori* reason exists for a precise relation between a square mile and an acre. Edmund Gunter (1581–1626) brought it off by inventing and gaining general acceptance of "Gunter's chain" of 66 feet, with 100 links of 0.66 feet each. Gunter's chain is, then, four rods or 22 yards long. A square chain, 66 feet squared, is 4356 square feet. By defining an acre as ten square chains, 640 of them will fit exactly into a square mile: $4356 \times 10 \times 640 = 5280^2$.

Gunter (in a [1673] reprint of one of his books) confronts himself with the problem of a square acre in a curious table and then ignores it. The table provides conversions of areal measures above a diagonal in a rectangular format. Below the diagonal, in corresponding spaces, it provides the corresponding linear measure (the square roots). Thus, square mile above, 5280 feet below. But, while acre is given above, the

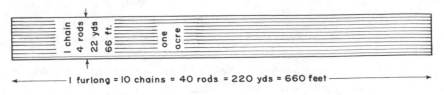

[Figure 1. The rectangular acre.]

space below for the length of its side (if it were square: 208.71 feet) is left blank. Probably he knew that no one was interested in a square acre.

Certainly, no one who farmed was interested in a square acre. An acre was a furrow ("furlong") in length by enough width to give an area that could be plowed in a day with appropriate equipment. And so, while the side of a square containing an acre can only be defined precisely as $66 \times \sqrt{10}$ feet, a properly shaped rectangular acre is ten chains by one chain; 40 rods by 4 rods; 220 yards by 22 yards; one furlong by one chain [Figure 1]. One can, if anyone cares, fit 640 of such shaped acres precisely into a square mile, 80 across by 8 down.

In the Ordinance of 1785, Congress, as prerequisite to disposition of the new public domain, prescribed a survey by townships, each six miles square and subdivided into sections of one square mile, 640 of Gunter's acres, each [Figure 2]. The sections are always numbered, a matter of intimate familiarity to most American farmers. But the

6	5	4	3	2	1
7	8	9	10	11	12
18	17	16	15	14	13
19	20	21	22	23	24
30	29	28	27	26	25
31	32	33	34	35	36

[Figure 2. The township, as prescribed by the Ordinance of 1785.]

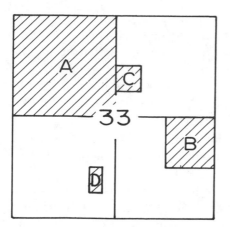

[FIGURE 3. Various subdivisions of a township section.]

system does not lend itself to subdivision by enumeration of acres within a section. Neither does it lend itself to decimal subdivision. . . .

Even though the Congress may have envisioned a seciton for every applicant, subdivision soon became necessary and it was commonly binary or quaternary. And subdivisions by quarters (which abbreviates the process) or by halves persists—although probably more in the recorders' offices than in the fields. Thus, in the accompanying diagram [Figure 3], the shaded areas would be described as follows: (A) NW ¼ Sect 33; (B) NE ¼ SE ¼ Sect 33; (C) NW ¼ SW ¼ NE ¼ Sect 33; (D) W ½ NE ¼ SE ¼ SW ¼ Sect 33. In the last of these parcels we are down to only half a square furlong, still five days' plowing by Elizabethan standards. This sort of subdivision remains far more common in the records than any decimal mode. And, in vernacular, the homestead tract was referred to as a "quarter section" more often than as "160 acres."

Finally, had Congress been able to wait a few years for establishment of a better system, our landscape might have been metric from the start. But, in fact, the French and American revolutions were too closely intertwined, and the Ordinance of 1785 preceded by six years the adoption of meters and kilometers, of ares and hectares. Thomas Jefferson did propose a more "rational" system based on a "geographical mile" of 6086 feet. He would have had the survey establish squares that were ten of such miles on a side, and divisions into 100 "lots" or sections of one square mile each. With such miles, each such lot would contain 850.31 of our acres. Paul W. Gates [1968], from whose history of the public lands I retrieved this item, does not say whether Jefferson would have proposed subdivisions of sections (did Jefferson, too, believe there would be enough sections to please everyone?). But, if driven to it, he might well have suggested a second decimal subdivision into parcels of 8.5031 acres each. What would he have used for a name for such a parcel, a parcel which, if square, would have measured exactly 608.6 feet on a side? Had he taken as his model the British nautical mile, 6,080 feet, a side of his decimal subdivision would have been exactly 608 feet.

The "geographical mile," as well as several versions of nautical miles, stems from the length of one minute of longitude at the equator. The trouble with all such definitions, as with the length of the meter, is that high precision in their determination is quite beyond us. The meter itself, originally intended to be 1/10,000,000 of a quadrant of the earth from equator to pole, later had to be primarily defined as the interval between two scratches on a bar of platinum–iridium alloy in Paris. Even that has been succeeded in more than one step to a present primary definition as 1,650,763.73 wavelengths of a certain spectral line of a certain isotope of a certain element. Not because it is more primary, more rational, more anything except that it can be measured more precisely. And, in the last analysis, the foot, the mile, and all English units of length and area also hang on that same wavelength measurement.

Even though all of these are easily decimalized, note that we do still have a deep-rooted preference for binary subdivisions: The circle of the compass itself is divided into directions by binary subdivisions. (Why are there no compasses with *six* primary directions? Was it because the Babylonians were not navigators?) This takes us back to where we began: the [northeast] corner of the [northwest] island of the western United States.

PART FOUR

ENERGY

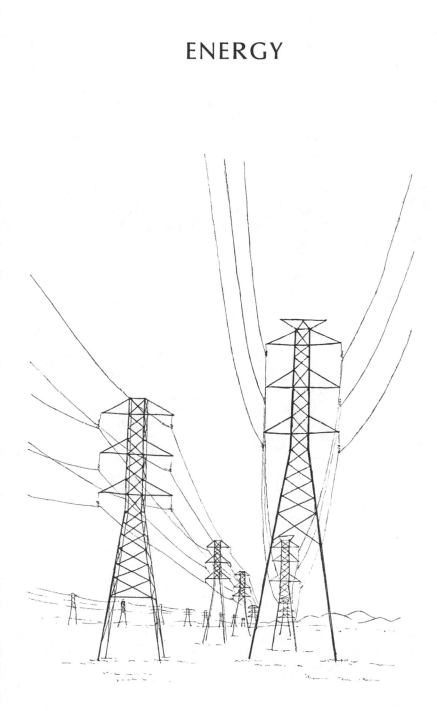

A key characteristic of Luten's writings (illustrated particularly well by the papers on population) has been his perceptive questioning of the assumed and the conventional. In these papers on energy resources, another major trait of Luten's is revealed: an expertise in technology. This expertise reflects Luten's academic training and professional career as a research chemist; however, he has transcended the usual boundaries of such a background by blending it with healthy skepticism. The combination makes Luten's papers on energy notable, and explains his reputation in this area of natural resource study.

THE ECONOMIC GEOGRAPHY OF ENERGY

At the beginning of the 1970s, as during the preceding decades, natural resource specialists were studying a myriad of policy questions regarding energy sources and uses. Environmentalists were worrying about the effects on the landscape of the construction of power plants and the mining of fossil fuels; they were also expressing concern over radioactive wastes from fission electric facilities. Yet most Americans did not yet view energy resources as the prospective basis for domestic and international crises. Nonetheless, a general awareness about energy supply and utilization was surfacing, as suggested by the focus of the September 1971 issue of *Scientific American*, subtitled "Energy and Power."

The contents and tone of Luten's article in that special issue reflect the time during which it was written. Luten did not deal in detail with the dilemma of radioactive waste disposal or the impact of strip mining. He did not mention such phrases as "energy independence," "China syndrome," "Three Mile Island," "core meltdown," "strategic oil reserve," "gasohol," and "synthetic fuels," which later in the 1970s would become familiar parts of our energy vocabulary. The article's restraint mirrors, in part, a time when energy was still seen in a noncrisis framework.

The paper also reflects the particular approach of its author to natural resource issues. His objective was description, illustration, and analysis of a chronological sequence of activities by which people utilize energy sources. The presentation allows us to understand more clearly how such sources are used, and it stresses both the similarities and differences of energy sources in terms of potentials and limitations. Although Luten concentrated here on conventional fuels, his framework could, and can, illuminate the use of so-called alternative fuels.

This article reveals two other aspects of Luten's thinking on energy. We see him as anything but a blind denouncer of advanced technology; yet we can also see skepticism about technological advancement in his suggestions that "the end of the road of increasing scale is close at hand," and that energy innovations of the future "seem to have less potential for working revolutions in our lives than the heat engine, small electric motors, and the automobile." We also see him as a successful prophet: He suggested that large pipelines would become "international political issues," and the subsequent concern over the natural gas pipelines from Alaska across Canada to the lower 48 states, from Mexico to the United States, and from the Soviet Union to Western Europe has borne him out. Moreover, Luten anticipated a questioning by Americans of the previously assumed link between growth in energy use and increased human welfare. During the 1980s, use of energy declined far more than could be explained by a sluggish economy alone. Luten's comment that "resistance to the purchase of industrial energy is increasing" has proven true, although he underestimated the conservation of energy at home and on the road. This decrease in energy utilization, which many forecasters say will continue, has been forced by higher costs, a circumstance only wondered by Luten in 1971: "Where on the rising consumption curve is the breaking point between gains and losses? Are we likely to find that point by encouraging growth until the customer—no longer interested in more energy or unable to afford it—finally offers resistance, and growth ends?"

All men have fire and have used it to change the green face of the earth, and those who live near fuel can have heat in abundance. Only those men who can convert heat and other forms of energy to work, and can apply that work where they will, can travel over the world and shape it to their ends. The crux of the matter is the generation of work—the conversion of energy and its delivery to the point of application. This article will explore some of the interrelations among the location of energy resources, the feasibility and cost of transporting energy commodities, and the evolution of technology for converting energy.

Consider for a moment the three crucial developments of the past two centuries that have worked successive revolutions in the human utilization of energy. The first was the steam engine, invented and developed in England primarily as an answer to the flooding of deep coal mines by groundwater. Removing the water was far beyond the capacity of human porters or of pumps driven by draft animals. For several centuries the task was accomplished by pumps driven by water mills. There was no realistic way, however, of conveying the action of water mills beyond the immediate site. Was coal mining to be forever confined to the streamside? The response to that challenge was the steam engine. It could operate wherever fuel could be delivered. In the 19th century its efficiency improved enough to make possible the steam locomotive, which could carry enough fuel with it to do work in transport.

The next big step came with the electric generator, the transmission of electricity, and the electric motor, which freed work from its bondage to belts and shafts connected to the steam engine's flywheel; work could be provided wherever it was wanted, and in small or large amounts. The final step of this kind was the development of the automotive engine: a small power plant that was less convenient than an electric motor but was not even tied to a power line. Other fuels and conversion devices have appeared and will appear in the future, but they would seem to have less potential for working revolutions in our lives than the heat engine, small electric motors, and the automobile.

Man's exploitation of an energy resource comprehends seven operations: discovery of the resource, harvest, transportation, storage, conversion, use, and disposal.

[DISCOVERY AND HARVEST]

The discovery of the resource may be explicit and material, as in the case of a coal seam or an oil field. It may be conceptual: the idea of a reservoir or a scheme for capturing solar energy. Often it is the discovery of a conversion, as in the case of fire, the steam engine, and uranium fission. And sometimes discovery comprises an entire series of technological improvements, as will be the case when shale oil is finally exploited successfully.

How much has resource discovery influenced human events? The United States ran on fuel wood until it had burned up the forests on croppable land as far as the prairies. England and Europe had done about the same thing, and when people ran out of wood, they turned to coal. (They complained; they preferred the old smells and smoke to the new, but they stayed warm with coal.) Whether it was the presence of coal that turned them to industry is another matter, one that is much more difficult to establish. Admittedly wood would not have sufficed, but a few lands with limited fuel have done well (notably Japan) and some with abundant fuel have not. Certainly local fuel does not seem to have been a sufficient condition, or even an entirely necessary one except for a pioneering society.

Gas and oil were adopted rather differently. It is said that as early as 1000 B.C. the Chinese drilled 3000 feet down for natural gas, piping it in bamboo and burning it for light and heat and to evaporate brine for salt. Elsewhere candles persisted for millenniums and were only slowly succeeded by fatty oils in lamps. Coal had little to offer as an illuminant, but the coking of coal provided gas as well as coke. Handling gas required innovation, which came through the chemical studies of the late 18th century. In England "town gas" soon undercut the price of fatty oil for lamps in the new factories; in the less urban United States oil lamps persisted until kerosene appeared in the mid-19th century.

Discovery comes first in the exploitation of a resource; use and then disposal are the next to last and last steps. The sequence of the intervening steps can vary depending on the resource and on the economics and geography and the specific set of operations they dictate. In some cases a preliminary conversion step is introduced: Wood may be made into charcoal or coal into coke, and petroleum must be refined.

[TRANSPORTATION]

A commodity can move by land either in a continuous process in a conduit or as a batch in a vehicle; shipping by sea must be by batches in vessels. The batch shipper has freedom of destination; a conduit constrains shipment to the chosen destination. The batch shipper, however, needs terminal storage facilities at both ends of every trip so that he can pick up and deliver his cargo with minimum lost time. For some commodities there are many possibilities; for others there are few choices or none.

The constraints on transport have had a significant effect on the adoption of new energy technologies. Primitive people can carry wood easily, coal less handily. The handling of liquids calls for pots and baskets; gases are uncooperative and elusive. Before the advent of simple and efficient equipment for containing and pumping fluids at high pressures, a development largely of recent decades, petroleum moved in barrels or in wood vats on flatcars, and long-distance transmission of gas was impractical. At sea, however, there were tankers, which began carrying oil from the Caucasus almost a century ago.

The combination of tankers and pipelines brought the fossil fuel industry to a momentarily stable condition in the years after World War II. All the possibilities seemed to have been exploited. Now, with competition tightening, innovations are again being pressed hard and marginal improvements are being squeezed for any advantage. Oil brought great distances is made competitive by increasingly large tankers, but the million-ton supertankers now being proposed must be near the limit. Larger pipelines also shave costs, but most of the pipeline routes that have enough potential also raise international political issues; the proposed trans-Alaska pipeline has become a domestic political issue.

As technology advances, the feasibility of transporting some commodities improves. The fact remains that most commodities that can be transported at an acceptable cost today could also be transported economically long ago, although admittedly the distances have grown a great deal in this century. Some movements are still impossible; we do not know how to move electricity by sea, for example [Figure 1]. The only recent real innovations in transport (except for the appearance of nuclear sources, with their trivial costs of transportation) are the movement of natural gas by sea as a refrigerated liquid and the development of new technologies for electrical transmission.

The power provided to any electrical-conversion unit is the product of the drop in voltage within the unit and the flow of current; the loss of energy as heat in a transmission line is the product of the square of the current and the resistance of the wire. Lower currents, higher voltages, and large wires (less resistance) therefore reduce waste. There are limits to the size of a wire, and so improvements in transmission were achieved primarily by utilizing alternating current (which could be transformed easily) and stepping up the voltage. Transmission voltages have increased as demands have grown and as transmission technology (insulation, for example) has improved, but the gains have required successive doublings of voltage rather than incremental increases, and the end of the road seems to have been reached for alternating current at less than 500,000 volts.

These gains, combined with the high growth rate of the electric power industry in the United States and with the large economies of scale in the construction of power plants, have changed the look of the land. The oldest power plants were small and widely scattered about the cities; the countryside had no electricity and no prospect of having

		Wood	Coal	Petroleum	Gas	Heat (Steam)	Electricity	Hydropower
LAND	Batch							
		Armload	▓						
		Pack	▓						
		Basket		▓					
		Pot			▓				
		Wagon	▓	▓					
		Truck	▓						
		Rail	▓	30	>15				
		Vehicle Fuel Tank			▓				
	Continuous	Aqueduct							▓
		Pipeline			10	20	▓		
		Transmission Line						50	
		Slurry Pipeline		30					
SEA	Batch	Cargo Ship	▓	<30	▓				
		Collier		<30					
		Barge		<30					
		Tanker			5				
		LNG Tanker				>20			
		Supertanker			<5				

[FIGURE 1.] Transportation of energy commodities can be by land or sea; on land it can be in batches or continuous, by sea only in batches. The [shaded] boxes in the matrix indicate the feasible means of transport for each commodity. The numbers in some of the boxes give the approximate lowest cost for the major means of transport in cents per British thermal unit [BTU] for a 1000-mile haul.

it. Today power plants have become even larger; they are moving out of the cities, and high-voltage lines dominate miles of the countryside. Electricity is provided where it is wanted; transmission is not as cheap as moving fuel, and yet it is attractive to build big power plants and move electric power more than 100 miles to consumers. Still, the pressure for innovation continues. The privately owned public utilities that provide most of our electric power, even though they are entitled to prices that guarantee them a "fair profit" and are therefore in a sense free to rest on their laurels, are driven by their own imperatives to seek every possible increase in operating efficiency. (For one thing, as utilities lower their costs the public utility commissions that set utility rates seem to lag in lowering the prices of electricity.)

The result is that even a trivial innovation may earn thousands of dollars a day, and the tendency is to judge its value by that potential rather than by its capacity to initiate a substantial revolution. Thus power companies adopt small improvements to alleviate some of the following inherent problems: (1) The demands of customers vary systematically by the time of day and the season, but unpredictable demands also arise and emergency shutdowns do occur. An isolated system must have enough spare equipment to handle such contingencies, but linking systems together with lines of high capacity makes some of the spare equipment unnecessary. (2) Peak demands are closely related to urban time schedules as well as to the sun. When a time-zone boundary is crossed, the period of peak demand shifts by an hour. Bringing in electricity from a neighboring time zone broadens the peak, reduces its magnitude and thereby again reduces the amount of generating equipment needed. (3) Some of the great hydropower facilities—Grand Coulee is the best example—can sell power very cheaply; others were built with the intention of selling power for premium prices, mostly at the hours of peak daily demand. Outlets for such peak-hour power may be many hundreds of miles away.

For all these reasons the power grids of the 48 states are now fairly well interlinked. It must be doubted that the resulting savings come to as much as 10%. Still, the interest in ever cheaper transport persists. Recently the devices of solid-state physics have provided means for transforming voltage (and current) with direct current. Because direct current is more tractable than alternating current at high voltages, utilities are now turning back from alternating to direct current and are beginning long-distance power transmission at extra-high voltages (EHV) of 750,000. The next step may be the use of superconductors. All metals, when cooled to near the boiling point of helium, become superconductive, or quite without resistance to the flow of current. The use of superconductors could change the technical task involved in transmission dramatically, from the reduction of energy loss as heat to the operation of an elongated ultra-low-temperature refrigerator. The first commercial application of superconductor transmission may be to bring power into urban areas too crowded for the wide corridors required for conventional high-voltage lines.

[STORAGE]

Storage presents its own set of constraints. Electricity is hardly storable as such in commercial quantities. Instead we resort to a subterfuge: building artificial reservoirs into which water can be pumped electrically and from which electricity can be retrieved by reversing the flow of water and letting the motors and pumps act as generators and turbines. Although this is quite efficient, it is a clumsy sort of thing; still, it is the best we can do. Storage batteries are not a substitute because they are expensive and have little capacity. One would think that about as much electricity could be stored in a battery as oil can be stored in a tank, because the same kinds of forces are being manipulated. Unfortunately, reliable storage batteries are very heavy because they use chemical elements at the heavy end of the periodic table, notably lead, and provide only about as much energy as would result from an equal number of atoms at the light end of the series. (Clearly what is needed is a good storage battery in which lithium is oxidized and reduced instead of lead!) The same phenomenon gives electric automobiles an unsatisfactory performance and cruising range compared with automobiles that depend on hydrocarbon fuels.

The difficulties of storing electricity impose exacting constraints on the operation of electric utility systems, as residents of many U.S. cities have learned in recent years. When customers demand more electricity by switching on lights or air conditioners or other machinery, the production of power must be increased to meet the demand. Little flexibility exists; electricity does not stretch or squeeze easily. To keep a system in balance requires minute-by-minute attention; at least, since electricity moves at a notably high velocity, increased production does reach the customer without delay.

If gas customers ask for a greater flow, on the other hand, gas will simply expand to a considerable degree within the pipeline and so meet the increased demand. Minute-by-minute flow is therefore no problem. The other side of the coin is that gas comes down the pipeline rather slowly, and so if the neighborhood supply runs short, it may take a day or two to make up the deficiency. Accordingly the marketers of gas usually have to arrange some kind of local storage. The large gasholders one sees on the outskirts of cities do not hold enough. To meet the possible peak demand for a day in the San Francisco Bay Area, for example, would take a gasholder equivalent in volume to a cube 1000 feet on a side; existing ones have perhaps 1% of that capacity. A common provision is therefore storage in depleted gas fields or in the transmitting pipeline itself. Gas is compressible, and if the upstream pressure is increased, not only can the gas be sent along faster but also larger amounts can be stored in the pipeline near the demand. A pipeline three feet in diameter running at 400 pounds per square inch contains about a million cubic feet of gas per mile, or a billion cubic feet per 1000 miles—equal to the capacity of the 1000-foot cube.

The third case is that of the supplier of liquid fuels. Here storage is so easy and so much of it is provided all along the distribution chain that no real technological problem remains. It is easier than keeping grocery shelves stocked.

In the synthesis of these unit operations both technological advances and economies of large-scale operation have contributed to lowering the cost of the alternatives for meeting demands. In general great economies of scale result only from the phenomena of liquid flow, which cause the capacity of a pipeline to increase as a high power of its diameter. One very different example of such economy is seen in strip mining: The stripping away and movement of overburden is now being handled by outsized equipment, making operations economically attractive that would have been unacceptable a generation ago. Yet one suspects that here too, as in the case of supertankers, the end of the road of increasing scale is close at hand.

[CONVERSION]

Energy is almost never harvested in the form in which it is to be used, and therefore it must ordinarily go through a conversion step [Summers, 1971]. The most significant conversions are those of latent energy to heat through combustion, and of heat to electricity. Once energy is in the form of electricity all the gates are open, even though the toll through some gates is excessive.

[USE AND DISPOSAL]

Centuries of development, innovation, and growth have built up an intricate pattern of physical facilities and economic relations that connect discovered and harvested resources with sites of conversion, use, and disposal [Figures 2, 3, 4, 5, 6, 7, 8]. For the most part, the patterns reflect the movement of energy from resource sites to the

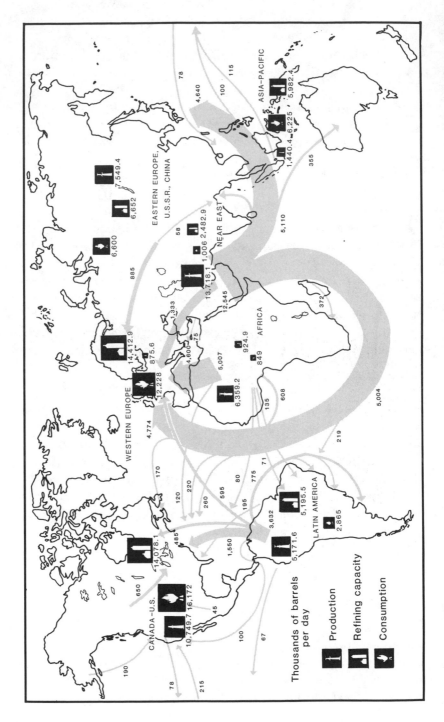

ASIA–PACIFIC
5,982.4
1,440.4–6,225
355

78
100
115
4,640

EASTERN EUROPE,
U.S.S.R., CHINA

7,549.4
6,652
6,600

885

NEAR EAST

58
1,006 2,482.9
13,718.1
12,545

5,110

372

1,333

75
4,600
5,007

AFRICA

924.9
849

608
135

5,004

6,359.2

WESTERN EUROPE
14,412.9
875.6
12,228

4,774

170
120
220
260
595
195
1,550

80
775
71

219

LATIN AMERICA
5,195.5
3,632
2,865

5,171.6

485

650

45

CANADA–U.S.
16,172
14,078.1
10,749.7

190

100
67

78
215

Thousands of barrels per day

Production
Refining capacity
Consumption

[FIGURE 2.] Worldwide patterns of oil production: refining, shipping, and consumption are summarized by this map based on maps from the *International Petroleum Encyclopedia.* The data are for 1970. All quantities are in thousands of barrels per day. Export figures for eastern Europe, the U.S.S.R., and China refer only to exports from those areas to other parts of the world. The arrows indicate the origins and destinations of the principal international oil movements, not the specific routes. The United States is a heavy net importer.

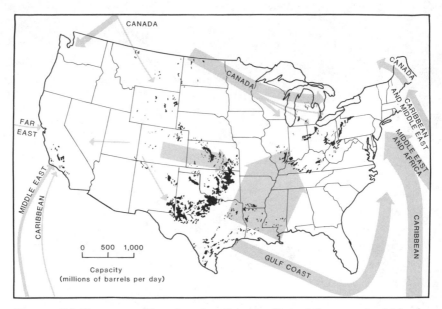

[FIGURE 3.] Transportation of crude oil to the United States and within the country is shown by a map adapted from the *National Atlas*. Data are for 1966. Arrow widths are proportional to movements by pipeline (land) and tanker (sea). Areas in [black] are oil fields.

homes and places of work of growing populations at the various times and in the various amounts and forms that are needed.

In a sense the customer has been king; he has received what he wanted when and where he wanted it. It might be argued, as a matter of fact, that societies in which energy costs have been excessive have simply not prospered. In the United States the consumer has usually paid the price and paid little attention to paying; in return, the energy industry has ordinarily met his demands while asking for a very minor share of his income. To estimate that share is difficult because so much of it is paid indirectly and because one scarcely knows whether to apply retail or wholesale prices, what to do about gasoline taxes and so on. Very roughly, every American consumes each day about 15 pounds of coal (200,000 BTU) for 10 cents; two and [a] half gallons of petroleum, half of it as gasoline (350,000 BTU), for 50 cents, 300 cubic feet of natural gas (300,000 BTU) for 20 cents, and 24 kilowatt-hours of electricity for 45 cents. If one subtracts the 250,000 BTU of the fuels that are used in generating the electricity, or 15 cents, the total comes to $1.10. Marked up to retail level, that would be about a tenth of the U.S. per capita personal income. Other inquiries have arrived at lower estimates, such as 4% or 7%, for the share of personal income spent on energy, but my own feeling is that a figure of 10% more nearly represents the situation from the consumer's point of view.

The resistance of the consumer varies. Two-thirds of his consuming is done for him in industry, commerce, and transportation other than his own, and is beyond his direct control. It is hard to tell how much he resists buying industrial products, but his interest has been turning toward spending for services and it does seem that in some vague way his resistance to the purchase of industrial energy is increasing. In his home he behaves differently. No one can measure the extent to which he turns down the heat, turns off electric lights, or skimps on

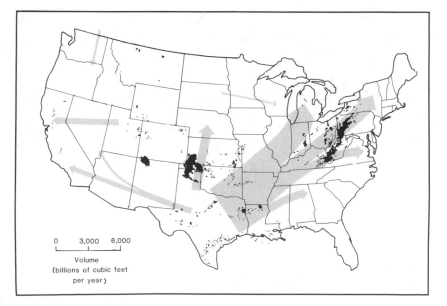

0   3,000   6,000

Volume
(billions of cubic feet
per year)

[FIGURE 4.] Natural gas movements are charted, based on figures for 1965. The development of techniques for transporting gas at high pressures in pipes has led to the sharp increase in the use of natural gas since World War II. Areas that are shown in black are gas fields.

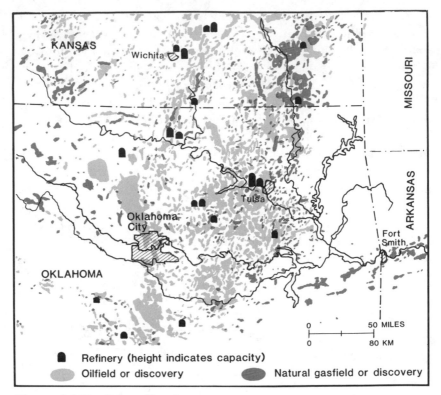

[FIGURE 5.] Pipelines radiate from the rich oil fields and natural-gas fields of Oklahoma. Crude oil is piped from wells to refineries in the region or farther away; petroleum products from the refineries are piped to industrial and commercial centers, primarily in the Middle West.

gasoline, but the general impression is: not much. (Has anyone under the age of 30 ever turned off an electric light?) He pays a good deal more for electricity than he does for fuels but is easily persuaded to use electricity as a fuel, even though it costs him many times as much per unit of heat.

How about the rest of the world? First, it seems plausible, since fuels have long been available to men, that a highly technological society should show a high ratio of work to total energy, as expressed perhaps by kilowatt-hours per million BTU. Second, it can be argued that the construction of a thermal power system requires an intricate structure extending from mining through diverse forms of consumption, whereas the construction of a hydropower system (perhaps with assistance from a more technological society) can precede and is often intended to initiate development. Accordingly, a high fraction of hydropower should be common in developing societies. Certainly the general experience is that the fraction of hydropower diminishes in the highly technological societies. Third, growth rates of electricity, for example, should be higher in the developing societies.

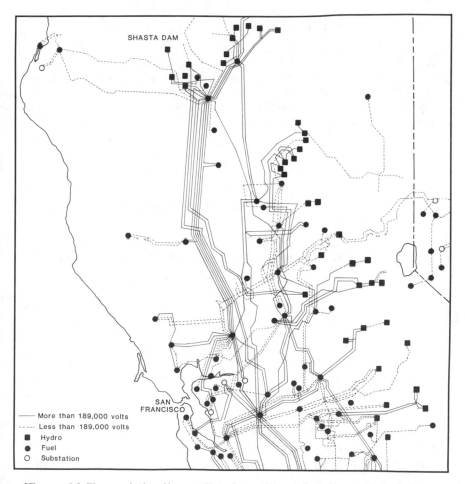

[FIGURE 6.] Transmission lines radiate from power plants in northern California, the largest of which is Shasta Dam plant. Most of the electric power goes to the San Francisco area.

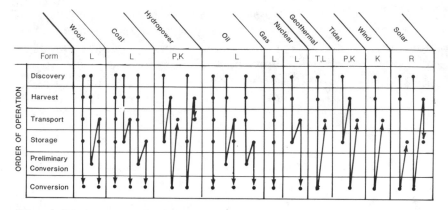

[FIGURE 7.] Sequence of operations between the discovery and the use of an energy commodity is diagrammed. Energy is discovered in various forms: latent (L), potential (P), kinetic (K), thermal (T), or radiant (R). The resource is harvested, transported, stored, and converted; sometimes there is a preliminary conversion step. The sequence of these steps varies for different commodities; in some cases there are alternate sequences. Arrows indicate the order in which the operations can be accomplished for ten kinds of energy.

Such patterns do appear in the statistics but are far from infallible [Figure 9]. The United States is by no means the highest in kilowatt-hours per million BTU. In fact, it uses 35% of the world's electricity, just as it does with total energy. The reason is at least partly obvious: It is our excessively high consumption of gasoline for private automobiles. Brazil and India come in too high on the kilowatts-to-BTU ratio, but the formalized statistics on which these numbers are based take no account of contributions from "primitive" sources: notably fuel wood in Brazil and cowdung fuel in India. If these sources are counted in, the ratio drops from 32 for Brazil to six; for India it falls from 15 to six. (Perhaps as energy economies evolve the ratio should pass through a maximum and then decline.) The electrical growth rates are much what one would expect, except that Brazil's seem low. The hydro-power percentages are generally in line, but they remind one not to forget climate and topography: Japan and the United Kingdom are both insular, midlatitude, and humid, but the former is mountainous, with a great many hydropower sites, and the latter is flat.

These, to be sure, are only the most superficial of the patterns associated with energy. Close examination of any society will reveal the

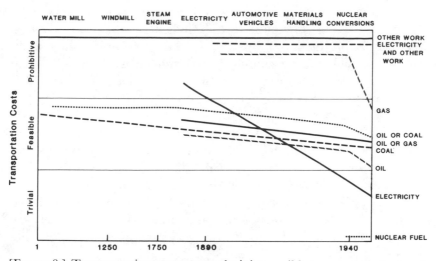

[FIGURE 8.] Transportation costs may make it impossible to move some forms of work, such as wind or water power, from the site where they are developed. The costs of other commodities have varied through history; in many cases technological changes make a cost feasible that was once prohibitive. The curves relate the general level of costs for transportation by sea in batches (*long dashed lines*), by land in batches (*short dashed lines*), and by continuous methods such as power lines or pipelines (*solid lines*).

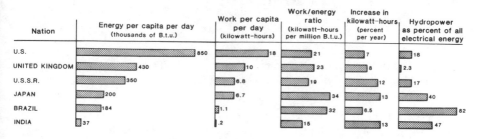

[FIGURE 9.] Energy patterns are revealed by some international statistics. Energy per capita is about as expected, with a large advantage in the developed nations. (BTU figures for Brazil and India would be about 150,000 and 22,000, respectively, if "primitive" fuels were included.) One would expect kilowatt-hours per million BTU, a measure of the ratio of work to energy, to reflect technical expertise in the advanced countries, but the inefficiency of gasoline engines reduces the ratio there instead. The figures for hydropower's share of total electrical energy reflect not only the state of development (hydropower comes early) but also the geography of the countries.

influences on it of its particular experience with energy resources and energy conversion. The patterns one finds depend not only on such physical factors as the waxing and waning of resources but also on cultural variables: the development of technologies, changes in social patterns and the constraints of tradition, governmental policies, and local fads and preferences. The resulting patterns are seldom simple, and it is particularly difficult to foresee the future. I should like merely to raise a few questions: Is the correlation between increasing use of energy and human welfare good enough, and is the hypothesis that more energy means a better life plausible enough, to warrant any hopeful extrapolation? Where on the rising consumption curve is the breaking point between gains and losses? Are we likely to find that point by encouraging growth until the customer—no longer interested in more energy or unable to afford it—finally offers resistance, and growth ends?

THE ELECTRICAL POWER INDUSTRY: ITS PROSPECTS FOR GROWTH

Unlike the preceding article, which was largely a detached analysis of how we use energy resources, this lecture advocated a point of view. Its position was (and is) classic Luten: Continued growth (in this case, in the use of electricity) over the long term is impossible; changes in policy can be used to constrain growth in the short term and thus ease society into the inevitable state of no growth.

This lecture was given in the year preceding the Arab oil embargo, and thus just before the beginning of the "energy crisis." Yet we can detect a

Reprinted by permission from A. S. Silverman (ed.), *Western Montana Scientists' Committee for Public Information Lecture Series* (pp. 122–132). Missoula: Western Montana Scientists' Committee for Public Information, 1972. Presentation and publication made possible by a grant from the National Science Foundation, 6Z-1773.

sense of urgency in its message: Luten asked his listeners to recognize not so much the dwindling of fossil fuel energy supplies, but, rather, the ultimate limits of society to use energy and the environment to absorb waste heat.

Luten's predictions on the constraints to the continued growth of electricity use have proven to be perceptive. He suggested that "in the short run, nothing seems likely to stop growth"; during the 1970s, the use of electricity did continue to grow, although at about half the rate of the preceding decade. He continued that "in the middle run, economics will [stop growth]." Indeed, the cost of a kilowatt-hour in the United States increased over the decade, the first such sustained growth in cost since electricity became available in the 1880s; this economic factor has contributed to the decline in the growth of electricity use. We have yet to see whether society will impose upon itself the constraints needed to avert the realization of Luten's ultimate prediction: "In the long run, the environment will strike back, if nothing else works."

The curve of electrical energy growth plotted on semilogarithmic paper is a straight line, the most seductive of all curves to the forecaster. It takes character to resist the temptation simply to continue the line onward. The act is easy; it seems simple and logical; it is subjective; it is self-serving for the forecaster, for his boss, for the utility employing him, for the industry, [and] for the economy. It may even be self-fulfilling.

And it has been the practice. The literature, everywhere you turn, is full of a general gleeful, thoughtless prostration before the 8% growth curve. Even the Federal Power Commission [1964], in what should be the most thoughtful of all projections, has done little more than obtain the consensus of the utilities. These temper the most extravagant hopes by reducing the 8% to 6%, and by limiting the projection to 1980, perhaps as far as is necessary for scheduling construction. Even those few who see reason for alarm must indeed go along with the higher rates in order to substantiate their fears ["Engineers Project Heat Rejection Requirements," 1970]. And so must I.

It has been said by an economist, "No obvious reason exists why it should not continue . . . [and] . . . many arguments to prove that technology can overcome increasing shortages of natural resources *ad infinitum*." But obvious reasons do exist. The first is simply that the earth is finite, a matter more familiar to geographers than to economists; the second is that exponential growth will surpass any finite limits, given a little time—a matter still known to too few.

Thus, 8% growth per year leads to a doubling time of nine years, a ten-folding of 29 years, 2200-fold per century; enough, carefully applied, to vaporize the earth in the year 2370.

To say this is to say simply that growth must end. The question I am trying to force on us is two-fold: Shall we let growth continue until "natural forces" bring it to an end, and perhaps us too; or shall we try to decide where it should end, and seek to identify and establish policies to bring it to such an end? Who's in charge around here, anyway?

I see three sorts of constraints, of so-called "natural forces." First, the extractive resource. It is hopeless to evaluate this at the moment. Hubbert [1969] has shown clearly that the age of fossil fuels is limited, and he and many others have argued persuasively that reasonably priced power from the current generation of nuclear fission power plants is limited. But limits to the potentialities of breeder reactors are hard to define. More, fusion energy is beginning to perk up a bit and I think we should assume it will work. If it does, then we can well-nigh vaporize the earth with the deuterium in the seas.

Second, let me come up with a new term for a class of resources. I have deliberately used "extractive" just a moment ago. Now, let me use "assimilative resource" for the capacity of the environment to accept the energy we throw away, the waste heat. This is in the area of environmental quality. Energy is less messy than beer cans; energy is radiated from the earth and never returns. But the earth must warm up if it is to radiate more energy; fortunately, the rate goes up (barring albedo changes) as the fourth power of absolute temperature (Wien's Law).

I want to argue some generalities on the assimilative energy resource, and ask your pardon for using some big numbers. The sun's annual input of energy to the earth is 5300 Q [one Q is one billion billion BTU]. The human use of energy in 1950 was about 0.1 Q (100 milliQ); I suppose it is about 0.2 Q today. If all men used as much electricity as the American[s], and if American electrical growth continues at 8% per year, the human output of energy in about 2100 A.D. would be 5300 Q, and the earth, according to Wien's Law, would be 100°F hotter. I can't imagine what we would use this power for until close to the end, but then, it is painfully clear we would use it all for air conditioning. In about a century from now, with the same assumptions, the earth would be 10°F hotter and the ice caps would be melting. [There would be] gondolas on Fifth Avenue and all that; Cairo, Illinois, [would be] a seaport; [we would have] 30 billion people and a lot less cropland. Before panicking, note that you have 70 years before the warmup reaches 1°F.

Shorter-term problems do arise locally. Washburn [personal communication] has noted that if you believe in such growth, you should anticipate by the end of the century on the average a million-kilowatt nuclear power plant every six miles along the California coast. Peter Mason [1971] has summarized plans for 1990, which, while restricted to 12 sites, total 40 million kilowatts, with the largest site having 6.6 million kilowatts.

Jaske and his associates [see "Engineers . . . ," 1970] have estimated recently that by 2000, heat rejection from the [Boston to Washington] metropolitan [corridor] area in January will come to half of the solar input. Microclimatology will be a growing field. While hotspots have long existed where local output exceeds input of heat—any campfire, for instance—these will grow and spread.

New York already has trouble finding enough electricity for existing air conditioning equipment, but the more air conditioning is localized, the hotter the outside air becomes, the more air conditioning is needed, and the less effective it becomes. I think I may have been in a few places where air conditioning failed to work because it was warming up the outside air too much. The natural response is for the most heat-sensitive occupant to order more equipment, which will force the neighborhood to do the same, which in turn will simply increase the external temperature. Here we have an "externality" with a vengeance, a magnificent example of Garrett Hardin's "tragedy of the commons" [Hardin, 1968].

These heat burdens on the assimilative resource can also be expressed in terms of evaporative load. The sun's input, if all spent in evaporation of water, would vaporize 190 inches per year. Current world total energy use, 0.2 Q, would then evaporate 0.007 inch per year, a trivial layer. For the [continental] 48 states it is 0.04 inch for electricity alone, and would be 0.4 inch at the end of the century. Stream runoff in the 48 states is about 8 inches. But in the metropolitan East, the intensity of energy use must rise to at least 1000 times the national average, or equivalent to 40 inches of evaporation. These regions may already be preying on external water supplies for cooling and are compounding their air conditioning problems with increased humidity.

This is why power plants will be seeking the coasts from now on. Washburn, though, concerned for the aesthetic value of the coasts, would require them to be several miles inland, and thinks we might as well admit that cooling water is to be evaporated immediately in cooling towers. [The] Sacramento Municipal Utility District is building a big one now at Rancho Seco near Ione. It is something like 400 feet tall and 400 feet in diameter.

So much for the assimilative resource. We cannot prove that disaster faces us immediately, only presently.

Turning to the third constraint, what will we do with so much electricity, and can we afford it? [A projection of] 8% growth to the end of the century means eight to ten times as much altogether, perhaps five times as much per capita. Does anyone have the ghost of a notion how we will use so much? The plausibility of the exponential projection can be no greater than the plausibility of prospective use. From the point of view of the proponents of growth, yesterday's tomorrow had much more in it than today's tomorrow. In 1930, aluminum, other electrosmelted metals, television, better lighting, a host of appliances, and a world of improved electrical industrial equipment [were] on the horizon. Today, I see little: more air conditioning, which is still a long way from saturation, and the "all-electric home," already a controversial matter.

On the matter of cost, an older generation was brought up to turn off the lights because electricity cost money; some of us are still compulsive on this score. A younger generation believes electricity is free, and can't be bothered to throw the switch. We even have a mythology which says you shouldn't turn off fluorescent lights; I hope this is about to be smoked out. One utility is said to leave fluorescent lights always on in its own building, for heat as well as light. This is as bad an example as I can imagine for others who must pay for their own lighting as well as for the utility's.

At today's 8000 kilowatt-hours per capita, costing perhaps 1.3¢/kilowatt-hour whether paid directly or indirectly, our annual personal share is $100 each, with some uncertainty whether it is a retail or wholesale price. This is less than 5% of income and essentially trivial. Will it continue to be trivial when approaching 10% of income? By the end of the century it would be $1000 per capita, and in 60 years, $10,000.

We believe that electricity has always become cheaper and are told that no reason to believe otherwise exists. But, in fact, the price of electricity, which has been falling throughout our lives, has about hit bottom, and throughout our children's lives, it will be rising. Even if power plants become slightly more efficient, the increasing cost of fuel, of wages, of maintenance, and especially of administration, will increase costs for the consumer. When will we begin to resist and to insist that the kids turn off the lights? . . .

Again, for so long as costs were declining, [the] return on utility investment should have been good because, in the nature of things, regulatory agencies were slower to reduce rates than utilities were to reduce costs. Under such conditions, expansion of capacity with its increasing production of efficient generators make a good thing look even better. With rising costs and with very limited prospective gains in efficiency, will expansion look so good? Will, perhaps, the utilities cease to urge us to use more electricity?

To sum up on the constraints: In the short run, nothing seems likely to stop growth; in the middle run, economics will; in the long run, the environment will strike back, if nothing else works.

I should like to close with a few notes on another path. This stems from my belief that we suffer from having established a resource policy for an empty land and a poor society, a resource policy which won't work in a full land and for a rich society. I have suggested in [a subsequent] paper that we must begin to regard our natural resources as finite and inherently valuable, as the common property of the society, and that we must begin to discourage their exploitation in order to shift the emphasis of our economy from growing extraction to growing service. To this end, I have advocated charging, whether by tax or severance fee or whatever, for the use of those resources which are in the market, but not for those which are aesthetic.

Before I itemize some recommendations, please consider these items. If you heat a house with natural gas, with coal, with wood, you thermally pollute this world with the heat liberated by the fuel you burn, no more. If you heat the house electrically (except [if] by hydro-electricity, an unlikely event), you thermally pollute the environment by three times as much. If you heat your house with a fuel containing sulfur, you pollute the environment with sulfur dioxide; if you heat your house electrically from a power plant using the same fuel, your share of sulfur dioxide is tripled. Next, and quite different, we expect to get lower rates if we are big customers for energy; [the same logic should prompt us to] expect lower tolls if we use the [toll] bridge at rush hour. Neither makes any sense today; they are empty-land policies. In contrast, we expect to pay higher rates if we use the telephone at rush hour.

Specifically, I recommend that we:

1. Tax the fuel resource so that the tax falls on the consumer and so that it escalates with increasing use.

2. Charge for the privilege of using the assimilative resources, certainly for heat and sulfur dioxide, and perhaps for carbon dioxide— with again escalation, both for total amount and regional intensity.

3. Penalize the power industry for using natural gas for electrical generation. The public welfare will be better served if gas is reserved for domestic heating.

4. Penalize the use of electricity, except hydroelectricity, for domestic heating, especially if natural gas is available. (However, when nuclear energy has become dominant, domestic electric heating may become inescapable.)

5. Substantially abandon the development of additional hydroelectricity. I suggest to you that moving water is more to be admired than used, that the primary purpose of water is to beautify the earth.

6. Penalize the power industry for advertising for growth.

7. Constrain the siting of thermal power plants to ease and distribute the burden on assimilative resources, and to protect aesthetic resources.

8. In regions of acute air conditioning burden, provide systems for collective heat removal.

9. Do not consider regional integration and pumped storage any boon. They increase the overall assimilative resource burden. Storm King pumped storage, for example, will only aggravate New York City's microclimate.

10. Encourage retirement of old plants, but only modestly. While they aggravate the heat burden, they are trivial.

UNITED STATES REQUIREMENTS

America's growing perception of energy as a problem in the mid-1970s is more apparent in the content and tone of this chapter from a 1974 book than in the preceding two selections. The incipient awareness of energy as a limited resource was by 1974 transformed into a widely perceived "energy crisis," the legacy of the Arab oil embargo. Energy would become the dominant resource issue, and a vital societal issue, in the next decade.

In this chapter, Luten anticipated at least some of the dialogue over energy resources of the late 1970s. "Confrontations" have indeed "come on, wave after wave" between those devoted to maintaining a society of continued energy growth and those dedicated to the slowing and eventual stopping of growth. The confrontations have involved "industry versus conservationist," but they have also involved advocates not so easily dichotomized; for example, it is difficult to identify industry spokespersons and conservationists in arguments over coal versus nuclear fuels versus hydropower versus geothermal energy versus solar power. Moreover, "policy statements" have been and continue to be "issued by everyone," including, as examples, the Mellon Institute, the Ford Foundation, the National Research Council, and the Solar Energy Research Institute. "The institutions" have begun "to bend," as the economic system and government policy inch slowly toward the realization that energy resources and their use are limited. For Luten, the "new path" to that realization has the same general route as that which has led to the realization that population cannot continue to grow. It is a journey along which "the basic question [is] 'what of the future,'" and at each crossroad the people "will insist on arguing for themselves whither they should go."

The American argument over "whither they should go" in regard to energy use progressed through the 1970s. Production of petroleum by the United States had peaked by 1970, and natural gas production showed little change over the decade. Yet oil imports continued to grow until 1977 before they declined; in the early 1980s, they were actually about the same percentage of total petroleum use (34%) as in the early 1970s. Most importantly, total energy use peaked in 1979, and has since decreased.

Reprinted by permission from A. J. Finkel (ed.), *Energy, The Environment, and Human Health* (pp. 17–32). Acton, MA: Publishing Sciences Group, 1974.

Luten ended this chapter with the hope that "we set our minds to getting along on no more than our present consumption of energy." At the time, such a hope seemed an unrealistic dream of those advocating the "energy ethic" of using less energy because it is morally right to conserve the earth's resources. Today, however, such a prospect is a widely accepted possibility, even probability, forced by increasing costs. We now have the "pricing policy" that Luten realized was necessary "to persuade the unethical." But while the declines in energy use are encouraging, we should not be complacent; read, in particular, Luten's warnings at the end of this chapter.

With respect to the energy requirements of the United States, the first reality we must face is that the costs of energy, which have diminished throughout our lifetimes and also, I should think, through those of our immediate ancestors, are destined to increase throughout the lives of our children. This is one of our legacies to them. A corollary can be phrased rhetorically by asking: How much energy will Americans buy as its price rises? Inklings of the answer to this are beginning to appear.

A second reality is to forget the myths of "energy as the ultimate resource," of the "unlimited energy" that will let us recover everything we need from the earth despite the progressive depletion of its riches. This is the economists' myth, shyly assented to by the technologist, that technology's capabilities will increase faster than resources are depleted and that, accordingly, the product of waxing technology times waning resources will never cease to grow. And so they say, "Everything will come out all right; follow me as sheep and I, the good shepherd, will lead you into green pastures, and you shall not want." But what if they be false prophets? What if, having followed the pied piper, there be no salvation? Who is to pay? Has anyone posted bond? No. In fact, you are on your own and will have to make up your own minds.

(Looking back on that delightful paragraph, I can reflect that about the only privilege a generalist is granted in this society of specialists is to mix metaphors in a manner to outrage scholars!)

Technology, in fact, will not continue to expand as it has during this century. If the growth of the postwar production rate of scientists and technologists were to continue, by the end of the century, I am told, all of the children of this society would have to become scientists and technologists.

BACKGROUND

. . . In energy discussions a decade ago you heard from "coal-equivalent" men, "BTU" men, "millions of barrels per day" men, "millions of tons per year" men. Now, you hear from "kilowatt-hour" men, "kilowatt" men, and a few more. Presently, "joules" will be the word. And we have all heard of calories, large or small. Everyone says we must go metric, and I suppose we must. But do not imagine this will help much. Diverse manifestations of energy are truly incommensurable and cannot be entirely reconciled simply by a better choice of units [Figure 1].

Worse, all of the numbers are so huge that everyone, except engineers in their detailed proposals, slips a decimal place—or two or three—now and again. The first task is to reduce the numbers to magnitudes where one has a chance to cope with them. Palmer Putnam [1953], 20 years ago, defined a new and huge unit suitable for national and world energy economies. He called it Q and set it at 10^{18} BTU. One BTU, a British thermal unit, is the heat required to warm a pound of water through 1°F. Q, a quintillion BTU, is ten times the world's energy use in 1950, five times it in 1970. That is, mankind's present energy use is 0.2 Q or, we might say, 200 milliQ. A supplementary and very helpful device is to reduce national energy use to a per capita and a per day basis. The numbers are still large but are more manageable. We will use both in this chapter. . . .

WHERE WE ARE

Currently (1970), mankind's annual use of energy is about 0.2 Q. The United States, with 5.7% of the world's people, uses one-third of its energy. If everyone were to come up to our level, that 0.2 Q would rise to about 1.15 Q. If, on the other hand, present use were uniformly divided, our share would be much less. Instead of our current 850,000 BTU/day/capita, we would have 150,000, about one-sixth as much.

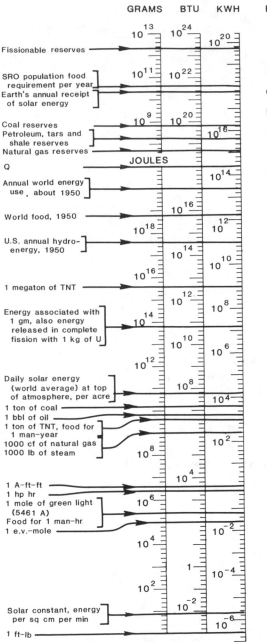

GRAMS   BTU   KWH

Fissionable reserves

SRO population food
requirement per year
Earth's annual receipt
of solar energy

Coal reserves
Petroleum, tars and
shale reserves
Natural gas reserves

Q

JOULES

Annual world energy
use, about 1950

World food, 1950

U.S. annual hydro-
energy, 1950

1 megaton of TNT

Energy associated with
1 gm, also energy
released in complete
fission with 1 kg of U

Daily solar energy
(world average) at top
of atmosphere, per acre
1 ton of coal
1 bbl of oil
1 ton of TNT, food for
1 man-year
1000 cf of natural gas
1000 lb of steam

1 A-ft-ft
1 hp hr
1 mole of green light
(5461 A)
Food for 1 man-hr
1 e.v.-mole

Solar constant, energy
per sq cm per min

1 ft-lb

British thermal unit (BTU)
  0.25200 kilogram-calorie or
  large calorie
  777.65 foot-pounds
  1054.35 joules
  1.05435×10^{10} ergs
Gram-calorie
  3.08597 foot-pounds
  4.18400 joules
Gram-centimeter
  980.665 ergs
Horsepower-hour (hpgr or hph)
  0.74570 kilowatt-hour
Joule-joule (absolute)
  0.73756 foot-pound
  1 watt-second
  1×10^7 ergs
Kilogram-calorie or large calorie
  3.9683 BTU
  1000 small or gram-calories
  4184.00 joules
Kilowatt-hour
  3414.4 BTU
  2.6552×10^6 foot-pounds
  1.024 acre-feet (of water)
  3.600×10^6 joules
Horsepower (hp)
  0.74570 kilowatt
  550 foot-pounds per second
  33,000 foot-pounds per minute
Kilowatt
  1.3410 horsepower
  737.56 foot-pounds per second
Watt
  0.73756 foot-pound per second
Metric ton coal equivalent
  28,880,000 BTU
Short ton coal equivalent
  26,200,000 BTU
Bbl/day
  50 metric tons per year
Metric ton
  7.30 barrels
  1.16 kiloliters
  306 gallons
Barrel
  0.137 metric tons
Kilogram of crude oil
  39,700 BTU
Barrel of crude oil
  5,400,000 BTU
Kilogram of fuel oil
  38,900 BTU
Barrel of fuel oil
  6,400,000 BTU
Kiloliter
  6.29 barrels (petroleum)
Barrel (petroleum)
  42 gallons
  0.159 kiloliter
Gallon (U.S. liquid)
  3.7853 liters
Imperial gallon
  1.2009 gallons

[FIGURE 1.] Order of magnitude and conversion chart.

We obtain three-fourths of our energy from petroleum (37%) and natural gas (38%) in almost equal shares, one-fifth from coal (21%), and 4% from hydropower. Nuclear power and other contributors are still trivial.

We use one-fourth of it to generate electricity. Of that, perhaps one-third (9% of the total) is used in households and the balance in commercial and industrial establishments. Another one-fourth is used for transportation, three-fifths of it personal. The remaining one-half is used for space and process heat, one-sixth of the total in households, the balance in industry and commerce.

	Industry	Commerce	Household or personal	Total
Electricity (input)	12	6	9	27
Transport		10	15	25
Heat	28	5	15	48
Total	40	21	39	100

Perhaps the most important point to make of this distribution is that about two-fifths of our energy consumption is subject to our personal control: how we elect to heat and light our houses, what appliances we use, how far we drive our automobiles and in what fashion. Three-fifths is determined indirectly by our other habits: whether we frequent brilliantly lighted stores and are drawn by electric advertising, how much we fly, whether we buy exotic or local products, how much we support industry by our purchases. But it is unrealistic to imagine that we have much short-term control over such matters other than in terms of our general affluence and total spending patterns.

That is the present state. How has it come about? How has it grown? Two patterns are clear: First, total energy growth has been dramatically small and has been at a remarkably steady rate of 2.7% per year since 1850 [Figure 2]. Until about 1900 it paralleled population growth. Then population growth slowed, but the energy continued. Its sources have changed. Until 1850, we had a fuelwood energy economy. After the Civil War, we began to change to coal and had about

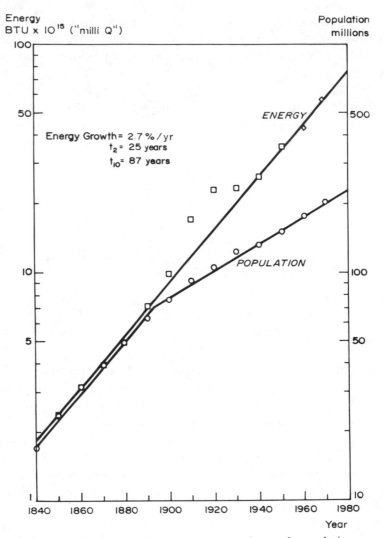

[FIGURE 2.] United States total energy consumption and population growth.

completed that when petroleum became important. Coal ceased to grow, and oil, and then gas, carried the burden of growth [Figure 3].

That 2.7% per year was surprisingly small. Cogent reasons for it to be so small included a diminishing extravagance in the use of fuel-wood as the forests of the Ohio Valley were cleared for agriculture and, to a lesser degree, the increasing efficiency of the steam engine. Growth

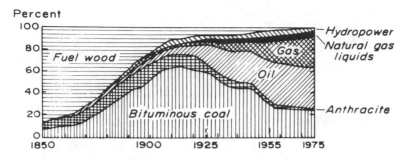

[FIGURE 3.] Sources of energy in the United States.

was promoted by a growing population, an increasingly urban and industrial economy, and, in this century, by the mechanization of all mobile activities, in part by internal combustion engines and in part by electricity. Little vocational muscle remains in the American scene.

In contrast to this overall picture, a second pattern is the rapidity of growth of new sources of energy. When coal was replacing wood, its use increased at better than 8% per year (1870–1910). When automobiles came in, petroleum grew at 9% per year (1900–1925) [Figure 4]. And the growth of electric power was 8% per year almost from its first recording in 1902 until the present time. Surely, with such a record, it must continue [Figure 5]. As the man who fell off the skyscraper said while passing the fifth floor, "Everything's going fine, so far."

THE FUTURE

Until quite recently, the people of the industry, the growth economists, the growth engineers all talked as if the future were straightforward and clear, 8% growth per year for electric power, doubling every nine years, increasing ten-fold every 30 years through the foreseeable future. It was, in fact, a most thoughtless, unreflective, and emotional attitude. Do not let anyone tell you American businessmen are cold-blooded keen thinkers. Instead, they are the most hot-blooded and emotional of our people. Is love of beauty, love of the landscape an emotion? What, then, is love of money? What is the insecurity that drives men to squirrel their money away—is it intellect or emotion?

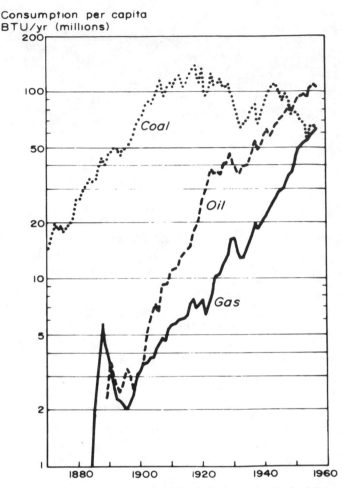

Consumption per capita
BTU/yr (millions)

[FIGURE 4.] Growth patterns of fossil fuels in the United States.

But in a finite world, growth must end. Twenty-five years of a growing literature (which itself must stop growing) has almost persuaded the American public that population growth must end. Now the argument has turned to economic growth—which also must end—and a part of the argument is that the energy economy's growth must end. The simplest, if least persuasive, argument was that continued growth, at present rates, of American electricity consumption would lead in less than two centuries to an outpouring of heat that would cook the entire earth (S Day) [Figure 6].

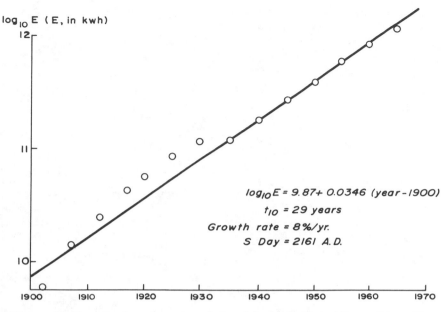

[FIGURE 5.] Growth of consumption of electricity in the United States. (Note: "S Day" is when the rate of human use of energy equals the energy received from the sun.)

A second constraint has been argued by Hubbert over a period of 25 years [e.g., 1949]. He has by now almost convinced the fossil fuel industry that these resources are finite and that the probable pattern of consumption is one, first, of exponentially increasing use, then of a lesser growth to a maximum production at about half exhaustion of the resource, all followed by a decline in similar pattern. He has, for a number of years, forecast that American petroleum production would reach its ultimate peak at about 1970 [Figure 7]. As it looks now, he may have hit it just about on the nose. Unquestionably, we are well on our way to becoming one of the great have-not nations as far as petroleum is concerned.

Finally, a third constraint is that if present growth patterns for electric power were to continue, we would find ourselves handing over entire paychecks for electric power. Somehow economic resistance will insure that no single activity dominates the entire economy.

These three constraints are inescapable. But what this debate has achieved thus far is barely an admission that the historical patterns of growth must end. We have not really come to the second stage of the

Annual Energy Use

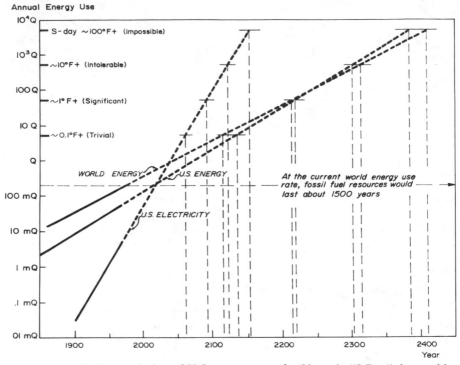

[FIGURE 6.] Extrapolation of U.S. energy growth. (Note: At "S Day" the world would be about 100°F hotter than today and would be uninhabitable; accordingly, the condition is unrealizable. At one-tenth the S-Day energy use, the earth would still be 10°F hotter and much of it uninhabitable, an intolerable condition. Note how long it is before even trivial heating occurs and how quickly it worsens.)

argument: Will this fearful condition arise in my lifetime, or can I continue in my traditional growth patterns secure in the knowledge that not I but my children will have to cope with it? The third stage will be an appeal: Can we in good conscience persist in our addiction to growth and then, having addicted our children, tell them in our wills to kick the habit? No. If we can foresee this problem, we must begin to attack it now. If mankind has any special talent, it is an extra degree of foresight, a more pervasive concern for the future, a willingness to work on problems, even those that will not be the death of us until tomorrow. The question, "My grandchildren, what have they ever done for me?" is a denial of humanity [Figure 8].

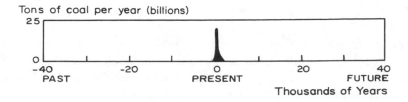

[FIGURE 7.] Hubbert's 1949 representation of the "age of fossil fuels."

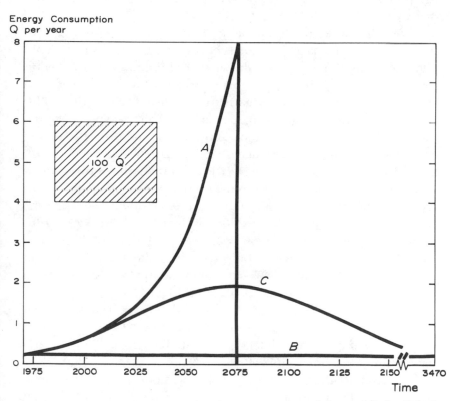

[FIGURE 8.] Conceivable alternatives in consumption of the world's fossil fuel resources. (A—At present world growth rate of about 3.5% per year, it will all be gone in 105 years. B—At present consumption rates, it will all be gone in 1500 years. C—Under Hubbert's hypothesis, it will mostly be gone in 200 years.)

REQUIREMENTS AND NEED

For several decades now, most of us could not have cared less about energy costs. We built our houses with picture windows; we kept them at whatever temperature was the going pattern; when the architects told us insulation could not be justified we left it out. We bought electric appliances according to our capacity for monthly payments. We bought as much premium gasoline as our tanks would accept and went where we wished. With other expenses we might seek a bargain, but energy was a social expense dictated by location and social class. Some of us, yes, bought economy cars, but the industry learned how to compromise our targets. Some of us bought discount gasoline, but not many.

We believed the myths about not turning off fluorescent lamps, that leaving the furnace on overnight cost less than to warm a cold house in the morning. We were drawn to the bright lights, whether on theater marquees or in daylight-bright supermarkets. We subsidized and encouraged energy-extravagant truck transport over rail freight. We turned to the single-occupant car for urban transport. We destroyed rail passenger service in one brief decade and turned to the air and more energy, again, for interurban transport.

Does anyone remember the electric interurban cars of two generations ago? The Traction Terminal in Indianapolis had eight tracks each long enough to load four or five of those rambling electric cars, and spewed them out in all directions at the rate of dozens per hour. They used little energy. But you could not do that today. When you got to Lafayette, or Wabash, or South Bend, how would you get around? Walk? Automobiles have rebuilt our cities so that only with automobiles may they be occupied. We ask ourselves the whimsical question: Who's in charge, men or automobiles? Do cars go where men wish, or do men dutifully come forth in the morning to guide automobiles to their tidy midday conclaves? Recall Thoreau's, "[For we are] the tools of [our] tools" [1854/1964, p. 292].

But automobiles are not solely to blame. Look farther afield; look at new patterns of home ownership that made it possible for an ordinary guy to become attached to a house, and to the automobile that permitted him to keep the house despite changes in direction and distance of the journey to work. So, not merely Detroit, but the Federal Housing Authority is part of the energy crisis.

If anyone had suggested the resource was limited, we would have laughed. We knew it was infinite, just as we had known all along that all of this great new world was infinite. Some had carped, yes; some were Cassandras, conservationists even. They had told us back in the 1920s that we only had enough oil for ten years. They said it again in the 1940s, in the 1950s. But each time we defiantly doubled our use, and still it came forth. They called wolf so many times—how could it ever end? Our entire world was built on cheap energy; it was the basic myth of America.

But it *is* ending; the world *is* changing. We *are* beginning to concede it to be finite. While we really do not know how big the resource is, Hubbert has told us clearly that, as long as we remain addicted to growth, resource magnitude makes little difference. We have also heard it, clear and explicit, in the book by Meadows *et al.*, *The Limits to Growth* [Meadows, Meadows, Randers, & Behrens, 1972].

And presently we will be ready to ask, how much do we really need?

* Enough to keep us warm.
* Enough to run our households.
* Enough to provide us with mobility, but not in Cadillacs; nor to commute, one per car. But we do need mobility; such individuality as we still have may be preserved in considerable measure by our freedom to move.
* Enough to operate a reasonable industry and commerce. Growth here must end, too.
* Enough to mitigate a number of insults to the environment. But while some of this will cost (especially smog control in the next generation of cars), other measures may save more than they cost, for example, the recycling of aluminum, paper, and glass.
* Enough so that we are not cramped into mass institutions for the sole purpose of saving energy, for the purpose of better serving a cramped economy. We must always remember that this society does not exist to serve its economy; the economy exists to serve the society and when it does not do this well, it must yield and reform.

And, in fact, the economy is changing. Economists are willing now to internalize the externalities, to assent that industry should pay the costs of cleaning up effluents [and] of straightening out land uprooted in the grubbing for coal, and to agree that perhaps industry should stay out of beautiful places.

But still, why should natural gas remain such a bargain because of a strange combination of the technology of its transport, a public power tradition in a regulating agency, and the still enduring shadow of the "invisible hand" of Adam Smith? Is there no way for us to recognize the very special value of this resource and to insure that it not be used where other fuels suffice?

Will we perhaps one day come to agree that the society still has some title to the resource, that the resource has an intrinsic value, and that a severance tax large enough to insure that use is moderate and selective is an appropriate measure? This is a far cry from our tradition of giving our natural wealth to the first comer in order to stimulate development. But that was an infinite world; this one is finite. Such a system of severance taxes large enough to discourage growth and to encourage selective use would be clumsy and full of inequities and would require repeated adjustment. Nonetheless, it could hardly fail to be superior to the present mess.

To sum up on the issue of "need" and "requirement," no matter how much we rail at our past and our lack of vision, no matter how humanistic our phrasing, we must still set prices that will lead to acceptable demands. How much do we "require"? Only as much as we are willing to buy at the prevailing price. It is hard to say we require more. It is easy to say it would be nice to have more; it is easy to say it would be nice for us to get along on less. But in the absence of clear principle, we must rest on the empirical test and must find ways to set prices so they will serve our purposes.

RESPONSE TO CRISIS

As these difficulties build up, one tends to become depressed, to believe [that] the society cannot manage its affairs. But, in fact, we do respond.

First a feeble literature appears, based on uncertain fact, confused thought, obscure principle. It generates a limited academic and public concern and then more voluminous writing. The first recognition that something may be happening is the appearance of counterattacks, of a defense of the status. After several rounds of this back and forth before an increasing public, suddenly, quite suddenly, one of the mass media, usually television, senses an issue that will bear watching. Then with the rush to center stage, the confrontations come on, wave after wave.

We see it happening now; in this case it is industry versus conservationist. The conferences come on in legions, promoted by both sides, but also by the middle. Policy statements are issued by everyone, and steadily, carefully, they become clearer, more competent. A new literature of careful inquiry begins to appear. It is much easier to learn today how we use our energy than it was five years ago. The economists are beginning to sense how demand will be affected by price. We are beginning to understand where we are extravagant in energy use, where prudent. Pamphlets appear telling us how to apply this information.

The institutions begin to bend; pricing regulations for natural gas are changing; big electrical customers are not being given the advantages they have traditionally had. We can, in fact, look forward now to a steadily spreading overhaul of all of those institutions of infinity.

SOME WARNINGS

Let me conclude with a small budget of warnings. Those that I have already argued for, I will only mention now.

Take a skeptical view of:

1. The myth that if we do not build more power plants we will end up living in caves. Do we consume power plants or just power? If we build no more power plants we will still have as much power as we have ever had. The industry that has generated this myth sounds more driven by emotion than intellect.

2. The myth of national security. Which provides better security—a land of undeveloped oil resources or one of wells pumped dry? If it is security we want, then let us drill up all of the fields and shut them in still unused. They tell us we need a trans-Alaska pipeline for national security. Ask them to guarantee that the oil will not go to Japan.

3. The [myths] that [say] to leave the fluorescent lights on and the heat on overnight. They have little substance.

4. The myth that environmental quality will demand vast new energy developments. The next generation of cars will, yes, require more fuel. Thereafter, I would suspect not. For water quality, mass transport, recycling, there would be an increase of a few percent, nothing near a doubling.

5. The mystical phrases of "foreseeable future," "need," and several others are almost always used to stop you from thinking and are self-serving. Whenever they are used, ask for elaboration, explanation, justification.

You should also:

1. Be warned against the all-electric home. It costs a bit less, it may end up the winner a century ahead, but for the middle run it is going to hurt every month when the power bills come in.

2. Be warned, of course, against the exponents of growth.

3. Be warned against the exposition of growth as a panacea for the poor. Poverty is a relative thing; recent growth hardly seems to have eliminated it. Poverty may stem more from the complexity of this society than from its overall affluence or lack of it. There is little reward nowadays for those who only understand simple things, for those whose virtue is to work hard. If we really seek to do something for the poor we will have to look elsewhere than at growth.

4. Be warned against dependence on the Middle East for oil. Most of the world's oil seems to be there and we may have it for our pledge. Economists are now guessing that we might end up owing the Middle Eastern states as much as $150 billion by the time that oil is gone. What would the Middle East do with all that foreign exchange? What else could they do but buy $150 billion worth of productive America? So with the oil gone, the United States would be committed to provide the Middle East with, say, half a dozen billions a year in foreign exchange to the end of time. And what would we get for it? Merely 10 to 20 years of relaxation. If we are to resolve the energy problem, let us get at it now, and in high gear. Let us get at a crash research and development program to bring fusion and solar energy within practical research at the earliest possible moment. The Manhattan Project of World War II and the space programs are reasonable models of how to go about it. We have had enough of penny-pinching research in this area.

5. Be warned against the "energy ethic," the theory that we need to learn to use energy more carefully because it is right to do so. This is quite true, and we should, but it is not enough. We must also have a pricing policy to persuade the unethical.

CONCLUSION

My general thesis has been that we have paid too little for energy, that we have created institutions to encourage the profligate use of energy.

We cannot continue; neither can we turn back. Now, we must find a new path. I suggest that we set our minds to getting along on no more than our present consumption of energy. We will overshoot this target but if we do not go too far over, we can come back. When, finally, our population comes down to a level which can be sustained at a decent level on our portion of North America for perhaps 100 million of us, there will be enough energy.

WESTERN COAL MINING

Part of the response to the "energy crisis" was a call for increased mining of coal. One reaction of conservationists was to pressure for regulation of strip mining, activity that resulted in the Surface Mining Control and Reclamation Act of 1977.

The action of the conservation groups was prompted by their perception, and the popular image, of "strip mining" as negative; the phrase typically conjures up visions of steep bare slopes, polluted streams, and devastated landscapes. In this short paper, Luten responded to the stereotyped concept of "strip mining" by suggesting that surface coal mines need not result in landscape ruination, at least in the West. The paper serves as an example, once again, of Luten's proddings for conservationists to be more thoughtful and less "knee-jerking" in their reactions to resource issues. The paper also illustrates, for a particular energy source (coal), the application of some of the "unit operations" (especially regarding transportation) that form the structure of Luten's appraisal of energy resources, as presented in the first paper in this section.

Coal strip mining is easily diagnosed as a plague on the American landscape. Yet it is a complex plague. Surface mining has been going on for a long time, and little of it can be called cosmetic. The United States is pockmarked with sand and gravel pits; the West is ulcerated

Reprinted by permission from *Landscape*, 1980, 24(1): 1–2.

with great copper pits; in California the skin was sloughed away by the disaster of hydraulic gold mining a century ago; the gold dredges left slow-healing wounds in the outwash from the Sierra Nevada. This is not all. Add to the patient's record the leprous aspects of granite, marble, and limestone quarries in the East, clay and iron pits in the North, and phosphate rock surface mines in the South. Each has its pathological symptoms. And now the infectious itch of coal strip mining!

By 1965 3.2 million acres (5000 square miles) had been disturbed by surface mining—41% by coal and 26% by sand and gravel, followed by stone, gold, phosphate, iron, and clay. And this was before Western strip mining was initiated. Coal ranked first because surface mining began around 1910 in Pennsylvania, West Virginia, and the states just to the west. Surface mining occupies many acres, but, looked at another way, coal-stripped lands are only 0.07% of the 48 states, or about the size of five midwestern counties. Nonetheless, in contrast to gold and iron, coal strip mining is growing.

Because airplanes fly so high today, travelers have to look intently to see anything but movies. However, if you do look closely as you pass over southern Illinois, you may see spoil heaps in ragged, recursive lines, looking as if the earth's abdominal skin and muscles had been torn away and the intestines exposed. Over West Virginia and south-eastern Ohio, you may see the long cliffs of "high walls" following the contour of the underlying coal seams, up each ravine, back down the far side, and so on to the next watershed. This mining has been going on for two generations. But until recently surface mining was only a minor component of the coal industry.

Coal began to replace wood after the Civil War, but only in those locations close to high population and industry. The anthracite of northeastern Pennsylvania kept pace with bituminous coal until 1870. Then bituminous coal from western Pennsylvania became dominant.

The urban landscape also came to reflect the use of coal. Winter in Eastern cities meant coal smoke and soot everywhere. Early commercial airline pilots navigated by smoke palls over cities—big ones for Chicago and Cleveland, smaller ones for Dayton and Fort Wayne.

Bituminous coal production grew from 200,000 tons in 1810 to 20 million in 1870, an increase of more than 8% per year. From 1870 to 1910 production continued to grow, but at the slightly lower rate of 7%. By 1918, however, growth had stopped, reaching the first production peak of 579 million tons. Of this total only 1.4% was strip-mined. Production then turned downward, hitting bottom in 1932 at 310 million tons. By 1944, with recovery from the Depression complete, another production peak was reached—620 million tons, with strip mining accounting for 16%. From 1944 production declined and by 1954 it had sunk to a low mark of 392 million tons. Now it's climbing again, 671 million tons in 1976, with more than half strip-mined, and currently it may exceed 700 million tons.

Petroleum, fairly enough, gets the blame for killing the growth of coal by 1915. Some markets, notably the railroads, were entirely lost; railroads used a quarter of production in 1920, but virtually none by 1960. Use of coal for domestic heating fell about 80% between 1940 and 1970. Although coal's share in the fuels used for power generation fell from 92% in 1920 to 53% in 1975, this is the market that has saved coal. The growth in our use of electricity has been so great that coal used for power generation grew from ten million tons in 1910 to 330 million in 1970.

This is where the West enters the picture. Western coal, in beds of great thickness, comprises the great bulk of the American coal resource. Its heat value is less than other types of coal but, in compensation, it has little sulfur. Environmental legislation limiting the release of sulfur dioxide from power plants has made Western coal competitive. Still, the demand for Western coal is lessened by the fact that power plants pay for coal only by the million BTU, and railroads charge freight by the ton. Accordingly its advantage is far from overwhelming, and market penetration has gone little beyond the Mississippi River.

Despite such restrictions, many "unit trains" of 100 cars, with each car carrying 100 tons, rumble east out of Colstrip, Montana, at 45 miles per hour through Bismarck, North Dakota, to power plants near St. Paul and to river barges. They are joined by more trains carrying lignite from Beulah, Zap, and Stanton, North Dakota. But their number is small because lignite, the bulkiest of the coal fuels, is more economically transported as electricity. Instead power plants tend to appear at the lignite mines, and the energy moves east silently, but more visibly, through a landscape becoming a wirescape. Electricity also flows out of Colstrip both east and west.

Kemmerer, Wyoming, has a dramatic set of coal seams, perhaps 120 feet thick, but dipping steeply to the west. Coal from Kemmerer feeds first a local power plant, and then the unit trains of the Union Pacific. Near Farmington, New Mexico, Navajo Mine produces a low-grade subbituminous coal for the expanding power plants at the Four Corners. Energy flows southwest by wire to Phoenix. From Black Mesa, high above and 20 miles southeast of Kayenta, Arizona, coal literally flows by slurry pipeline to power plants on the Colorado River near Davis Dam. Coal also leaves the mine by a ten-mile-long conveyor belt to a special railroad. This line, connecting with no other railroad, was built solely to haul Black Mesa coal 60 miles to power plants at Page, Arizona. It is electrified and has welded rails and concrete ties.

All of these centers pale beside Gillette, county seat of Campbell County, Wyoming. The only railroad construction of consequence since World War II (except for the Black.Mesa operation) is being carried out by the Burlington Northern Railroad from Orin to Gillette. Currently, coal moves from Gillette southeast to Alliance, Nebraska, over a line already choked with traffic. Leaving Gillette last summer, we saw two unit trains in town and four more, each a mile long, on sidings, waiting to be loaded.

Gillette currently has eight mines in operation and another half-dozen under construction or planned. Growth has been phenomenal— from only 6% of Wyoming's production in 1972 to a projected 65% in 1982. Production of 17 million tons in 1977 necessitates four to five unit trains a day. This year's capacity is expected to be in excess of 32 million tons or nine trains a day, but production may be considerably less because of rail traffic problems. If the estimate of 95 million tons for 1982 is achieved, traffic density will be one full train per hour out, and one empty train in.

One hears of much higher targets for production. These may not be credible. Somewhere, the ability of Western coal to displace Eastern will be limited by transportation costs and by the waning growth in electric demand. But if the demand for synthetic liquid fuels made from coal ("synfuels") increases significantly, mining will also increase.

Regardless, 100 million tons of coal a year soon will be mined in Campbell County. With coal seams averaging a hundred feet thick and containing 200,000 tons of coal per acre, this requires 500 acres per year. What is happening to that land? What, in fact, is happening to all of the strip-mined land in the West?

Mining and reclamation techniques differ little in these operations. Topsoil is first removed and set aside. The overburden is broken by blasting and then removed by a dragline bucket. In at least one mine at Gillette, overburden is trucked away to reconstruct the landscape into some topographic resemblance of the original. The topsoil is replaced; the surface smoothed, cultivated, seeded, [and] sometimes watered; and with luck in rainfall, a crop of mixed grasses or wheat is produced. The more recent the mining operation, the better the reclamation being done.

Unquestionably, the cost of reclamation far exceeds the land value, either initially or afterward when used for crops, hay, or range. Economic or not, we have made the decision by legislative process to require that the land surface be restored. It is possible in the West, although unlikely in the East, that reclaimed land may be more productive than it was before mining. In the West the costs of reclamation are trivial compared to the value of coal recovered: at most reclamation costs are $5000 per acre, whereas the 200,000 tons of coal per acre are worth $1.2 million. With Eastern coal seams as thin as three feet, reclamation costs loom much larger against a gross return of only 6000 tons at $16 per ton. Perhaps this is why resistance by Western miners has been weak.

Add to the reasons for greater Eastern impact the fact that strip mining in the East has been far more extensive. In 1976 three-fourths of strip-mined coal was from the East. More land is damaged in the East because the seams are thinner. More land value is lost because, at least in southern Illinois, some of the mined land is excellent cropland. In Eastern hill country, contour mining is particularly likely to damage, not merely the mined slopes, but downstream drainage channels. Horror stories about lack of concern for these consequences have been told in vivid detail. Furthermore, much Eastern strip mining was done before reclamation was required or before requirements were enforced. The effects are overt: the peculiar landscape of windrows of conical spoil-heaps growing up into scraggly forests with intervening ponds, pools, lakes, and linear drainage channels. It is a bewildering landscape for people, but apparently comfortable for wildlife. Some of these ravaged Eastern countrysides have now become acceptable recreation areas.

In the West, evidence of early strip mining is clear in the untouched residues. One sees them at Four Corners, at Colstrip, and at

Stanton. But they are minor compared to the East. Why then, the enormous opposition to Western strip mining? Has the East simply become numbed by the excesses of earlier practices? Or are they grateful for some progress? Or is it simply that the environmental movement has more strength in the West?

Driving west out of Stanton, North Dakota, we passed the new, rolling, graded, manicured slopes reconstructed over the vanished lignite beneath. I wondered if a good physical geographer a few years from now would be able to tell this was not a natural surface. A few miles farther we passed an utterly unreconstructed digging. An offense to the eye. Yet there it was, clothed in scrubby cottonwoods, and gullies filling in the sharp little recesses. "An offense to the eye," I conceded to myself, "but if I were a deer, I'll bet I would learn this place inside and out, how to come into it unseen, ten ways to get out unseen, where the blizzard drifts end, where there's browse all winter, where there's a bit of fresh water in October." But, as everyone knows, deer have a limited comprehension of environmental quality.

HEATING OUR HOMES

The "energy crisis" prompted us to view questions about energy use only in terms of the problem of maintaining a functioning society. As illustrated by the first article in this section, however, energy resources and their use constitute a field of interest that extends beyond dilemmas of adequate supply and excessive pollution. This paper, like several in Part Three on food and agriculture, is an encouragement to wonder about resources in ways that are freed from the bounds of crises. To paraphrase Luten, we must plow the energy field if we are to harvest understanding from it.

In 1978 the Census Bureau printed an eight-page report [U.S. Bureau of the Census, 1978a] that summarizes a good deal of information

Reprinted by permission from *Landscape*, 1980, 24(3): 10–11.

obtained in recent censuses about household heating. One part of it that gets down to really interesting detail is a set of three maps showing the "primary home heating fuel" for the last three censuses (1950–1970) [Figure 1]. . . .

In 1950 coal was primary. By 1960 it had become minor and was restricted to classical coal-mining regions. By 1970 it had almost disappeared. In the East it was the primary fuel only in southeastern Kentucky, a few neighboring Tennessee counties, [and] perhaps two dozen scattered counties in West Virginia, Ohio, and Pennsylvania. In the West it had shrunk to 17 counties in the northern mountain states, all either coal-mining counties or adjacent to them.

Wood declined similarly. In 1950 most counties south of the Eastern coal-heating region warmed their houses with wood, except those in Florida. New Mexico, Navajo Arizona, large parts of the Pacific Northwest, and the upper lake states also burned wood as their

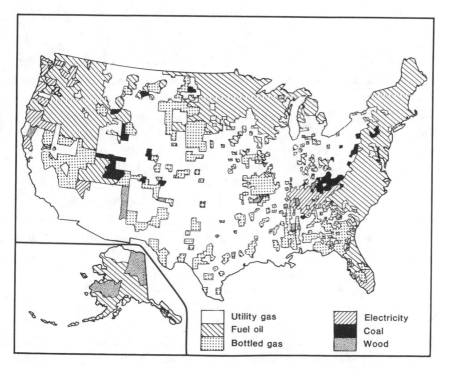

[FIGURE 1. Primary home heating fuel by counties of the United States: 1970.]

main fuel. By 1970 barely two dozen counties in the entire nation relied primarily on wood—all notable for poverty and most for hardwood forests. Most are in the Southern states.

Gas grew immensely during the 20-year interval, but chiefly it was from a core already established in 1950. Its greatest new conquests were the southern lake states. Curiously, Illinois and Indiana went from coal to fuel oil to gas.

Fuel oil expanded, too, but it filled gaps, replacing coal and, to a lesser degree, wood. By 1970 fuel oil had pushed wood out of Virginia, the Carolinas, the Northwest, the northern lake states, and the eastern Dakotas, but gas had pushed up out of Kansas to replace fuel oil in Nebraska.

In 1950 electricity claimed only Clark County, Nevada (Las Vegas)—an obvious consequence of Hoover Dam. By 1970 TVA–Tennessee and neighboring areas were [heated primarily by] electricity, as were coastal Oregon and Washington as a result of the Bonneville Power Authority. Beyond that, only southern Florida, previously reporting no heat at all, now reported electricity as the major method of home heating.

Last is bottled gas (liquefied petroleum gas or LPG). In 1950 it dominated 30 rural west Texas counties and eight in Louisiana. It expanded widely, replacing wood in the rural deep South, in southern Missouri, [and] in sparsely settled high plains regions such as the Nebraska sandhills, and replacing fuel oil in half of Nevada and trans-Sierra California.

The set of maps is revealing, but at the same time much is concealed. The maps show area, not size of population or amount of consumption; nor do they show the degree of primacy of the favorite fuel, whether 30% or 99%. Yuma County with 10,000 people is immense on the map compared to Cook County with five million people. Although we know this, it is still difficult to keep in mind that the picture presented is dominated by rural counties. Surprisingly, other data in the report suggest that this distortion doesn't matter much, except that bottled gas, an almost exclusively rural fuel, shows up well beyond its entitlement compared to electricity.

In 1970 gas was the primary fuel in 55% of American households; the 1970 maps makes it look a bit larger, perhaps 65%. This is surprising, too, for how does gas, the fuel most dependent on specialized, capital-intensive transport, find its way into so many rural counties?

But then, it only has to reach a few towns to become designated as the primary fuel for an entire county. I realized that a small town can dominate a rural county.

Clearly, an immense amount of steel pipe is buried beneath the American landscape. In the 1950 and 1960 maps, we can see the location of at least two gas pipelines by the counties using gas along their rights-of-way.

This set of maps and, I suppose, many other such sets should make magnificent teaching tools. With 3000 counties to ask questions about, an instructor could plague students unendingly. "Why does Fountain County, alone in Indiana, prefer bottled gas?" "Why did fuel oil replace wood in the Carolinas while bottled gas was replacing it in Georgia?" "What will the 1980 map show?"

PART FIVE

WATER

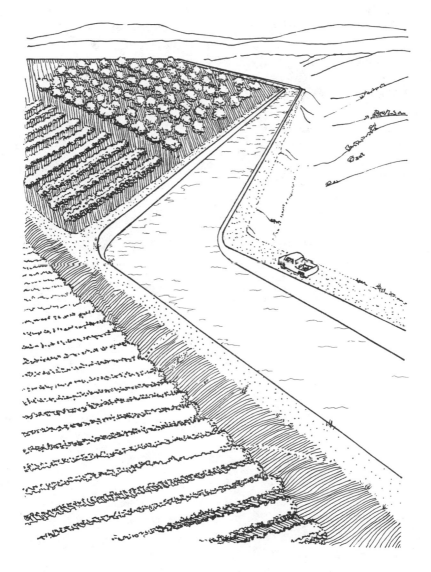

Luten's writings on water have covered a variety of issues and questions. Still, these papers, taken as a group, reveal a strong link between Luten's interest in water and his concern for wild landscapes. This association is not unique with Luten; proposed water developments, particularly dams and reservoirs, often generate unusually intense opposition from admirers of parks and wilderness. Perhaps the metaphor of rivers as living biological entities lies deep in the human heart.

WASTE WATER MANAGEMENT— A CONSERVATIONIST'S LONG VIEW

In spite of its title, this presentation was a discussion of resources generally and water specifically. Moreover, Luten made no attempt here to go into careful analyses of particular water issues. Rather, he presented ideas about how we think about water resources and ways that we allocate and utilize them. The presentation serves not only as an introduction to this section of articles on water, but also as a more general illustration of some critical questions about resources: How much of a resource do we use? How are variations in quality important to an understanding of a resource? How much of a resource remains for the future? How do the political and economic institutions by which we use a resource reflect our vision of the future?

Luten's perspective on water, then, like his views on food and energy, was not inalienably linked to crises over excessive or abusive use. For example, he mentioned the 1960s water shortage in the New York City area briefly in this paper, but it was not the focus of his discussion. Similarly, even though vituperative disputes over proposed dams in the Grand Canyon raged in the 1960s, Luten did not concentrate his attention on them here.

In papers presented earlier in this book, instances have been noted in which Luten was a successful anticipator of change. Here, in one matter, he seems to have been overly optimistic about the persistence of clean water "where man treads lightly." The water in Glacier National Park's McDonald Creek, which he felt was so clean that it was "outrageous" to question its purity, is today, like water in most parks and wildernesses, a potential source for human infection from gastrointestinal bacteria spread by people and other animals. As Luten himself would appreciate, too many people, even if they individually "tread lightly," can have a large collective impact.

I wish to begin by disclaiming any intention to go into details on waste water treatment. My concern today is with water as a resource,

Paper presented at the meeting of the California Water Pollution Control Association, Fresno, CA, April 1964.

and as a fascinating kind of resource. It is essential: We drink it and would be hard put [to do] without it. The natives of the Kalahari Desert have had to develop a remarkable technology to recover even the small amounts required for drinking, but for most of us water is so abundant that we have little conception of the volumes used. It has, accordingly, been possible to bamboozle New Yorkers into voting for unending water supply bonds by the simple expedient of proclaiming a water shortage in order to alleviate it and asking that restaurants not serve water to guests except on specific request. In fact, though, a stream flowing at one second-foot will supply the drinking water needs of one million people. The entire world's needs could be met by a flow of 3000 second-feet, 6000 acre-feet per day, 2,000,000 acre-feet per year. This could be provided by [one of many minor rivers so small that they are known only locally, such as the Yuba of California, the Cedar of Iowa, the Saco of Maine, the Genesee of New York, or the Hatchie of Tennessee.] . . .

Water is a resource because we use it. But it is also a resource simply because, under some circumstances, we admire it. I hope we can agree with Henry Thoreau [1854/1964] that some things are "more to be admired than used," and that admiration of Lake Tahoe is a use of the lake.

Our principal use of water [is] to transport things, and mostly to carry thing away—low-grade energy and waste matter—things we are bored with and wish to be rid of, to forget about. This is pervasive: Irrigation water moves upward through the plant transporting nutrients, but then evaporating to carry away heat—heat more often than not in excess of the plant's needs, and, therefore, a waste to be rid of. The excess liquid irrigation water percolates out of the fields and carries away minerals, mostly unwanted minerals. This is the big end of the scale. At the other, the small end of the scale, when we drink water it is also for those purposes: to carry away heat by evaporating water, and to carry away unwanted waste material by voiding it. Most of the intervening uses are in the same category. Instances do occur in a technological society where water is used otherwise—where, for example, it is changed chemically. The manufacture of water gas comes first to my mind. But these are minor.

When we say we wish to use some water, usually we are saying we wish the privilege of contaminating it, of adulterating it, of polluting it, and we are saying implicitly that we are thus interested because we are confident it will go away quietly when we have used it.

How completely water has been used depends on your point of view. Man's used water is another organism's daily bread. Water which has been used may or may not have been fully used. That is, it may or may not have additional usefulness. Water has been fully used, perhaps, when it costs more to bring it back to a useful condition than it costs to tap the next cheapest source of usable water. If this is an acceptable notion, then fully used water is simply water we are willing to abandon.

In simple theory, waste water ought to have the same meaning. Now, though, we come to the question of its going away quietly. The water these days still goes away quietly, but the downstream neighbors are in a continual uproar. The mixing of two streams of different quality almost always leads to a loss in values. No matter how much the efficiency experts extol the merits of homogeneity, there is value in diversity almost everywhere you turn in life.

We begin to think about waste water treatment when the folks downstream don't want our used stream mixed with their unused stream, or worse, when they want the water we have used, but don't want what we have put into it. Furthermore, because the management of the volume of water is a major problem in treatment for reuse, they will argue strongly for treatment before dilution rather than after. They may also have in mind that only under such conditions will you be more apt to pay for it than they.

How heavily water is used before it is fully used depends on geography, [including] the supply and the burden of men on the landscape. Where man treads lightly on the landscape, he can be finicky in his choice, and where water is also abundant, he can be profligate in its use. This is transparent: You don't find cooling towers where water is free; you don't find treatment plants where effluent is minute in terms of supply, and you shouldn't.

The urbanized American, though, has little sense of proportion in such matters and, while ignoring the technologist at one moment, is piteously dependent on him at another. Thus, one day last summer, as I sat at the edge of McDonald Creek, which flows from Logan Pass and the Garden Wall and other admirable places in Glacier Park, a city type stopped and asked me if the water was safe to drink. I'm not entirely sure it was, though I had been drinking it and intend to continue, for there is some human activity upstream. But I told him it was outrageous even to ask such a question, and I have not changed my mind.

Conversely, where men press heavily in their environment, and especially where water is not abundant or its management is bad, drinking water is taken from what we would regard as sewers or cesspools. I don't think any of these people prefer such water, but many of them know nothing we would call better. And, anyway, all of us put up with what we must. T. E. Lawrence tells, in *The Seven Pillars of Wisdom* [1935], how in one traverse of the desert, they missed a waterhole one night, found the next one dry, and then after three days without water, came upon a third which the Turks had polluted by killing a camel in it weeks earlier. The water, rich, high, yellow and frothy, he described as excellent. . . .

Next, . . . consider the matter of the magnitude of a resource, [of which water is but an example]. It is usually desperately hard really to see the limits of a resource. Even when we are assured of a total fixed amount, as, for example, [with] copper, we see ways in which the notion of a fixed ceiling is rendered pretty much untenable. The ceiling is raised by a technology which finds ways to process leaner ores, to transport ores and metal from remote places. For a resource which is really part of the economy, and copper seems a reasonable example, increased prices both raise the ceiling and protect the supply by inviting substitutes. Aluminum is a conspicuous substitute for copper.

Whether any resource ceilings are fixed and immutable, I don't know. None come to my mind. However, collapsing ceilings are common; the passenger pigeon is an adequate example. Most of our wildlife resources fall in this category; many of our fisheries; many, perhaps, of our forests; and some, certainly, of our croplands.

Now, in general our activities and our numbers increase with time in a manner describable only as "exponential and probably more than exponential." What happens when depletion of a fixed resource increases exponentially? At first, nothing. The use is minute compared to the resource. Always our forefathers on this continent spoke of the limitless forests, the unbounded promise, the infinite resources. No matter how prodigal their use, the resource stood unblemished. But it is in the nature of exponential growth to tend to exceed any finite limit. And these resources were not, in fact, infinite. Look at this schematic table:

Time	Total original resource (%)	Resource used (%)	Resource left (%)
0	100	0	100
1	100	0.001	99.999
2	100	0.01	99.99
3	100	0.1	99.9
4	100	1	99
5	100	10	90
6	100	100	0

If the measurement which is being made is the residual resource, and if it can only be measured to 10%, then essentially no warning is given that the resource is about to be exhausted until that exhaustion is imminent. . . .

This [growth] feeds back into the resources picture in two interesting fashions. First, as a general principle, when pressure on the environment grows, property rights intensify and new property rights tend to appear. . . . So far as new property rights are concerned, consider the insistence on rights to a view, on a right of preservation of a [river], a right to expect to catch fish in that [river], a right to clean air, a right not to be hemmed in by tall buildings. Today we have governmental agencies defending, to some degree, all of these rights.

But this also brings in another aspect. We used to imagine that such property rights could be effectively administered through the machinery of the market place, by economic criteria. On these matters resulting from crowding, we have usually found no such way. What is the price of a day's personal supply of clean air? Instances have arisen where a price is exacted for the privilege of polluting a stream, but I know of none in this country.

I suspect that steadily we move away from the notion of an economically determined society, not merely in our public lives, but in our private lives as well. The management of water is a conspicuous example. In an earlier decade, we undertook the irrigation of Western lands under government auspices. Justifications had economic overtones, but they were as shoddy a set of economies as one could imagine. They worked, but only because no one was in a position to question them excepting those who espoused them philosophically or who stood to gain from them.

When such possibilities ran out, we turned to hydropower to justify irrigation. Now with a long background of this, it seems plausible to build power plants on the Colorado River in order to raise money, not electricity, to finance the movement of water into Arizona. It would be fully as logical to tax the tuna fishery to build salmon ladders at new dams. They are both aqueous. The illogic spreads everywhere. The sound head will scorn the hoot-and-holler conservationist who writes from his redwood house demanding the preservation of the redwoods, but a Chamber of Commerce will use the same secretary the same day first to write letters demanding more economy in government, and next to demand a special local appropriation.

Free enterprise has almost shrunk to the freedom to influence legislation. The economic criteria are going; decisions on resource administration are becoming heavily political, and the political machinery is not very good at this. It is too much to expect that we could devise a rational system for reaching detailed decisions in such matters, but we do desperately need some overriding concepts of resource management. We need an ethics of resource use. We can barely see some straws in the wind which suggest that such an ethic may appear. . . .

THE USE AND MISUSE OF A RIVER

No piece of the American landscape has stood out more prominently and more recurrently in recent conservation history than the elongated strip of canyons of the Colorado River. The great depth and narrow width of the canyons make them attractive to dam builders and landscape admirers alike. As a result, dams and dam proposals on the Colorado, notably at Echo Park,

Reprinted by permission from *The American West*, May 1967, pp. 47–53; 73–75.

Glen Canyon, Marble Gorge, and Bridge Canyon (the latter two being within what is usually perceived to be the Grand Canyon), have been major conservation controversies of the mid-20th century.

In the two papers presented next, Luten focused on water development on the Colorado River. The first serves as a kind of stage-setting discussion of the physical environment of the river, and the history of water allocation to various users. In it, Luten also introduced his philosophy about the difficulties of knowing "what is the part of wisdom in resolving between utility and beauty," particularly concerning the effect of compromise on beauty. The article illustrates the importance to the antidam viewpoint of both the landscape setting and the image of a river free to flow unhindered over long periods of time. Luten's sympathy toward that viewpoint, if somewhat muted in the first of these papers, can be seen clearly in the second.

The Colorado River, like much of difficult Nature, calls to mind the complaint that if the good Lord had been foresighted he would have arranged to have the sun rise at day's end so as to provide light at night when needed. The Colorado, in an arid, parched land of high mesas, sandstone cliffs, and deep-cut canyons, is only one river, not large, not clean, barely sweet, seasonally difficult. No wonder it is abused.

Statistically, it is a mighty stream. Its basin is a twelfth of the area of the 48 states, 245 thousand square miles or 157 million acres. It stretches 1400 miles from the tules and shifting channels at the head of the Gulf of California up to its remotest source at the far end of the Wind River Mountains in northwest Wyoming.

At its source, the Colorado contends for watershed with the Columbia's ultimate tributary and with one of the many streams carrying tribute to the Mississippi. If the Rockies are the ridgepole of the continent, then the Colorado Basin is its south-facing roof.

The first Caucasians to cross the belt of the continent went directly, if tortuously, from east slope to west slope, from Missouri to Columbia waters. But in later years more than 95 of each 100 travelers have made the crossing through the Colorado Basin. Whether by horse, by wagon train, by rail, by automobile, or by plane; whether through Green River, Wyoming, through Vernal or Green River, Utah, through Needles, Blythe, or Yuma; whether with feet cooled in the river's silty water or head lost in the airline's movie—all of those westward bound have encountered the Colorado Basin and its river.

The basin is rimmed by great mountains, as a great river's basin should be [Figure 1]. From northeast to east are the Wind Rivers (13,800 feet), the Rockies (14,400), and the San Juans (14,400). On the west are the Wasatches and the Uintas (13,500). Through two gaps in the eastern rim, the one just south of the Wind River Mountains in

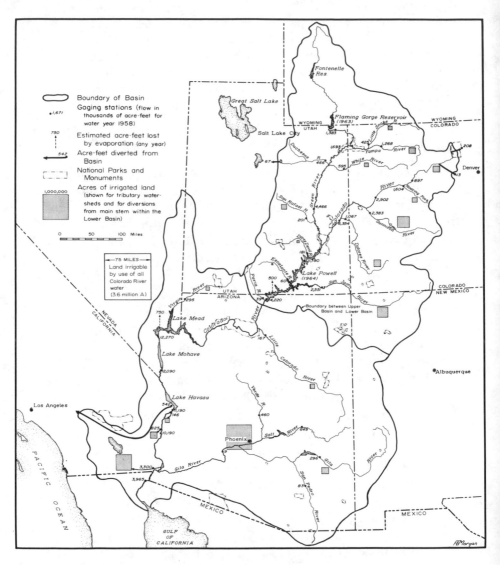

[FIGURE 1. The Colorado River Basin.]

Wyoming, the other west of Albuquerque, most of the people have passed.

Here is the Colorado, then, with a grand setting, with a fair share of the land for its province, with its face to the sun. What makes it special? What purpose does it serve that would cause it, if it could, to petition against man's interference? Why should it complain?

In other lands, a river's birthplace is a mountain in alpine meadows; its youth is spent brawling and carving the lower slopes of forested hill country; in its full maturity it meanders through verdant, flatland farms. Its workload is light, its free time high. It has not lost its right to go on a rampage now and then to remind men that it is still a free river, that it will cooperate only on its own terms. The Colorado's youth, too, is in mountain brooks, but it drops quickly from forest meadows to a dry land, where for millions of years it has worked as a drudge, hauling dirt to the end of time, and the task only begun. No help comes to it from lowland tributaries; all of its strength springs from the northern mountains. Incised deep into the rocks, it has no chance to escape from its ancient meanders, to explore new ways. Never a free day, never a moment's relief from work.

But while at this endless task, it has still built a land of magic and witchcraft.

One would suppose that a river with the character to cut such canyons would have a history clear and distinct, sharp and purposeful. Regrettably this is not so. Geologists still find some things not clear at all. Through much of the past, the heart of the basin—the canyonlands from the Grand Canyon to 500 miles upstream—was flat and low-lying, or under the waters of the ancient midland seas that covered the region of today's Rocky Mountains. Accordingly, it is largely a region of sedimentary and metamorphic rocks which go back one and a half billion years to well before the beginning of the Paleozoic era. At one interval during the Jurassic Period, the region was desert with dunes of red, pink, and white sand that swept in from the west, ultimately leaving deposits almost 2000 feet deep. Later the sea returned and covered the dunes with sediment, thus preserving them as sandstone.

Late in the Cretaceous period, the sea retreated slowly to the east as western North America began to rise. New hills appeared to the west of the basin, and they washed away to the east as they rose, leaving great depths of sediment. The Kaibab Uplift, a southerly fringe, may have occurred at about this time. It is a fold 100 miles long and 25 miles wide, running north-northwest from Flagstaff almost up to Kanab, on Utah's southern border. When you drive northward from Williams to the South Rim, or southward from Kanab to the North Rim, you are climbing up the spine of a broad swell that has been cut through at the crest by the river. The Grand Canyon is sliced through the top of a plateau. It hardly seems the easiest way to the sea, but conditions change and, presumably, it was once the line of least resistance.

By the end of the Cretaceous period, the region had become a great plain sloping off to the east—but then the eastern edge of the land began to rise. This was the beginning of the Rocky Mountains and of the Colorado basin, too, in a sense. Before the final development of the basin began, however, most of those enormous depths of Cretaceous sediments disappeared. Only their fringes remain to form the high plateaus on the margins of the basin. Where they went is uncertain. Apparently, they did not end up in the Gulf of California and were not, therefore, carried away by today's river. Perhaps when coastal mountains rising to the west made the region dry again, the sediments simply blew away, as the red Jurassic sands had blown in earlier.

Quite recently, perhaps 10 to 20 million years ago, the streams which exist today settled into their drainage pattern. Because these modern streams meander as if wandering across a flat, featureless plain, we must suspect that the basin was just such a land, close to sea level, when the stream patterns became established. Only then did the Colorado River find its way across the top of the Kaibab plateau, already an elevated fold, but still at a low altitude.

During the past few million years, the entire region, especially near the Grand Canyon end, has risen more than 5000 feet. Along with this lifting and tilting, a good deal of gentle folding and faulting has occurred, the basis for the great series of plateaus, edged by bright cliffs that lie within the basin today. Despite all of these changes, the bedding remains almost flat.

With this last uplifting, the rivers, caught in their meandering paths, set to work at erosion again.

Much of the region's past shows in the shape of the canyonlands. Quite apart from the canyons, it is a region of plateaus, usually sloping gently upward toward the south, then terminating in abrupt

cliffs that stretch for miles across the land. These cliffs are not the
canyon walls, but quite a separate feature [Figures 2, 3, 4].

The river itself—what is it really like? First, it is in an arid land;
the rainfall over the entire basin averages but ten inches per year. The
only parts which are at all well watered are the highlands. On the
plateaus, annual precipitation may reach 20 inches per year. Such
areas include the drainage of the Green River in the foothills of the
Wind River Mountains, the highlands reaching southwestward from
the Uinta Mountains of Utah, a long stretch of the western slope of the
Rockies from the northern to the southern border of Colorado, and a
surprisingly large strip of Arizona highland, extending southeastward
from the south rim of the Grand Canyon along the height of land
separating the Little Colorado from the Gila River drainage.

In the high mountain crests (especially those which lie athwart
the eastward-moving winter storms), precipitation may be as great as
40 or 50 inches. Most of this comes to the mountains as snow and can
accumulate in cirques and leeward basins to great depth. But, except
in such sheltered reservoirs, snow is largely gone from the highlands
by June. The seasonal pattern in river flow shows a great wave of snow
water in the spring, reaching a peak in June. By September and
October it is gone, and the main stream's flow may be but 5% of what it
was at flood [Figure 5].

Flood flow is deceptively inconspicuous in many parts of the
river's course. In Glen Canyon, the river rises only ten feet at flood, but
the current is astonishing. At low water, the stream wanders among
sand bars, almost lost. In the Grand Canyon, rock-strewn rapids are
totally submerged in a mighty flow at high water. In 1869 John Wesley
Powell saw high-water mark (indicated by debris caught in crevices)
100 feet above stream level in Cataract Canyon. Was there some ob-
struction there that backed water up, or was this a record of a flood far
greater than any we have seen?

One other pattern of rainfall must be mentioned. In the arid basin
lands, summer thunderstorms are a spectacular part of the landscape.
Occasionally, precipitation from these may be great, and rarely, it may
cover wide areas. In contrast to the high-elevation winter snow, or thin
rain percolating into the soil, these summer rains are intense and fall
on land which often has no topsoil at all. As a result, stream flows
respond as quickly as on city pavement. The overall contribution of

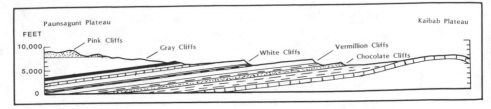

[FIGURE 2.] Erosional cliff lines from Grand Canyon north to central Utah [after P. B. King, 1959].

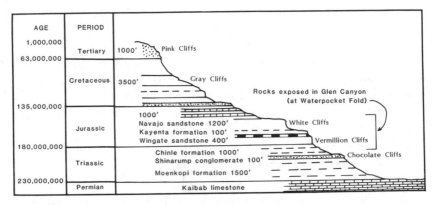

[FIGURE 3.] Rock sequence in southern Utah [after P. B. King, 1959].

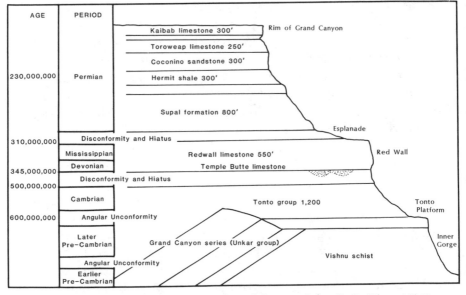

[FIGURE 4.] Rock sequence in the Grand Canyon [after P. B. King, 1959].

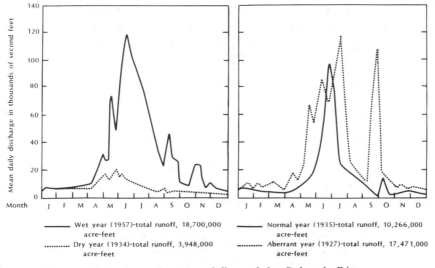

        Wet year (1957)-total runoff, 18,700,000
        acre-feet
.... Dry year (1934)-total runoff, 3,948,000
        acre-feet

        Normal year (1935)-total runoff, 10,266,000
        acre-feet
.... Aberrant year (1927)-total runoff, 17,471,000
        acre-feet

[FIGURE 5.] Comparative annual flow of the Colorado River.

summer rain to annual flow is small, but record floods on most of the tributaries originating in the canyonlands have been measured in the thunderstorm months of July and August. Powell mentioned several occasions on his first trip down the river when the precipices above the party became alive with waterfalls within minutes after rain began. He also spoke of flash floods in the side canyons, but said of one that he could outrun it, so greedily was the first water drawn into the sand.

The abundant water from the snow fields comes down through cool valleys of little cropland and limited meadow areas into a lower-latitude desert, the hottest land in the New World, a land with fertile alluvial bottoms—and with virtually no rainfall. Here is a land for agriculture and here is water to make it bloom. Whose land, whose water?

The water is really not very much. Caught in the rapids of Cataract Canyon or in the June flood in Glen Canyon, some might not agree. But of that average of ten inches of rainfall over the basin, only an eighth (called "virgin" flow) ever becomes river. Most of the water evaporates from the ground or is transpired by the leaves of the basin's plants. Today, the fraction of rainfall which gets to the Gulf of California is even less, and irrigated agriculture threatens to consume the virgin eighth to the point where the river at its mouth in summer will become only an effluent trickle of brine, a vehicle for the minerals and salts which percolating waters pick up on their way to a stream.

A great river, yes. A long river, yes. But big, no. The Colorado's mean annual virgin flow has been set at 15 million acre-feet at Lees Ferry and about 18 million at its mouth. By comparison, the Amazon averages 5400 million feet at its mouth per annum, the Congo 1000 million, the Mississippi 440 million, the Columbia 184 million, and the Yukon 130 million. By these standards, the Colorado's flow can hardly be considered more than the spurt of a garden hose. If all of its water were used in the hot lowlands of Arizona and California at the rate of five acre-feet per acre per year, the land irrigated could be included in a square only 75 miles wide on a side.

But there's more to a river than basin and stream. A river's task is erosion. It is done with its task when its watershed is flattened to sea level. No river succeeds, but some come close. Its weapon is the energy of water on high slopes, all of which has been dissipated before reaching the sea. Most of the energy turns into heat, but a little goes into the work of wearing down the watershed.

The Colorado displays an impressive record of erosion, but the point it makes is not that the task is done, but rather, how much still remains. The main streams, fed by dependable annual floods, have carved impressive canyons. The lower tributaries, fed by undependable summer thunderstorms, have not been able to keep up. Even the main canyons have a long way down to go. Geological uplift is far ahead of degradation. . . . An old stream, nearly finished with its work, would show low elevations until close to its sources. The Colorado begins its climb to its source in its lower canyons. For this reason, it has the potential for substantial hydropower development in its main stream [Figures 6, 7]. Compare this to the Mississippi, where major hydropower developments have mainly been limited to such remote tributaries as the upper Tennessee or the far Missouri.

Nonetheless, erosion *is* proceeding, and the best testimony is the enormous burden of sediment and dissolved solids carried by the river. Sediment burden is not easy to measure, but a rough value given for the Colorado is 0.5% by volume. Half a hundredth of 15 million acre-feet of water each year is 75 thousand acre-feet of sediment. If the runoff of water is 1.25 inches per year (one-eighth of the ten inches of precipitation), the runoff of sediment is 0.006 inches per year, or six

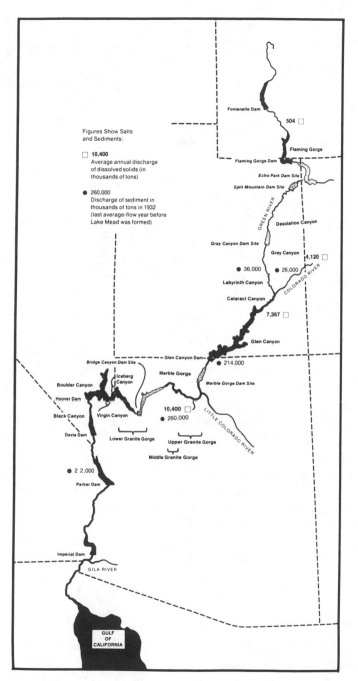

[FIGURE 6. The canyons of the Colorado River Basin.]

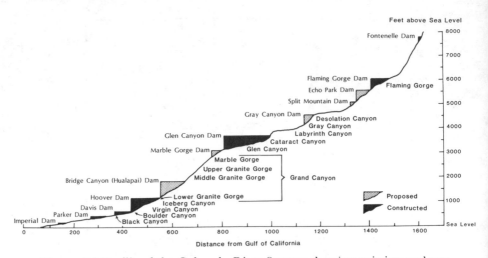

[FIGURE 7.] Profile of the Colorado River System, showing existing and proposed dams and reservoirs.

inches per millennium. The present rate of uplift in the canyonlands region may be about the same. While it appears, then, that the river keeps up with the rising land, it does not do so uniformly, and we may suspect that the canyons are deepening their bottoms and approaching sea level while the mesas are still rising. The landscape is becoming more spectacular as we watch it, at a rate of one-half foot a millennium, 500 feet each million years, and 5000 feet in ten million years—and that, perhaps, is how long it has taken the river to carve 5000 feet of canyon.

The distribution of sediment and dissolved salts is given [in Figure 6]. As might be expected, little comes from the snow-melt waters of the high mountains; most comes from the arid basin regions, the Little Colorado, the Dirty Devil, the Paria, and the Escalante.

And most of it moves at high water. The small streams pour vast loads into the main stem's channel in their summer floods. The river sweeps it downstream with next spring's snow melt, spreads it across the bottomlands, and fills the head of the Gulf of California with smooth, rich, and irrigable land.

Look now at what we have done to this region, to this land of endless high plains, of range after mountain range, of narrow beaver-meadowed valleys, of intermontane "parks," but also of juniper- and sage-clad plateau lands, of bare sandstone rocks, and incised canyons. Keep in mind the nature of the 19th-century invasion. The floods of migrants moved onward to the promise of yellow California gold or green Oregon fields, but some—perhaps with a greater Biblical literacy—saw in this region a land of both oasis and wilderness. They had left the East in a spirit of wanderlust, but also in search of a new security. The former urge might well have expended itself before arrival. The latter found, in the irrigable land and snow-fed streams, a substratum upon which, with infinite industry, they built an oasis of security and usefulness. Around it remained a wild land, a Biblical desert of scorching summers and bitter winters. It was reminiscent of ancient memories but so foreign to the forested hills, the swamps and river bottoms, the marshlands, and prairies of the eastern New World as to be a new kind of wilderness.

All of the old conflict between love of wilderness and need for pastoralism, between wanderlust and homesickness, between concern for what is beautiful and what is useful rode with them into these mountain valleys, these desert ranges, these sparse canyon streams. They built little dams everywhere in the headwaters and diverted water onto the beaver meadows. They raised fruit trees, a few vegetables, grain, hay, and livestock. Lower down, the dams were a little bigger, the meadows broader, the canals, tunnels, and ditches, longer. The water they used depleted the river flow but little.

While this was going on, however, the migrants who had gone on swarmed against a limiting western coast. They also learned how to use water, more and more of it. While those of the upper basin diverted small streams into cool fields, those in the lower basin, especially in southern California, had expanding ideas. First they turned to nearby coastal hills, then to the California mountains, then, finally, to the yield of the remote mountains of Wyoming and Colorado. The land they sought to irrigate expanded from the narrow alluvial plains of coastal valleys first to the bottomlands of the Colorado River where it bounds California, and then to the Imperial Valley and Arizona's central lowlands of the Salt River. All of this was hot, thirsty land. It needed not just one or two feet of water a year as the meadows did, but four, five, and even ten feet. The prospect of limitless demand aroused concern upstream. Attitudes toward water and water law had developed in a time of limited need and local use. The 20th century saw the rise of an ogre of unlimited need and interstate demand.

A first attempt at resolution was the Colorado River Compact of 1922. It divided the water equally between the upper and lower basins, with Lee's Ferry as the dividing point. Expecting that virgin flow would average 15 million acre-feet a year at Lee's Ferry, but knowing that individual years would vary widely, the upper-basin users agreed not to deplete the river's flow below 75 million acre-feet for "any period of ten consecutive years."

Unfortunately, the 20-odd years of records on which the Compact was based appear, in retrospect, to have been unusually wet, whereas more recent years, especially the early 1930s and early 1960s, have been unusually dry. Tree-ring evidence going back to the "great drought" of the 13th century suggests that few periods have been wetter than the first decades of this century.

The Compact assured the lower basin that upper-basin states would never make "area of origin" demands on all the water, and, at the same time, assured the upper basin that lower-basin states would not develop uses for the entire flow and then seek enduring rights through court or Congressional action based on the fact of development.

Subsequently (in 1944) a treaty assured Mexico of a tenth of the river's flow, or 1.5 million acre-feet, half of which might be made up of irrigation waste water from developments close to the border. The most recent major allocation of Colorado River water was by the United States Supreme Court, which settled contention between California and Arizona by cutting California's share of the river to 4.4 million acre-feet and granting Arizona rights to 2.8 million feet. Nevada got 300,000. The court decision is of little importance, of course, until Arizona and upper-basin developments actually take the water to which they are entitled.

Pending upper-basin development, California has withdrawn larger amounts of water, in part to retrieve earlier damages resulting from overpumping of the groundwater in the Los Angeles basin. Up until the most recent years of extremely low flow, no one in Los Angeles has really suffered from water shortage, although hydropower generation has sometimes been less than desired. Never has concern for supply in the lower basin been great enough to require full use of Lake Mead. This reservoir, filled only twice in its history, was by no means full even in the wet year of 1952 when 8 million acre-feet of water reached the Gulf of California. The requirements of flood control and the wish to increase power income have outweighed any notions of providence with water.

But with the dry years of the early 1960s and the simultaneous need to fill the enormous new reservoir behind Glen Canyon Dam, pinches have been felt. Water was discharged from Lake Powell before levels were high enough for power generation, so that Hoover Dam generators and downstream irrigation could continue. The Colorado River Compact would not seem to have required that this be done. But the Compact envisioned beginning with reservoirs full, not empty.

With assurance by the Compact that the lower basin would continue to get water, Hoover Dam was built in the early 1930s to create a reservoir capable of storing two years' flow of the river, capable of controlling floods, and capable of generating enough power ultimately to pay for itself and provide financial aid for downstream irrigation works. Prior to the Compact and Hoover Dam, the actual uses of the lower basin had been limited to irrigation in the bottomlands of the California–Arizona border. In 1939, however, shortly after the dam's completion, the All American Canal, the largest diversion from the entire river, began to move water into the Imperial Valley. That same year, the California Aqueduct of the Metropolitan Water District began to move water into the Los Angeles basin.

The next stage in development was to be the preparation by the upper basin of storage facilities to permit it to develop and use its half of the river and at the same time to meet its commitments under the Compact. This was to be followed by facilities to take water from the river across western Arizona into the Salt River Valley near Phoenix, where farmers were already overpumping groundwater in the confidence that deficits would be made up before the wells ran dry. The first step in this stage was to be the construction of Echo Park Dam near the junction of the Green and Yampa Rivers. The resulting reservoir would back water up into Dinosaur National Monument. The next step was to be Glen Canyon Dam, which would create a reservoir equal to Lake Mead and would, if it ever filled, back water up into Rainbow Bridge National Monument. The third was to be two dams in the Grand Canyon, one above the National Park, the other below it but backing water up through the length of Grand Canyon National Monument and well into the Park. With the interference of World War II, it was not until 1955 that plans were ready.

But at this time another element in American culture intervened.

Up until 1955, concern had only been for the river's usefulness. Now the landscape of the basin was beginning to arouse an American concern for beauty and wildness that goes back two centuries. It was first tuned to Atlantic shores, then to forested hills, then to snow peaks. At last we began to see beauty in painted deserts and canyonlands. Here again the issue came up: Are some things more to be admired than used?

It had come up many times before. It had arisen in an empty land when objections to wilderness reservations were minor and easily overcome—Yellowstone and Yosemite. It had come up later when beauty and usefulness met head-on—and usefulness had won—Hetch Hetchy. At Echo Park, beauty won, perhaps in large measure because the case for usefulness was weak. In Glen Canyon, beauty lost, in perhaps the most grievous loss of all, simply because no one knew what was there. Now the battle for Grand Canyon is in its third year. It is not yet lost to beauty, but it is far from being won.

Over the century since Yellowstone was dedicated to beauty, the land that was empty has filled. Simultaneously, the contention over any proposal for land use affecting the general welfare has grown from less than a whisper to at least a babble, sometimes a roar. If the problem of an empty land was to encourage development, the problem of a full land is to know what is the part of wisdom in resolving conflicts between utility and beauty. . . .

The arguments on usefulness and economic attractiveness run on and on, in intricate detail. Congressional hearings on these matters suggest that few people have mastered the intricacies, that probably no Congressmen have had the time to do so, and that decisions will not be based on the logic of economics.

On the other side, on the question of beauty, the matter is no simpler. Conservationists have argued that National Parks must not be invaded by incompatible uses and that a reservoir is an incompatible use; that reservoirs will destroy unmatched natural landscapes; and that reservoirs will make impossible the experience of following the wild Colorado down its length. In rebuttal, the reclamationists have said that only a few privileged individuals have traversed the length of the canyons by boat. In contrast, they say, the reservoirs will let millions see the canyon safely by motorboat. Furthermore, they will provide trout fishing. . . .

Such controversy is not about to end. So long as Americans continue to value both the useful and the beautiful qualities of the landscape, so long as they cherish both fields and wilderness, so long as they are beset by both nostalgia and wanderlust, for so long will the problems of conflicting demands arise.

In such dilemmas, we usually speak of compromise. The compromises are never true ones, for beauty does all the compromising. Splitting the difference between utility and beauty again and again ultimately will leave nature next to nothing; half of a half of a half of a half is a 16th.

Suppose someone were to counter a suggestion to compromise on the Colorado dams by saying, "Certainly. Two dams block the river today, Hoover and Glen Canyon. You may keep Hoover, if you will remove Glen Canyon Dam and let Glen Canyon begin its return to the world of beauty."

"Ridiculous!" is the only possible reaction. And for so long as such a statement is ridiculous, the cause of the American landscape is a losing battle, to be fought from barricade to barricade, but always backward.

When will the tide turn?

CENTRAL ARIZONA PROJECT: HEARING STATEMENT

In the 1960s, a plan (the Central Arizona Project) to provide Arizona with its share of Colorado River water involved two proposed dams in the Grand Canyon, one at Marble Gorge and the second at Bridge Canyon. As Luten pointed out in this statement, the true but sometimes hidden purpose of these dams was to generate electricity for sale. The resulting revenues were

Statement made at the hearing of the U.S. House of Representatives Interior Committee, August 30, 1965.

to help pay for the water delivery system and thus to subsidize the cost of the water; this was particularly important for farmers. Therefore, as Luten noted, "the American taxpayer is subsidizing Arizona agriculture just as fully as if he personally were paying off the notes for the construction costs of the Central Arizona Project." Such a "cash-register" function of large dams has been a characteristic part of water developments of the Bureau of Reclamation.

The fundamental argument over the Central Arizona Project was between groups with contrasting concepts of the best use of the canyons: development for reservoirs or preservation as wild landscape. The issues, like those over population growth or energy use, were debated in magazines and on television, on street corners and over the backyard fence; also, of course, they were argued in Congressional hearings. The dialogue in all its forms was a dispute over which of the two viewpoints was wiser, but typically the discussion revolved around matters that seemed more objective and thus easier to deal with—matters like the importance of Arizona farmers to American agriculture, the need for reservoirs for water storage, or the demand for hydroelectricity. It is particularly when such topics arise that Luten's advice to conservationists, as stated in earlier selections in this book, seems most appropriate: Be skeptical about assumptions, and be sophisticated in the use of numbers and information. This short discussion exemplifies that advice. (Luten has also suggested that conservationists address directly the value, or importance, of wild landscapes—a topic that is more fully explored in the next section of this book.)

The Central Arizona Project was approved by Congress in 1967. The dams at Marble Gorge and Bridge Canyon were not included in the authorization.

I am speaking today on behalf of the Federation of Western Outdoor Clubs, an affiliation of some 40 clubs devoted to outdoor activities and to the conservation of the American landscape. These clubs have an aggregate membership of close to 45,000 American citizens living in nearly all of the states.

The Federation is on record, by resolution at its annual conventions in 1963 and 1964, as opposed to construction of any dams between Lake Mead and Glen Canyon Dam, and in support of the extension of Grand Canyon National Park to include all of Grand Canyon National Monument and the Colorado River and its gorges from Lee's Ferry, just below Glen Canyon Dam, to the Grand Wash Cliffs, just above the head of Lake Mead.

In this matter, the Federation [has] just simply joined with the unanimous position of American conservationists. From the point of view of conservationists, the arguments in favor of inclusion of all of this reach of the river within the park and against the construction of the proposed dams are so overwhelming that it is difficult to understand how anyone could call himself a conservationist and still advocate the dams.

Let me also note at the outset that the Federation has raised no objection to the Central Arizona Project aside from the dams. Once the waters of the Colorado have passed through this region of our concern, the magnificent untamed scenery of the great canyons, their subsequent use seems unlikely to disturb the canyons significantly.

A great deal of concern has been expressed for the plight of the Arizona farmer, and I am sure that if I were an Arizona farmer I would be out drumming up support. But let me suggest a little perspective: Among American farmers, the Arizonan is a rare bird. There are only 8000 of him, less than 0.1% of the number of all American farmers, and his average net income last year was first among all American farmers, Californians being a close second. His 8000 farms are not large, averaging only 125 acres more or less of cropland, and the total cropland of the state is only a million acres, one-tenth the cropland of the small state of Indiana. A million acres is a square of land only 40 miles on a side. Arizona's first crops are cotton and alfalfa, and Arizona's crop support payments over the years have about equaled Indiana's. Cotton gets more support than corn.

Let me next express my bewilderment that any of the arguments in support of these two dams, the ones in Bridge Canyon and Marble Gorge, should be given more than a moment's credence. The argument is, first, that the dams will conserve water and make it available for Arizona. This argument fails quickly, for it is conceded that the reservoirs behind them will increase the evaporation loss from the reservoirs of the river by 100,000 acre-feet annually. Mr. Dominy, earlier in this hearing, testified, I am told, that if all of the reservoirs built and planned on the Colorado were ever to become filled, then the evaporation loss would be in the neighborhood of three million acre-feet. This would cause a diminution in yield of liquid water about equal to the diminution of flow from the wet-cycle flow on which the Colorado River Compact was based to the current dry cycle. In other words, because of all this reservoir construction, there is little expectation of relief from the conditions of the current dry cycle. The Bureau of Reclamation has insured perpetuation of dry-cycle conditions. Most of this reservoir construction serves no purpose in conserving the waters of the river, as has been adequately proven by W. B. Langbein [1959] and L. B. Leopold [1959] in two classical government documents, Geological Survey Circulars 409 and 410.

The next argument is that electrical energy from the dams is needed to pump water up into Arizona. But we are also told that the energy from the dams will be sold at premium prices, for peaking service. Peaking energy is usually bought by householders; water pumping is ordinarily emphasized in off-peak hours. Apparently, the energy from these dams is to be sold at premium prices, and part of the income is to be used to buy off-peak energy for pumping. This is sensible, but energy from the dams is not being used for pumping; it is being used to generate income. No shortage of energy, current or anticipated, exists for the task of pumping.

In fact, it is quite clear that the dams are technically not a part of the Central Arizona Project at all. Their relation to it is purely fiscal. They are a fiscal artifact whose chief purpose is to conceal the fact, the legerdemain, of subsidy to Arizona irrigated croplands.

It is conceded they would not be attractive ventures but for the low interest rate for repayment. We are asked to believe that low government interest rates are simply a gift, perhaps of divine origin. In fact, though, they stem from banking policy laws, [from] the policy of tax exemption for government obligations, [from the] graduated income tax bracket, and from the belief that no risk is involved. Even though admittedly no forfeiture is risked, this is so only because the federal government underwrites any risk. In fact, the American taxpayer is subsidizing Arizona agriculture just as fully as if he personally were paying off the notes for the construction costs of the Central Arizona Project. Since the water to be moved into Arizona under this project, 1.2 million acre-feet annually, is only enough to irrigate a quarter of Arizona's cropland, the subsidy in the construction of these two huge dams comes to about $3000 per acre for that quarter of a million acres.

We are not, though, objecting to the movement of this water into Arizona, but only to the construction of the dams in the canyons. We suggest, if subsidy is demanded, that another way be found to hide it.

Next, we are often told that additional water is needed for the teeming new millions who seek the richness of living in the clement

Southwest. And, also, we are told that water is the most valuable of all resources and that it must not be denied to anyone. Let me remind you that a city man uses from 0.1 to 0.15 acre-feet of water a year, [while] an acre of irrigated land [uses] from three to five acre-feet per year. Only a minor fraction of the Colorado River goes into city mains. Each million acres of land withdrawn from agriculture will provide enough water, and also enough room, for 30 million urban dwellers. If Arizona's population continues to double a little faster than California's population doubles, then late in this century there will be eight million Arizonans, almost all of them urban, to use this water. They will be able to pay for it. Water, to them, may really be a valuable resource; to the farmer it is essential, but not valuable. They may even be able to pay $25 per acre-foot for it in the river. They can pay $100 per acre-foot for it delivered and never know the difference. By the end of the century they will be numerous enough, if the current growth rate is maintained, to pay for these facilities—without the dams.

Really, although we speak of water as a valuable resource, we don't treat it that way. Scarcely any American pays for water as such; he pays only for its management, its harvest and delivery to his doorstep. It is still a free good. Land once was also free, but as we have increased in numbers, we have become accustomed to paying for it and its fruits. Timber was once free, but now we are accustomed to paying for the right to cut it, to pay for the resource itself. Water is still free, but perhaps as we become more crowded and more demanding, it, too, will have a value, will cease to be a free good. To call it dirt-cheap is an understatement. Water at $25 per acre-foot is only 2¢ a ton. The superlative of cheapness is "water-cheap." . . .

I have spoken in some detail in an area of economics. Perhaps I should not have done this, because the real issue in the Grand Canyon is only half economic, and my major concern is for a resource which cannot be valued in economic terms. The resource we are talking about is not the water in the Colorado River; its disposition has already been arranged. It is the river itself, its wildness, its scenery, its aesthetic values, its revelation of the earth's history—and its restless energy. The issue is not easy for us to decide because we cannot compare the alternatives on a single basis. That is why it must be settled through a political process. . . .

I spent a day at the south rim of the Grand Canyon this summer, right in the center of the traffic jam, watching people. My purpose was to see if I could judge in some way the good which stems to Americans from the Grand Canyon. Not the use; we measure that with traffic counters, but the good. I think I learned a little about judging it. Not much of it went to the man from Florida who barreled up to the parking slot, spat over the brink, said, "Ain't nothing like this in Florida," and drove off. His wife didn't even have time to get out; perhaps she was hunting for "Grand Canyon" on the check list. I doubt if the people from the flatlands who had difficulty getting near the brink could benefit much. Not until they had stayed long enough, days perhaps, either at the rim or in other steep country, for the acrophobia to wear off, was the wildness of the canyon any good to them. But as you near the head of Bright Angel Trail, the feeling of a benefit to everyone around begins to well up. Those who go down to the river . . . get the most good. Those who go part way get part of it. And everyone up on the rim knows this.

But if the day comes when they go down to a dead river, a spiritless river, a river broken to harness, a river where the jet boats flash by, then the glory will have gone out of it. And another iota of the vitality of America and Americans will be lost.

These matters cannot be measured by their economic components. But they must be judged by you legislators, whose principal task, always, is to make judgments where the two sides of a question cannot be weighed in the two hands, in the two pans of a balance. If your judgment is that the resources of America are so hard pushed that there is no room for wild rivers and wild lands, that the economic component must dominate, then you are in fact and explicitly saying that the difference between the United States and the poor overcrowded lands of the earth is diminishing. Must we, then, turn to China for guidance in the management of our resources?

If you believe, instead, that we are gaining, then you must find that we do have room for wild rivers, that we are quite able to afford them, and that we cherish them.

In conclusion, I should like to suggest that the Bureau of Reclamation's . . . job is done; the vein is running out. I still see three fields in which opportunity exists, and I wish the Bureau would devote its attention to one or all of these.

The first of these is the explicit generation of peaking power. The private utilities seem reasonably willing to let the Bureau pull this chestnut out of the fire for them. Apparently, the return is not great enough to attract private capital. But I should like to see them explore this in terms of explicit pumped storage proposals rather than of proposals so complex as to defy analysis of attractiveness.

The second is the reclamation of land—not the claiming of land, which has been the task thus far, but rather the reclaiming of land once fruitful but since drastically changed by our technology: the waste heaps of strip mining. Their management is not simple; it may not be wise to try to recover them for agriculture. Thus, they seem in some instances to develop into superb wildlife habitat, simply because mere people get lost in the complexity of their drainage patterns.

The third is the reclamation of polluted, of used, water. Sea water is the choice for the head-on approach to new water supplies. But while we will certainly get city water from the sea, we have at this time no prospect of obtaining irrigation water from that source. But the used water of our cities, of our industry, of our farms, all of it is less burdened with impurities than sea water. Thermodynamics suggests it to be a better starting material than sea water—but it will take more wisdom to manage it.

NAWAPA: AN EDITORIAL AND LUTEN'S REPLY

The Central Arizona Project is but one example of water transfer systems that have through the years involved increased amounts of water, longer distances, and greater costs. The most extravagant water transfer system of all is the vision of moving water from northwestern North America, notably Alaska, to the lower 48 states. In the middle 1960s, while the future of the canyons of the Colorado River in Arizona was being argued, a version of this

Reprinted by permission from *Science*, 1965, 147: 113 and 149: 133. Copyright © 1965 by the American Association for the Advancement of Science.

plan—called the North American Water and Power Alliance, or NAWAPA—was also under study in Congress.

Philip Abelson, long-time editor of *Science*, wrote an editorial endorsing NAWAPA as "grand and imaginative." His unhesitating praise for the project, including its "large storage lake in the Rocky Mountain Trench," its diversion of "a substantial fraction of the flow of the Columbia River," and its use of "very cheap electric power furnished by huge nuclear reactors," seems to reflect a time when many technical scientists looked upon such engineering feats with emotional affection.

Luten's response to Abelson's editorial invoked themes that he had presented in earlier articles: a concern for the future, the limitations of engineering and science to serve human needs, and the fundamental importance of population growth. But two additional points, particularly important in water development, were initially presented here. First, Luten noted that water "demand" or "need" is equivalent to water made available and thus used; therefore, "forecasts and definitions of [water] use . . . are self-fulfilling, subjective, and self-serving." Second, the identification of a "foreseeable future" simplifies the engineering and economics of planning, but the concept is logically incomplete. Luten queried, "After the water 'for as long as 100 years' supplied by this development has all been 'used,' what next?" Whatever the water proposal, or whatever the resource, such questions were and are good ones to ask.

[ABELSON'S EDITORIAL:] WATER FOR NORTH AMERICA

The United States currently uses about 1.25 [billion] cubic meters (350 [billion] gallons) of water per day. Consumption is growing, and water shortages are becoming more serious in areal extent as well as severity. One answer is desalination of sea water. . . . In large-scale projects, in which nuclear reactors were used, fresh water perhaps could be obtained at about six cents per cubic meter (22 cents per 1000 gallons) at sea level and at the plant. Distribution of this water to points distant from the sea would entail very large additional expense.

An alternative approach is that of effectively utilizing part of the continent's natural water supplies. For example, in the northwestern section of North America, more than 800 [billion] cubic meters of water flow almost unused to the sea each year. Use of the potential supplies would solve most of the continent's water problems for as long as 100 years.[1] Unit cost of the water, delivered inland, would be a small fraction of that of desalted water even at sea level. Through a series of dams, lifts, tunnels, and canals, water from Canada and the northwestern United States would be conducted to the Great Lakes and to the southwestern United States and Mexico. By this means, the level of the Great Lakes would be regulated and maintained, and the amount of power generated at Niagara Falls and related sites would be increased. The canal conducting the water to the Great Lakes would be navigable, and huge blocks of hydroelectric power would be generated en route.

In the West, large areas in Utah, Nevada, Arizona, New Mexico, and other states, as well as three states in Mexico, could be irrigated. In Mexico alone, eight times more area could be served than will be supplied in Egypt by the Aswan High Dam. The needs of southern California also would be met. In all, 33 states would obtain some form of benefits from the plan. Canada would receive the equivalent of about $2 billion a year. The cost of the development is estimated at $100 billion; 20 years would be required for construction, after authorization.

Much of the water would be drawn from the Peace and the Yukon rivers. One of the features of the plan is a large storage lake in the Rocky Mountain Trench, just west of the continental divide; the lake would extend 800 kilometers northwest into Canada from the vicinity of Libby, Montana. A large storage basin is crucial, since most of the river flow of the region occurs during spring and summer. This projected flooding of Canadian territory could prove to be a major point of friction, even though the region is sparsely settled. In any event, past experience suggests that there would be long delays before the necessary international agreements were formalized.

However, many of the benefits for the United States could be obtained in a way not mentioned in the report. A substantial fraction of the flow of the Columbia River could be intercepted, near Hanford, Washington, and at other points, and lifted and caused to flow eastward and also southward through tunnels and canals. Very cheap electric power furnished by huge nuclear reactors could be used. The

1. A conceptual plan for accomplishing this objective, NAWAPA (North American Water and Power Alliance), has been prepared by the Ralph M. Parsons Company, a large engineering and construction firm. The scheme is presently under study by a Senate subcommittee headed by Senator Moss of Utah.

present NAWAPA concept is grand and imaginative. It is to be hoped that the Canadians will join us in this great project, but alternatives should be studied.

[LUTEN'S LETTER:] NAWAPA

Let me respond to your editorial . . . on the $100-billion-plus North American Water and Power Alliance by agreeing that it would be large and that it is imaginative, but only within engineering limits [Figure 1]. Four sorts of criticisms may be voiced.

1. It would destroy a great deal of the low-altitude wildlands of Alaska and Canada and a large fraction of the vestiges of such wildlands in the Western states. No one, thus far, has undertaken to compare our need for these wildlands a century hence with our need

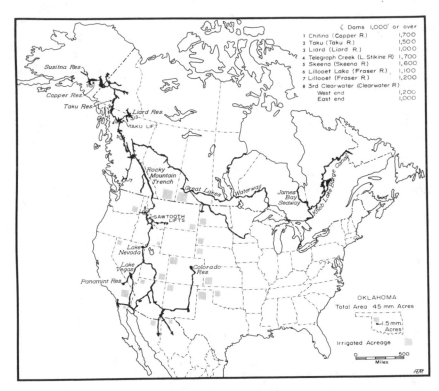

[FIGURE 1. Map of NAWAPA.]

for NAWAPA's boons, and no one on earth is either competent or in a position to do so objectively.

2. As premises, NAWAPA takes forecasts and definitions of use which are self-fulfilling, subjective, and self-serving. Burton and Kates, in a review . . . (1964) of three books published by Resources for the Future (RFF), have said:

> Demand for [water] . . . is not to be interpreted in conventional economic terms. . . . Water "demand" for the base year 1960 is really an estimate of the amount of water actually supplied. Similarly, projected "demand" for the year 1980 is really that amount of water expected to be supplied. . . . [The RFF authors] are caught in the prison of their own assumptions . . . [namely] that things will change but only in the way and at the speed that they are now changing. . . . The danger which we foresee is that projections may become self-fulfilling prophecies.

3. The NAWAPA proposal is in no sense an optimum, because imagination in seeking alternatives has been limited to engineering alternatives. Imagination must not be limited to alternate conduits or tanks. It must also ask whether we should electrodialyze the Colorado River to reduce the surplus of water required for irrigation in order to carry salts out of the soil; whether we should distill treated sewage in order to escape the free energy of removal of salt; what the economies of scale in desalination are. And we must be just as sure about the economies of scale and the technology of desalination a century hence as we are about the technology of water storage and transportation. Imagination must also inquire into the nature of "use." By and large, water is used only to carry something and, excepting for the transport of nutrient in irrigated plants, to carry away something not wanted, including heat. Is our imagination really so narrow that we can envision no other way to serve these purposes?

4. The major problem is quite separate: Common practice among those concerned with resource development is to take population as an independent variable, and population projections as immutable, sacred. Discarded by the engineers are the host of "if's" either tacit or explicit in the demographers' projections. . . . In fact, we do not know what the future will bring. While a ten-year projection seems to leave little room for uncertainty, still the halving of Japan's birth rate between 1949 and 1957, the failure of the American birth rate to drop as Sweden's dropped following a post-World War II "bubble," the per-

sistence of California's growth, each of these has shown that earlier projections were not prophetic. The 100-year projection should have uncertainties at least as great as the tenth power of the uncertainties in the ten-year projection.

One point comes clearly out of this: If we must plan for the century ahead, we cannot regard population as the independent variable. Whether or not we wish to plan populations as well as the facilities to serve them, we cannot escape the proposition that virtually everything we undertake will in some obscure way affect population changes and, thereby, the facilities needed. Even if we can identify all the significant influences and ask our computers where we go, the answer that results will itself be a significant influence. And when we include it in the computation, will we have an iteration sequence that converges or diverges? For, whereas the short-range forecasts seem to have a self-fulfilling quality, in the long range they should be self-defeating, whether they forecast "our plundered planet" [see Osborn, 1948] or "enough and to spare" [see Mather, 1944]. Certainly a society convinced by the pessimistic forecast will modify its course to avoid such a fate, and a society convinced of the other will probably expand until there is nothing to spare. How far ahead does "self-fulfilling" neutralize "self-defeating"?

NAWAPA is a program of bankruptcy. After the water "for as long as 100 years" supplied by this development has all been "used," what next? And if we find a way to wiggle out of the predicament of A.D. 2065, how about that of 2165? No problem of population growth stemming from a static pattern of family size and death rates can be solved either by emigration or by technology. It can only be solved by a changing pattern of family size or of death rates. Science, technology, emigration can only postpone the issue. If the time gained by postponement is not used to find a solution in smaller families, then the problem will only have been enlarged. At today's growth rates, in each 35 years the piper's bill is doubled. It would seem the part of providence to attack the issue now rather than when time has come to an end. It would seem the part of providence not to lull an audience by telling them they may go their way secure in the knowledge they will be cared for.

If we must build NAWAPA, let us wait until we know our doom is at hand, and when our last realizable ambition is to amaze future archeologists.

THE 160-ACRE LIMIT

Probably no other water issue has generated such strong accusations of special interest as the lack of enforcement of the 160-acre limit. Until recently changed, this Congressional directive limited to each farmer federally subsidized water (provided by Bureau of Reclamation projects) for no more than 160 acres. It was a law of the progressive conservation movement at the turn of the century.

As Luten noted in this essay, the application of the limit has been inconsistent, with large landowners receiving large amounts of cheap water. Yet he recognized the difficulty of identifying "fairness" in resolving the matter. In addition, he saw parallels between the allocation of federal water and the more general disposition of land and resources by the federal government, a giveaway most rampant in the last century but endorsed by contemporary political conservatives.

Luten was not hopeful of major changes in water policy, so strong were the interests that benefited from existing regulations: "We must learn not to expect profound reform when dealing with such a real instinct as territoriality." Luten thus anticipated the 1982 Congressional modification of the 160-acre limit, which increased the maximum acreage that could receive federally subsidized water to 960 acres.

In 1902, when Congress passed and President [Theodore] Roosevelt signed the Reclamation Act, some bitter lessons from history already were recorded. Even so, the 160-acre limit imposed on landowners who wanted federal water for irrigation has inspired more bitterness than could have been foretold. The new law was also called the Newlands Act after its author, Nevada Representative Francis Newlands. It sponsored both reform and enterprise and may have tried to define the future too narrowly. Or, perhaps, another war between the states, this time frontier West versus settled East, was inevitable. The same antagonisms had surfaced in many previous attempts to dispose of the public domain.

Reprinted by permission from *Landscape*, 1978, 22(2): 1–2.

Thomas Jefferson had hoped we would become a nation of land-owning "yeoman farmers," but virtually everyone on the scene or with influence in Washington thought land speculation or acquisition of baronial holdings held more future. However, by the time of the 1862 Homestead Act, 160 acres had been established as enough land for a farmer: 40 acres in woodlot for fuel and construction materials, 80 acres in pasture, the balance in crops. The reasoning seemed sound at the time. Cropping 40 acres meant forty days of plowing each spring; was there time for more?

But the Homestead Act's limitation may have come at the wrong moment. We were just about to occupy the short-grass prairie where farmers needed more land; also, the mechanized equipment that would allow a man to cultivate more land was starting to appear. Whether 160 acres was precisely right for irrigated land in the arid West, or too little, or too much, still is being argued. But the strict provisions of the Reclamation Act were not open to debate. It reads: "No right to the use of water for land in private ownership shall be sold for a tract exceeding 160 acres to any landowner, and no such sale shall be made to any landowner unless he be an actual bona fide resident of such land. . . ."

The acreage restrictions worked well enough in the more than 30 reclamation projects where land was still predominantly in federal ownership. Entry by individuals was limited by the terms of the Homestead Act to 160 acres. Other projects were far more complex: Much of the irrigable land already had passed into private ownership, so sponsorship and financing of irrigation involved other parties. For example, even today the Southern Pacific Land Company owns checkerboarded railroad grant land comprising 170 odd-numbered sections in Westlands Irrigation District on the west side of the San Joaquin Valley northwest of Fresno. The state, with its California Water Plan of the 1960s, participated in construction of facilities for delivery of water to Westlands. Similar arrangements prevailed in California's Imperial Valley. Under such conditions the applicability of the requirement to dispose of "excess holdings" was not clear, and the Bureau of Reclamation did little to enforce the limitation. But in California, other ferments, involving migrant farm labor, ideas about land reform, and a new populism attacking corporate activity have led to litigation resulting in recent judicial and administrative decisions. These decisions are bringing the long-hidden 160-acre teeth of the law sharply into view. As a result, owners who for years thought themselves exempt from the limitation may now be subject to it.

One might sum up the controversy by saying the gift of water on top of the grant of land grated on those left without, and they have reacted effectively against it. But, as always, it is really not so simple. In the early years, reclamation of arid lands was no bonanza, even with the federal government supplying water. Perhaps American farmers had a lot to learn about irrigation agriculture; perhaps prosperity depended more on access to markets than on water. At any rate, both restrictions on the freedom of prior owners and relaxation of requirements on new owners came along year after year, sometimes by legislation, sometimes by administrative action. The "bona fide resident" clause became anachronistic as automobiles encouraged farmers all over the country to live in towns near their farms. Currently, the quarrel is whether such "bona fide residents" must live within 25 miles or 50 miles of the farm or within 50 miles of the district.

Owners of excess lands who wanted to continue to use federal irrigation water were required to sell within ten years at a price reflecting the value of the land prior to the irrigation project, and to do so by "recordable contracts," that is, contracts on record at the county courthouse, so as to constitute a lien on the land. The Reclamation Bureau planned and engineered reclamation projects that were allocated among the Western states. The Reclamation Fund financed these projects, and farmers contracted for water under the terms of the Act. But if a large landowner chose not to participate in the new water district, he could not be forced out of his holdings. True, he could get no water from it directly. But as pumping equipment improved in many places he could irrigate with water from his own wells. And, as often happened, if his neighbors and he were grossly overdrawing their groundwater supply, the defection of any of them to the new district reduced the overdraft to the advantage of him and other holdouts. Better yet, some of the district's water might make its way into the aquifer and be available to him. Perhaps the moral here is that the Bureau of Reclamation never should have bailed out such a "water-mining" region until all of its pump irrigators, desperate for water, were ready to join up and sell excess holdings.

The Reclamation Act's supporters originally thought that prior owners would be forced to sell excess holdings, because they would not be able to compete successfully with farmers on the newly irrigated neighboring land. But since property owners were only to be paid the worth of their land without water, the landholders found themselves in no hurry to sell. In fact, prior owners had to be bribed to sell. The provision granting landholders ten years to deliver the land and the acquiescence of the Bureau to unrealistically high "before water" prices may have been necessary to get action. Such practices insured that prior owners realized some, and perhaps much, of the benefits from the new irrigation districts and that the new owners, the presumed beneficiaries, carried more burden than was envisioned. Also, of course, prior owners showed a strong tendency to sell to relatives, friends, and even themselves under pseudonyms. On the other side of the fence, the requirement to repay the costs of the new water district from water fees, at first prescribed to be completed in ten years, had to be relaxed to 20, then 40 years, and even more later on. Even then, projects didn't seem to be paying off. The yield from hydropower, a separate resource, had to be dumped into the pot, and later, oil royalties from the public domain as well. And no one wished to raise the bogeyman of paying interest on the costs of construction. Waiving even the low-interest charges of those days was forgiving, on a 40-year repayment, half the debt. From an economic point of view, irrigation districts were not gold mines, but, of course, they were not supposed to be. These were the projects that private enterprise would find unattractive. One wonders if the social, or perhaps the geopolitical, benefits were great enough to outweigh such an outrageously uneconomic enterprise.

But perhaps this question misrepresents the issue. Could the Department of the Interior and the Bureau of Reclamation, in fact, have been engaging in a fraudulent exaggeration of the difficulties of the irrigation farmers? It wouldn't have been the first time Washington had been told a different story from that seen by the man in the field. And wasn't it something of a paradox that, while the new farmers were having so hard a time making it, the previous landowners were strenuously resisting efforts to dislodge them? . . .

With such intricate complexity, with such intense competition, few holds barred, to gain or to keep land, how could the Reclamation Act ever have led to a simple answer? No one could have foreseen much of what has happened. The Bureau of Reclamation has been vilified for procrastination. But who, with full consciousness of all the complexity, would not have been tempted to meditate rather than act? Now, though, court rulings are intruding, and judicial action is forcing legislators and administrators to comply with the Act. The intent of the 1902 law was, after all, clear enough, even though phrasing it succinctly was beyond our powers. But the losers still find it profitable to delay in all possible ways.

And for the winners—the advocates of land reform, of egalitarianism—will the fruits be sweet or taste as dust? If land is allocated from now on by a lottery from a pool of "qualified applicants," and if the value of water for the 320 acres a man and his wife may win is a half million dollars, that man is hardly a farm laborer, doubtfully a yeoman farmer. Is it land reform to take land from multimillionaires and to make quasi-millionaires of lottery winners? It should be quite a lottery: perhaps a thousand winners at half a million dollars each.

And who will be the "qualified applicants"? In the past, when chances of success were dim, homesteaders were required to have two years of farming experience and adequate equipment. Now, with the stakes so much higher, will it be possible to screen applicants objectively?

Before we gag at the ethics of government sponsorship of such gambling, let us ask ourselves if the disposition of all the public domain was so much different. We must learn not to expect profound reform when dealing with such a real instinct as territoriality. With water so muddy, no sieve, especially no legal sieve, can be expected to produce clarity.

PART SIX

WILD NATURE

For Luten, few topics have inspired such persistent attention and thought as wild species and wild landscapes. Reacting against the allegation that love of nature is merely a whim (he likes to point out that love of money is no less emotional), Luten has tried to demonstrate that wild nature is a legitimate resource. His support of wild nature has appeared as an aside or a secondary issue in many papers presented earlier; in the papers appearing here, he has addressed the resource directly.

BERKELEY WATERFRONT MASTER PLAN: HEARING STATEMENT

Luten's thinking and writing about wild nature as a resource reveal progressive development through time. In this early statement, Luten defended the wild nature of a small shoreline park and challenged potential destroyers of the park "to dedicate one day of your lives this week to a conscious effort to erase all the influences of nature from your [lives]." This rhetorical challenge was meant to emphasize the ubiquitousness of nature in human existence, although why wild nature is important was not addressed. Such rationales were explored in later articles, written after Luten's thoughts had matured.

The circumstances that led to the hearing from which this statement is taken require some comment. The city of Berkeley, California, extends across the gently sloping plain that flanks the east shore of San Francisco Bay. It is bordered by parkland in the hills to the east and by other cities on the bay plain to the north and south. Like most other cities along the bay shore, Berkeley owns the shallow waters that border the city limits; also, like most of these other cities, Berkeley had used its bay acreage for dumping garbage and earth in order to create dry land for development. Such filling of the bay had continued in various parts of San Francisco Bay for a century before appreciation of the water as open space and as an aquatic system had developed. In the late 1950s and early 1960s, local groups generated support for constraining and eventually stopping the filling of the bay. This hearing statement, which questioned the economic justification for the fill and defended the bayside lagoon called Aquatic Park, was a manifestation of the then growing recognition of the bay as a resource.

At the time of the hearing, Luten was President of the Regional Parks Association, a local conservation group whose primary interest was the management of the parks in the East Bay Regional Parks District.

Statement made at the hearing of the Berkeley, CA, City Council, December 11, 1962.

[THE PLAN]

The present proposal is bad in general. It starts out with the implicit assumption that Berkeley is in dire straits because it is land-locked and has no place to grow. As public officials should already know, the general public should be learning, and even the business community should be coming to appreciate, the fact that growth and progress are not the same things, and cannot be identified with each other. While through much of our national history they have been compatible, and, in fact, growth may well have supported progress, this is no longer true. The time is coming rapidly when they will be in utter opposition to each other, when progress will be impossible in the face of growth.

The present proposal is bad in detail. It suggests residential development in the tidelands, and this is unwise. It reserves land for the university [i.e., land for a new campus of the University of California system], a university which is now mature and will cease to grow shortly. This would be tax-free land. At the other side of town, we complain when the university takes land off tax rolls. The university neither needs nor has it asked for this land. No effort has been made in this proposal to minimize industrial land. At the very least the Aquatic Park area, proposed for destruction, should be replaced out of privately held land farther west. So far as the economic arguments in favor of this development are concerned, enough has been written and said to show that they are, at the very best, shaky.

[THE PLAN AND THE FUTURE]

Another matter: You are a body charged with making decisions in a most difficult region of decision theory as the mathematicians would look at it. For you must reconcile economic arguments, which can be compared quantitatively, with social arguments, which can often not even be placed in order of desirability and which can be assessed against economic considerations only in terms of your individual values—what the sociologists call "value judgments." I am not going to belabor you with any discussion of decision theory because it doesn't get you anywhere in this field of decision making. But let me make one point. This society is changing; its values are changing. You are faced with a decision which is going to have consequences a long way into the future. Try to envision what public attitudes are apt to be in that future, and try to make a decision which the public of the future will endorse—not one such that your grandchildren will say of you bitterly, "They had no concern for the future."

When you try to envision the public attitude of the future, you have a tough problem. No one can know for sure what it will be. Let me suggest that you recall the changes which have occurred over the past 20, even 50 years, and imagine that they may continue into the future. Who cared for the bay 50 years ago? No one, except to make a killing from it. Who cares for it today? A lot of people. Who will care for it tomorrow? Will this attitude grow, or is it a flash in the pan? This is the question to ask yourselves.

[THE PLAN, THE FUTURE, AND WILD NATURE]

The present proposal is a bad proposal in another regard. We are opposed to any disposition of the Aquatic Park other than for Berkeley to give it a little care and support instead of the back of its hand. Even in its present condition the Aquatic Park is heavily used, not merely by the handful of people who manage to find their way into it, but by thousands of the scores of thousands who pass it daily. For north-bound traffic, after the prospect of Yerba Buena Island between the towers of the [Bay] Bridge, it is the first break in an oppressive atmosphere of smog generation, of commerce and industry. It is enjoyed by those who at the moment of passing have a moment's respite from the quiet desperation of their lives, and it gives them some cause at that moment to regard California as a good place to be and not merely a good place to be passing through.

You may, nevertheless, decide to destroy the Aquatic Park. Your decision may be based on the notion that economic criteria should be weighted heavily over social factors, and you may, by choosing economic arguments carefully, persuade yourselves this is wise. If you should take such action, which our organization considers unwise, then we must fall back to our next line of defense, which is to insist that a new Aquatic Park be complete and functioning before this one is destroyed. This is necessary because while you may intend to take only one step downward, your successors on this Council may consider your actions as precedent for having no Aquatic Park at all. Moreover, this Aquatic Park is an essential base for some of the wildlife of this region. It is not improper even to say that it belongs to them, and that to take it from them is no less than common thievery.

I know that some of you have been saying to yourselves, "A concern for the wildlife of this shore—what sort of tommyrot is this?" To those of you who feel this, let me suggest to you that you dedicate one day of your lives this week to a conscious effort to erase all the influences of nature from your life. Should you see a flight of geese overhead as I did Sunday morning, avert your eyes, close your ears to their clangor, and remember [that] we have this year reduced our waterfowl population to its lowest level yet. When you walk out to your car, turn your eyes away from your lovely garden; it will look better done up in high-rise apartments or under pavement. As you step across the parking strip into your car, cross out the trees in that parking strip; we will widen the pavement, the better to serve man. Focus your attention instead on the marvelous functionality of the intricate pattern of ducts which the intensity of your consciousness tells you lies beneath the asphalt—the ducts which bring you energy, water, [and] communication, and which dispose of your effluents. What more does man want to gratify his needs?

In your offices, in your homes, turn your eyes away from all the decorations and furnishings with symbols of nature. Turn to the walls all of your paintings except for those abstractions in which no inspiration from nature can be discerned. Let no bird song come to your ear; let no vagrant smell of seashore or lilac reach your nose—we can synthesize for you, from oil, coal, air, lime, and water, smells to gratify the senses beyond anything in nature. Given time, even, we can provide odors which will not stimulate anything in nature, neither butyl salicylate for gardenias nor hydroxyethoxybenzaldehyde for vanilla. We can give you foods which have never felt the touch of nature. Try for all of one day to imagine yourself in such a world before you make the decision to destroy more of the natural scene.

If, in spite of all of this, you still persist in your efforts to create such a world, let me say that your grandchildren, if they ever manage to escape the traps you are setting for them, will envision and create a new sort of Independence Day, one in which they may include as an essential ceremony the burning in effigy of those of their ancestors who sought to create such a way of life for them—a life from which nature was excluded.

Gentlemen, this battle has been fought over once, in the England of the early Industrial Revolution. It was learned then that labor is not merely a commodity, that a society does not exist merely to serve its economy. In this age there is no justification for a retrial of those issues unless you are convinced that our society is, in fact, in such desperate economic straits that we can afford to give consideration only to economics and that all social considerations must be sacrificed.

Before you finally make the decision which is recommended to you tonight, I ask you in addition to trying a day without nature, to read, to reread, Aldous Huxley's *Brave New World* [1932], in order to get a clearer view of the Utopia you are planning. Huxley still lives, and, one of the wisest men of our times, he still stands unswerving behind these convictions of 30 years ago. Read, also, a poem; it is about 50 short pages, and it gives a most clear impression how life in 19th-century England seemed to one gifted poet. This was the century when the theorem that if one serves the economy to his best ability, the economy will best serve the society was assumed to be true. Read James Thomson's poem, "The City of Dreadful Night" [Thomson, 1895].

ENGINES IN THE WILDERNESS

In the statement to the Berkeley City Council, Luten simply observed the high value of nature to humans. In this subsequent article, his thoughts developed into an explanation for that importance. Luten began the paper with some "parables," which well exemplify his flair for the pointed use of stinging satirical wit. Weaving into his proposal numerous other anecdotes and situations to give it strength, he theorized that the genetic need of people for "wanderlust" may be served by wild landscapes: ". . . just as each of us suffers from or glories in some degree of weakness and strength, of timidity and boldness, or improvidence and providence, so each of us also has inborn, in varying degrees, . . . *both* wanderlust and homesickness. And

Reprinted by permission from *Landscape*, 1966, 15(3): 25–27.

our environment will be adequate only if it provides opportunity for expression for both of these attributes." The idea sounds as if it were derived from a consideration of sociobiology, but E. O. Wilson's book of that title—the initial statement of the importance of genetics to human behavior—was published in 1975, nearly ten years after this article.

Luten's purpose in presenting these comments was, in part, to demonstrate that wilderness is a legitimate resource and not merely a sentimental whim. He explored a second rationale for wild nature in articles to be presented later in this section.

A few years ago Erle Stanley Gardner, more famous for his writing in other fields, undertook a defense of off-highway motorized vehicles in an article published in *Sports Afield* (September 1962). The following excerpts may give his sense:

> Perhaps the person who owns property on the lake would like to sleep late on a Sunday morning, but he now recognizes the fact that the noise made by outboard motors is something he has to live with.

And, later:

> . . . Under the guise of preventing "attrition" to trails, an attempt is being made to use legislation to preserve "solitude." Preserving solitude is one thing. Preserving liberties is another. . . . I claim that anyone who wants to drive a scooter, an airplane, a helicopter or a Jeep into the vast desert wastes which still remain public property . . . is entitled to do so and to use any means of transportation that he wishes.

An acquaintance, on being shown the second excerpt, said that he certainly agreed with it. Knowing that, while he was no wilderness type, he was an avid trout fisherman, pheasant hunter, and horseman, I conceded the point and said I'd go even a bit further. "What I like to do on the public lands," I said, "is to walk along trout streams and throw rocks at trout. I prefer company, of course, and if I can find a trout fisherman I like to work up a stream ahead of him, showing him good pools and, by tossing rocks where trout might be, showing him where to cast. I have had, quite commonly in fact, objections raised to my conduct, but I have pointed out to such a fisherman that it's a free country and if he wants to preserve his solitude, maybe he should climb a mountain. Liberties are just as important as solitude, or more so, and it is important to my sense of liberty to throw rocks into trout pools on publicly owned lands where and when I see fit.

"At other seasons, especially in November, I like to walk along the field edges in the Valley to watch the pheasants fly up. I can't always tell where they are, but when I see some pointers in a field I go over and start working along with them and am really pretty good at this. I usually manage to find the pheasants before the dogs can stir them up. Once, when I made the point about the preservation of my liberties, I got a load of birdshot in my backside, and the other gent said he was sorry but he had to preserve *his* liberties."

My friend, when I got done, left in a hurry, saying he had to inquire about extra tickets because he meant to ride his horse in to the opera that night, it being a public place.

I have a lot of other liberties to defend and other people do, too. A year ago up in Glacier Park, it took me half an hour to get a coveted picture of St. Mary's Lake from a notable point. Mostly this was because of other people who were having their pictures taken to prove they had been there.

I'm such a nut on stereo hi-fi I've got one in my camper and, when we camp, I try to get near the underprivileged who haven't any radios at all and I give them all 50 watts.

Then there's the question of garlic.

And whether I can throw a beer can farther out in the lake than the next man.

Next, let me quote from a San Francisco sports columnist:

> . . . I had motored up the Putah Creek arm of the lake where a few other fishermen were slowly trolling among the weather[ed] tree trunk snags. The lake was calm. Sounds traveled easily so we could hear the "plunk" of an angler's lure as it splashed the water, the purring of slow outboards and when a flight of ducks sailed overhead, we could hear the whistle of their wings. . . . Then the roar of a speedboat shattered the quiet and suddenly a boat with a water skier behind—in a skin-diving suit, mind you—charged into the trollers. The speedboat veered sharply to send the water skier flashing sideways. . . . My fishing partner muttered, "I hope he breaks his damfool neck!" [B. Boyd, 1964]

Again, the same writer says:

> . . . The bright colors of fall, mountain-maple yellow and poison-oak red, were splashed in wild profusion on the green, and in the distance the tops of powder-blue mountain peaks dissolved into the hazy sky. It was very quiet. Completely still. . . . Then from down the ridge I heard

the noise, like a power saw or a lawnmower. Soon I saw the hunter on his trail bike as he skidded and swerved uphill, revving the engine until it roared. He came to a halt beneath the rock I rested on and asked, "Any bucks up there?" "Not any more," I answered. . . . with that, [he] took out a portable walkie-talkie set and started yakking with a friend. . . . "Nope, Sam, there's no bucks up thisaway. Let's head back to camp." [B. Boyd, 1963]

This is not new on this continent. Leo Marx, in his recent book, *The Machine in the Garden* [1964], takes his theme really from Hawthorne's *American Notebook*:

> . . . a thriving field of Indian corn, now in its most perfect growth, and tasselled out, occupies nearly half of the hollow: and it is like the lap of bounteous nature. . . . But, hark, there is the long shriek, harsh, above all other harshness, of the locomotive.

And Thoreau pondered the railroad, then newly built, which still thunders by Walden Pond.

Professor Marx in his book has followed, in our literature, the invasion of the machine and the rather tantalizing images we have had of wilderness, the pastoral scene, technology and the city. But another thread weaves through the parables and citations above.

This is the matter of competing uses of a resource. We are wont to speak of "multiple use," and have specified it in our legislation. The concept of multiple use was an experiment, noble in purpose. It came from a vision, not particularly foresighted, that what was once an enormously rich country was becoming markedly, perhaps disastrously, less rich. Today, the most conspicuous change is from a country which was once empty to one which is now perilously full. This stems less from increase in numbers than from increase in mobility, in affluence, in *uncommitted* time. (I despise the word "leisure" for the company it keeps, but its root *licere, to be permitted*, is appropriate.)

Now, we do have multiple uses of natural resources which are not competing, but fewer of them than we used to have. While the chipping for pulp of mill slabs seems hardly a competitive use of wood substance, logging and watershed perhaps got along better together a generation ago than today. And when you look at our large water developments, manifestations of the competing, difficultly compatible uses of the resource insistently intrude: flood control, irrigation, power, mass recreation. Quite apart from who wants the water level low, variable, high, or constant, note the intrusion of forebays, afterbays, and other ingenious devices designed to reconcile competing demands for the same water. We are also finding that the use of air for breathing and as a vehicle for effluents can be competing, and not entirely compatible.

How should such competitions, such incompatibilities be resolved? By letting "normal evolution" take its course? Would we have any forests today in that case, or is the conservation movement a part of normal evolution? Rather, "normal evolution" is simply a refuge of ignorance. A separate factor is clearly involved. It was enunciated at the fifth Northwest Wilderness Conference (Portland, 1964) during [a] discussion by William Burch, of the Pacific Northwest Forest Experiment Station. It is very simple: *Convention* is a most important factor in the use of the landscape.

The ignoring of conventions, sometimes strong and current, at other times failing, was the common pattern in my initial examples. It is easy to argue for, but also against, conventions. It depends on who is ignoring them: whether it's students at the University of California in Berkeley, or you who drive an automobile but are the grandson of a man who only drove a wagon. People love to distinguish between progress and revolution, between tradition and reaction, but I think if you seek patterns of consistency in such attitudes, you had better start off with a far more durable lantern than Diogenes possessed.

Turning next to conservation, its definition as "wise use" is a good definition. It leaves the door open: What is the part of wisdom? Who amongst us is the wisest? Where is the oracle? Is today's wisdom tomorrow's folly? And yet, we do find ourselves able to agree in large measure that some actions, some policies, are wise; others are foolish; and still others are debatable today but probably will be clarified tomorrow.

Which is the wiser, the conventional or the unconventional use of the landscape, especially the wild landscape? I am going to argue in this instance for the importance of the conventional use. Please do not expect me to do so in other matters.

Parenthetically, let me note that my discussion will not encompass all of the currently cited uses and exploitations of wildlands: ecological sanctuary, scenic spectacle, wilderness experience, mass recreation. And so I hope to keep clear of any involvement in the issue of "wilderness sentimentality" or of its complementary ill, "mass sentimentality"—the programmed, regimented, lossful consumption of leisure, that portion of the American life no longer demanded for gainful production.

To support the argument for convention, I want to introduce what seems a most important polarity in human nature: at the one end wanderlust, at the other homesickness. Their symbols are opportunity and security. We could dredge up many examples before considering people—some more, others less convincing. Consider only two: First the seasonal migration of birds. The waning of the great arctic ice sheets and the continental seasonality, especially of North America, spelled opportunity, and a host of bird species responded to it by migration and by confining their breeding cycle to this opportunity. Retreat to the tropics in winter was a retreat to security. I would hazard that the most successful of bird species, measured by numbers, not by durability, are those which migrate. In quite another pattern but still dealing with birds, Ernest Thompson Seton speaks of the "mad moon" in late fall when the ruffed grouse travel and disperse erratically.

Each of the two attributes of wanderlust and homesickness has such a potential for survival that it is hard to escape the proposition that they should be separate genetic qualities, peaks in a bimodal curve of distribution of attributes, rather than the extreme manifestations of a single genetic quality. While among early men, those who clung to the group, who stayed at home, were essential to the stability and succession of generations, it was the rarer ones who wandered away, discovering new opportunities, who sired new tribes and founded new cultures. No one living today has an ancestry of undeviatingly settled people going all the way back to those earliest human dwellers on the shores of East Africa. The waves of human migration have swept back and forth over all of the old world and much of the new. But each of us has many more ancestors who settled for security than who wandered for opportunity. In consequence, there has been a genetic development of both attributes.

Those who stayed home did so for a variety of reasons: They were strong and mature and could dominate the community; they were timid; they were provident; they could get along with the group; they saw the wisdom of elder counsel. Those who left or were thrown out included the weak, but also the young, the bold, the ingenious, the improvident and a host of other nonconforming sorts. And just as each of us suffers from or glories in some degree of weakness and strength, of timidity and boldness, or improvidence and providence, so each of us also has inborn, in varying degrees, but always *both* wanderlust and homesickness. And our environment will be adequate only if it provides opportunity for expression for both of these attributes.

Neither is easily fulfilled in this century of revolution. Some of us who seek, in homesickness, the site of our childhood can only say, "I grew up somewhere under this freeway."

For wanderlust, some of us may seem to find opportunities in the mind, in the exploration of the margins of science and literature, many of us by reading of adventure, others in the city. But this trait is really geographic; its eternal companion is solitude and its essence is insecurity. I have said opportunity before, let me now call it insecurity.

I bring in security and insecurity because I want to turn to the matter of security symbols. In this geographical context, the first security symbol coming to my mind, perhaps curiously, is the motel. I cannot escape the feeling that in the days when we were relatively immobile, the distinctions between the city slicker, city dude if you wish, and the country hick were much sharper than today. Going to the city posed substantial problems of conduct in hotels. Can you trust these people with your bags, thievery is rife; how about tipping; how about table manners? Our ribald literature is thick with these stories, now becoming obsolete (the Indian murdering his urban wife in the hotel room). The motel, to my way of thinking, was the answer. It has now, of course, become much more than that and quite different, but this was its start.

There were similar problems in the country. Any dude knows that one end of a horse bites and the other kicks. The real problems, though, are how much do they cost, where are they, how do you go about hiring a packer? And the upshot is that the only secure way to approach God's great out-of-doors is in the custody of that all-pervading security symbol, the gasoline engine.

Tourism today has as its chief problem to maintain the illusion of wanderlust while guaranteeing security. But our acute secretary, after reading a deluxe world tour prospectus, said, "It almost convinces you that you could go around the world and see nothing new."

After all of this preparation, I come to my primary conclusion quite abruptly: The wise use of our wildlands is to manage them to satisfy the human need for wanderlust. The conventional use of wildlands has come to us from experts in wanderlust and is sparse in security symbols. These conventions should be honored and, in particular, the profligate introduction of security symbols into wildlands should be discouraged because this, more than anything else, destroys the essential qualities of such places.

Robert Marshall, of southern California, put it beautifully in a statement of opposition to ski development of the San Gorgonio wilderness when, in speaking of a Boy Scout troup heading up the mountain into the wilderness, he asked, "If there is a ski development at the top of the mountain, what will they be going away from?"

This is a flexible criterion. It speaks of convention and of security symbols. But convention varies with time and place. Every man has limits to his wanderlust. No one, to my knowledge, has asked to be sent to the moon to carve his own life out of *that* wilderness. Few have wanted to go unsupported into Antarctica. And few, barefoot and naked, have gone into the mosquito-ridden barrenlands of Canada. (Read, again, Seton's chapter in *The Arctic Prairies* [1923] on mosquito censusing.)

Conventions regarding equipment vary with circumstances. Thus I see no conflict in assenting to air drops on Mount McKinley while deploring them in the Sierra Nevada. I can oppose the use of land rovers, or tote goats, or what you will in the Golden Trout Wilderness of California's Kern Plateau while assenting to them in many extensive arid regions of the United States. (Let me reserve for another time the issue of the damage they may wreak if driven at random across the fragile desert landscape.) I can condone the use of motorboats on Lake Tahoe while deploring them on Lake Yellowstone and condemning them in the Boundary Waters Canoe Area.

One concluding, perhaps appendicular, matter deserves to be brought up. This is the problem of communication. I don't know what to suggest, because I think I see both too little and too much. Let me give some examples of the problem and drop it there:

If I ask one man where to seek a job, I can end up in any American city or town with about equal chances of its being in any size range, because American city size follows the harmonic rule reasonably well. But if I wait until two men tell me to go to the same town, I will never end up in Poplar, Montana, and if I wait for a third confirmation, I can only end up in Los Angeles.

In spite of my wanderlust, I can, in fact, do very little that I know *nothing* about; I can only go to the places I am told of and in the manner familiar to me. If I ask the man on Atlantic City's beach why he chooses to vacation there, his only answer is "But where else is there?" If *Sunset* magazine tells me Death Valley is wonderful at Thanksgiving, I, thousands of me, will swamp its sewage system.

How can I ever find my way to those empty Forest Service camps? No one I know has ever been there. Everyone I know has been to the crowded ones. Everyone can tell me where to find full camps; no one where the empty camps are. I am not sure it is desirable to overcome this problem, because I like to come on the unknown, unoccupied camps by accident, but if it is to be overcome it must be through communication other than word-of-mouth.

Why do the motorized vehicle advocates push into the wilderness? Because the wilderness enthusiasts have bragged of its beauties and of their wilderness exploits. But they have failed to communicate the conventions. That is why I walk up trout streams, rock in hand, but, as I age, farther and farther ahead of the agile fishermen and their flies.

AN INTRODUCTION AND
A WELCOMING ADDRESS

The biennial Wilderness Conferences were sponsored by the Sierra Club from 1949 through the early 1970s. Luten described these meetings as "heterogeneous . . . neither a completely scholarly inquiry nor a gathering and exhortation of clans of wilderness advocates, nor indoctrination for the

Reprinted by permission of Sierra Club Books from the following:

M. E. McCloskey and J. P. Gilligan (eds.), *Wilderness and the Quality of Life: Proceedings of the Tenth Biennial Wilderness Conference* (pp. 119–121). San Francisco: Sierra Club, 1969. Copyright © 1969 by the Sierra Club.

M. E. McCloskey (ed.), *Wilderness, the Edge of Knowledge: Proceedings of the Eleventh Biennial Wilderness Conference* (pp. 1–2). San Francisco: Sierra Club, 1970. Copyright © 1970 by the Sierra Club.

laymen." The degree to which the conferences contributed to an understanding of wildnerness and the support for its preservation was due, in part, to Luten, who felt that conservation groups might profit from being more analytical and introspective about themselves and the movement in which they are the prime participants.

The first of these two short statements was an introduction to a session of the 1967 conference, "Wilderness and the Quality of Life"; the second was a welcoming address to the 1969 conference, "Wilderness, the Edge of Knowledge" (for which Luten acted as chairman). Both statements reflect the tone of urgency so often heard in Luten's demands that we continually reexamine our basic assumptions about the conventions concerning and the definition of wilderness. They both illustrate extensions of the "wanderlust" thesis presented in the preceding article.

[WILDERNESS AND THE QUALITY OF LIFE: INTRODUCTION TO PART FOUR]

The infant who crawls from his mother's knee has begun his exploration of the world. But with each foot of separation, his feeling of security dwindles and, sooner rather than later, he returns to establish his confidence before turning away again. (What miniskirts, and the difficulty of reaching them, will do to the human psyche has not yet been told us by those concerned with our minds.) The duality of our nature, which causes us to probe the unknown and then to shrink back from it, is not new, nor is it unique to us.

All of animate life is faced with the problem of securing its future. Each organism has come to have instincts, tropisms, behavior patterns, call them what you will, that direct it and instruct it to seek opportunity, but also to secure its continued existence.

The patterns are almost as diverse as life itself. I have not the time this morning even to suggest them, but they will come in hosts to your mind. Repeatedly, insistently, emerging from among these patterns is a polarity—the search for security against the search for opportunity, nostalgia against wanderlust. These are not essentially at odds, of course. Opportunity fulfilled provides security; security may be a base from which to seek opportunity. Each promotes the purpose of the animal, which is, after all, to survive, first as an individual, next as a lineage.

This polarity is not absent in mankind, even though man is perhaps the most adaptable of all animals and perhaps the least instinctual. The great emigration of men from the ancestral regions of southeast Africa, enduring perhaps a quarter of a million years, 10,000 generations, has quite plausibly modified the human mind, just as their efforts to shape stone tools have shaped our minds and our hands as well. While other animals have been content to conform in most things, to seek opportunity narrowly, man the heretic, the deviant, the nonconformist, has upon occasion rejected his culture and has turned away from his environment.

Inescapably, we are the children·of our past. And it is proper to ask, Who in fact were our ancestors? Were they the men who stayed in the settlements? Were they the men who stayed even though the situation, once secure, had become desperate? Or were they the men who moved onward, whether from curiosity, from simple refusal to put up with crowding, or because they were thrown out? Those who stayed raised families, but did their grandchildren die of privation? Those who wandered mostly died of unforeseen hazards, but, when they survived, they sired entire tribes.

Whose children are we? I think we are the children of both, and I think this still shows in our nature. Each of us is, in some degree, endowed with both wanderlust and homesickness. How much of each, and of what quality, on this we vary. At one extreme, I may mention John Ledyard, who in the 18th century set out by canoe from central New Hampshire to sail with Captain Cook's third expedition, to walk across Russia to Irkutsk, and to die in Cairo on the threshold of exploration of Africa. At the other extreme stands William Ellery Leonard, seared in his infancy by a locomotive and ending afraid to go beyond the limits of a Wisconsin campus.

Whether wanderlust comes first or whether it awakens only when security hard-pressed becomes desperate, I do not know. Whether wanderlust is a search for opportunity only, or for insecurity, I do not know. But when you see, or imagine, an infant venturing from and then returning to his mother's knee, imagine also those 10,000 generations of your ancestors who lived while men were walking from southeast Africa to Cape Horn, and back and forth and in and out and up and down. Because they wandered and survived, it is instinctive in you. That is why you need wilderness; that is why you must seek what is not known.

Let me call on Henry David Thoreau [1854/1964] for support with his "Most men lead lives of quiet desperation" [p. 263] and "Our village life would stagnate if it were not for the unexplored forests and meadows which surround it. We need the tonic of wildness. . . . At the same time that we are earnest to explore and learn all things, we require that all things be mysterious and unexplorable, that land and sea be infinitely wild" [p. 557].

But still a question remains unanswered: Is wilderness in the landscape or in the mind? To the boy brought up on the pavements of Brooklyn, the Catskills may be remote and wild. To the boy brought up on the fringe of Montana's statutory wilderness, the mountains are home, the Catskills a cityscape, and Brooklyn a wilderness. Do wildernesses of the mind satisfy the need for wanderlust, or must the need be met on the land? Is wilderness the edge of knowledge? Is it personal or universal, subjective or objective?

We do not intend, I believe, to attack this question today. We have enough without it. Instead we will start from two propositions:

1. We have been on this continent for three and a half centuries, most of this time narrowly confined to the Atlantic seaboard. We had been here two and a quarter of those three and a half centuries when Thoreau went to Walden Pond. Our traditional views of wilderness have developed, as Roderick Nash told us yesterday, in large measure from the writing and painting of it. For most of our tenure, well-watered, forested valleys rising to wooded hills lay to the west of our homes. Only in the last century have new wildernesses come into our literature and our art: the Mississippi's waterways, the plains, the arid rangelands, and finally the alpine meadows and, rising above timberline, the stony slopes of Western peaks.

2. Three years ago Congress passed an act to preserve certain wild lands in their primitive state. We did this because of the persuasiveness of dedicated advocates of wilderness. Why they are thus dedicated has never, it seems to me, been said clearly. But I have tried to suggest some qualities of human nature itself which may be responsible.

We have now a considerable body of conventions concerning wilderness and we have a legal definition of it. Inescapably these reflect much of these past 350 years. But we must not imagine the matter to be settled; we still must ask: Has the literature guided us wisely, or have we overlooked something? Have we defined wilderness broadly, or have we defined it narrowly and in doing so forgotten other wildernesses?

In reflecting on what may have been forgotten, we will think first of the desert, the original Biblical wilderness, and next of the sea's edge. Later, we will recall also the Arctic wilderness, wild rivers, caverns, and submarine and island wildernesses. And we may wonder about a host of others, about bogs, marshes, and even microwildernesses.

We have brought to you today a group of distinguished experts to initiate a discussion of the first two sorts of wildlands that we tend to forget: the desert and the edge of the sea. We hope, with the start they will give us this morning, to come to see more clearly what we wish to do with these places and what we mean when we say "wilderness."

[WILDERNESS, THE EDGE OF KNOWLEDGE: WELCOMING ADDRESS]

[The] Wilderness Conferences have been, and continue to be, heterogeneous. They are neither a completely scholarly inquiry nor a gathering and exhortation of clans of wilderness advocates, nor indoctrination for the laymen. This might be deplorable in a well-established discipline. However, in any inquiry into wilderness we must first recognize the complexity of the matter, and also [acknowledge] that inquiry is exploratory in a way rather different from established disciplines.

In the latter, probing fingers of exploration have long since clarified the major outlines and the basic patterns of the field. Subsequent inquiry serves largely to fill in the gaps, to flesh out the bones, to complete a structure whose outlines are already visible.

In contrast, in any inquiry into wilderness we are still in exploratory phases on many counts. We see simultaneously the need for statutory protection for wilderness as we understand it at this moment. We see also the need for education of those who are puzzled by our concern. And we remain puzzled intellectually about the idea itself. And so a Wilderness Conference may turn in any direction, and perhaps at any moment. Because no other recognized medium for reporting the results of inquiry into wilderness exists, new ideas are likely to turn up here.

People ask me the meaning of the theme of the conference, "Wilderness, the Edge of Knowledge." Usually I just shrug my shoulders and say that a conference has to have a theme. After you have heard one theme, how many more? Others know immediately what it means. In these divergent reactions there is a clue to our feelings about wilderness. To some, wilderness is acreage to be set aside, protected by statute, and perhaps managed. To others, it is an edge of knowledge and what lies beyond that edge. To resolve these differences is itself an edge of knowledge.

Through most of the millennia of human existence, of human consciousness of surroundings, explicit terra incognita always lay just beyond. Only in recent millennia have men in fact inhabited all the habitable earth. While gradually we have come to suspect that our wilderness is another man's back yard, still for us it is wilderness, because it is beyond the edge of our knowledge. Even though Utah cattlemen ran cattle in and rounded them up out of Glen Canyon's Cathedral in the Desert, it was still Eliot Porter's *Place No One Knew* [1963]. But now with an explosion of information, explicit terra incognita are almost gone. Even Ultima Thule becomes an air base. It is no longer necessary to go around the world to count the cats in Zanzibar, for they are numbered in some statistical abstract. Where then lies the edge of knowledge?

To sum up, the question of wilderness does not end with the signing of the Wilderness Act of 1964 and completion of the details of wilderness classification. It is also in the blood and in the mind. We are faced with an enigma. Do we destroy wilderness by learning more of it, or as we lengthen the edge of knowledge do we add to it? This is why we have quoted from Thoreau [1854/1964] in the conference program: "We need the tonic of wildness . . . At the same time that we are earnest to explore and learn all things, we require that all things be mysterious and unexplorable, that land and sea be infinitely wild, unsurveyed and unfathomed by us because unfathomable. We can never have enough of nature" [p. 557].

RESOURCE QUALITY AND VALUE OF THE LANDSCAPE

Rationales for wild nature proceed along at least two lines. Some rationales attempt to explain why people value wild nature, and others try to explain how humankind benefits from preserving these values. Luten's identification and discussion of the contrary human traits of wanderlust and homesickness, as presented in the preceding paper and statements, exemplify the first line of argument. In this book chapter, he presented another rationale, one that exemplifies the second line of argument. He contended that wilderness is "perhaps the most essential of all resources . . . because it is essential for the long-range welfare of man." It may also help to explain the biological advantage of valuing wild nature, and thus to account for the apparent genetic propensity that people have for wilderness.

The essence of Luten's discussion is that wild landscapes function as references against which human activities can be evaluated. Other thinkers too have suggested that pristine nature provides a datum to judge human alteration of the environment, but no one else has couched the idea so well in the framework of systems, a complex framework that is presented in a novel way but in plain language.

When we speak of the "quality" of a natural resource, two aspects may come to mind. The first is well symbolized by water. The "quality" of water is often an issue in the management of water, but it can usually be measured in terms of the quantity of impurities. While the qualitative epithets "good" or "bad" may be applied to it, they always lead to the queries, "How good?" "How bad?" And the answers must be made in quantitative terms. In sharp contrast is the second aspect: [the

Reprinted by permission from S. V. Ciriacy and J. J. Parsons (eds.), *Natural Resources: Quality and Quantity* (pp. 19–34). Berkeley: University of California Press, 1967. Copyright 1967 by The Regents of the University of California.

quality of things that cannot be measured in quantitative terms. Consider, for example,] the "quality" of a sparrow compared to that of a robin.

Two theses are examined in this essay: The first pertains to divisions and boundaries, matters necessarily associated with the latter sort of quality. It is discussed partly because the topic of resource quality pervades this book, but also because it is a reasonable preliminary to the second argument, which is an effort to justify the landscape itself as a natural resource.

[DIVISIONS AND BOUNDARIES]

Any discipline has divisions, which must be arranged. An arrangement of divisions is properly called a "taxonomy" (Gr. *nemein*, to arrange; *taxis*, a division), but the word is commonly used only in biology. The first part of this essay undertakes to broaden the idea by referring to divisions of the material objects in the landscape.

Divisions are usually separated by boundaries, and boundaries are important because that is where qualities change. It is at the boundary that a robin might become a sparrow. But both robins and sparrows are birds, a generic quality, and can be counted on a common basis: Quantity transcends boundaries.

Boundaries which separate domains of differing qualities have their own attributes. In nature, some boundaries are clear-cut; others are vague. The earliest recognition that species exist came perhaps for animals and plants. Birds are birds and do not grade imperceptibly into mammals or plants, or from crows into crocus, from dogs to dogwood. Wood's book, *How to Tell the Birds from the Flowers* [1907], is not serious, at least not very much so. Most of the individuals of a biological species closely resemble the average individual, but one species resembles a second more closely than it does a third. So it is helpful, it exposes a pattern, it appeals to our instinctive search for order, to arrange these divisions in an orderly manner.

In chemistry, the search for divisions was not fruitful in its early stages: earth, air, fire, water. The boundaries were not satisfactory; the individual examples were not tightly clustered around a type. In the 18th and 19th centuries the situation changed dramatically. Now it is clear that chemical substances are diverse, have specific qualities, and, almost inescapably, are classed as species. The species are arranged, in one fashion or another, according [to how] we discern their relations. In organic chemistry the arrangement is the structural theory. So we have a taxonomy of chemistry because we have an arrangement of divisions. It is not the *purpose* of chemistry to prepare a taxonomy any more than it is the purpose of biology. But in each science, at an early stage in the search for order, the development of a taxonomy might have seemed a primary purpose.

Since chemistry is concerned with the transformation of matter [Luten, 1964b], it can be concerned only with understanding the rates and equilibria of chemical transformations. The structural theory of organic chemistry is only one of a number of accessories to that understanding. It is the greatest of these, and a highly complex and successful abstraction, but it is only an accessory. The purpose of the structural theory is to assist in the understanding, to reveal the patterns of order in the transformations of matter.

Chemical taxonomy shows what species may exist, and shows good and bad paths for transformations, for travel, from one species to another. It speaks of these paths in terms of equilibrium and rate. It can and often does speak authoritatively of equilibrium, a timeless matter. In contrast, when chemists speak of rate, they cannot be strongly predictive and must bring in a new entity, the environment. At an early stage, it seemed a reasonable undertaking to try to change lead into gold; later the possibility was denied; still later, chemistry suggested that a path might exist, but the equilibrium seemed unfavorable. To my knowledge, the environment for encouraging this transformation has not been defined.

Again, chemistry says that you cannot easily change methane to carbon dioxide except in an environment of air. Measurement has shown that the equilibrium is favorable, and, in a proper environment of temperature and concentration, the transformation is easy, sometimes too easy. The taxonomy of chemistry, then, guides us quickly to the conclusion that ethane and a host of other chemical species will behave in a similar fashion.

Chemists long ago learned the importance of environment and pretty well how to define it, having in mind the entities of reaction partner, temperature, medium, and concentration. Environment, though, is not a part of the taxonomy. We can envisage a boundary—perhaps "envelope" is a better word—which divides what is in the environment of a chemical transformation from what is not. But the only division here is between "in" and "out." It is not a division of one part from another. And so we do not have a taxonomy of chemical transformations. If we had, might we not have a full understanding, a synthesis, of the transformation of matter? But if we have not solved this problem in chemistry, it is hardly surprising that it remains an obstacle in other fields.

The divisions of chemistry have been arranged to show relationships, and these relationships are useful in predicting the transformations of matter. What of the divisions themselves, of the boundaries between them? They are not arbitrary; chemical substances do not intergrade continuously in all conceivable directions. Chemical substances occur in species and in groups of species just as biological organisms do. The speciation, in concept, is utterly sharp. And it is *objective*. There are a number of instruments which will, when traversing some quantitative property of a group of substances, draw a curve closely representing this perhaps infinitely sharp speciation. Mass spectrographs and gas–liquid chromatographs are two such instruments. The curve [is] illustrated in Figure 1. The quantity measured in the one case is essentially molecular weight, the mass of an individual of the species; in the other it is the volatility of an individual species. The curve shows that for most values of volatility *nothing exists*, but that at certain values a species is found. Two species are actually separated by emptiness. You could hardly find a foundation in this world which would sponsor a search for an intermediate between methane and ethane. The taxonomy says clearly that there should be none.

No *a priori* reason for such speciation has been brought to my attention, and I believe none exists. No *a priori* reason exists to say that elements should not intergrade continuously, that their compounds should not vary continuously in composition and properties.

POPULATION ↑

QUANTITY OR QUALITY ⟶

FIGURE 1. [Curve representing sharp speciation, as found in chemistry.]

So deeply imbued with the notion of sharp speciation are we that it is hard for us to envision the problems early chemists encountered in establishing that such is the nature of matter.

In biology, matters are different. The taxonomy does not predict transformations very well. Underlying biological taxonomy is again the idea of relatedness, but in a one-way temporal scheme, the idea of a ramifying evolution. Biological taxonomy displays the patterns of order of the evolutionary process. As in chemistry, it does not include the environment directly. If we could manage to include the environment in the taxonomy, would we have a more predictive taxonomy? Could we know what to expect of the future?

In the living world, just as in chemistry, speciation occurs. Robins are not sparrows and do not intergrade into sparrows. They are thrushes, but thrushes other than robins exist. Species exist and groups of species exist, and patterns of order among them can be discerned, and so we can establish an arrangement of divisions which aids the mind in encompassing what is known. But the taxonomy of biology will not help us to transform robins into sparrows. Instead, it will tell us something of when and how some common ancestor came to be transformed into both robins and sparrows.

Speciation in biology is less sharp than in chemistry. Individuals do deviate from the typical, but the distinctions even between closely related species are usually objective and substantial (Figure 2) Thus in both chemical and biological taxonomy, sharp boundaries exist between species and, without doubt, quality changes at the boundary.

Another example that comes to mind, perhaps because pedologists have done so much classifying, is soil. The environment has been directly involved in the arrangement of divisions, and its influences, climate, parent material, and age are easily seen in the taxonomy. This arrangement of divisions seems to aid our understanding of the ramifying evolution of soils and the prediction of transformations. But its

Figure 2. [Curve representing less sharp speciation, as found in biology.]

precision is not high, and perhaps this stems from the nature of the species of soils. Species certainly exist, and boundaries separate them, both on the land and in the taxonomy. But speciation is no longer sharp, and the variation of soil quality as we alter some quantity, whether it be miles across the earth's surface or a parameter such as acidity, is rarely sharp (Figure 3). This stems from the absence of sharp boundaries in the environmental factors which generated the soils, but also from the absence of factors tending to eliminate soils which intergrade, which tend to deviate from a type.

Thus, in three instances chosen from a discontinuity of phenomena, a continuum in the nature of the boundary seems to arise. Schultz [A. M. Schultz, personal communication] has suggested that this should be related to the complexity of the systems in which the manifestations are found. When a system may be defined with but a few parameters, boundaries should be sharp; when many are needed, discontinuities become weak.

In three other examples, chosen from a host of closely related sorts of arrangements of division, no real discontinuities or even rapid changes of quality occur at or near the borders, but only changes in quantity. But in the first of this group, changes in quality certainly occur within the arrangement of divisions. Where is the border between hard and soft water, or between small cities and large? Still, hard and soft water do have differences in quality, and small and large cities as well. But the borders now are set arbitrarily, and a continuous range of quality closely related to a change in quantity must be expected. In the second example, the arrangement of divisions may be an administrative device. What change occurs at the border between the 16th and 17th assembly districts? None; but an astute observer can itemize many differences in quality between the two districts, each taken as a whole. However, this is largely descriptive; pattern, order, is not disclosed by the arrangement. The third example in this group is simply a pigeonholing device, employed for mnemonic reasons.

FIGURE 3. [Curve representing low-precision speciation, as found in the classification of soils.]

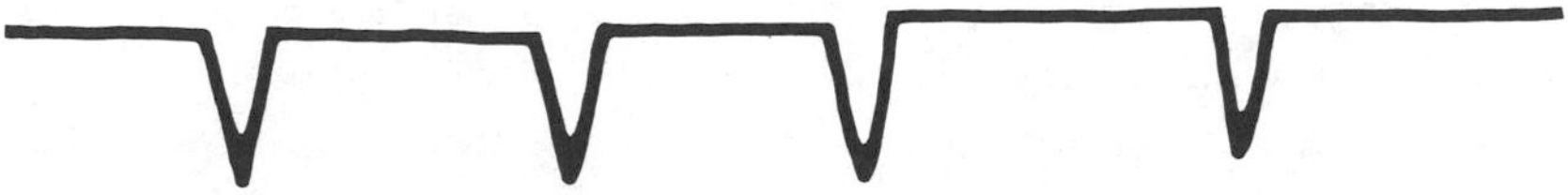

FIGURE 4. [Curve representing arbitrary boundaries.]

The common attribute of all these examples is that the boundary has become needle-sharp, as it was for the boundaries of chemical species, but the curve is inverted (Figure 4). Here, in place of sharply defined species separated by emptiness and discontinuous changes in quality, we have a fully occupied region with arbitrary boundaries at which no sharp changes in quality occur. Quality now varies continuously and more or less uniformly.

We must refer to the boundaries of chemical species as natural boundaries and to these last as artificial. From all of the above we conclude that *quantity transcends boundaries*, and *quality changes at boundaries*. But, also, inevitably we shall say that *the better the boundary, the more quality changes at it.* . . .

[SYSTEMS AND THE STRESSES OF CHANGE]

The "envelopes" of systems, apart from being very different from taxonomic boundaries, may be quite diverse among themselves. But their diversity reflects the attributes of the systems they envelop. Thus an envelope surrounding a system may be material and may separate the system physically from the surroundings, or it may be imaginary and serve only to focus our attention on what lies within it, to focus our attention on the system. Chemists, especially, have created but also imagined systems in which no energy passes through the envelope. These are called "adiabatic" (Gr. *diabatein*, to pass through), but there is no particular reason to stress energy as the entity which is not to pass through.

Examination of an adiabatic system usually begins with a disturbance which displaces it from equilibrium, followed by observation of the processes of its return to equilibrium. This can be reasonably approximated in the laboratory, less so in the field, where we more often encounter steady-state systems, whose adiabaticity is impaired by a flow through them. Most commonly, perhaps, this is a flow of energy, and we are familiar with biological systems into which energy flows as sunlight, and from which it leaves as infrared radiation. Or matter may enter as a stream of water and leave in much the same condition. If such flows are limited in number and reasonably well understood, they may be no handicap. Sometimes they may even be helpful. Take, for example, what chemical engineers call a continuous stirred tank reactor. This is a vigorously stirred vessel into which reactants flow continuously and from which an equal stream discharges. The chemical reaction kinetics of the processes occurring in the tank are often simpler than those of an isolated mass–adiabatic vessel, and especially of an isolated mass–energy–adiabatic vessel.

So we may have material or conceptual system envelopes of varying adiabaticity surrounding a contiguous region in space. But there is no reason why a system must be contiguous. Instead of having sunlight pass through the envelope, the system may reasonably be extended to include that part of the sun which is generating the incoming light and that part of the cosmos which is receiving the emitted infrared radiation.

This alternative idea of an envelope is that it should include not only the object of interest but also its significant environment. Entities, even though remote in ordinary space, should be included if they influence the object of interest. Entities, even though neighboring, to which it is indifferent may and should, in the interests of simplicity, be excluded.

The envelope for this system may become a curious sort of surface: It may be discontinuous, but one side of it will be "in" and the other "out" of the system. However, it is also selective; so some items of matter, or of energy, which at first seem "in" are actually "out." This is because they are without influence on the object of interest. Thus sunlight may be "in" while radio waves in the same region are "out" of the envelope. The crucial test is whether such items are part of the significant environment. Perhaps we can go so far as to ask whether, in some resource discussions, economic matters might be "in," but aesthetic factors "out" of the system.

Having played hob with all reasonable ideas of arrangements of a system, let me now stipulate one more outrageous condition: Imagine that the significant parts of the environment are located in a pie-shaped region centered on the object of interest at distances proportional to their influences. Thus we have an object of interest at the center of a system, and arrayed around it most closely are the least influential parts of its environment; at a greater but still modest distance are the most influential parts of the environment. The object is at the center; the greatest influences are at the rim.

The object of interest is taken to be biological, an individual, the members of a species in a region, or all the members of a species. We shall call it a biosystem, not an ecosystem. Were we to include all the members of a community of different sorts of organisms we might have an ecosystem, but this is a thornier notion and I should like to shy away from it, except for a passing note later on.

I have chosen this kind of arrangement in order to consider what happens to the system with the passage of time, and this arrangement provides an explicit analogy to a simple physical system. In one device used by physicists in accelerating nuclear particles, the Bevatron, electrons are guided on a circular course by an array of magnets and electrical fields located on that course. The environment of an electron, or a small group of electrons, [consists of] the magnetic and electrical fields within which it finds itself. They constrain it, guide it; they dominate it. At any instant, the environment of an electron is the field of the nearest magnet and the immediate electrical field, not the fields of the magnets farther along. In a later instant, the field of a subsequent magnet and the electrical field in that neighborhood will be the environment. The environment is pie-shaped at any one moment; over a period of time it resembles a cylinder, and, with the Bevatron, it is a bent cylinder. When I speak of the "bent cylinder" as the system moves in time, I am trying to suggest an environment which may be changing, an environment which disturbs, which modifies, the electron's path; not that time itself is curved.

In the Bevatron, some members of a group of electrons, because of secondary forces, interactions, perturbations, disturbances, stray from the central path essential for success. As they do, focusing forces in the fields tend to bring them back on the paths desired for them by the designers of the equipment.

In the biosystem, the environment which is significant to the organism is, by that token, the part of the environment which constrains the organism, which directs it on its course through time. We can view the organism as constrained within this pie-shaped region. What lies outside the rim has no influence; within the cylinder, what lies behind or ahead is a past or future environment. As a corollary part of the analogy, picture the well-adapted organism as being close to the center of the pie, secure in its adaptation and free, momentarily at least, of pressure from the environment. But when an individual strays from the center, because of perturbations current or recent, it is subjected to constraints, to pressures, to forces. The more the straying, the greater the forces. The strongest forces come into play only with increased straying. The most positive constraints are the most remote, not the most immediate, parts of an environment so arranged. An individual which strays too far will completely escape the system and disappear.

Since biological speciation is not perfect, individuals do tend to stray from the course of perfect adaptation, of conformity. In the biological environment, I think I see some direct focusing forces which tend to bring individuals back into line. Perhaps more commonly, however, individuals which tend to stray, whether geographically, or physiologically, tend simply to disappear, to be wiped out. But over long periods of time, surely a focusing effect exists. In each generation, the offspring of mild deviants contain more deviant, but also less deviant, individuals. The more deviant are eliminated in favor of the less, and the less deviant provide the next generation. We must keep in mind that the environment is not immutable. An organism deviant today may, without changing, be conforming tomorrow because the environment has altered.

At this point I want to try to identify "ecosystem" in terms of the last few paragraphs. An ecosystem would appear to be an association of biosystems such that each organism is a part of the environment of every other organism of the ecosystem. The concept of space devised in earlier paragraphs to describe a biosystem is distorted enough; the intertangling consequent on the extension to the ecosystem is much more involved. Perhaps, indeed, so much that the image becomes fruitless.

Returning to the simpler idea, picture the environment as a guide which keeps the organism on course, as it were, but as a guide which itself may vary with time. If the environment were to remain unchanged, would the biota remain unchanged? Perhaps so, but, because much of the environment is itself biological (the biosystem is a part of an ecosystem and entangled with it), the chances of evolution coming to an end are remote.

In fact, though, the environment does change, and as it does, it guides the organism at its nucleus. The electron's nature is to go in a straight line; the Bevatron's magnetic and electrical fields cause it to veer and constrain it into a circular path. When the environment changes, the organism rubs against one side and rides free on the other. On one side, the environment is constraining; on the other, beckoning. If the organism generates deviants that veer toward the beckoning opportunity, it adapts; it evolves, generation by generation; it is viable. If the environment changes too rapidly for the adaptability of the organism, the organism escapes the environment altogether and becomes extinct. While the environment persists, the biosystem vanishes with the escaped organism, for the organism is as much the essence of the system as is the environment.

How and why does the environment change? For my immediate purposes, ignore the changes in the inorganic world. They are by no means negligible: Glacial periods, subsidences, new surfaces, chemical changes, all these have affected innumerable biosystems drastically and rapidly, and have influenced evolution, but that is not the immediate issue. Let us consider only the changes due to the activity of our central organism or of other organisms in its environment.

The most obvious way in which an organism changes its environment is by eating it up, but many others come to mind: by shading out one's offspring, by changing the pH of the soil, by building a nest, by claiming a territory, by developing a sod, by producing smog. Eating up the environment might have been dramatically rapid when this world's first freely reproducing organism went to work on the ocean of broth which nurtured it [Hardin, 1963]. There may well have been oscillations in the nature of that environment so spectacular, so much beyond adaptive capabilities, that the creation of life itself had to be repeated. Still, at some point, and long ago, a relatively stable accommodation was reached. Since then, alterations due to activities of the biota have been mostly slow. As one organism changed, owing to the constraints and opportunities of the environment (the rubbing and the beckoning), it, being a part of the environment of its neighbors, caused changes in the neighbors' constraints and opportunities. If the neighbor could adapt and respond to opportunity, it thrived; otherwise it vanished.

Next, consider two limiting cases; in the first, the organism has no effect on the environment. Its associates change its environment. It is, perhaps, in no biosystem but its own. That is, it has no significant influence on any other organism. This is the predicament of the rare organism, which must conform and adapt, as circumstance dictates, or die. Its survival depends on the rate and manner in which the environment shifts, and on the organism's ability to adapt, to stay somewhere near the center of its biosystem. The species need not remain invariant. The important test is whether it has descendants, whether of the same species or of derived ones.

The record suggests that not many organisms have met this test: The limbs of the phylogenetic tree are intricately branched. Few primitive organisms have left descendants, but those which have succeeded have left many and diverse descendants. The environment of most organisms of the past has at some time veered so sharply that the organism could not stay within it and was accordingly wiped out. But while this was happening, the environments of other organisms were opening up and ceasing to constrain. And the opportunity for diversification, for individuality, was expressed in ramification [Hardin, 1959].

In my second limiting case, the organism is completely in control of its environment in the sense that all influences on the environment come from the organism itself, not from any independent source. It influences, often dominates, the environments of its associates while they have no influence on, are not part of, its biosystem. Here is an organism which can do no wrong. No matter how it veers, its environment veers with it and it continues unimpaired on its own course.

This is a curious situation, for we must exclude any idea that the course is guided. This leaves us in a predicament: If the course were utterly random, without constraints of any kind, it would also be discontinuous; here this instant, there, perhaps remotely there, in the next instant. It becomes a rather useless sort of limiting case unless we impose some restraints on how the course may vary. Yet, if the course is not to vary without restraint, it must be guided in some fashion.

[GUIDANCE OF SYSTEMS]

Three kinds of guidance come to mind: foresight, inertial, and by a fixed reference point.

Much has been said of foresight, of purpose, of setting out for a target, but, by general admission, hindsight is sharper than foresight.

Nonetheless, all life is concerned for the future, so all life has some vision of the future, and a notion of what it will be like, and prepares for anticipated events. Much anticipation is genetic, but not all. Foresight serves to avoid a serious rubbing against the environment, and leads to a veering when it is judged the environment is about to veer. "Go to the ant, thou sluggard." It is as if the organism were probing ahead for turns in the road and had learned from the past to prepare for such turns, to maintain a conservative course even when constraints appear remote.

Currently, we hear much discussion about whether humanity, while apparently in full control of its environment, is in fact approaching a corner too sharp to be rounded, or even creating a corner too sharp to be rounded. An easy example is the human use of energy. For millennia we have been great users of energy, converting chiefly from chemical latent energy to heat. In recent decades our rate of energy consumption has rapidly accelerated, and now we vacilate between the belief that fuels are limitless and the fear that they are nearly exhausted. One appraisal has suggested a 7% increase in energy use each year ["Fusion Power—Future Necessity," 1956]. This is too high, perhaps twice too high, but it is a convenient number because it comes to 1000-fold per century. If 3.5% a year is more accurate, think of a 1000-fold increase every two centuries.

Men are essentially in control of this part of the environment. Perhaps we can continue on the exponential growth curve, in our use of energy. At this moment the energy resource seems to impose no limit, and the amount we use today is still small, about 1/30,000 of the sun's input to the earth. But a 7% increase for the next 150 years would amount to a 30,000-fold increase in human use, and would cause it to equal the sun's input to the earth. It is hard to imagine what anyone would want with so much energy until near the end of that interval, but then a need becomes terribly clear [Fremlin, 1964; Luten, 1961; see also "Parks and People," elsewhere in this book]. With double the amount of energy released and double the amount to be radiated from the earth's surface, the average temperature would be 100°F higher than now. I envision most of that energy being used for air conditioning. Would such a circumstance be an unmanageably sharp turn in the road, an intolerable constraint by the environment, an unescapable trap? The answer is that our foresight should be adequate to guide us away from this particular hazard, but our prevision of other hazards may be less sharp.

Human foresight can do wonders with such problems. That it can serve as guide for the environment must be denied. That would be possible only if a target, a clear human purpose, existed. Who is wise enough and respected enough to define such a purpose?

The second sort of guidance, the inertial, may be criticized on the score that it defines the future in terms of the past. But if the future is to endure, it must look to the past for guidance. A host of inertial guides may be imagined: rate of genetic variation; dominance of the group over the individual, that is, convention; rate of communication within the system—how quickly is the information that the organism has changed its course communicated to the environment so that it can veer to match? Alternatively, how much of the information thus provided reaches the environment so as to modify it? These guides encompass memory, tradition, conservatism, be it learned or genetic.

An organism dominating its environment, its biosystem, and controlled by inertial guides may be realistically imagined. Most such systems, I suspect, are associated with population outbursts. However, do not include in this category systems whose transiently unconstraining environments permit an outburst of population, for they do not modify the environment in their own favor. In contrast, some examples of marginal control of environment are the tree which modifies the soil in which it grows to make it better for its requirements; the bird which builds a nest and claims a territory.

An organism in this category would dominate the environment of its associates without being affected by them. No matter how much it might veer, its environment would veer with it. Fixed reference points and foresight being excluded for the moment, this biosystem has no Polaris, no fixed star for the helmsman, no clear target. At best, its guides would be memories of the past, the ghosts of history peering into the heavens for a Polaris, for a purpose. Instead of these, it would have inertial guides: the inertia of innovation (How fast could technology solve the problems it has created?), the inertia of delay in communication (but both communication and change in cities seem ever to accelerate). What portion of advocacy of a new course would be heeded? What conformity would a society demand? How fast could traditions change? To what degree could the repositories of traditions be shielded from the pressures of a society?

How fast could such a course change? Would it be an exponential spiral? Genetic adaptability would eventually become an external constraint to limit the fate of such a system. Exactly how is unclear. Mankind appears to be gaining so much control over his environment that he is approaching this condition. But there is no guarantee of perpetual control. Inevitably, control will pass back and forth between organism and environment, and disaster beckons at each transfer. The image, in my model, is one of getting into too tight a turn, of losing control and being abruptly wiped out.

The third kind of guidance is the reference point. If a system in which the organism controls the environment is to maintain a stable course, if it is not to veer uncontrolled, if it is to be homeostatic, it must have a reference device, an immutable Polaris.

A familiar instance of homeostasis is homeothermy. A simple control system such as an ordinary thermostat has a reference temperature device, perhaps a bimetallic element, perhaps a mercury thermometer with electrodes in it. We have these familiar devices in our laboratories, in our homes. We also have something of the sort in our bodies. A competent textbook on physiology [Guyton, 1956] says a great deal about how information is relayed in the body to modify the output of heat, but not a word is said about the reference device except that it is probably located in the hypothalamus. How does the body know that 98.6°F is the normal temperature? How do three billion human bodies each know this same thing? Only because a reference device is there to keep body temperature constant, on course, in spite of drastic changes in the environmental temperature, until the verge of death. It is hard to imagine what the device might be other than a phase equilibration (resembling the melting of ice) or a group of opposed chemical reactions. Its nature is unimportant just now; its existence is important.

We should not expect to find reference devices in biosystems, for they are dependent on their environments and have no use for such devices. We might consider the tangled web of biosystems which make up an ecosystem, for it has a measure of stability, and could have something similar to a set of opposed reactions. Whether such a control depends unequivocally on a reference point or is really inertial is not clear, but neither is it important at the moment. While a reference device may be small, this is not necessarily true. Conceivably it might have to be very large. How large is Polaris?

I have cited three influences which may serve to keep an organism on a course, despite a growing dominance over its environment. One of these is inertial, the rate at which the biosystem can change. Another is foresight, a probing into the nature of a future environment with responsive modification of the course. A third is the existence of a specific reference mechanism, be it Polaris, a bimetallic regulator, a mixture of ice and water, or what not.

[GUIDANCE OF HUMAN SYSTEMS]

If human society should become independent of its environment, what might its course be? Is there any limit to the wandering of the system, or in the rate at which it veers? [Mumford, 1962]. The answer has been sought in an outpouring of writing during the past two decades, in the controversy between "enough and to spare" [see Mather, 1944] and "our plundered planet" [see Osborn, 1948]. The answer seems to be that there is a limit but heaven only knows where.

Should we suppress mankind's dominance so that we become subservient to our environment? No; that is impractical, unrealistic, unachievable.

Does mankind have foresight? Yes, a great deal more than we can perceive in other organisms. Does it keep us on constant course? No; on the contrary, foresight serves only to increase human adaptability, to accommodate the tendency toward exponential spiraling of our environment, itself resulting from the diminishing of inertial controls. Does the human biosystem have a built-in reference device? None that is obvious to many of us.

I can see only one possibility for such a reference device: the traditional environment of mankind, the native landscape, the natural scene, the wilderness. This environment, to which we were subservient for a million-odd years, is now greatly altered, and survives unchanged only in a few remote or forbidding retreats. (Does enough of our traditional environment remain to provide an adequate reference device?) The manner of operation of such a reference device is not clear. Whether it is a promising one must be argued, but even if no answer is forthcoming, it is still the best hope until a better one is suggested.

While it is probably inborn for men to struggle against the dominance of nature, it is probably inborn also to recognize this dominance and submit to it. The more people remove themselves from the natural scene as they accede to the pull of the cities, the more we find them seeking, as opportunity permits, a return to the open land. Olmsted's words of a century ago citing the need expressed by government leaders for contact with the natural scene are worth remembering [Roper, 1952]. As urbanization grows, the descendants of men who saw no good in the natural scene now turn back increasingly toward it. Is the oscillation between city and countryside perhaps a manifestation of the need for guidance by the unique reference device?

Concerned with such matters these days, we find two sorts of people. One group can be categorized as those who understand immediately and are awakened by and sympathetic to Sigurd Olson's phrase, "The Singing Wilderness." For the second group, the wilderness is only land awaiting development, and the symbolic phrase is "a howling wilderness." Who, in terms not of the immediate but of the longer-range wandering of the human-dominated environment, is the deviant and who the conformist? Against whom does the human environment rub and whom does it beckon?

It must become clear to all who are concerned for the future that the natural scene is the only conceivable reference point. Further, it must be retained, even though we cannot understand how it could work, until the day we are able to prove that it cannot work.

How much of the natural scene is necessary depends on such matters as the amplification of information it provides and on how much it is disturbed in the process of providing that information. The amount needed might be very little, perhaps a 40-acre natural prairie; the bimetallic unit needed to control the temperature of a house is very small. Still, prudence would suggest maximum retention until the needed level is clearly established. Common sense would suggest that the more abundant the natural scene, the more effective will be its control and the less erratic the veering and yawing of the environment under the guidance of man.

How perfect, how unimpaired must the landscape be to be effective? No good answer is at hand. Landscape of any quality exerts some sort of control, whether of an inertial nature or as a reference point, but, because only an unimpaired wilderness can be independent of the human influence, only it can be a dependable reference point.

I have not tried to say that wilderness is admirable, or that it should be made useful, or that it is admirable to be useful and useful to be admirable. I have not mentioned wilderness aesthetics or wilderness sentimentality. I have not tried to persuade anyone that the howling wilderness is really a singing wilderness. Instead, I have argued that, howling or singing, it is a resource, perhaps the most important of all resources, both in its quality and its quantity, because it is essential for the long-range welfare of man. Nature is the final helmsman; no other reference point can be imagined.

THE ETHICS OF BIOTIC DIVERSITY AND EXTINCTION: FROM PLEISTOCENE TO ALDO LEOPOLD AND A STEP BEYOND

Perhaps no other name is more familiar to contemporary environmentalists than that of Aldo Leopold. Moreover, perhaps nothing about which Leopold wrote is more quoted than his discussion of a "land ethic." Yet, the meaning of that concept remains elusive, even obscure. Luten, in this paper, did not explain away the difficulties, but he did explore interpretations and implications of them. In addition, he tied the concept of a land ethic in with his own ideas about wild nature as a reference device; thus, this paper serves as a logical sequel to the preceding article. Finally, Luten made it clear that the sort of precision demanded by narrowly conceived science is not easily found in this area of human relations to the land: "[A]ll of this does not get us away from the several dilemmas of decision or interpretation of 'land ethic.' But it does add an iota of the sense of 'land ethic. . . .'" Still, Luten did not despair of this inability to dispel dilemmas. He expressed confidence and conviction about his basic theme, the importance of nature for guidance of human society:

> [W]e will have a land ethic when we come to believe, whether by consensus, or by faith in the wisdom of a prophet, that the elements of the natural landscape, from form, soil, and biota to wilderness and wildness, that these alone can provide the information we need to guide us in our winding course into the future.

Paper presented at the annual meeting of the Association of American Geographers, Milwaukee, WI, April 1975.

A Sand County Almanac, written not far from here, was published in 1949 after Aldo Leopold's death in 1948. The first edition was followed by a second and amplified edition in 1966. Later, Oxford University Press brought out a nicely done paperback of the first edition, followed presently by a cheaper Sierra Club paperback of the second edition. Any references today are to the second edition, with paging the same whether hard or paperback. Initially, the book sold at best a few thousand copies a year; in a recent year, in contrast, sales exceeded 300,000. If one were inclined to argue that it will endure, he might cite some elements of similarity with *An Essay on the Principle of Population* [Malthus, 1798/1926] or with *Walden* [Thoreau, 1854/1964], each well into its second century and vigorous with controversy.

Leopold, among many other things, argues for a "land ethic," and the phrase has become a universal watchword among environmentalists.

Before entering a discourse on ethics, one might reasonably display one's qualifications on such matters. The best I can do is to enumerate my disqualifications. I have gone to the library to learn that a 17-volume *Encyclopedia of Ethics* may be found there. "Land ethic" is not in the index, but the volumes are too old and were published too far away. I found an analysis of Spinoza, Joseph Butler, Hume, Kant, and Henry Sidgwick in *Five Types of Ethical Theory* by C. D. Broad, a reputable philosopher of science. Most helpful, really, was the article on "Ethics," by Abraham Wolf, in the *Encyclopedia Britannica* (1947), perhaps three pages. Throughout all of these is the obsession to validate "good" and "evil," whether by revealed divine authority, by recourse to argument or human nature, or [by recourse] to doctrine propped up by calling it "natural law," or howsoever. Only weakly does the idea of "community," or common interest come through; not at all [is] the idea of explicit "purpose" [discussed].

Broad does think [that] Kant would say, "It is no more the business of ethics to provide rules of conduct than it is the business of logic to provide arguments. The business of ethics is to provide a test for the rules of conduct, just as it is the business of logic to provide a test for arguments."

By and large, I came out by the same door where in I went.

But then I recalled, from some 20 years earlier, an afternoon (1952) when Bertrand Russell was being interviewed on television on the occasion of his 80th birthday. When asked how the world had changed since his childhood, he made one comment that has stayed with me. He recalled, he said, that when he was a child his elders were deeply concerned about their "goodness," not about anyone's welfare, but about their own "goodness," that they should take all possible measures to be personally "good." He implied [that] this was not achieved by service to others, [nor] by any sense of duty to a larger community; [it was] simply that they, in their personal conduct, should in no wise commit evil, but rather in each action, be good.

In contrast, at the time of the interview, in the postwar year of 1952, he felt that a widespread concern for "human welfare" was well nigh paramount in the thinking of thoughtful people. Let me suggest that he had, in fact, identified a transition, from concern for a smaller to a larger community.

When I turned to more recent, and less profound, literature, I found little more: C. H. Waddington's *The Ethical Animal* (1960) was recent enough to have mentioned "land ethic," but too remote, [too] Scottish, to be interested in something said in Wisconsin. After all, Broad had already set us in our place with "all good fallacies go to America when they die, and rise again as the latest discoveries of the local professors." *Bioethics* (1971), by V. R. Potter, despite a careful chapter on Teilhard de Chardin, and despite a Wisconsin author, was little help. The same [went] for *Ethics for Environment* (1973), edited by Steffenson, also recent and from Wisconsin. Christopher Stone's *Should Trees Have Standing?* (1972) is a legal tract. Stone did remind me of Erhard Rostlund's citation of Nathaniel Shaler, whose *Domesticated Animals* of 1895 has a chapter on "The Rights of Animals," and who, in *Man and the Earth* (1905), spoke of our obligations to nature and of the need of a "new attitude," a sense of kinship with nature. Also recent is Garrett Hardin's *Exploring New Ethics for Survival* (1972a); again, no mention of "land ethic," but helpful, nonetheless. But again in the main, I came out by the same door where in I went.

Bertrand Russell had warned me to think about human welfare, broadly, but only Hardin would bring the nonhuman world into the matter as well.

Let me turn directly to Leopold; the matter is covered in one chapter, pp. 217–241. Major elements of the arguments are [as follows]:

1. The extension of the community, the group of common interest from family to the entire biotic association. Pleistocene ethics were

limited to the family; Greek ethics to the family and the city-state; today's to the family, the nation-state, and, tentatively, to all of humanity; tomorrow's, hopefully, to all living organisms who partake of this immense journey. He supports (p. 231) the inevitability of such a progression by arguing that the "trend of evolution is to elaborate and diversify the biota"; whence we, as a corollary, may add "including to elaborate and diversify symbioses." A. J. Lotka would agree and may have come close to saying it 50 years ago (*Elements of Mathematical Biology*, 1925, p. 416).

2. [Leopold] refers (p. 219) to the conservation movement as embryo of a land ethic and also to an ethic as a constraint on conduct. Let us combine this with Walter Firey's (*Man, Mind and Land*, 1960, p. 209) naming of conservation as a constraint on conduct, commonly a sacrifice of present gratification in favor of the future. This suggests a close affinity, perhaps identification of "land ethic" with "conservation." Leopold, quite clearly, is for the preservation rather than the utilitarian side, though he has to use "conservation" both ways in his discussion. Perhaps he sums up his position when he says, "Conservation is a state of harmony between man and the land."

3. The relinquishing of dominance over the community, the biota, to become instead merely a member of it (pp. 219–220). We will return to this.

4. On the question of how an ethic originates, he is ambivalent. Sometimes (p. 241) [he simply equates it with] "consensus"; [elsewhere] (pp. 218–219), [he explains it as] a mode of guidance too intricate for the average individual, that is, an enunciation from one of recognized wisdom.

5. Finally, corollary issues come in:

a. Stability demands preservation (p. 225) of the subordinate organisms of the landscape because stability requires diversity and diversity demands maintenance of the integrity of the entire community. Returning to the matter later (p. 236), he asks, "[W]ho knows for what purposes cranes and condors, otters and grizzlies may some day be used?" We will come back to this, too, but let me digress for a moment.

I have a small watercolor, only 6 × 7 inches, of a hunting shack my grandfather used to have where the Monon Railroad crossed the Kankakee River in the midst of its great marshes in northwestern Indiana. When I was a boy he used to tell me of having seen the courtship dance of the whooping cranes in the marsh. Today the shack is long since gone; the marshes have been drained; the railroad is bankrupt; and the cranes, never common, may be doomed. But those same cranes may still have had something to do with my being here today, and this may be a minute part of their purpose. The watercolor itself was painted by a great type designer, Bruce Rogers, whose Centaur type graces all of the Sierra Club exhibit format books done by David Brower. Bruce Rogers, too, may well have seen the cranes' courtship in the marshes, and they, conceivably, may be reflected in the grace of Centaur type.

Leopold can only speculate that cranes and condors may some day be of use. He could, of course, have cited many instances where an organism that seemed utterly useless turned out quite differently. The first such to come to my mind is the mold *Penicillium*.

b. He is also aware of the conflict between ponderables and imponderables, between tangibles and intangibles, and of the incommensurables of use and of beauty. While recognizing that budgets are real and constraining, he ends up damning economic determinism. He calls it an "A-B cleavage" between those, the utilitarians, who view land as a commodity, and those who view land as a biota. As a mnemonic device, let A stand for "application" and B for "beauty" or "biota." Don't try to think of better words; you'll only muddy the mnemonic!

While recognizing that budgets are real, he says explicitly (pp. 229, 240, 224) that a "system of conservation based solely on economic self-interest is hopelessly lopsided." He could have made it stronger. Economics, the market and all its appurtenances, evolved and adapted to deal with quite different sorts of problems. More than being surprised that they do not work well, we ought to be amazed if they [do] work well in such situations. (But they don't—so don't be amazed.) Leopold can only suggest that an "ethical obligation on the part of the private owner is the only visible remedy for these situations" (p. 230).

But still, he cannot provide a test for A versus B: Dams or rapids in the Grand Canyon? Corn or cranes in Indiana (Figure 1)? Recreation or preservation in the National Parks? His position is clear, but he has

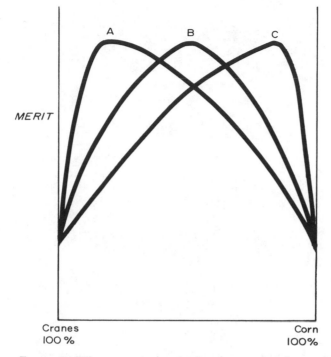

FIGURE 1. [The comparative merits of use versus beauty.]

no way of proving his case, no way of identifying an optimum proportion, no way to say, "So much corn, no more."

We have, by now, laid the way to propose three ethical dilemmas.
When Leopold says to quit thinking about decent land use as solely an
economic problem, and, instead, to examine each question in terms of
what is ethically and aesthetically right, we must ask: But what of
survival? The American farmer who does what is ethically right is not
apt to stay on the American land—the competition is too severe. But,
on the other hand, the society that practices only economic expediency
will also not endure, even though its fate will come more slowly. So
much for one dilemma.

For the second, take a look at . . . Figure 2. It is my own estimate
of the response of a reasonably wildlife-conscious middle-class American to the request: "Rank your likes and dislikes in the animal kingdom above and below the black line." It is a couple of years old;

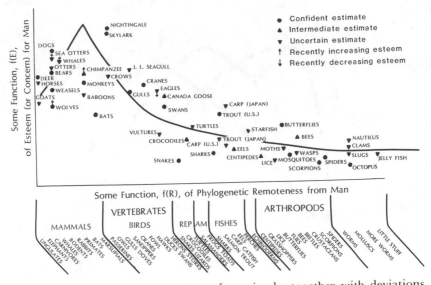

FIGURE 2. Pattern of human concern for animals, together with deviations from "ideality."

Jonathan Livingston Seagull is forgotten, but we may well rate sea-gulls higher than we would have done before him. Our concern declines with phylogenetic remoteness—I cannot recall ever having heard a voice raised against the impending extinction of the poliomye-litis virus. The second dilemma is how much to care for the little ones, how much to deter the extinction of forms greatly dissimilar from us in contrast to our nearer neighbors.

The third dilemma comes via Garrett Hardin, but is in the same region: How much one may ethically disturb a system depends on the state of the system; the immorality of killing the last elephant far exceeds that of, thus, killing the 10,000th from the last. But where is the line to be drawn?

There are many more. Hardin's "[The] Tragedy of the Com-mons" [1968] raises the question of competition versus cooperation within the community much more broadly than Leopold [has done], and yet leave[s] some obvious ramifications unexplored. We have, thus, almost parallel questions of how much pollution is good for us.

Let me now propose, as a small step forward, that we consider the future of a system and ask about its purpose. I prefer not to use the language of systems theory because I tend to get tangled up in it. . . . But I tend to think of a system as more in the mind than in the landscape. My simplest example has nothing directly to do with the landscape, but it does show how the central object of a system is guided. Here is a schematic cross-section of a Bevatron, wherein protons are guided in a circular path by synchronized electrical and magnetic fields (Figure 3). Deviant protons are subjected to greater focusing forces that generally bring them back into line. The constraining environment is least at the center, greatest at the edge. It is a simple example of "systems guidance."

Next, the system of robins is robins together with the environment of robins, whatever it is that affects the welfare of robins (Figure 4). For the moment, cats and climate will have to do. Cats constrain robins. Robins, generation after generation, tend to have some deviant young that don't learn soon enough what cats are up to. But, also, [they have] other [young] that do. They also tend to have some young that cannot accommodate themselves to climatic rigors, deviants of another sort, but also additional young that can accommodate them-

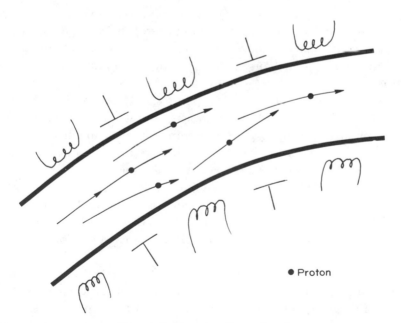

● Proton

FIGURE 3. Bevatron [cross-]section.

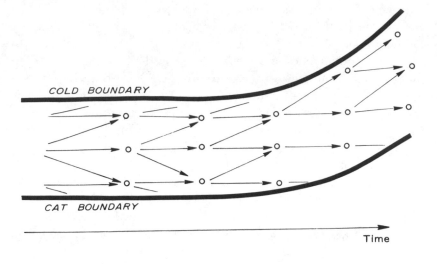

o Robins

FIGURE 4. [Schematic representation of the system of robins.]

selves. In fact, of course, constraints on robins are myriad, but, with two-dimensional paper to display an image of their plight, two constraints must suffice. So long as cats on the one hand and climate on the other remain unchanged, for so long do robins find a niche between them.

If now cats become cattier and progressively take more and more of the robins, the future of robins darkens. But if at the same time, the climate moderates so that, perhaps, robins can move to where cats are not so catty, then robins can survive. Converting the diagram into [drawings], thanks to T. M. Oberlander, my image of the system of robins is of its descent down a winding valley where now one wall, now another, presses harder on the success of robins [Figure 5], or where, in contrast, the constraining elements of the environment relax and robins come out into a vast plain of abundance, a land of milk and honey (Figure 6).

One major point with regard to robins [is that] they do not need to plan their future. Fate is simple: Conform or die. This is generally true for all of these organisms that are influenced by their environment but have little influence *on* their environment. Robins do not control the cattiness of cats, [or] the coldness of climate. Their plan of action is simple: Conform or die; adapt or abdicate. This is the predicament in general for both the rare bird and the meek: Conform or die.

Next, in contrast, consider the organism that influences its environment. We are familiar with many such—the early stages of many successional sequences. These influence their environment adversely to the degree that presently they disappear. In contrast, other organisms certainly influence their environments favorably. Systems analysts would say "negative feedback" and "positive," but I can never keep straight which, so I'd rather say "adverse" or "favorable." I should like for the moment, and unconventionally, to identify those that influence their environment favorably as "dominants." One, for example, may generate a soil more favorable to its own survival and prosperity. Another may cultivate the soil and grow its food rather than hunting and gathering what is naturally present.

FIGURE 5. [Representation of the system of robins under moderate environmental pressure.]

FIGURE 6. [Representation of the system of robins under relaxed environmental conditions.]

Some organisms may be so successful for long periods of time that geological eras are known for them: the age of trilobites, of ammonites, of dinosaurs. They have, [like the robins in Figure 6,] come into a broad valley of opportunity with constraints far removed. Whether they influenced their environment, shaped the valley or simply fell into some luck by being adaptive at the right time and place, I do not know, and it is not important just now. When we call them "dominants" the sense is different.

To return for a moment to my images of the valley with its walls as constraining guides for a system [see Figures 5 and 6], the dominant system, by definition, shapes the walls of its valley as it proceeds. Does the possibility exist that it may push its luck too far and that the wall will ultimately fall in (Figure 7)?

Any organism that does strongly influence its environment, such as mankind, has a far more difficult intellectual problem than the rare bird or the meek. The dominant organism may behave in a profligate fashion, changing the pH of its soil to its own disadvantage, eating all of the rabbits to its own disadvantage, whether thoughtlessly or content in the belief that everything is cyclic and that another golden age will come for some later generation. And what, after all, have our grandchildren ever done for us?

But [this organism] may also sit down and think about such matters. And [it may] reflect that it should plan for its future and have a purpose. Purposes can, of course, be diverse, but one suspects that when laid out explicitly they will almost always include continuing survival as a major element. While the contrary may make more sense, one suspects that the biological instinct of any planning agency will surface at such times.

If, then, concern for the future is to be an ubiquitous element, what measures, especially what principles, may one invoke to promote such a future? Only three have come to our minds, and some of us

FIGURE 7. [Representation of a system that may have "pushed its luck too far."]

locally have discussed these matters repeatedly. They are (1) the maintenance of tradition; (2) foresight; (3) [the use of a] reference device. First, to maintain tradition is to suppress innovation, to extrapolate the growth curves, whether arithmetic, exponential, or whatever. Second, to identify foresight is exasperating; of course, we know what we mean. Let me go on to the third. A thermostat in a room is a reference device; so is whatever it is in the human hypothalamus that says 98.6°F is the right temperature for each of four billion living people. So, also, is the diameter of the earth. The argument over whether the earth is finite or infinite is an argument over the reality of a reference device. The north star, Polaris, is another.

Quite commonly, perhaps almost universally, more than one of these three principles is used in a planning effort. Thus, if we believe the earth has a limit (a *reference* device), we can *foresee* that *traditional* growth will lead to a problem that may prevent us from fulfilling some purpose.

The matter should be argued in more detail, but we lack time today. Instead, I wish to focus on an essential attribute of all reference devices. This is that their merit is diminished to the degree that they are affected by the system for which they provide controlling information. What of a thermostat whose set point edges up a trifle each time the furnace goes on? What of a body temperature that increases by a tenth of a degree with each fever its owner suffers?

How shall we describe in most general terms this attribute of independence? What, looking at all of the phenomena about us, characterizes a reference device that is uninfluenced by humanity? It is, in the first place, undomesticated; it is *wild*. Polaris is uninfluenced by man, undomesticated, wild; and until we tilt the earth's axis it will be a useful reference device. What else? The diameter of the earth; but also, the hermit thrush in my backyard, so long as he remains wild. He, too, has something to tell me.

Let me cite two literary authorities in support of wildness. One of them, I think, would endorse the citation; as to the other I am not sure. Emerson, in the essay on *Nature* [1836/1957], says:

> Hundreds of writers may be found in every long-civilized nation, who for a short time believe, and make others believe, that they see and utter truths, who do not of themselves clothe one thought in its natural garment, but who feed unconsciously on the language created by the

primary writers of the country, those, namely, who hold primarily on nature.

But wise men pierce this rotten diction and fasten words again to visible things . . . [p. 34]

Thus "An enraged man is a lion, a cunning man is a fox, a firm man is a rock" [Emerson, 1836/1957, p. 32]. What if there [were] no lions; what if no one could recall what lions were like? We can, in fact, define words only in terms of what we see in the world around us. Definitions can endure only if the reference images in nature remain wild. Circus lions will not do.

What if we had, following the exemplary case of George Washington, set as a definition, "as honest as a president"? Presidents are influenced too much by their culture, and make poor reference devices.

Here is the second quotation [Shakespeare, 1623/1969, pp. 1132–1133]:

> [Siward:] What wood is this before us?
> [Menteith:] The Wood of Birnam.
> [Malcolm:] Let every soldier hew him down a bough,
> And bear't before him: thereby shall we shadow
> The numbers of our host, and make discovery
> Err in report of us. . . .
>
> [Messenger:] As I did stand my watch upon the hill,
> I look'd toward Birnam, and anon, methought,
> The wood began to move.
> [Macbeth:] Liar and slave!
> [Messenger:] Let me endure your wrath, if't be not so;
> Within this three mile may you see it coming;
> I say, a moving grove.
> [Macbeth:] If thou speak'st false
> Upon the next tree shalt thou hang alive,
> Till famine cling thee; if thy speech be sooth,
> I care not if thou dost for me as much.
> I . . . doubt the equivocation of the fiend
> That lies like truth: "Fear not, till Birnam Wood
> Do come to Dunsinane," and now a wood
> Comes toward Dunsinane.

If one takes a forest as reference device, be sure to take one that remains undomesticated. This is what is wrong with plastic trees; this is what is wrong with a wilderness designed by foresters to provide better for the "wilderness experience."

Let me suggest that we should regard the 25-year-old debate whether we live on a "plundered planet" or in a world of "enough and to spare" as a veering back and forth of the guidance system for humanity (back and forth across the valley floor), seeking identification of the limits of the earth, and employing tradition, foresight, and reference devices.

I do not know what went on in Thoreau's mind when he said, "In wildness is the preservation of the world," but it may have been a 19th-century equivalent of what I am trying to communicate.

Now, all of this does not get us away from the several dilemmas of decision or interpretation of "land ethic." But it does add an iota of the sense of "land ethic" by saying that any bit of life on this earth, especially if in its natural, undomesticated, wild condition, may have something to say to mankind that is of importance to the fulfillment of the purposes of humanity.

We cannot, of course, anticipate these messages. They must, though, be different from what we can learn by tradition alone, by foresight alone, or by the two together. One of the messages may be to abandon the role of superdominant, "to change from conqueror of the land-community to plain member and citizen of it. It implies respect for his fellow-members and also respect for the community as such" (Leopold, p. 220).

And so, to close, we will have a land ethic when we come to believe, whether by consensus, or by faith in the wisdom of a prophet, that the elements of the natural landscape, from form, soil, and biota to wilderness and wildness, that these alone can provide the information we need to guide us in our winding course into the future.

PART SEVEN

CONSERVATION

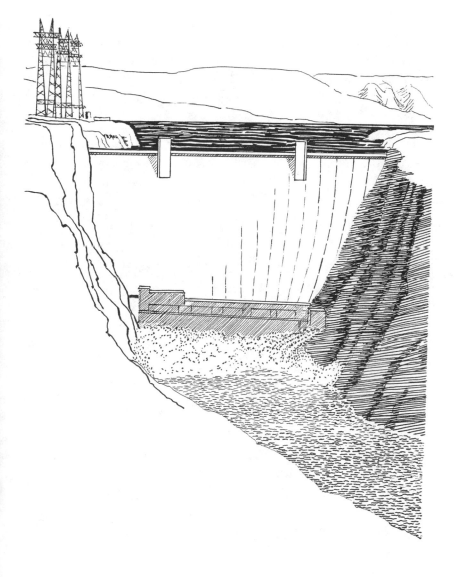

Luten has been involved with American conservation both as a detached scholar and as an active participant. In the latter role, he has served as an executive for such groups as the Sierra Club and as an advisor for David Brower, probably the most important figure in conservation since John Muir. (Brower describes Luten as his "coach.") Still, the papers appearing here are not simply expositions of conservation rhetoric; rather, they represent searching analyses of the meaning of conservation and the anatomy of the conservation movement.

EMPTY LAND, FULL LAND, POOR FOLK, RICH FOLK

If I were forced to choose one piece of writing that epitomizes Luten and his work, this chapter of a 1969 yearbook for geographers would be it. In it, Luten clearly enunciated his classic themes concerning people–resource interactions: population as a major resource factor; human purpose as the common denominator of resource issues; and variability in those human purposes. The chapter is characteristic of his style in general: questioning of the conventional; writing in simple language; and adding emphasis to his points with original, unexpected, and often humorous examples. Luten also gave voice here to persistent frustration over the failure of geography to embrace the conservation movement and contemporary resource issues as matters central to the discipline. Developing a thought from a quote by Wilbur Zelinsky, Luten asked, "Is the day nearing when geographers will peer, surprised, on a landscape which has been molded by forces under their very nose, forces which they preferred to ignore; and all because geographers failed to march into this 'breach that seems providentially designed for them'?" Since this chapter was written, other disciplines and interdisciplinary programs have "marched into this breach," although geographers continue to make contributions.

But this chapter is not included here merely because it is representative of Luten's themes, style, and philosophy. It also is more fundamental in concept, more pregnant with possibilities for application in a variety of situations, than most of his other papers. Luten here examined ways of addressing resource issues as they occurred in societies of different times and places. He then presented a "model" by which such resource problems may be analyzed.

Luten's basic subject here was the changing nature of the questions asked and the decisions made regarding landscape use over the history of the United States. He treated in detail the dichotomy between decisions that emphasize "utility" versus those that stress "beauty." This distinction shows

Reprinted by permission from J. F. Gaines (ed.), *Yearbook of the Association of Pacific Coast Geographers*, Vol. 31 (pp. 79–89). Corvallis: Oregon State University Press, 1969.

up strongly in Luten's other writings on conservation; it was, in fact, a central concept in the paper to be presented next, on the American conservation movement.

My thesis is simplicity itself. We came, poor people, into an empty continent. We devised resource management policies for an empty land and for poor people. Now the land is full and we are rich beyond earthly precedent. Our needs have changed and, ever faster, still change. But we have failed to abandon, to adapt, to invent resource policies to keep up. And so we stretch, warp, patch, wire up, lick and promise. But it won't work.

[To explore why it won't work, we need to explore] a little about "systems" from an earlier paper [i.e., the final paper in the preceding section of this book]. A system is simply some object of interest, a nucleus together with its significant environment. Its significant environment is what influences it, what constrains it, what guides it on its course through time.

In natural resources inquiry the inescapable nucleus of the system is man. But try as we may, the task of understanding this system is beyond us. [Instead, we] must turn, and it is a token of defeat to do this, to subordinate systems, to resource systems. In such subsystems the nucleus may be the resource itself—a few dozen whooping cranes, a Douglas fir forest, a salmon population, the North Cascades wildlands.

The boundaries of the system will have to include all of the environment which is significant and should exclude that which is not. Perhaps a major part of the significant environment will be human influences and perhaps it will help if we categorize many of these under the heading of "disturbance." What we are largely concerned with is disturbance, existing or proposed, and the response to disturbance. The test of significance is whether it influences the future within the degree of precision sought or attainable. The overwhelming task of resources inquiry is to decide what must be included and what may be excluded. Here is where genius takes the high road and pedestrian the low.

But why say all of this, that everyone knows, in words less easily understood? Using such phrasing does not simplify the problem. True enough, but let me try now to fit some rough patterns into this machinery.

Without going into detailed history, accept my proposition that in three centuries the United States has changed from an empty land to a quite full land. Once if we wanted work done, we dammed a rill and diverted its water. Once if we wanted to get rid of anything, we threw it in the river, confident that it would never be seen again. Once if the passenger pigeons nested nearby, we harvested as many as we could. If ever anything was in infinite supply, it was passenger pigeons. Once if we plowed up and down the hill and our cropland washed away, we moved on to new land. When men wanted land, we gave it to them. If the effete East, becoming crowded earlier, had doubts and restricted the gift of land, we in the West subverted their rules. Our policy was to occupy and develop. If *we* had not, others willing to occupy would have appeared.

These things that we did bothered no one else. It was a land of infinite resources. On this all agreed. Stuart Chase [1936] said in a book from a generation ago, *Rich Land, Poor Land,* "The whole system is wrong. . . . It started under the American concept of infinity."

In recalling that period, think, please, in terms of systems of widely dispersed families and settlements. One man's actions did not disturb his neighbors; he was not a part of his neighbors' significant environment. The boundaries of their systems did not overlap.

The symbol on the map of this era is Yellowstone Park (Figure 1). To define the boundaries of the Park took eight lines [in the original document]:

> . . . commencing at the junction of Gardiner's river with the Yellowstone river, and running east to the meridian passing ten miles to the eastward of the most eastern point of Yellowstone lake; thence south along said meridian to the parallel of latitude passing ten miles south of the most southern point of Yellowstone lake; thence west along said parallel to the meridian passing fifteen miles west of the most western point of Madison lake; thence north along said meridian to the latitude of the junction of the Yellowstone and Gardiner's rivers; thence east to the place of beginning. [17 Stat. 32 (S. 392, H. R. 464, 42 Cong. 2 Sess.].

That is all. No one knew what else was there; no competing demands existed; no one cared.

But times change. Our technological capacity to change the face of the earth grew beyond all precedent. Our numbers, too! We began to rub against each other. Cattlemen quarreled with sheepmen for a place on the range—that once infinite range. One man's sewage becomes

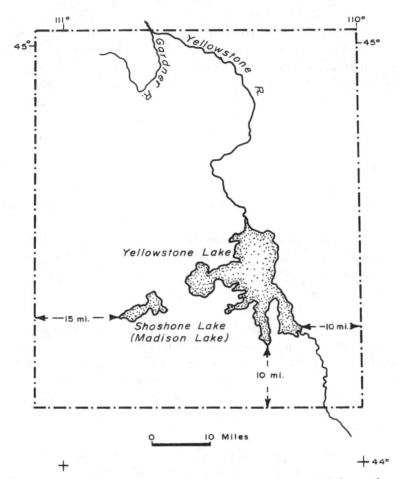

FIGURE 1. [Original boundaries of] Yellowstone National Park in northwestern Wyoming.

another man's drink. Water developments now are focused on great dams with "forebays," "afterbays," "fishways," recreational development, flood control criteria, and must conform to demands for irrigation water, must be integrated as peaking units in great power systems.

We found that if we permitted free access to the natural wealth of the land, someone, always someone else, would take more than his reasonable share. We began to develop a legal code constraining what might lawfully be done to the landscape. It can be said with both fairness and bitterness that we locked stables already well robbed.

Thus, Stuart Chase [1936] continued: "By the time the theory of forest inexhaustibility became clearly fallacious . . . America's magnificent forest [had fallen] before an economic system which had no philosophy of conserving natural wealth." We finally demanded replanting of timberlands. We denied access to the market place of virtually all inland wildlife; we imposed inefficiencies on the harvesting of marine wildlife. We devised legislative hearings so voluminous that it is asked whether we will one day cut our forests to provide the paper which records the Congressional hearings on their fate.

This simply says that in a full land what one man does affects his neighbors. Each man is now a part of his neighbors' significant environment. The subsystem boundaries overlap endlessly. The entire resource system seems to encompass all activities, to be continent-wide.

The symbol on the map today is the proposed North Cascades National Park (Figure 2). A century ago the significant environment would have included little but the geographic neighborhood, and the boundaries of the system could have encircled the mountains in any fashion. Today every section line is a quarrel. Every man has different plans for every valley. Wilderness as unwanted and unknown land is gone. Influences of remote places are manifestly significant: the prospective price of copper, of lumber, of electricity, the remote fortunes of Congressional politics, the population of hunters and of the North Cascades Conservation Council and its friends. All of these may affect the future of the North Cascades.

But we continue to act as if we had an empty land to fill. In the arid Southwest we came to call this "reclamation." But also we came to have qualms over our record of giving away our natural wealth in support of development. We had given land to all comers; we had condoned, perhaps encouraged, widespread fraud in the sale of timberlands. Perhaps our moral sense in those times can be expressed by a paraphrase of a rhyme by Ogden Nash; ". . . robbing is a crime, unless you rob the government ten million at a time." So finally we felt obliged to demonstrate that development was beneficial and accordingly we began to calculate benefits to prove to skeptics that such undertakings would promote the general welfare.

But we quite ignored reasonable notions of a system and tended to define the significant environment as that region in which benefits could be shown, not as the region significantly influencing or influenced by the activity. To take as homely an example as I can coin, a

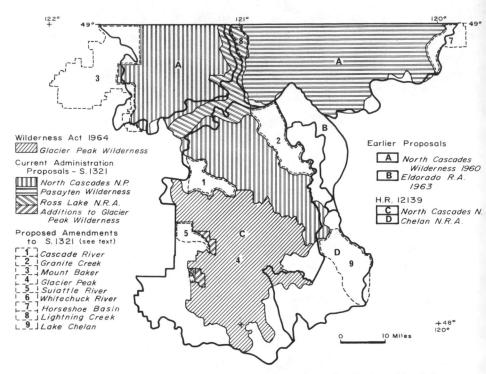

FIGURE 2. [Various proposals for North Cascades National Park.]

new recreational lake can be argued to be beneficial because sales of beer at it will go up. But perhaps church contributions nearby will go down, the money having been spent on beer. Who is to say which is the more beneficial? Carefully, though, we do not ask such questions, even though we could turn for help to Houseman's [1924] couplet:

> For malt does more than Milton can
> To justify God's ways to man.

It was a policy for an empty land; can it possibly be germane to a full land? Is it wise to load the southwest corner of the nation with people? The land is already tilting!

So much for the empty versus the full land. How about the poor versus the rich society? In our early days on this continent we were poor, not as poor as most of the people of the earth, but poor by today's standards. We agreed on what we wanted from a tree: we wanted to burn it to keep warm, to build something from it, or to sell it. It seemed unlikely that we, or any of the world's people, would want more from it. J. B. Say [Heilbroner, 1953/1961] stated, in a premise to Say's Law, the proposition that human wants are infinite and can never be satisfied.

But in the 19th century in the Atlantic community, signs of a change appeared. The combination of the raw materials and markets of new worlds, of land to absorb population growth, of an explosive technology, [and] of declining birth rates led to an affluence more widespread than ever envisioned. And so today we hear of the "man who has everything." While he is not common, neither is he royalty. Even though many still want, more and more we hear, "I have enough." More and more we see a rejection of the scramble for a place on the ladder of conforming achievement. Our attitudes are influenced by such people. Say's premise is not dead, but it is dying.

Ambivalence in human ambitions is not new. The church made demands at odds with economics. Charles Dickens, concerned throughout with the 19th-century factory economy, brought the matter clearly to light in *A Christmas Carol* [1843/1954]. Even Scrooge, the symbol of the pure economic individual, flinched when brought face to face with the issue. But American affluence today, unlike earlier societies, is not directed toward the greater glory of God, neither toward hedonism. Americans in their search for a national identity have made much of nature and of the idea of wilderness [Huth, 1957; Marsh, 1864/1964; Marx, 1964; Nash, 1967]. The demands of the 19th-century geologists for more time than the Bible could grant may have helped, as certainly did Darwin's unification of man with the rest of life.

But just now let me recall Thoreau's [1854/1964] "some things are more to be admired than used." Here is the signpost to two roads. Gifford Pinchot took one and brought forth a conservation movement dedicated to the proposition that natural resources should be saved because they are useful. John Muir, with a splinter of the conservation movement, took the other road with the proposition that the landscape should be saved because it is beautiful.

Efforts persist to nullify the difference by arguing that beauty is valuable and therefore useful. You can usually stir up a quarrel by asserting that the value of beauty is not adequately measured by its price. Thus the Mona Lisa is said to be beautiful and is worth five million dollars. How beautiful is my $5 print of the Mona Lisa? One-millionth as beautiful? Only to a connoisseur of dollars, not of art. In fact the quality of beauty stands apart from the quality of usefulness. Thoreau's distinction has merit.

We try to gloss over other distinctions in quality by putting dollar values on them. But it won't work. Does the man who goes to the beach in a Cadillac have twice as much fun as he who goes in a Volkswagen? It costs him twice as much. Is our wildlife resource valued because we spend 20 billion dollars annually on services and facilities for hunting and fishing? If so, how valuable is the cotton boll weevil, on which we spend a half billion dollars annually? Whose answer will you prefer, the pesticide manufacturer's, the cotton grower's, or the man who pays the taxes for cotton price support?

Let me try one more example: Recently a beautiful old eucalyptus tree on the Berkeley campus took ill. It was argued that a small new parking lot nearby was responsible, although general campus unrest was just as likely a cause. At any rate the parking lot was removed and the soil surface restored. It was then argued, since replacement of the parking spaces at going rates would have cost $30,000, that this shows the tree was worth at least $30,000. None of this argument stands close inspection. The alternative lot was not built so no one spent $30,000. The effect on parking was, in a sense, that the few people who parked in the lot instead must park at the outer limit of campus parking a half-mile away. More realistically, a good many people must park one space farther away. Further, they don't know they are parking farther away and haven't been asked if they prefer this hardship rather than the tree. The tree died anyway.

In a subsequent tree controversy also on the campus, some handsome, quite sizable redwoods were threatened by a road relocation. An alternative existed, but it would have cost $60,000 and would have come out of the university's budget. The budget people thought it preferable to remove the trees. Were the redwoods less beautiful than the eucalyptus?

I want to suggest now that usefulness and admirability are, in fact, incommensurable quantities. In Figure 3 I have shown several pairs of antitheses: "used" versus "admired," "quantity" versus "quality," and so on. On the vertical scale in the simple vector diagrams are measured changes in what broadly may be called economic attributes; on the horizontal scale, changes in aesthetic attributes. Only positive values appear in this quadrant; negative values would appear in the three

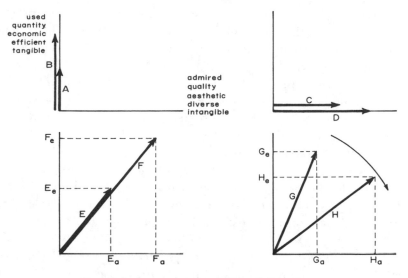

FIGURE 3. Incommensurability of disturbances.

unused quadrants. In the first diagram, of two proposals to disturb the landscape which do not change its beauty but which increase its usefulness in different degree, B, the larger, is preferred. In the second diagram, of two proposals to disturb the landscape which do not change its usefulness, but which change its beauty in different degree, D, the larger, is preferred. In the third diagram, of two proposals to disturb the landscape which increase its beauty and usefulness in equal degrees, F, the larger, is preferred. Thus far the matter is trivially simple. What, though, is the decision when one proposal leads to greater usefulness but less beauty than its alternate: Which of G and H is preferred?

No unequivocal answer can be given; however, as a society becomes richer, it will tend to prefer H over G. As affluence increases, preference in this quadrant rotates clockwise. Perhaps, given a bit of mystical license, I can say, "This is the clock of progress."

One final comment on this symbolism: Rather than two incommensurable attributes as suggested in the figure, in fact a host of incommensurables must be envisioned. The present versus the future is a notable example. The practical question which will not cease to plague us is: How many of these are significant?

Another phrasing of the situation is that the economist works in economic space, the modern conservationist in aesthetic space, and that someone had better come along soon who can work in a manifold of such spaces.

When we were poor and the land was empty, the economic criteria for decision[s] were reasonable. The market is a fine device for making small decisions on allocation of sparse means. It has not proved its merit with great decisions, neither for disposal of abundant means. And on the available evidence the economists again working with baling wire, tire patches, and paint are not succeeding brilliantly. And yet in the field of resources management, society has given them the ball, the rules, and the referee, and has let them come up with "externalities," "opportunity cost," "shadow pricing," and "benefit–cost analysis."

The schemes of benefit cost analysis used to evaluate major resource disturbance proposals combine qualities so grossly incommensurable that they have no meaning. Answers rest on irrational assumptions. Anyone who works backward from the desired answers to the necessary assumptions is no more honest than he should be; anyone who does not is no wiser than he should be. Any prestidigital computer, any numbersmith, can take an intricate mess of unsound data, run them through a host of calculations until the idiocy of their birth has disappeared, and come out with impressive results fully and predictably capable of convincing legislators. The legislators, after all, simply want to be able to say they did what the calculations said was wise. This was not invented with fancy electronic computers; they only make the act more impressive. The basic computer warning still holds: "GIGO, garbage in, garbage out." If you put in lies and junk, you will get out, in silk and satin, lies and junk. A better way must exist. And yet Wilbur Zelinsky [1967] recently wrote: "It is abundantly clear that neither ecologist, economist, geographer, planner, nor any other professional has really bothered himself about the global wholeness of our emergent North America, and, from the evidence . . . that they don't yet know how. (I like to daydream about my fellow geographers heroically marching into a breach that seems providentially designed for them; but I know better.)"

Again, George Macinko [1968] has recently written, "Were America dependent on the university alone for the ethical and aesthetic vision necessary to the establishment of a conservation attitude things would be in a sorry state."

Traditionally the teaching of conservation has fallen to the geographer. Yet today the geographer has recoiled from his task and prefers to look backward to easier times when the patterns on the land were leaden rather than mercurial.

Meanwhile, proceeding without help from the university, proceeding in defiance of the dicta of the resource economists, a conservation movement based on the thesis that beauty cannot be reduced to dollars has come on the stage. Still only a shadow, it grows in strength perhaps more rapidly than any directing element in our society and soon will shape the face of the land.

The geographer's rejection of a directing role in and failure to study this movement may end up merely hurting geography. Is the day nearing when geographers will peer, surprised, on a landscape which has been molded by forces under their very nose, forces which they preferred to ignore; and all because geographers failed to march into this "breach that seems providentially designed for them"?

FADING AWAY?

In the preceding selection, Luten identified a historical swing in the outcomes of controversies over use of landscapes in the United States away from utilitarianism toward preservation: ". . . proceeding in defiance of the dicta of the resource economists, a conservation movement based on the thesis that beauty cannot be reduced to dollars has come on the stage." In this article, Luten explored in more detail the arrival "on the stage" of the concern for the beautiful. He viewed that concern as being opposed, not by interests against conservation, but by other conservationists who enter the play with a concern for the useful. But he went beyond this dichotomy by providing a chronological anatomy of the American conservation movement that should provide "a basis for discussion" about today's conservation movement, whenever "today" may be.

Two characteristics (Luten called them "images") form the basis of that anatomy: a conservation movement that has steadily expanded the issues for

Reprinted by permission from *Western Outdoors Annual*, 1973, 40 (Spring): 8-12.

which it battles, and a conservation movement that has swung from utility to beauty and then from beauty to utility as its primary concern.

In regard to the second characteristic, Luten seems to have changed his assessment of the conservation movement in the four years that separated the publication of the preceding selection from the appearance of this paper. In 1969, he confidently predicted that concern for the beautiful "will soon shape the face of the land"; by 1973, in contrast, he observed that concern for the useful had gained dominance: "More and more [the conservation battlefront] begins on the preservationist side and swings quickly across into utilitarian issues." By the mid-1980s, would Luten see a resurgence of interest in "parks, wilderness, [and] the pure quality of natural landscape"? This shift is suggested by the success of Alaskan lands legislation, the heated debates over threats of oil development in wilderness areas of Wyoming and Montana, the increased worry over survival of grizzly bears, and the outcries against the federal land policies of President Reagan and former Interior Secretary James Watt. Or would Luten see the continued conservationist interest in such issues as nuclear war, solar energy, toxic waste dumps, and acid rain as evidence of a "utilitarian" movement—one reacting to a society that sees itself too poor to worry about "the pure quality of natural landscape," or one so entangled in side issues that "principles [have been] forgotten" and "objectives" [have become] confused"?

Recently Presidential Counselor (also Secretary of Agriculture) Earl L. Butz was noted to have said in 1971, "I am informed that attendance was down substantially from what it was [during Earth Week] a year ago" [Carter, 1973].

And indeed it was.

Again, a current newspaper feature article is titled, "Where Have All the Ecology Freaks Gone?", and it observes that numerous environmental news publications are in difficulty, that *Ecology Today* and *Clear Creek* have given up.

Enrollment in some courses under my instruction seems to have crested, and now to be decreasing (Figure 1). But concern for energy still grows.

The Sierra Club's membership, after 25 years of growth, has paused. Apparently, thousands who joined in the hot enthusiasm of 1970 are not renewing. Anxious queries are heard, asking if the conservation movement has peaked out and if it now must reconcile itself to a declining old age, to a diminishing influence? Is it just another old general, duty done and fading away?

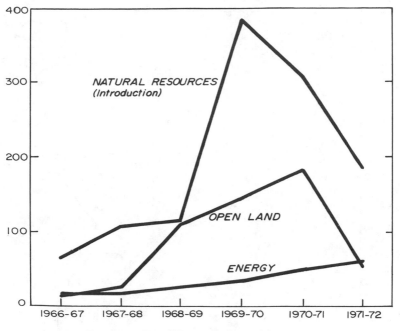

FIGURE 1. Enrollments in Luten's courses.

But the Sierra Club, as everyone knows, is much, much bigger than when it was formed, and its growth has always been dramatic and interesting. From 1892 until 1914, the year of John Muir's death and of defeat at Hetch Hetchy [Jones, 1965], it grew at 10% per year, faster even than electric power (8%/year), doubling almost three times in 22 years. Then, from 1914 to 1945, it grew and lost membership by fits and starts. After World War II, growth began to pick up. And in the 1960s, with victory in the Grand Canyon, with exhibit format books, with new National Parks and Seashores, with the Wilderness Act, and with taking up the population issue, it grew even more rapidly, sustaining a peak rate of almost 30% per year for several years. The full curve is given in Figure 2.

Maybe 10% is enough. Continued from the original thrust, it extrapolates to a million in 1977. The present membership is not close to the original curve, and now seems unlikely ever to reach it. The increased competition is one reason. *Clear Creek* may be gone, but *Not Man Apart* and *ZPG Reporter* continue. And there are more organiza-

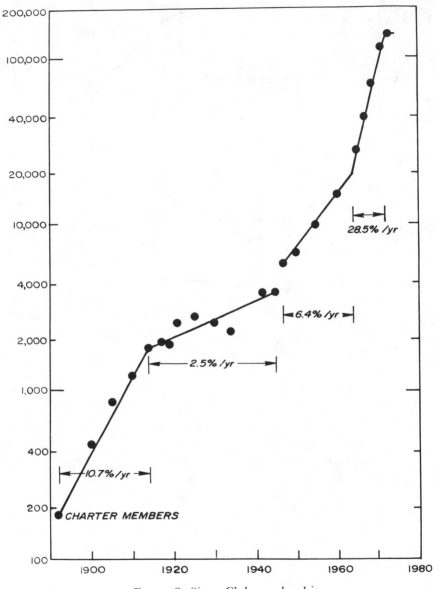

Figure 2. Sierra Club membership.

tions. And, recalling for a moment the complaint on dwindling course enrollment, there are more courses. But the question remains unanswered: Is the conservation movement fading away; is it changing into something else?

Diverse views are held of the conservation movement. One, a favorite among those geographers concerned academically with conservation, has been to picture it as a dichotomy, a contest between two ideologies: utilitarian and preservationist, personified by Gifford Pinchot, the forester, and John Muir, the mountaineer. Hawkes [1960], for example, cites the successive utilitarian concerns for forests at the turn of the century, then for petroleum after World War I, then for soils in the Dust Bowl years, and, after World War II, for water management, wildlife management, energy resources. Counterposed against this, and initially in a losing role, was the concern for parks. Hetch Hetchy is the symbol of this early phase. But after World War II, the preservationist wing gained a fair share of the victories. Hawkes's story is summarized in [Figure 3]. . . .

Utilitarian Concern (Pinchot)	Resource (and Time)	Preservation Concern (Muir)
Timber	Public Land for National Forests 1897	Mountain Landscape
Urban Water (San Francisco)	Public Land for Watershed 1901–1913	National Parks (Hetch Hetchy)
Fuel (Teapot Dome)	Petroleum Reserves 1920s	
Soil Erosion ("Dust Bowl")	Land 1933	
Reclamation (Irrigation)	Water 1950s	Open Rivers (Echo Park)

[FIGURE 3.] Hawkes's dichotomy.

Throughout most of its history, "conservation" has been a "good" word. Thus William H. Taft is reported to have said, "There are a great many people in favor of conservation, no matter what it means." In contrast, "utilitarian" and "preservationist" both have been stigmatic. In reasonable consequence, something of a struggle has gone on for ownership of "conservationist."

Quite clearly, by about 1968, the Sierra Club, emerging in strength from the successful battles for a Wilderness Act and for preservation of the Grand Canyon, had clear title to the word in the eyes of the public. The foresters had lost it. McConnell [1954] judged that this was already the case.

The Sierra Club, with 135,000 members and all of them paying enough dues to know they are members, is hardly fading away. And with scores of associated organizations competing with it for members, the movement is not disappearing. But is its attention still focused on preservation? How much of its time goes for parks, wilderness, the pure quality of natural landscape? Was the Wilderness Act perfect? Is the job done? Is it time now to turn preservationist concerns toward urban amenities, to accept the dicta of public health and physical scientists regarding air quality and water quality? Is the energy crisis a preservationist concern? Should the Sierra Club prosecute this as its first order of business?

Recall Hawkes's image of a utilitarian concern for natural resources gradually giving way to a preservationist concern for the landscape. Was this to be the whole of the story? Preservation to triumph after generations of contention and then to ride off with the enchanted princess to live happily ever after? Or is there more? Two new images come to mind.

First, imagine a host of issues, each with deep roots in the past, gradually approaching a maturity which brings them into the public eye. Forget about the classical dichotomy. Think of a conservation movement concerned with the problems of society's relations to the land. Think also of the resource institutions developed in a land which everyone agreed was infinite and of the strain of modifying them for a new and very finite situation, one of resource shortage on every side. Think of the conservation movement as a catalyst helping to move the society out of its traditional view of infinity, helping to change institutions into a condition compatible with the finite limits of natural resources. Think of the movement, alternatively, as a prod, a goad, trying to drive those who profit from archaic institutions into an acceptance of a reality which has changed.

It will be a problem to identify the significant issues which are arising, and even more of a problem to establish when they began. The accompanying table [Table 1] can be only preliminary, a basis for discussion, a hint to urge better analysts, better historians to join the inquiry. The table is arranged in columns in an effort to show a most terse chronology (persons, events, books, organizations) of several strands of concern for environmental matters. Population is put on the left side, not because it is the oldest (although it may be) but to show some of its relation to conservation, which still appears to be the central idea. (A two-dimensional table is not always adapted to show complex relations, but it will have to do for now.) To the right of conservation, other environmental issues are listed. They do become younger in progression to the right, but only in very broad terms. Did concern for wildlife begin with Audubon, after Malthus, or with St. Francis, before Malthus; and was Malthus first in his field?

The intent of the table is to support an argument that the conservation movement has gradually expanded its interests, embraced new matters, affiliated with others. Some related affiliations have been quite explicit, as that of Planned Parenthood with world population. The former is almost purely a social movement without environmental implications, the latter is strongly environmental in its broad concerns, but dominantly utilitarian. Accordingly, it has been comfortable to place it next to the utilitarian side of conservation. To bring in wildlife as a separate strand may generate protests that John Muir was intensely involved with all of nature. Nevertheless, it is the Audubon Society which stands out for its defense of the snowy egret. The Sierra Club's concern is much more recent and still decidedly minor. In similar fashion, the Audubon Society has broadened its concerns to include many issues which, earlier, were only the Sierra Club's. The documentation becomes more sparse to the right, not because nothing could be cited, but because what can be cited becomes obscure.

Some entries bridge two columns because, in my judgment, both concerns are major. Some [are] extended, by an arrow, into other columns to indicate an associated but hardly major concern.

Finally, a heavy line passing across and up and down the table indicates when the issues, the movements, the organizations became part of the conservation movement, viewed quite broadly. No one has

[TABLE 1.] Anatomy and Chronology of Recent Environmental Issues:
A Platform for Argumentation

When (by decades)	Population		Conservation		Outdoor recreation	Wildlife	
	Family planning	"Population problems"	Develop (useful)	Preserve (beautiful)		Management	Preservation (endangered species)
1800	MALTHUS (1) (1766–1834)						
1830							AUDUBON (2) (1785–1851)
1840				THOREAU (3) (1817–1862)			
1850							
1860				G. P. MARSH (4) (1801–1882)			
1870				American Forestry Association (1875)			
1880							
1890				National forests	Sierra Club (1892)		BURROUGHS (5) (1837–1921)
1900			PINCHOT (1865–1946) T. ROOSEVELT (1858–1919) Reclamation	MUIR (1858–1914)			Snowy egret LACEY (1841–1913) National Audubon Society (1905)
1910	Family Planning Association (1918)			Country-Life Movement Save-the-Redwoods League (1918) National Parks and Conservation Association (1919)			HORNADAY (6) (1854–1937) E. T. SETON (7) (1860–1946)
1920	SANGER (1883–1956)		Petroleum Pulpwood			National Wildlife Refuges (1929–1966)	
1930			TVA Soil H. H. BENNETT (8) (1881–1960)	ROBERT MARSHALL (1901–1939) Wilderness Society (1935)		National Wildlife Federation (1936)	J. N. ("DING") DARLING (1876–1962) Trumpeter swan
1940		VOGT (9) (1902–1968)	Nature Conservancy (1946) Conservation Foundation (1948)				International Union for Conservation of Nature (1948)
1950		FAIRFIELD OSBORN (11) (1887–1969) HARRISON BROWN (12) Multiple use irrigation Resources for the Future (1952)		Echo Park	Mission 66		Whooping crane
1960				ZAHNISER (1906–1964) Grand Canyon BROWER UDALL Redwood	Outdoor Recreation Resources Review Commission (1962)		World Wildlife Fund (1961) California condor
		EHRLICH (14)	Trans-Alaska Pipeline (TAPS)	National Park Alaska WAYBURN		?	
		ZPG (1969)		Friends of the Earth (1969)			
1970			Energy crisis MEADOWS et al. (15)	Off-road vehicles			

[Persons are indicated by CAPITAL LETTERS; organizations by underlining; symbols by regular type; triumphs by *; disasters by **; and books by *italics*, identified with author by number in parentheses.]

Ecology (land ethic)	Environmental contamination	Urban amenities	Steady state		Happenings along the way
			Economy	Communication	
					(1) *An Essay on the Principle of Population* (1798)
					(2) *Birds of America* (1826–1838)
←——————→			J. S. MILL (1806–1873)		(3) *Walden* (1854)
		OLMSTED (1822–1903)			
←——————→					(4) *Man and Nature* (1864)
					Yellowstone National Park* (1872)
					Buffalo**
					(5) *Wake Robin* (1871)
					Forest Reserves Act (1891)
					Lacey Act* (1900)
					Reclamation Act (1902)
					Murder of G. Bradley on Audubon Refuge**
					Antiquities Act* (1906)
					(6) *Vanishing Wildlife* (1913)
					Passenger Pigeon**
					(7) *Two Little Savages* (1903)
					Hetch Hetchy**
					Fur Seal Treaty* (1911)
					National Parks Act (1916)
					Migratory Bird Treaty* (1916)
·········· ←——————→					(8) *Soil Conservation* (1939)
LEOPOLD (10) (1886– ·····1948)					(9) *Road to Survival* (1948)
					(10) *A Sand County Almanac* (1949)
		Radio-activity			(11) *The Limits of the Earth* (1953)
					(12) *The Challenge of Man's Future* (1954)
←——————→	RACHEL CARSON (13) (1907–1964) Scientists' Institute for Public Information (1963)				(13) *Silent Spring* (1962)
					Glen Canyon Dam**
					Wilderness Act (1964)
					Public Land Law Review Commission** (1964)
					Blue whale (?)**
					(14) *The Population Bomb* (1968)
					Hardin's "Tragedy of the Commons"* (1968)
G. HARDIN ··············	{ Air and water quality Oil spills	MCHARG	MISHAN H. E. DALY	Who and when ?	National Environmental Protection Act* (1970)
·········· ←——————→					Torrey Canyon** (1967)
					Ivory billed woodpecker (?)**
					(15) *The Limits to Growth* (1972)

to agree with this representation. Hopefully, though, it will stimulate amendment, correction, contradiction.

So much for the first of the two images of what has happened and is happening.

The second image goes back to Hawkes and is an image of successive environmental issues arising and being dealt with by all of the concerned components of the society: individuals and their conservation and environmental organizations, government agencies, and the communications medium. A crucial question, not attacked in this paper, is what determines the paramount issue of the day: Whence comes the viable seed, where is the nutritious soil from which an issue will grow to fill the public eye, to engage the decision making forces of the society, and to be resolved? It is an old question, much discussed [Glacken, 1967,] and cannot be summarized here.

One element of the second image is the role of the mass media in the new growth of public issues; of these, television is probably most influential. Each of three major networks, nationally competing for advertisers' dollars, is continually seeking out the next issue which will be paramount in the public's attention. To be the first to identify it means growth in advertising revenues. To fail to join in support of a winner means excessive, unneeded loss of revenue. So, each of the networks is engaged in an unending search for the next issue which will draw the attention of all the nation. When one has found such a winner, the others immediately join in. This stabilizes the gain and starts the search for the next winner. As we are drawn ever more rapidly from one issue to its successor, our attention span diminishes. Small wonder that the "year of the ecology" passed by so fast. One wonders if the "energy crisis" will make it through the spring and the cherry blossoms. What's next?

Another element of the second image is also basic to the entire problem. Most of the members of most of the world's societies have been poor for a long time. Their concern has been for the traditional essentials: food, clothing, and shelter. Competition for them has been institutionalized in the market place. These things have a price, they are "in the economy"; they are "utilitarian."

With the rise of a new affluence in the late 19th and especially in the mid-20th century, economic pressures have slackened on numerous people. Quite commonly they have responded to this slackening of pressures by an increasing affinity for the natural environment. These are the people who formed the preservation wing of the conservation movement.

These values, utilitarian and preservation, remain incommensurable; they cannot be compared on a common scale [see the preceding selection in this section]. Such incommensurability of values is not new, nor is it unique. "Ye cannot serve God and mammon." The division of the conservation movement into two parts, is, therefore, hardly surprising.

It follows that so long as we were poor, conservation should have been utilitarian; when we became rich, it should have become preservationist. And it should remain so until we become poor again. What in fact is happening? Is it becoming utilitarian; are we becoming poor? Is smog prevention preservationist, or utilitarian? Is the energy crisis a preservationist concern for wild beaches or a utilitarian concern for warm houses?

Or is it rather that the two sorts of problems are overlapping, becoming confused with each other? I am driven back to another conclusion of my earlier paper [see the preceding selection] that in an empty land competition for natural resources is inconsequential; in contrast, in a full land competition is universal and diverse. An example in that paper was the boundaries of Yellowstone, which were chosen offhand and without controversy, in contrast to the incredible quarrel over the boundaries of the North Cascades National Park. What we are seeing today is that each conservation issue has ramifications clearly recognizable as both preservationist and utilitarian.

The preservationist wing could, of course, remain purist and fight these issues solely on their preservationist merits, but it finds it tactically to its advantage to fight on all fronts. The other face of the coin is that it is being drawn out of its own territory and into quarrels which have only ancillary relations to preservationist issues. So long as such quarrels are minor components, it can be argued that the forest will not be lost sight of (pun intended). But if the utilitarian components become dominant, then principles may be forgotten, entanglements may become unending, objectives may become confused. We may find ourselves simply pulling chestnuts out of the fire.

[Figure 4] ends this paper. It endeavors to suggest, as a continuation of Hawkes's thesis, that now the conservation battlefront is across

Utilitarian Concern (Pinchot)	Resource (and Time)	Preservation Concern (Muir)
Timber	Public Land for National Forests 1897	Mountain Landscapes
Urban Water (San Francisco)	Public Land for Watershed 1901–1912	National Parks (Hetch Hetchy)
Fuel (Teapot Dome)	Petroleum Reserves 1920s	
Soil Erosion ("Dust Bowl")	Land 1933	
Reclamation (Irrigation)	Water 1950s	Open Rivers (Echo Park)
		(Lake Powell)
Hydropower	Water 1960s	(Grand Canyon)
Starvation 1960s	Population	Crowding 1950s
Managed 1950s	Wildlife	Endangered 1960s
"Mass Recreation" (National Seashores)	Outdoor Recreation	Wilderness Act 1956–1964
Smog, Water Pollution NEPA 1970s	Environmental Contamination	Bird Kills 1962
"Energy Crisis" 1970s	Land–Coastlines	Power Plant Sites 1960s

[FIGURE 4.] An extension of Hawkes's thesis.

the board. More and more, it begins on the preservationist side and swings quickly across into utilitarian issues. Where are today's successors to the confrontations of the sixties? Where is today's Grand Canyon, today's Redwood National Park?

GAME THEORY, STRATEGY, AND GAMESMANSHIP ON THE COLORADO

In Part Five of this book, several selections explored the issue of water development on the Colorado River. Those papers focused on water both as a "useful" resource, for potable use, for irrigation, for hydroelectric power, and as a "beautiful" resource, for wildland uses. In this paper, Luten's emphasis was different: How does the history of dam proposals relate to the conservation movement, its leaders and its opponents, its policies and its tactics? Luten traced and analyzed the workings of conservationists and their adversaries in the recurrent plans to fill the canyons of the Colorado with reservoirs. His questioning of the motivations and the strategies of participants in these battles illustrates a type of analysis that can be applied to other resource issues. Moreover, Luten, even though obviously supportive of keeping wild the undammed portions of the Colorado River, did not blindly endorse the strategies of the conservationists. As in the preceding paper, he once again questioned the course of the conservation movement. It "might pull itself together and decide what it does want, what is doomed, what it can expect to save, and how to go about it. It can devise strategy, tactics, and trade-offs. Or can it?" The question has continued in Luten's subsequent writings, and it remains unanswered today.

Passage of the Newlands Act in 1902 changed management of water for irrigation in the arid Southwest from small, private undertakings to

Paper presented at the annual meeting of the Association of American Geographers, Salt Lake City, UT, April 1977.

federal projects. The former were often underfinanced, sometimes ill-conceived, incompetently built, but may have been highly profitable when well done. The latter began small but have grown in imaginative scope, in engineering scale, and [in] administrative competence, seemingly without limit. Have these federal reclamation projects at the same time become progressively less attractive economically? Would not, almost automatically, the most attractive projects have been the first undertaken? Not necessarily; the economies of scale in water management so far outrun those in most human activities that what is worthless when small may save empires simply by being large. . . .

When postwar programs [for water developments on the Colorado River] got under way in the late 1940s, a major proposal was Echo Park Dam on the Green River, with a reservoir reaching into Dinosaur National Monument. Its ostensible purpose was to provide additional storage to permit the upper-basin [states] to meet [their] obligations [under the Colorado River Compact to deliver 75 million acre-feet of water per decade to the lower basin]. The site, at a high elevation, was chosen at least in part because evaporation losses would be less. . . .

Why could not the Compact have been modified to permit the upper basin to store some of its committed water in Lake Mead? After all, Lake Mead had proven to be more than adequate, not merely for flood control, but also for whatever providence in water conservation that might seem appropriate for the lower basin. Admittedly, discharges in excess of commitments have been made in wet years, primarily to take advantage of opportunity for power generation at Hoover Dam. But banking of upper-basin water in Lake Mead would have increased the power head at least marginally, would have increased evaporation losses minimally, and [would have done this] at a trivial capital expense.

Instead, they went for Echo Park Dam with the argument of reduced evaporation losses. The conservation movement, at that time, was little concerned for the fate of the river. But the drowning of Hetch Hetchy Valley in Yosemite 40 years earlier had sensitized them to invasions of National Parks by water development projects. As one element of their campaign against Echo Park Dam, they added trips on the Yampa River, an involved tributary, to their budget of outings. Experience had already told them that their legislative campaigns were more effective with a letter-writing cadre that had actually seen and been in the places at issue. The clincher, though, was the success of

David Brower of the Sierra Club in entangling the Bureau's spokesmen in their own evaporation calculations at Congressional hearings. Committee members lost patience and the dam lost their support. Such obfuscation of an issue is an old legal and legislative trick and a fairly dependable one, but it was being used by the "wrong" side.

Frustrated at Echo Park, the Bureau of Reclamation turned their sights downstream and did secure authorization for Glen Canyon Dam, and, more, raised its height (to "High Glen Canyon Dam") so that it would be sure to invade, conspicuously, Rainbow Bridge National Monument. Did they wish to establish a precedent; did they wish to reject any possibility that Echo Park would be a precedent against their invasion of the National Park System? They justified the higher dam on the score that extra storage would help meet the commitments of a dwindling river.

The Sierra Club may have responded too slowly to the Glen Canyon invasion. They fought it vigorously in Congressional hearings; they initiated raft trips through it; they focused the big guns of their exhibit format books on the matter. But Eliot Porter's [1963] title was telling: [Glen Canyon:] The Place No One Knew. And so, despite all opposition, Glen Canyon Dam was authorized and has been built.

During the quarrel, the Bureau mousetrapped the conservation movement in spectacular fashion. In authorizing the dam, Congress had specified that the reservoir should not invade Rainbow Bridge National Monument. The Bureau assented and said, yes, that for four million dollars it could build an interesting little backward-facing dam and pumping plant to keep the reservoir out of the monument and to pump such water as comes down the small side canyon up into the reservoir. This was probably a fiction from the beginning because, while the ordinary flow is trivial, on the rare occasions of flash floods the flow would probably far exceed pumping capacity and the monument's part of the canyon would be well flooded (and perhaps the pumping plant as well). The Bureau did not ask for an initial appropriation for this task, which was perhaps reasonable; it could well wait until the reservoir began to fill. Meanwhile, though, the Bureau did encourage the conservation movement and its engineers to explore alternative sites, and thereby to save some more of the spectacular side canyons (Aztec and Bridge Canyons) by moving the restraining dam site downstream—and at the same time increasing its size and cost. They got it up to 20 million dollars. In fact, the Bureau never did ask for an appropriation and Congress never considered one. Finally the Sierra Club sued to enjoin the Secretary of the Interior from closing the diversion tunnels at Glen Canyon Dam because the expressed will of Congress against invasion of the monument was not going to be complied with. The Bureau replied that Congress had changed its mind by not appropriating funds for the restraining dam, whether four or 20 million dollars, and they made it stick in court. The Supreme Court refused to override a circuit court decision that the Sierra Club, "having no economic interest in the matter," had no standing in a Federal Court. They could, yes, have sued in a Utah or Arizona court, but those courts, whether or not confused by jurisdiction (the dam was in Arizona, the monument in Utah), would not have been confused by a preference for aesthetics over economics. Parenthetically, a comparison of the Supreme Court's 1962 attitude with its attitude expressed on Mineral King, ten years later, is dramatic. In 1972, the Court invited the Sierra Club to resubmit its case on the score that its members had important, if not economic, interests in Mineral King.

So the Bureau got its Glen Canyon Dam and its invasion of a monument. But with them it got a rather new little hornet's nest, or was it a bonus that might better have remained hidden? [L. B.] Leopold [1959] and Langbein [1959] . . . proved (at least to the satisfaction of many) that Glen Canyon Dam, rather than increasing the amount of water in the River, would instead, by its evaporation losses, cost more in long-term supply for downstream than it would be likely to store in any excessively wet years—storage that could not be held in Lake Mead. The Bureau took this blow with equanimity. Similarly, Floyd Dominy, Reclamation Commissioner, defended the Bureau against charges, stemming in part from Eliot Porter's [1963 book], that they had ruined a beautiful canyon. He published a handsomely illustrated brochure, *Lake Powell, Jewel of the Colorado*, so stuffed with pious platitudes it has come to be called *The Book of Dominy*. It argued they had created a beautiful lake; ergo, the benefit–cost ratio must be high.

Presently, the Bureau announced two new dams, at Marble Gorge and Bridge Canyon. The latter, with its deep narrow reservoir, would invade Grand Canyon National Park—but just a little, say 15 miles, and would be out of sight of the visitors on the rim. The Sierra Club countered that the Grand Canyon goes from Lee's Ferry to the Grand

Wash Cliffs and that both dams would be *in* the Grand Canyon. Let the other side defend itself against charges of wholesale invasion of a national park. (This, in passing, is just one of a host of examples of Vale's Law, which, stated with excessive bluntness, is: "Everyone in a conservation controversy, whether amateur or professional, whether pro or con, is lying as much as he can get away with." And in many other controversies, as well.)

The Bureau of Reclamation defended the two dams—first on the score that they were needed to store water for the Central Arizona Project, the facilities that were to get river water to Phoenix and Tucson, where irrigators had been overdrawing the Salt River aquifers for far too many years. When it was rejoined that these had effectively no storage capacity, they were too narrow, the Bureau conceded without embarrassment that this was so, but that they were needed to generate hydropower to pump water from Lake Havasu up into Arizona. But the generators were designed for peaking power, and the Central Arizona Project pumps might well be used mostly off-peak. So next, Dominy conceded the dams were really a cash register to generate funds to buy power for the pumping. The next counterargument suggested by the conservation movement was that the electricity could be generated more cheaply by building a fossil fuel plant at Lake Havasu. That plant has been built. (It [receives] coal from the Black Mesa, from the mine that has the conservation movement up in arms.)

Somewhere along here, I had a personal and private debate with Mr. Dominy (he had had, I think, somewhat the best of me in an earlier television debate in Denver) over the uses of water in central Arizona. He said it was a grand project. I said Arizona had only a tenth the cropland of the small state of Indiana and the water would make up only a part of the deficiency. I was quite right; Indiana, the smallest of the 48 states outside the lands of the original colonies, is a good deprecatory example—no one in our part of the world has much image of Indiana. Dominy conceded this, but said that Arizona was important because it produced "protective foods." I knew what he meant— fruits and vegetables—but I had to go to *Agricultural Statistics* to find that Arizona's croplands were then half in alfalfa, a quarter in cotton, and only the last quarter in fruits and vegetables. He had won again. The moral is: Know all the numbers before you begin to argue; principles will not suffice.

Finally, Marble Gorge Dam was dropped; there may have been

some real problems with leaky footings there, and the focus was on Bridge Canyon, renamed Hualapai Dam to throw the hounds off the trail—at least those that trailed by sight, not scent. The Sierra Club and most of the conservation movement were adamant; the National Wildlife Federation was undecided because, after all, the Bureau promised some magnificent fish in the new lakes. Perhaps the Federation was just learning that all those people who had become members by buying a dollar's worth of wildlife stamps were bird lovers not fishermen.

But at this point, the entire business came to a halt. Senator Jackson (Democrat from the state of Washington), Chairman of the Senate Interior Committee, made it plain that as long as he held that post, and he proposed to do so for a while, there would not be so much as hearings on more dams. For his stand, he received the John Muir Award as a major conservationist at the Sierra Club's Eleventh Wilderness Conference in 1969.

Why, why should all of these things happen? Well, there had been talk, quite a lot of it, of bringing a little Columbia Basin water down into the Colorado to bring it up to the hallowed 15 million acre-feet. And, yes, all of the hydropower plants were designed as peaking units, which is to say they had generating capacity for a lot more water than the river could supply. The Northwest had made it abundantly clear that it was not interested in such diversions; they would be from the upper Snake River, at least at first. Senator Jackson was no dog in a manger; he offered the arid Southwest all the water they wanted if only they would take it from the mouth of the Columbia. Some have argued that such transport might be feasible; I do not know. But no one was interested. Why not?

It never came out in the arguments, but the blunt fact is that water at 3000 feet elevation in the Snake River Plain is worth, with peaking energy at six mills per kilowatt-hour, $18 per acre-foot more than water at the mouth of the Columbia, *provided* that a completed staircase of hydropower plants down the Colorado River exists with excess capacity sufficient to extract all of that energy from the new water as it proceeds down the river. The incremental hydropower income from, say, three million acre-feet annually might come close to $50 million, enough at prevailing low interest rates to pay for an extensive diversion system. But every step that is missing from the staircase means that much less premium for high-altitude water.

Somewhere along the way, probably quite early, Senator Jackson had understood this. The Sierra Club got the credit—and the blame (they lost their income tax exemption)—but it was only a smokescreen. Senator Jackson got the conservation award; did he really deserve it? Was he doing more than protecting his regional interests?

Things have been quiet since then. Has the game ended? Or is it only halftime? What will be the next move by the Bureau? For interbasin transfer or for the Continental Water Plan? Is the age of growth coming to an end and is the time for NAWAPA, the North American Water and Power Alliance, now or never? It does seem to be raising its ugly Medusa head again.

Let me note some new elements: Energy costs are rising, for the first time; farming is up, not depressed; California has a severe drought. On the other side, public works discount rates are way up, and President Carter is down on water development for the moment. (Parenthetically, could he have proposed suspension of the Central Arizona Project in part to show that even Congressman Udall, the darling of the conservation movement, becomes a developer when his own turf faces browning?)

We might propose an answer if only we could answer some earlier questions:

1. Why Glen Canyon Dam instead of a [Colorado River] Compact amendment?
2. Why persistent proposals to invade national monuments, if not in anticipation of invasion of Grand Canyon National Park?
3. Why a built-in delay of crisis at Lee's Ferry, if not to give time for Congress to respond?
4. Why the early version of the full staircase and excess generating capacity if no vision of water imports from the Columbia Basin?
5. With so many hidden targets in the past, can we believe there are no more?

But we cannot answer these questions.

On the other side, the conservation movement, now called the environmental movement, might pull itself together and decide what it does want, what is doomed, what it can expect to save, and how to go about it. It can devise strategy, tactics, and trade-offs. Or can it? Can it spread itself over parks and wilderness, [over] wildlife and endangered species, [over] outdoor recreation, over rivers and dams, over energy from nuclear power, through pipelines and oil spills to coal stripping, over environmental contamination, and still act on population growth, steady-state economics, urban blight, and social reform, while defending itself against charges of elitism? Can it ever take the offensive on battle terrain of its own choosing?

Is it doomed by the nature of the game always to fight the battles forced on it and to fight only with troops that arise as if from dragons' teeth sown by an adversary?

THE IMMIGRATION BOMB:
AN ADVERTISEMENT, COMMENTS,
A SUPPORTIVE LETTER,
AND LUTEN'S RESPONSE

The *Yodeler* is the local monthly tabloid of the San Francisco Bay Chapter of the Sierra Club. In the April 1979 issue, the group Zero Population Growth (ZPG) paid for advertising space to run a 19-word message asking for support to help stop illegal immigration to California and the rest of the United States. The *Yodeler*'s advertising manager accepted the ad, but wrote a short article that expressed disagreement with ZPG's views; the following month, a reader wrote in support of the article's anti-ZPG stance. In June, Luten responded to both critics of the ad. (The names of the advertising manager and the letter writer are omitted here.)

Many conservationists often see their concerns as synonymous with traditional progressive or liberal politics. Yet, through the years, many leaders, and undoubtedly many more members, of conservation groups have not come from the left side of the political spectrum. Many have, of course, and perhaps more have than have not. But the motivations for preserving wild nature and for prudent resource use are varied. While the goals of an environmental group may be coincident with those of a liberal political

Reprinted by permission from *Yodeler*, April 1979, p. 10; May 1979, p. 14; and June 1979, p. 11.

group in many issues, the purposes of the two groups are not identical. Luten suggested in his letter, in fact, that the two viewpoints have a fundamental ideological difference.

The worry over illegal immigration as an impediment to a stable population is not idle. Data on numbers of illegal aliens are understandably uncertain, but if the frequently used number of one to one and a half million is close to the truth, it would equal the number of people added to the U. S. population by births each year.

THE ADVERTISEMENT

Concerned about California's population growth?
Help stop illegal immigration.
Write ZPG-Livermore,
P.O. Box 575, Livermore, Calif. 94550

THE ADVERTISING MANAGER'S COMMENTS

On this page of the *Yodeler* is an ad on illegal immigration purchased by ZPG-Livermore. As advertising manager I am running this ad, but I want to offer, as well, the other side of this issue.

ZPG advocates stringent measures to keep out immigrants as a way of controlling U.S. population. They propose population control on a nation by nation basis, as in President Carter's request for an additional $100 million to further militarize the United States/Mexico border. ZPG says, "Funding for the Immigration Border Patrol is . . . grossly inadequate. . . ." But is military action an acceptable form of population control?

According to the U.S. government and ZPG the cause of immigration is overpopulation in countries like Mexico, and Haiti. ZPG proposes U.S. aid to Mexico and an easing of trade restrictions on Mexican exports to the United States. In fact, according to the North American Congress on Latin America, unemployment in Mexico is 40%–50% because Mexican and transnational corporations (most United States based) have a vested interest in exploiting Mexico's poor workers by encouraging this desperate employment problem. Mexican farmers cannot compete with transnational agribusiness, which is literally pushing Mexicans off their land and in search of work in the United States. Most economic aid and export rules benefit corporations. Until Mexico's people can take economic control from the corporations they will continue to suffer from this problem.

It is also disappointing that ZPG discusses population control in the Third World without mentioning the deplorable practice of forced sterilization.

The Sierra Club has not taken a position similar to ZPG's on (illegal) immigration. The Club firmly supports slowing population growth to zero. I hope Sierra Club members will consider carefully that the same governmental and corporate policies that threaten our environment are causing much of the immigration problem worldwide. . . .

The Bay Chapter has declined to embrace ZPG's position on illegal immigration but does favor world population growth slowed to zero.

THE LETTER IN SUPPORT

1. I wouldn't have seen the ad if you hadn't commented. Thanks for commenting!

2. ZPG evidently believes that any means necessary to achieve zero population growth is ok. Does the Sierra Club? Essentially ZPG here appeals to racism–brown peril. I wonder what the next ad will appeal to? Does the *Yodeler* have a process for screening ads? Does this include consideration of sexism, racism, militarism, and other more specifically conservation of nature for human enjoyment? If not, please institute such.

LUTEN'S LETTER

[The] advertising manager accepted an ad from ZPG (*Yodeler*, April, p. 10) and then spent twice the space (presumably free) attacking it. Now comes [a reader] (*Yodeler*, May, p. 14) in her support. Both attacks are capricious and malicious.

[The reader] charges ZPG with "appeals to racism–brown peril." No basis for this exists in the ad. In fact, ZPG simply asks for enforcement of a law. Do [the advertising manager] and [the reader] oppose enforcement of laws? Do they believe one should choose what laws to obey? Does this principle apply to each of us? To individuals, to corporations? To speeding, to taxes, to illegal immigration, to rape, to murder? Will they, perhaps, set themselves up as a commission to advise us on what laws we should, severally and collectively, obey? (Before they put themselves in Henry Thoreau's position and claim conscience against an immoral law, let them read and reflect on at least the first paragraph of "Civil Disobedience.")

Both writers stigmatize ZPG by epithet. Easy incitement by stigmatic epithet has plagued the Sierra Club for decades. Carl Pope learned recently on television how hard it is to argue against the spurious charges that the Club is "elitist." Is this a game at which the Sierra Club can win?

[The advertising manager] comes up with [the] following, if I understand her: United States-based transnational corporations force Mexicans off their lands and into illegal immigration to the United States in search of (presumably exploitive) employment. It seems a complex conspiracy. It can be extended to argue that its purpose is to destroy the [United Farm Workers] and to compete elsewhere unfairly with Americans (because, vulnerable, these people work for illegally low wages). Does [the advertising manager] support that? She demands, perhaps revolution, perhaps reform in Mexico; does it improve either to have their safety valve of emigration, [which] removes the most enterprising, the most desperate of Mexico's people from the Mexican political scene? Is she then a reformer or a closet reactionary?

The ad did not focus on illegal immigration from Mexico, but that *is* a large and probably major fraction of the total. [The manager] asks, "[I]s military action an acceptable form of population control?" In fact, the Mexican border is the most porous in the developed world. She could better protest every nonmontane border in Europe, and she might have cited the Berlin Wall, the 38th parallel in Korea, the Chinese–Russian border. Many of them involve societies commonly extolled to us as progressive and humane compared to our exploitive, conspiratorial society. In fact, the U.S. government has proposed no machine guns, no mine fields, not even a fence the length of the Mexican–United States border, but fences only where uncontrolled traffic is densest. What would [the advertising manager] propose, traffic lights?

When [the manager] charges ZPG with advocating population "control," she may be close to revealing a totalitarian set to her own thinking. ZPG has asked Americans to recognize the limits of this land and to limit family size in order that future generations may enjoy a rich life. With sieves for borders and with hundreds of millions of poor people around the world seeing merits in attributes of American life that many Americans see as curses, family limitation by Americans will be futile.

The day is past, unfortunately, when emigration from poor lands to the empty parts of the globe can accelerate the demographic transition—the change from high birth and death and growth rates, misery, and no education to low birth and death and growth rates, reasonable living conditions, and good education. There are no empty parts. From now on, the problems cannot be solved by export; they must be solved where they exist.

It is a liberal viewpoint that immigration laws are immoral; it is also a liberal viewpoint that the world is infinite and, if society were properly organized, that no difficulties should be found in accommodating all of its people. If this is true, why is there need for conservation organizations; why cannot we all focus our attentions on social reform? But, in fact, the polarization between conservation versus exploitation (of resources and landscape) does not precisely parallel the polarity between political liberalism and conservatism. A conservationist (or an exploiter!) cannot find his guidance from the latter polarity.

Finally, [the reader] asks if the *Yodeler* has a process for screening (objectionable) ads. The answer is yes. [The advertising manager], by devoting twice as much free space to countering the paid ad, will insure that all advertisers ask her approval before venturing cash for space in the *Yodeler*. But is "advertising manager" the proper title for a censor?

WHO OWNS THE ATOM?

The preceding selection suggested the importance of political progressivism as a factor in population policy within the contemporary conservation movement. In fact, the populist attitude pervades many conservation issues, including water allocation (see "The 160-Acre Limit" in Part Five of this book), food production, federal land policy, and wildland recreation, as well as population and energy. Historians have identified progressive motivations for the institutionalization of American conservation early in this century, but the distinctiveness of the thread is often lost in modern conservation controversies.

At the time when Luten wrote his letter in defense of ZPG, he was apparently thinking about the relationship between conservation and liberal social doctrine more generally, because he published this short article in the same year. In this paper, he wondered about the role of progressive political sentiments in conservation issues over energy development, notably hydroelectricity and nuclear power. My comments preceding the exchange over the ZPG ad are thus equally appropriate here.

The American landscape is always changing. The natural landscape dwindles and is infringed in uncountable ways; the cultural landscape expands bit by bit, changes, evolves, and commonly, but not always, becomes more complex.

Some changes can be seen only from the air, such as center-pivot, irrigated fields, those round fields most often seen from planes over the North Platte River valley while flying from Chicago to San Francisco. Visible from both air and land are the gigantic, natural draft, hyperbolic cooling towers of great inland power plants. Some are nuclear. The twin towers of the Rancho Seco power plant of the Sacramento Municipal Utility District, about 25 miles southeast of Sacramento near the small town of Ione, are easily the most conspicuous element

Reprinted by permission from *Landscape*, 1979, 23(3): 1–2.

against the horizon for a score of miles. And, by now, everyone in this nation has seen the twin towers of the two nuclear units at Three Mile Island. The acronym "TMI" joined the language in the spring of 1979 as rapidly as "Elvis Presley," two decades earlier.

The "incident at Three Mile Island" will be the focus of serious inquiry by those concerned with hazard perception. But that should not deter us from preliminary speculation. The expanding literature in this field was ably initiated by the geographers of the University of Chicago, notably Gilbert White, Robert Kates, and Ian Burton. Lamentably, one of the reasons for its growth is that the investigator doesn't really need to know anything about reality; the issue is not what is, but what people perceive to be. An investigator in this field must be an able interrogator and analyst of questionnaires but need not know nor be concerned with the truth of the matter.

Environment recently published a series of papers on perception of hazard. I haven't been able to get my hands on all of them, but from what I have seen, I can only conclude that even the authors are afraid to come to terms with reality. Instead they elect to compare the perceptions of the common person with those of "experts." From what little I know, I am prepared to take exception to some of the experts' judgments.

One of the articles [Slovic, Fischhoff, & Lichtenstein, 1979] gives expert opinion that 100 deaths a year stem from nuclear power, and 50,000 from automobiles. The first number suggests the experts have included for nuclear power fatalities all deaths upstream of the power plant, inasmuch as no deaths directly attributable to operation of nuclear power plants can yet be established.

In contrast, the number of deaths for automobiles suggests that it begins and ends with traffic deaths—that it does not include deaths in the manufacture of automobiles, in antecedents to that industry, in the construction of highways, or in the petroleum industry from Tehran and Prudhoe Bay to a service station attendant murdered during a gasoline high-jacking.

Regardless of details, it is abundantly clear the American public is terrified of nuclear power, even with zero directly attributable deaths, and is completely unconcerned with another very American hazard, the automobile, [which] has thus far claimed 2.1 million lives and will claim another 200 this weekend. Three Mile Island may have terminated the growth of nuclear power in this country; it might even lead to termination of generation of nuclear power, although this does not seem likely at the moment.

Why should this be? A common, but unsatisfactory, answer is that we cannot escape nuclear hazards, whereas the use of the automobile is voluntary. If we use automobiles, we should accept the hazards. But it is unrealistic to say that in the United States we can do without automobiles. They have shaped American cities and the American landscape. For better or worse Americans are stuck with them and their hazards. It would be easier to move and start a new life 500 miles away from a nuclear power plant.

I could propose, as an explanation of the different perceptions, that when someone dies in an automobile accident we can see the relation between cause and effect. A victim may be guiltless. If an oncoming car crosses the center line and hits you head on, there is little you can do to avoid it. Nonetheless, it is clear why the victim died, blameless or not. He just happened to be in the wrong place at the wrong time.

In contrast, with deaths from radioactivity it is utterly unclear who will die, or when, or even in large degree, why. We see numbers saying released radiation and radioactive material at TMI may lead to augmented cancer deaths of perhaps one to ten individuals. But who will that one be? And how will we ever know that the cause was the TMI "excursion?" The courts will hand down judgments, but I doubt that many of us will have much confidence in the findings, whichever way they turn out.

But such an explanation of the intense awareness of nuclear hazard just doesn't fit. John Gofman has given numbers, numbers that seem plausible to me, that cancers initiated by background radiation lead to 70,000 deaths per year. A fair part of these [are] from therapeutic and diagnostic x-rays. Do we shy away from them? Not very much. Some 700 deaths should be experienced by air travelers, because cosmic radiation is more intense at 35,000 feet. However, we are nowhere near a steady rate from these causes because the latent period for appearance of malignancy still has decades to run. Do people ask themselves about such hazards before flying?

So, unquestionably, fear of radiation and radioactive contamination occupies a unique position in American perception of hazards.

Does it stem from the horrors of atom bombs, past and future? If so, that fear also has had a substantial latency period—one almost unique in social phenomena.

The activities of a widely ramified environmental movement are largely responsible. Their effectiveness has been compounded by the dubious scientific competence and integrity of the nuclear power research industry, the less than candid attitudes of the Atomic Energy Commission, and now [the attitudes] of the Nuclear Regulatory Commission. (If the NRC continues to find safety deficiencies in plants long since approved, what confidence can the public have that all defects have been found?)

Why should the environmental movement have turned against nuclear power? Not so long ago nuclear power was to be the savior of the environment—the way to avoid damming the beauty of America's running waters and strip mining its fruited plains. The Sierra Club did not join the attack on Pacific Gas and Electric Company's proposed nuclear power plant at Bodega Head until David Pesonen, well-nigh single-handed, had slain Goliath. Even after that, the Sierra Club was concerned only that the next site, Nipomo Dunes, had landscape values too great to be wasted on power plants. And only minority opposition was expressed within the club over the choice of the Diablo Canyon site. The two-million-kilowatt nuclear power plant there awaits only final licensing for operation.

Let me speculate about another evolutionary path for this intense opposition. Go back a century. When electricity first became useful rather than merely fascinating, what did the term "electric power" mean to the American public? Recall that this was in the early days of populist–progressive protests against monopoly, against cornering America's resources, against speculation, and against ill-gotten gain. Did it seem that whoever controlled electrical power would also have political power? The position was easily supportable, at least [until] the collapse of the Insull empire in the 1920s. The public power movement continues to affirm that privately owned power facilities [are] corrupt, and that the utilities are ogres—conspiratorial and selfish to boot.

The public power movement has a great tradition of some enormous accomplishments. Senators Robert LaFollette, George Norris, Thomas Walsh, and William Borah have figurative monuments in the Tennessee Valley Authority, Bonneville Power Authority, Rural Electrification Act, "preference power," and the close to 2000 municipal power systems in the United States. Norris Dam of the TVA system is a literal monument to Senator Norris. Progressivism, although dead as a political movement, persists as a thread in the fabric of resource management. It appeared most prominently in those decades between the two world wars.

Turning to another aspect of the public power movement, the controversy over Hetch Hetchy Valley of Yosemite National Park in the first decade of this century is an environmental milestone. San Franciscans saw the valley as a magnificent reservoir site. John Muir saw a reservoir as destruction of a vital part of the park. Perhaps a fourth of the Sierra Club defected from Muir's leadership and supported San Francisco. Early in Wilson's administration, Congressman Raker introduced a bill, which became law, permitting San Francisco to use Hetch Hetchy Valley. Some say it broke Muir's heart; he died the next year.

Much has been written about the solution and geographers have cited it repeatedly as an example of the distinction between utilitarian conservation—the Pinchot philosophy—and preservation—the Muir philosophy. Much less attention has been paid to the following language in the Raker Act: San Francisco "is prohibited from ever selling or letting to any corporation or individual, except a municipality or a municipal water district or irrigation district, the right to sell or sublet the water or electric energy. . . ." San Francisco has often been charged with ignoring this language.

Holway Jones, who wrote *John Muir and the Sierra Club* [1965], says almost nothing about the public power clause in the Raker Act and attributes opposition to Muir simply to utilitarian conservationists in San Francisco. Samuel P. Hays in *Conservation and the Gospel of Efficiency* [1959] makes little of it. But Judson King writes in *The Conservation Fight* [1959] that Congressman William Kent inserted the public power provision, that Senator Norris made his first fight for public power in the debate on this bill, that Borah supported it, and that the opposition (Muir's side) was "power interests hiding behind well-meaning nature lovers." The thread of public power progressivism stands out in the fabric of this incident.

The next issue was the Federal Power Act of 1920. Again, a bitter congressional battle preceded the vote that led to federal control over hydropower. The Tennessee Valley Authority ensued, and it, too, was bitterly controversial. The Bonneville Power Authority might have become another battleground, but World War II provided alternates, and Grand Coulee, just completed, was too helpful to be criticized.

Another confrontation occurred after World War II over control of nuclear power. Civilian control won, the military lost, and perhaps the public thought this meant nuclear power would be public power. But it became clear that although the federal government would do much of the research, the power plants would belong largely to privately owned utilities.

Perhaps it took a while for this to sink in. In California protest began in 1960, but it did not generate widespread environmental support for nearly a decade. So far as I can learn, no one objected to the Rancho Seco nuclear power plant, but, after all, it was publicly owned. Is the thread of progressivism again visible?

The Clamshell Alliance is currently thwarting construction of a privately owned plant in New Hampshire, and the Abalone Alliance is trying to keep the Diablo Canyon plant in California from operating. Is it because they are nuclear, or because they are privately owned as well as nuclear?

In contradiction to this thesis, in the 1950s David Brower aligned the Sierra Club against threats to the canyons of the Colorado: first Echo Park, then Glen Canyon, then Grand Canyon. This was pure preservation, but so far as I know public power advocates were silent. Was the thread of progressivism hidden, or is it merely an illusion?

The municipal power issue is also reappearing. Two recent efforts have been made in Berkeley to authorize condemnation of PG&E's electrical facilities in that city and to issue bonds for their purchase. And the Raker Act's long-ignored terms are being argued in San Francisco. [But all of these efforts focus only on electric power and ignore natural gas, which is also supplied by PG&E. Is PG&E simultaneously a power ogre and a friendly gas giant?]

All of this leads me to the tentative conclusion that in addition to the long-established dichotomy in the conservation movement between Pinchot's utilitarian and Muir's preservation philosophy, an additional single interest persists through the entire fabric—the interest of public power progressivism. It remains alive; intermittently it becomes vigorous; and it will continue to be heard.

SAGEBRUSH REBELLION

No issue has been of greater or more recurrent interest to the conservation movement than the management of the federal lands. Part of the reason for this preeminence is the crucial role that the federal lands play in all three major traditions in American conservation. First, they contain the country's major wild landscape reserves, and thus embody the concern for the "beautiful." Second, they include important commodity resources, such as fuels, wood, water, and forage, and therefore are often linked to questions of utilitarian "wise use." Third, their public title makes them a focus for progressive interests who see in the federal lands a desirable public ownership of resources.

Each of the three concerns has been the basis for conservation positions in battles over federal land policy. A particular policy issue, however, encompasses all three, and that issue is the transfer of federal land to state or private ownership. In this short essay, Luten discussed a recent attempt to achieve such a transfer, although he placed it in the historical context of repeated similar efforts. Luten, who in the preceding paper seemed to be wishing for a less strong focus on progressive concerns within the conservation movement, here stressed a populist attitude himself.

Our history is, as everyone should know by now, a grand record of land thievery. Once it was decided that the prior Indian owners were not really owners at all, the ambition of the Caucasian newcomers to own land simply exploded. Opening the pages of Hibbard's [*A History of the Public Land Policies*] [1924], one rarely has to read far before finding abundant reference to outrageous manifestations of this pervasive, obsessive land greed. A paraphrase of a famous verse by Ogden Nash is "Robbing is a crime/Unless you rob the government ten million at a time."

After a century of this, with only the worst or most remote Western lands unclaimed by private owners, the nation's temper changed. Gradually various bits and pieces were reserved, held back from dispo-

Reprinted by permission from *Landscape*, 1980, 24(2): 1–2.

sition into private ownership. Examples are the national parks and monuments, national forests, and Indian reservations.

In a sense these were positive reservations, established because of unique values and for particular purposes. But remaining was a vast interstitial domain—most of it arid, infertile, and with unknown mineral wealth. It was kicked around for generations and finally given to an agency set up to deal with its headaches—the Bureau of Land Management. The policy of retention did not extend to the BLM's holdings. Only within the last 20 years has the BLM's land disposal trailed off to almost nothing.

The most recent raid on the public domain was suggested by the Public Land Law Review Commission. Setting up the PLLRC was said to be the price exacted by Wayne Aspinall, then Chairman of the House Interior Committee, for letting the Wilderness Act go through. The commission proposed to dispose of much of the remaining public domain. However, the conservation movement responded so vigorously that nothing came of the PLLRC proposals. The attack may have been influential in establishing a tacit policy to hang onto all or most of the residual public domain.

But this year, with land prices galloping upward, there is a rumbling in the West. Just looking at all that public land lying around, not really belonging to anyone, not really being used (except for epidemic overgrazing), not really being managed, not really being occupied except by the outliers of a remote bureaucracy, stirs a body to action! Is it shame that raises Western blood pressures to bursting and temperatures to boiling? Is it envy of the speculative spoils in real estate going to city dudes? Is it simple admiration at the ease of looting? We cannot tell.

At any rate, the West has saddled up and is off on another raid. A few months ago the Western Region of the Council of State Governments asked Congress to force the federal government to sell all its land to state and local governments, or to private buyers. Senator Hatch of Utah (where these attitudes seem to flower best) has a bill to transfer title to the public domain from the federal to the state governments. A Utah legislative proposal would turn all BLM-managed land over to the Utah Division of State Lands. Under this legislation federal land managers who continued to protect BLM lands would be "guilty of a felony of the second degree and subject to imprisonment." Apparently this nonsense is being taken seriously in some precincts.

When, after the Constitution was ratified, the frequent business of admitting new states came up, a lot of hard bargaining took place between its residents and Congress. Sometimes the territory was desperate to become a state. At other times a congressional majority was desperate to get more electoral votes.

Bargaining focused on land concessions, and the terms were written very clearly on durable paper before the deal was consummated. They are good contracts and stand up well in the courts. Some states got good deals; some, poor. But the bargainers never expected a state to get title to all the public domain within its boundaries. If Utah claims this land today, they are stealing it from absentee landlords—20 million in California, an equal number in New York, and 180 million in the other states. If their agent, the federal government, wavers for a moment, they should fire it.

LETTERS, 1979

The following two letters illustrate two points. The first letter was addressed by Luten as Treasurer of Friends of the Earth to the Executive Committee of that organization; he was submitting for their consideration a letter that he proposed to publish in the San Francisco Chronicle. Luten posed to the committee members a fundamental question about the functioning of the conservation movement—namely, how is conservation policy made? The letter is a statement of a problem, a matter to be explored by scholars but also to be wondered about by conservationists themselves.

The second letter is the one that Luten proposed to be sent to the Chronicle. In it, he questioned the near-universal condemnation by conservation organizations of President Carter's synfuel program. Luten saw the conservationist position as a knee-jerk reaction to strip mining, a stance that was both environmentally and economically "indefensible." Moreover, he linked that reaction and what he viewed as similarly unwise positions on

Unpublished letters, November 27, 1979.

related energy issues as an expression of the conservation movement's involvement with "political liberalism" in which "purely conservational objectives [have been subordinated] to conflicting liberal doctrine." Luten's worrying about the importance of populist attitudes in the conservation movement had been growing over the preceding years, judging from the previous papers, and in this letter we see a clear and direct articulation of that concern. The issue, moreover, remains significant for both students of and participants in the conservation movement. (The letter, by the way, was not submitted for publication.)

LETTER TO THE EXECUTIVE COMMITTEE, FRIENDS OF THE EARTH (FOE)

Somewhat against my judgment, [I have been] persuaded . . . to send a copy of a proposed letter to the *San Francisco Chronicle* for your reaction. By publication of this letter, I had hoped to draw attention of executive committee members and staff of FOE to certain by-laws:

> Art. IV, Sect. 1: The management . . . shall be vested in a board of directors . . .
> Art. IV, Sect. 13: The board . . . may designate . . . an executive committee . . . [which] may exercise all powers of the board between [board] meetings.

To the best of my knowledge, the Executive Committee has only once tried to set conservation policy (bowhead whale, 1977), only to have it largely ignored. Further, so far as I know, the Executive Committee (or Board) has never made a general delegation of authority on conservation policy. And yet surely policy exists. Who has set it? The answer is complex and not easily found.

Publication of the [proposed] letter before consultation would have left me defending a tactically secure position: When questioned, "By what right does the treasurer presume to set policy," the answer is, easily, "Is such action any different from innumerable actions by president, staff, NMA [*Not Man Apart*, the FOE newsletter], book authors which in one fashion or another end up as FOE policy?"

Now, instead, I shall be taxed on the details of what I argue for. I am much less confident of being able to persuade you of my view on national energy policy than I am of persuading you that it is appropriate for the Executive Committee to set conservation policy for FOE. So, let us debate the latter first, at our next meeting.

Before debating the former issue, please think carefully about how our conservation policy has been established. Who are we following? Who has made the decisions that we now accept as gospel? My own response is that to an unhappily large degree we are following any self-appointed guru, any self-anointed expert who can gain public attention. And, in view of the environmental incompetence of those who open the gates to public attention, TV and radio newscasters and the press, each with its need for spectacular attention-getters, it is no wonder that we take off after any banshee, will-o'-the-wisp, or foxfire and presently find ourselves selling its wares to a public disastrously undereducated for a technological world.

As it stands now, the conservation/environmental movement bids fair to be remembered as, if not the major, then certainly one of the most spectacular antiintellectual movements of the latter half of the 20th century.

PROPOSED LETTER TO THE
SAN FRANCISCO CHRONICLE

The current uproar in Iran underscores the basic wisdom of President Carter's synthetic fuels (synfuel) program. While we have thus far done very badly on energy conservation and innovation and must learn to do better, even the best performance would, within a decade, leave unmanageable deficits in domestic supplies of liquid fuels.

By 1990, the President's original target date, U.S. oil ("petroleum liquids") production, including a million barrels per day (mb/d) from northern Alaska, will have fallen to no more than seven mb/d; the number of cars and trucks may have risen from 1975's 133 million to 145 million; and, even with better mileage performance, they will require the gasoline and diesel fuel obtainable from 10.5 mb/d of crude oil (petroleum liquids) and synfuel.

Continuation of oil imports at the present level is intolerable, Iran[ian] intransigence or no. So long as the current excessively adverse trade balance persists, we are selling the United States to outsiders. Those new owners will gain with their purchases the right to the income from their investments, a burden for which our children and grandchildren will not thank us. It is not simply a "transfer payment," it is a change in proprietorship. It is idle talk to say, "When they have bought General Motors, we will expropriate it." The Third World has complained, legitimately, that too much control by foreigners over their internal affairs has stemmed from a similar outside proprietorship. We must change our course away from such a future.

The only answer in sight is the manufacture of liquid fuels from coal. The adverse consequences have been exaggerated. In fact, if enough coal were mined from 100-foot-thick Wyoming seams to produce 2.5 mb/d of synfuel (at 65% thermal efficiency), the reclamation requirements would be only 6.3 acres per day, 2300 acres (four square miles) per year. This is trivial by comparison with the reputed million acres per year (four square miles per *day*) consumed in urbanization. In passing, the tonnage of coal mined annually in the United States would increase enormously, by 400 million tons, some 60% over present levels.

Other factors dictating this as the only reasonable solution include:

1. No alternative at all is in sight for fuel for trucks, planes, barges, combines, and only an uncertain one for trains.

2. It will be impossible to adapt personal domestic transport to fuel shortages until close to 2000 A.D. Automobiles, especially big ones, last too long. American cities are ill adapted to mass transit. It is one thing to climb on BART [Bay Area Rapid Transit] in [suburban] Walnut Creek for the trip to work on Montgomery [Street in San Francisco]; it is quite another to take public transit from [isolated] El Sobrante to school at [almost as isolated San Francisco State University on the opposite side of the Bay Area].

3. Synfuel is feasible. Our best information is that Germany fought [World War] II on liquid fuels from coal, even though the size of Germany's liquid fuel ecomony was amazingly small. (In 1943, the United States produced two-thirds of the world's crude oil!) The chemical processes are not yet optimal and more research is required before major plant construction begins, but, if anything, Carter's original goal of 2.5 mb/d is too modest.

4. While the environmental impact is intolerable, the alternatives are not. We have already seen the violence of irrational reaction to quasi-shortages of fuel; major shortages may completely disrupt this society. It is not beyond imagination that Americans will burn refineries to force oil companies to disgorge gasoline!

Synfuel (from Western coal) is a case where the environmental/ conservation movement, faced with a hard choice, chose to erect its barricades on indefensible terrain. In other energy issues, the movement, now deeply involved with political liberalism (despite distinctions between the two), has sacrificed purely conservational objectives to conflicting liberal doctrine.

An example is [the] Diablo Canyon power plant, two million kilowatts, almost ready to go. If it does not run, the $1.6 billion spent on it is wasted and will ultimately come out of consumers' pockets. This economy is too hard-pressed for such waste. We should endorse its operation. However, to endorse operation of this completed plant is not at all to endorse the construction of new nuclear power plants, and it is not to assent to sloppy operation.

In a third category, the movement remains saddled with empty victories, such as the prohibition by Congress against shipping northern Alaska crude oil to Japan. Revocation of this prohibition would end demands for any new pipeline from the West Coast to midcontinent and would probably diminish total ton-miles of crude oil tankered worldwide, with a proportional reduction in oil spilled. The Federation of Western Outdoor Clubs has endorsed such revocation, but the conservation/environmental movement as a whole will rarely back down on any earlier position, whether well or ill taken.

If the conservation/environmental movement could concede such points as these more graciously than in the past and could control its turbulent components in support of such positions, then we might gain presently the badly needed protection . . . against invasions, sponsored by an unbridled Energy Mobilization Board, of more valuable parts of the native landscape, protection against reservoirs that should not be (or should not have been) built; against destruction of free-running streams; against wirescapes in wilderness.

PART EIGHT

THE FUTURE

Most of Luten's writings have expressed, in varying degrees, a concern for the future. These papers focus directly upon that time, and they illustrate the development in Luten's writing from the simple act of sounding alarms to the more difficult but positive role of providing prescriptions to the still more thoughtful job of wondering about why people vary in their assessment of the future. We see here Luten's most recent major papers, suggesting that he has also progressed in his writing from the problems of individual issues and resources to broader themes involving human personalities and human thought.

THE BICENTENNIAL LANDSCAPE

A discussion of the development of the American landscape, first from 1776 to 1976 and then from 1976 to 2176, serves as an introduction to this group of papers on the future and the limits to future growth. In this lecture, Luten made no statement of advocacy (except quite subtly) to curtail growth, nor did he present an analysis of the perils if such action is not taken. Rather, he offered a reflective look at the past, and a positive speculation about the future. Luten suggested that over the next 200 years "the fate of the landscape is pretty well set but for two variables: population and energy use," thus echoing concerns of earlier papers in this book. But here his scenario included a population reduced in numbers voluntarily and an energy use stabilized by greatly reduced resources. He also foresaw great gains in the dedication of landscape to wild nature, including "a national buffalo migratory corridor 200 miles wide from Montana to Texas." Society will turn increasingly to the husbandry of land and wildlife, he predicted along with Aldo Leopold, because in near-Utopian conditions our human instincts toward problem solving can no longer be satisfied by more traditional survival challenges. Before going on to the subsequent writings in this section, in which Luten has viewed the future with some apprehension, enjoy this expression of unbridled optimism.

Carl Sauer, great American geographer, shortly before he died last year at 85 said how almost unbelievable he found it . . . that he had lived half of American history since Lewis and Clark. And I am myself startled to figure that I have lived a third of the bicentennial. We think it a long time ago that Henry Thoreau went to Walden Pond, but the Anglo–Saxon settlement of the continent was two centuries on its way then, and is now only three and a half.

My focus today is the American landscape. By this word I mean the resource base, broadly defined, and thus including cropland, and

Public lecture given at the University of Tennessee, Knoxville, February 1976.

pasture, forested land, water, mineral resources (including some of the energy resource), the assimilative resource, fisheries, and wildlife. I also want to touch a bit on the urbanized portion of America.

More specifically, I want to look at the changing nature of the American landscape, both since the country was born (thus tracing change through the first American bicentennial) and onward for another two centuries when the nation will be celebrating its next bicentennial. I fear not to make predictions for such a distant American future because no one who hears me today will remember, in the year 2176, what I say.

[1776–1976]

My initial purpose is to present a look backward to see how the present American landscape has developed.

Let us start with the land itself. Glance first at the American territory:

1790	After Treaty of Paris	888,000 sq. mi.	1.9% per year, if you wish to
1867	After Alaska Purchase	3,608,000 sq. mi.	envision such a jumpiness as exponential growth
1917	The peak	3,735,000 sq. mi.	0.08% per year

Thereafter, it has declined with the Philippines' independence, and, perhaps, [that of the territories] still to come: Micronesia, [the] Canal Zone, Samoa, [and] Puerto Rico (especially if they'll take New York City with them). No one envisions exponential growth in this sector. Second, consider occupance of the land. If you will accept my guess of a half million 40-acre farms (20 million acres) in 1776, and not much else, to the closing of the public domain, perhaps in 1922, with 1.5 billion acres privately owned, then the growth rate in occupance was 3% per year. Since [then], it has been nil, and will continue so, Alaska excepted. Exponential growth here also ends. Third, think about the boundaries of the country. The Canadian boundary, it seems to me, could well remain peaceful. Canadians have sometimes been apprehensive of American aggression, but they need only remind us of the cost to us of overwhelming them: 20 more senators. Attractive as

Canada is, is it worth such a price? The Mexican border may well be a line of increasing tension. At present population growth rates, in 60 years there will be as many Mexicans as Americans—and they will be hard-pressed.

The rate of American population growth has steadily decreased, even as the country's total population has exploded:

1790	3.9 million	} 2.8% per year—and it really was close to exponential
1900	76.1 million	
1960	180.7 million	1.5%
Currently		0.8% (discounting illegal immigration)

Children ever born to women just past child-bearing age must have been [as follows:]

1776	5–6
1876	5.5
1976	2.5

Will it fall [another 3.0 children] to —0.5 in 2076? No. But why should it stop at 2.5?

Urban population [is also worth considering:]

1790	0.2 million	(5.4% of the total)	} 4.7% per year
1900	30 million	(39.5% of the total)	
1960	125 million	(70% of the total)	} 2.4% per year

And it will slow down more—to the overall growth rate, when the entire nation is urbanized.

Settlement in 1800 had reached into the upper Ohio from Pennsylvania, to White's Fort (in 1786), now Knoxville, and across Cumberland Gap into Kentucky and Tennessee as far as Nashville and the lower Tennessee River. See the splendid maps of the U.S. National Atlas. By 1850 it was well into Wisconsin [and] Iowa, straining at Nebraska and Kansas, and into eastern Texas. By 1890, the frontier was gone.

Cropland, first reported in 1850, was 113 million acres; it peaked in 1935 at 416 million acres; this growth comes to 1.6% per year. Since then, it has declined. Again, an end to exponential growth.

Now, let us look at certain resources. Lumber production:

1799	0.3 billion board-feet	4.6% per year
1910	44.5 billion board-feet	About the peak
1970	37.0 billion board-feet	Effectively zero growth; perhaps a slight decline

Mining—take pig iron as an example:

1810	60,000 tons	6.4% per year
1910	30,000,000 tons	1.9% per year
1970	91,000,000 tons	Growth rate here has declined

But next take energy:

2.7% per year from 1840 to 1970. Note the parallel growth of population to 1900, and the lower subsequent rate.

After 1970, it was starting to increase substantially, until the setback at the hands of the OPEC. Now it is undecided.

We could try to say similar things about water management—but they would be very hard to interpret.

[Next, consider] the assimilative resource—our record in polluting the environment. This also would be terribly hard to interpret, and I'm not going to say anything about it, except a word of caution. We are all supposed to worry about the "greenhouse effect," the warming of the earth that may result from the increase of atmospheric carbon dioxide concentration by 10% during this century, from about 0.029% to 0.032%. But we might also keep in mind that [carbon dioxide] is essential to photosynthesis; that the rate of photosynthesis in this concentration range should be close to proportional; and, therefore, that an increase of 10% of our food production may result from the increased carbon dioxide content of the air. I suggest this only as a caution.

Turning now to elements of the landscape not easily measurable, note that we have exterminated the passenger pigeon, once perhaps the most populous bird species on earth; we have almost done the same with the buffalo, and numerous other birds and animals. We have been [afflicted] with chestnut blight, starlings, and now Dutch elm disease. Finally, I have really no way of estimating what we have done to our scenic resources. Some of them we have probably improved; others we have drowned, burned, scorched, or buried.

Summing up the past and looking ahead to the future, energy and population are crucial factors. Population grew exponentially and always has the potential for exponential growth, given an infinite environment. Energy has shown symptoms of exponential growth, although in the future, 1976–2176, the myth of infinity rests on the myth of free energy.

[1976–2176]

Now, looking forward into the next two centuries, I wish to make two important assumptions. The first is that the American people will set their own course on population, despite the injunctions of the experts. Demographers are always projecting future populations. Sometimes they seem to do worse than the amateurs. . . . But demographers seem to have an emotional fear of declining populations (perhaps their instincts are showing).

The best-known projections of the approach of the American population to stabilization [were done] by Tomas Frejka. He assumed that the size of the American family would decline to replacement size at varying speeds and then calculated how the population would finally stabilize. The notable item is that it [would take] a century at the least. Further, the faster it [were to occur,] the more disruption of the proportion of various age groups [would accompany] it. If, for example, it were to stop growing now, completed family size would be only 1.4, but a generation later it would have to rise to 2.8, because of the scarcity of potential parents.

But neither Frejka nor, within my limited knowledge of the field, any other demographer has touched the field of declining populations. I am going to suggest that the American population will decline to 100 million by A.D. 2176—not from any deterioration of spirit or welfare, but simply because they see it as the way to a better world. Completed family size of 1.5, over the next bicentennial, would about do it.

Where will they live? More on the coasts and in the warmer parts of the nation than now. How much will they be urbanized? Perhaps no more than now will make their living in the extractive industries, but this dispersed population will be supported by more in the service industries. Smaller cities and towns will prosper at the expense of the megalopolis. . . . Cities will, that is, be more of a size than they are now.

My second major assumption is that the energy economy will be complex and energy will be *dear*. But we will continue to use a lot. [I think that] it should [not] be more per capita than today. Coal mining will continue; the oil and gas will be nearly all gone. Solar power will be substantial and [will be used] in many places. Houses will be carefully insulated; automobiles will be small. Deliberate governmental pressures to suppress use may well include taxing, rationing, laws (e.g., on car economy), subsidies for conservation.

Resources other than energy will pose fewer problems. Food requirements will, of course, be less—not so much less as might be imagined, because diets may improve and the fraction exported may increase. Still, my guess is that half of the present cropland can provide two-thirds of the present food. This should give an increased fraction for export. Note, in the figure, the reversion of cropland to range, to forest, to cities, to strip mining, and so on. Expensive energy will encourage this, because it will make poor cropland less competitive. Envision, please, the good lands of the corn belt and its surroundings still in crops; the irrigated orchards of the arid West; truck crops still on all the urban fringes; and specialty crops where they are now found.

Timber requirements should be met domestically; with no population growth, they will not be excessive.

The entire field of mining cannot easily be covered. Imports will be greater, but there will be much recycling. Perhaps we will be stripmining the borrow pits of our highways for their beer can content.

Water management will be no great problem; the assimilative resource will be improving. But can we ever get Lake Erie back to a mesotrophic, let alone the verge of an oligotrophic, condition as long as the nitrogen and phosphate that the Farm Belt farmers must pour onto their lands for that 100-plus bushels per acre production continues to leach into the lake? Again, Lake Tahoe, even if the contribution of human sewage to its waters is completely ended, will take millennia to get back to its quality of 1900.

So far as the wildlife and the wild flora of the continent are concerned, they will certainly suffer from occasional unlucky infections—more tough pests imported from the tougher Old World. There will be some more extinctions, but we should be able to avoid those of conspicuous elements of the biota.

Finally, returning to the matters of wilderness and scenic resources, note [in Figure 1] the reversion of land to less intensive uses. The croplands of New England turned to pasture long ago, then to forest, and now to small-tract private vacation habitat—second homes, if you will. Much the same will happen to the croplands that will be noncompetitive with the declining population of the next bicentennial.

Summing up, if we assume that society can manage its affairs well enough to survive, what comes through is that the fate of the landscape is pretty well set but for two variables: *population* and *energy use*. If, as I judge, we will reduce the population, [and] if, as I judge, energy

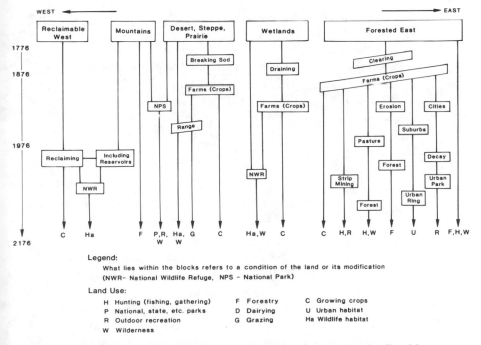

Legend:
What lies within the blocks refers to a condition of the land or its modification
(NWR– National Wildlife Refuge, NPS – National Park)

Land Use:

H	Hunting (fishing, gathering)	F	Forestry	C	Growing crops
P	National, state, etc. parks	D	Dairying	U	Urban habitat
R	Outdoor recreation	G	Grazing	Ha	Wildlife habitat
W	Wilderness				

[FIGURE 1.] Evolution of the American cultural landscape over the first bicentennial.

will be dear and used thoughtfully and with care, then some of the appearances of the land may transpire as I have forecast.

Where will the Americans be and what will they be doing two centuries hence? The basic and disquieting message from *Brave New World* [Huxley, 1932] is that if we solve all our problems, if we reach Utopia, then we are dead, we are no longer human. . . . If, in fact, central North America makes it through a second bicentennial, what unsolved problems will keep [its inhabitants] human? I have argued that they will take two bold steps: to limit their numbers and their energy use. Will they then be Utopian, and, so, less than human? I think not. If the survival hedges I have already inscribed do not give them enough warriors, their instincts will still come to their aid.

I envision an incredible complex of "territories"—really, of "status" in society obtained and defended by proprietorship of land—even though owners' freedoms will progressively be infringed: by proprietorship of other wealth, but also by being skilled, by being knowledgeable, by being arcane. [Here are some examples:]

You are rich and look down on me for being poor—but I am up on hummingbirds and scorn you.

You own productive farm land; I only own 40 acres of useless scrub woodland or meandering creek valley or a Sand County farm or a long-legged house or a strip mine's spoil heaps—but I am husbanding them, am beset with problems and am solving problems, and therefore will survive.

You are a community leader, but I have been up to 16,000 feet in Nepal.

These intricate and innumerable manifestations of territoriality will stabilize and diminish the efficiency of the society. In the landscape, they will be just as complex as elsewhere.

Last Sunday, in my territory, there were five television programs on wildlife. Perhaps fascination with wildlife is instinctive. There is also in this land an unheard, complex conservation movement, involving, all told, perhaps five million people, possibly still growing exponentially. [It includes] a dozen or so major, general organizations, all flanked by numerous major regional organizations, by numerous specially oriented national organizations, and by almost countless minor, weak, special-interest groups. Ecologically considered, the movement has the elements of durability and of success (and inefficiency). I expect it to continue.

Among its coming successes, I envision, for example, establishment of a national buffalo migrating corridor 200 miles wide from Montana to Texas, wolves in the Adirondacks, cougars in Tennessee, and defenders of such developments everywhere. I see already the Friends of the Sea Otter as a totemic group; [similar groups will be formed by] the defenders of the elk, green turtles, peregrine falcons, and, of course, wolves. There will be many more. Perhaps, even, these will have legal standing.

Look, finally, at [Figure 1] again, [and particularly at] all those places ending up designated to be used as Ha, H, P, R, [or] W. They will have grown greatly. C will have diminished but will still occupy the most productive soils. D and G will be less. F will be as it is now, and V also.

Some of you find all of this unabashedly optimistic. I might agree. But I might also point out that an authority on people's relation to the landscape, Aldo Leopold, suggested that the character of the changes that I have described forms a natural extension of what is the best of humanity. Certainly, the goal of a more humane world is a worthy goal of our next bicentennial.

THE END OF THE TETHER

The theme of the environment as a constraint on human activities, particularly on various forms of growth, is recurrent in Luten's writings. In this paper, he explored that theme in the general framework of societies suddenly and unexpectedly reaching environmental limits, "the end of the tether." At the core of his discussion is a series of five examples: "Each of them begins, in one fashion or another, with rising expectations, whether

Paper presented at a conference sponsored by the Federal Office of Emergency Preparedness, San Francisco, May 1969.

simply of greater numbers or of increased affluence." In each, "a plan which seemed well laid encounters minor difficulties. . . . [Each] revision leads to another difficulty until finally [disaster results]." Luten went on to argue that technological response to environmental constraints will often fail, not because of inadequate technology, but because adequate foresight is not possible. Weaving that notion into a discussion of systems, Luten concluded that "our only course is to abandon the role of ecological dominant, the role we have spent all this time reaching."

Luten did not chart in detail here a safe course for the human future. Rather, he let his thoughts progress from point to point, cautiously, even hesitatingly. The resulting riddle-like style of this paper is not always easy to understand fully, but it is particularly rich and provocative. Like so many of the papers in this collection, it illustrates Luten's special talent for the incorporation of numerous allusions and analogies to literature, history, and science. He pointed out here that these techniques "must not be pushed too far"; yet perhaps they help to bring often difficult concepts a bit closer to the reader's understanding.

The literature of tragedy pictures the way disaster closes in on a man. Not one misfortune, not even a series, suffices to bring a hero down in disaster. Instead, a plan which seemed well laid encounters minor difficulties, little vexations, as its execution proceeds. But each revision leads to another difficulty until finally, with all return to security, to simplicity, to virtue lost, the hero is trapped, ruined, or dishonored. [It is] thus always with tragedies, whether the hero be animate or inanimate, individual or group, whether a man, a ship, or a society.

Whether tragedies are real or figments of literature is immaterial. Certainly, the sense of tragedy is vastly enhanced if its chronicler has had the skill and foresight to establish that its central figure is, in fact, of heroic dimension by certifying his record of heroic achievement. A tragic hero is not a fumbling, groping incompetent: Before being overtaken by outraged fortune, he must first have triumphed over lesser, human forces.

We have phrases to describe such predicaments. Some of these are less tragic than ludicrous. Thus, we may "paint ourselves into a corner"—a plausible consequence of looking backward at one's achievements rather than toward the future. Did Gibbon [1776/1932], in describing the decline of an empire, put into some contemporary voice a recognition that the "grandeur that was Rome" was failing, or did the Romans, even to the end, persuade themselves that Rome's greatest days lay ahead?

Again, we may "bump into a ceiling." This is an expression, perhaps only implicit, that growth may suffer when it encounters the limits of an environment. We may find ourselves "in a straightjacket," our freedom to maneuver constrained.

Or, again, "The best-laid schemes o' mice an' men/Gang aft a-gley . . ." [Burns, 1786/1979]. Do we sense that Robert Burns thought little of the planning discipline? That he sensed an environment overpowering to men as to mice?

Joseph Conrad wrote of such a human predicament in a minor novel, *The End of the Tether* [1903/1960]. So far as my limited literary background tells me, this story never won much critical acclaim. Perhaps this was because, in contrast to other real successes, Conrad's image of tragedy just did not quite make the grade in this case. Perhaps he picture[d] Captain Whalley—a pillar of a man—in his declining years as trying to make too much of virtues which are too simple. Nonetheless, it is a tale of careful plans for the protection of integrity, property, and character, and all of these ultimately go down in disaster.

Allegories, figures of speech, and analogies are compelling and enlightening but must not be pushed too far. To compare human society to Captain Whalley's concern for his modest property and its disposition is not apt. To compare his progressing blindness to the failings of human foresight is inept, for the essence of Whalley's nature [is] providence.

Nonetheless, the phrase "end of the tether" is compelling enough to be used to introduce matters which need to be [discussed].

This meeting deals with disaster. It deals with a curious class of disaster. A Neanderthal society would hardly understand it, although they might understand a meeting called to inquire into the waning population of the Pleistocene mammoth. A contemporary subsistence society could understand parts of this meeting but not the bulk of it. Only a society immensely specialized, [only a society] immensely devoted to the gospel of efficiency, and only a society whose productive individuals find their time utterly committed, could have a real feeling for a meeting such as this.

None of the disasters with which you deal threaten the society; none of them are more than trivially regional; none of them except [a] major tsunami threaten the lives of more than thousands of people. Each of them, however, threatens to disrupt the intricate integration of a region of the society. In the event of such disasters, a great number of people will have to turn from their specialized routine and undertake tasks for which they are less well trained. Presumably, their efficiency will be less at such tasks.

In addition, substantial physical damages will be incurred, and incurred in some *natural* manner rather than in some *equitable* manner. That is, the penalty falls on the man who *bought* [a house] on the fault, not on the man who *built* there for immediate sale. If "acts of God" strike down sinners, it is for the sin of ignorance of the environment, not for the sin of exploiting the environment. Our society compounds this sin: We ignore the warnings of nature; we compensate losses of economic equity and subsidize sinning against the environment.

I am not suggesting that subsistence societies are immune to geological disasters. The collapse of stone huts on the Anatolian plateau traps and kills thousands; the collapse of tile-roofed, unbraced frame houses in Japan traps and burns thousands. Tidal waves spare no lowlanders in Indonesia. The collapse of terraced hillsides in Assam undoes the work of centuries. Still, once [such disasters occur], the task of recovery in such societies is not greatly different from the task of everyday living. For, in fact, everyday living is not itself remote from disaster.

The difference in this society is that it has become specialized, alienated from the land, and heavily populated. It has changed greatly from April of 1906, when a retreat to tent life in Golden Gate Park as a refuge after the San Francisco earthquake was imaginable, tolerable, and perhaps even fun. We have become unfamiliar with the fundamental tasks of a subsistence society, ignorant of husbandry of any sort, barely able to change a tire, unfamiliar with the sight of gasoline, some of us almost unable to walk. Could we, if left to ourselves, deal with the tasks of a subsistence society; could we hoe turnips for a living?

The disasters which concern this meeting are, none of them, of a scale to lead to such a predicament. We envision that emergency supplies, emergency facilities, emergency financing, and, above all, emergency administration will carry any afflicted region through such disruptions. In sum, our picture is of disaster which proceeds merely from the direction in which our society has evolved and with which it is inherently competent to deal.

If this were all that was changing within human society, we might have a degree of confidence. Unfortunately, this is hardly the gamut of possibilities. Other matters have more potentiality for catastrophe, in contrast to mere disaster.

I want to cite five sorts of situations which have catastrophic potential. Each of them begins, in one fashion or another, with rising expectations, whether simply of greater numbers or of increased affluence. It matters not which. [Before turning to the five examples, though, I want to comment on the nature of societies and their reaction to environmental limits.]

Throughout history, it has not been the little, stable societies which have torn up the face of the earth, but rather the aggressive, expanding empires.

In Mesopotamia, as demands on cropland grew, whether from increasing population or deteriorating soil, water had to be applied to the land. Whether the new yields of grain demanded imperialism for the administration of water or not, they supported empires and aggression. And part of this aggression [consisted of] extended demands on the forested uplands. Finally, with the forests gone, the hills came down and filled the ditches, and the empires failed. Or were the empires so lush and living so easy that they drew predators from outside who wore them down into failure? Most likely it was both.

Loss of soil was already legendary by Plato's time. It continued around the Mediterranean rim and was exported to the New World, until it seems that from Iran west to Alabama, mankind [has] scrubbed the soil from the earth's rock face.

Why, when [people] saw what was happening, did they not "call time"? First, because it happened slowly. Time was long; the world that even the rare aged man saw from his deathbed differed but little from that of his first memories. Records of the past were incompetent. Second, the world was not terribly full, and sometimes people could simply move onward. Third, if they could not move onward, neither could they contract. Who, even today, with the vision to say, "Our valleys are too narrow for our numbers," has the character to say, "We should be fewer?" Desperate societies seek expansion, not contraction. . . .

My first example [of a catastrophe] is a model. I do not know if this precise sequence occurs, but I believe it is beginning to be seen in certain parts of Africa, and perhaps in southeast Asia. Consider the agricultural system called "slash and burn," which is practiced in many wet tropical hill lands (in contrast to the rich alluvial flood plains). The soils there are profoundly leached, quite sterile, and deficient in ion exchangers—most of the ion exchange capacity is in the humus of rotting vegetation. However, given fallow periods perhaps as long as a human generation, a considerable amount of mineral nutrient is brought up by deep roots from the weathering regolith [and perhaps blown in with the winds,] and stored in the growing vegetation. Also, a considerable amount of humus may accumulate on the shaded forest floor. But not [much], for the nutrient is limited, the sun now reaching the humus oxidizes it, the ion exchange capacity fails, and leaching of nutrients out of the ash and down the river is fast. Secondary nuisances also discourage continued use of a fixed field. And, so, new fields are cleared, burned, and cropped each year, and exhausted fields are abandoned to the forest for a generation. Geographers generally feel that this procedure provides an enduring basis for an agricultural system, provided [that people] do not try to force it beyond its capacity.

Suppose, though, that the population begins to grow at 2% per year. Then the second year's field must be 2% larger than the first, the third [year's] 4.02% larger, and so on. This [in and] of itself is not too discouraging, but another consequence is that the hypothetical 30-year cycle will be reduced to perhaps 20, and new fields brought into cultivation will have had less than their full interval for recovery. Accordingly, they will not be fully recovered, and, if enough food is to be produced, the area to be cropped will have to be increased in some relation to the diminished fallow period. Instead of field size growing by the compound 2% annually, it has another factor of increase multiplied into it. The result, and it comes on very suddenly, is that presently [people] set out to clear a field and find it is one [they] have just abandoned, and abandoned because it was worn out.

Success depends on an inventory of nutrients and upon the root system which accumulates that inventory while still using it. The potential for this sort of disaster still seems not to be widely recognized. Does it require too much foresight? Does this sort of situation mean a tightening of the tether? The response is apt to be that the surplus population can go to the cities and make synthetic fertilizer for the land. Small subsistence systems are thus integrated into large, urban-centered market economies—empires, perhaps. With this, they become less stable, but perhaps more efficient.

My second example lays more stress on productive inventory. The productivity of a forest depends not merely on the forest land, with its nutrient minerals and ground water, but on the trees and the acreage of their foliage. There is an age for each commercial forest when the production of wood per year since it began is at a maximum. Most economic pressures lead to cutting before that age is reached. As economic pressures increase, cutting is accelerated. As cutting is accelerated, the growth of wood diminishes.

Japan overcut its forest land to the edge of disaster in its efforts to win World War II. Ever since, we have been supplying them with increasing amounts of forest products, coming now to 10% of our production. First, this was to give their forests time to recover; now, it seems more to support an outrageously explosive economy, an economy increasingly efficient—and less stable.

In the United States, quite suddenly, the price of timber stumpage has risen to undreamed-of levels. Partly, this reflects an expanded housing program; partly, general inflation; and partly, perhaps, a loss of concern by house buyers for price. Credit policy makes buying seem so much cheaper than renting—the total price is unimportant. No one ever lives in a house until it is paid for, anyway.

Letting the price of stumpage stay high might have some merits. Thus, it might reduce somewhat the demand, and it might encourage better management of private timber lands and even bring a lot of small holdings into the market. But we are tending to view our forests as if they were just factories, capable, with sufficient management and attention, of meeting any demand made on them. Such beliefs stem from an urban, economic, manufacturing ethic which says that production can be set at any level, if only the plans are well laid and the investment adequate. These beliefs have Marxist overtones and deny that the environment can be limiting. Currently, our forest managers, in their eagerness for greater research and management budgets, seem to have decided that technology can solve all. Personally, I feel the tether tightening a bit, and wonder if we can look forward to the day when 4 × 4 timbers with bark on all four corners will be found in our lumberyards, just as happened in Tokyo in 1950.

The productivity of other resources also depends on inventory. Wildlife and commercial fisheries are examples where reproduction and growth are so much faster than with trees that recovery can be rapid if pressure is remitted. Nonetheless, through carelessness, my-opia, and competition from other demands on the land, we have destroyed a wide range of animal species. And we will never get a single one of them back.

My third example deals with climatic cycles. To take a simple case, consider the use of semiarid rangeland for livestock. A stable society can persist on such a resource base indefinitely. It is not very aggressive; [it is] not very efficient; and it does not push its luck. When a grazing society becomes competitive, aggressive, and economically oriented, it will ask more of the land. When the climatic phase is one of increasing rainfall, herds are increased. When the climate turns its back, one hates to have to cut back, and all ingenuity is employed to escape the consequences. If successful, the next benign phase finds rain and ingenuity combining to reach new highs in stock population. When again, the weather turns dry, hope and false prophets always combine to promise a good year just around the corner. If the phase is really adverse, then the range is pushed to ruin, and a new desert is on the march.

The same can be said, of course, with respect to farming on the arid fringe of cropland. In this nation, we have repeatedly tried to expand crops into areas that just would not carry crops. The long story is of homesteaders coming to the high plains on the crest of a wet cycle and finally giving up as the rains waned. Then they moved on to the west, leaving more deserts on the march behind them. Up until now, we have been able to move onward. If our demands grow so that all the land must be managed to the utter limit that efficiency can provide, what margin will we have in reserve, what stability? Similar comments could be made on floodplain occupancy.

Fourth is the matter of simply superintegration. We have moved water from one drainage system to another, are moving it the length of a state, and have envisioned a water plan to take water from Alaska as far as Mexico and the Atlantic Ocean. If it is necessary for us to go to this extreme to meet our needs, how will we meet the increased needs of the subsequent round? Quite apart from a host of other objections to such plans, how much reserve, how much stability, does so efficient a proposal leave us? How many more extensions can be spliced into the tether?

Fifth is the matter of ecological blunders. No one could have foreseen them, but each one of them tightens the tether. Persistent pesticides seemed a godsend in the 1940s. Now, we come to have doubts. We were told that DDT would save us from hunger and that we could, anyway, always turn to the sea for the final solution to man's hunger. Now, when we turn to the sea, we find that DDT has beaten us there and may be making the sea's food unusable. In fact, though, the sea never did have much potential.

DDT has had one interesting and good side effect. If ever we wondered what peregrine falcons were good for, we now have one more answer: They told us first of the dangers of chlorinated hydrocarbon pesticides.

The high Aswan Dam seemed a good idea to "solve" the problem of Egypt's growing population. Now, almost finished, the population to use all of its [newly] irrigated lands is lined up and waiting. What is the next solution? In addition, the quite unexpected results are lining up, too, and waiting: Will the older irrigated lands stay fertile, with all of Ethiopia's sediments trapped up there in the reservoir? It is said that fishery production at the river's mouth is declining because nutrients stay in the reservoir. It is said that the deltaic shoreline is retreating because sediment supply has come to an end. Worst of all, the suspicion grows that schistosomiasis, the debilitating blood fluke disease of the irrigation ditches, is becoming pandemic. No one could have foreseen any of these things. How tight is the tether?

To counter this small budget of disasters, an impressive budget of technological achievements can be listed. You should remember, though, that these achievements are being cited for you by their creators. You should remember that you have paid them well for their work, and that they expect you to continue to do so. You are, in fact, in a sort of continual contract negotiation where you are offered, in return for your support, assurance that you need not worry about the future. Everything will come out all right. It is reminiscent of a tale by Arthur Guy Empey [1917] of trench warfare in World War I. When the Scottish Black Watch regiments came in as relief, they scorned warnings of the disasters facing them and bet willingly that they would suffer no harm until the replaced unit came back. And, in fact, all of the Scots who were in the trenches at the succeeding exchange collected on their bets. Those who lost were not there to pay up.

In a sense, it ought to be possible to tot up the credits of technology and the debits of population growth, destroyed resources, and ecological blunders and compute the length of the tether. To do that is not easy; a few people have tried, but there is no agreement on the answer, and I have no confidence that anyone has come close.

I have no answer, either, and I am beginning to suspect that we have so arranged things that there is no answer. Let me bring in three sorts of considerations which come out of ecological theory. The first one speaks of systems and hierarchies of systems and says, to simplify the matter utterly, that if you wish to know the mechanism of a system, you should examine its subsystems; if you wish to know the purpose of a system, you should examine its supersystem, the system of which it is a part. Look down for mechanism, up for purpose.

The second one is a set of uncertainty principles. Werner Heisenberg, years ago, won a Nobel Prize by enunciating an uncertainty theorem which says that you cannot learn precisely both the place and speed of a particle because the act of learning them changes them. The greater the weight of the information needed and the smaller the particle, the greater the uncertainty.

Garrett Hardin has posed an ecological uncertainty theorem: In any system you cannot maximize both efficiency and stability. The more efficient, the less stable; the more stable, the less efficient. I have been harping on this today.

Barry Commoner has phrased what I think to be another uncertainty principle: Science solves problems by isolating variables. Perhaps we should imagine a great, continuous problem stretching across this room. The scientific method is to break it up into compartments in order to solve it. The smaller the compartment, the better the solution. But the more we subdivide it, the more unresolved problems there are between adjoining compartments. Perhaps, then, for each problem we solve, we create a new one in the relation of this solved isolate to the adjoining solved isolate. So long as we are dealing with small, separate systems, the solution of small, separate problems is fine and science does well. But when we come to integrated societies, half of the problem is to put back together the solutions of the small problems—to synthesize them all—and Commoner is insistent and vehement that science fails utterly in this task.

And a fourth [uncertainty principle might be this]: You cannot plan in great detail, because if you do, you must depend on inexperienced planners whose work you will reject when the time to use it arrives.

Next, I want to allege that our early society could be viewed as a set of small, essentially independent, discrete systems. Communities were largely self-sufficient. If you had seen one, you had seen them all. They were not specialized and were inefficient. They did not all prosper, so it is hard to say that, taken singly, they were very stable; but their individual instabilities averaged out to a considerable stability, all considered. Their intercommunication was limited and slow. If one panicked, the others heard of it too late to react. If one set out on a false lead, they did not all follow. Some never heard; others argued the matter and rejected it. Decisions were local and independent. Mistakes, then, averaged out as well as successes. They should be regarded as independent systems, not as subsystems.

Today, in contrast, the entire society has to be considered as a single system, with an intricate hierarchy of subsystems. We are in it; we cannot be objective about it. We have difficulty in perceiving its purposes. Perhaps the closest we can come is to suspect that one of its purposes is to survive, this being a purpose of all biological systems.

Before concluding, it is fascinating to speculate on a possible transitional moment between the former small, discrete systems and today's integrated system. It was a moment when a few components of the entire society were in good communication, but not all. It was a time when you could tell a town how to stop a typhoid epidemic without worrying about the consequent population explosion. It was a time when you could corner the wheat market without worrying about either the Department of Agriculture or foreign famine. It was a time when the discount rate was a device to make money, not to control inflation. It was a time when science was proud rather than ashamed of transcending nationalism. Was it a moment when a higher hierarchy was in charge because it had learned to communicate across systems boundaries? Did it, by this token, make them its subsystems?

In conclusion, without being able to give any answers, I think we can come up with two interesting warnings:

First, if we cannot manage the system, we probably cannot foresee what is going to happen to it. Any disaster we can foresee, we can manage. Ergo, our real disasters will always be unforeseen. Did anyone foresee two years ago that the University of California would be disrupted by a one-acre mudhole [a reference to the "People's Park" controversy in Berkeley]?

Second, if we wish to escape these problems, our only course is to abandon the role of ecological dominant, the role we have spent all this time reaching. I know of no precedents to this effect, and I doubt that we will try to set one.

Finally, if we continue to meet each stringency with a technological solution, will we not inevitably end up in the predicament of the "wonderful one-hoss shay" [Holmes, 1858/1889]? [It] lasted a full century, but—

> You see, of course, if you're not a dunce,
> How it went to pieces all at once—
> All at once and nothing first
> Just as bubbles do when they burst.

TELOECONOMICS:
THE MICRODYNAMIC,
MACROSTATIC ECONOMY

In the preceding paper, Luten argued that societies that continue to walk the path of growth will necessarily eventually reach "the end of the tether." This paper, presented a year later, demonstrates the maturation and development of Luten's thinking. He expressed his views more clearly here (despite one's first impression of the title—paradoxically, Luten coined a tongue-twister and used it adeptly to give clarity to his perspective), and he moved away from Socratic warnings to prescriptive suggestions. These suggestions involved economic mechanisms by which resource consumption can be reduced: "[We should] put a price on those of our natural resources which lead to economic goods and a price sufficient to bring demand for them down to a level which can be sustained." Such market mechanisms are well within the domain of political conservatives (as subsequent efforts to deregulate the price of natural gas illustrate, for example). On the other hand, Luten revealed that he was hardly a laissez-faire capitalist in his rejection of economic measures, particularly the gross national product, as indicators of

Reprinted by permission from A. Silverman (ed.), *Western Montana Scientists' Committee for Public Information Lecture Series* (pp. 112–120). Missoula: Western Montana Scientists' Committee for Public Information, 1972. Presentation and publication made possible by a grant from the National Science Foundation, GZ-1773.

the "goodness" or "badness" of actions regarding natural resources. He advocated, in fact, quite the opposite: "My purpose here is to limit the impact of the economy on the resource, to direct economic activity away from resource deterioration." Once again, the lack of correspondence between conservation goals and particular political ideology is evident.

Luten, then, urged his hearers to manipulate the economic system, a variable human creation, so that it will reflect the physical reality of finite resources. He attempted to incite economists to "definitive action" by unqualifiedly labeling environmental optimists (often economists) as "wrong" and playfully urging them "to abandon their emotional hang-up on growth." He went so far as to give a convincing definition of an economist's true task as that of an "applied ecologist." But he made it clear that he had no intention of turning over the "china shop" to these hesitating "angels" of economics: "Brief mention only has been given to those resources which are not economic; to aesthetic resources, wild game, outdoor recreational opportunity, wilderness. These matters are too important to be allowed into the economy."

The title [of this paper], I guess, needs explanation. The root "telo-" is familiar in "teleology" and means "end" or "purpose." "Teloeconomics" is, then, purposeful economics. "Macrostatic" says that overall it does not grow; "microdynamic" says that it can change greatly within. Teloeconomics raises the question: Who is to be the master, we or the economy? Does the society exist merely to serve the economy, or does the economy exist to serve the society? If the latter, are we to be subject to "natural laws of economics," and to what degree? Or are these laws we can make or modify? Are they natural laws in the scientific sense of being generalizations of observation, or do they have a compulsive theological or moral quality to them?

J. K. Galbraith (1965) raised some of these questions five years ago. Kenneth Boulding [1968] has inquired into similar problems, as has Mason Gaffney (1967), as editor in *Extractive Resources and Taxation*. Many other economists must also have done as much.

But I wish to go a bit further. A major intellectual revolution now in the making, perhaps as significant to the 20th century as the Darwinian revolution was to the 19th, is the rejection of a notion tacitly accepted by many early economic writers, including Karl Marx—the notion of an infinite earth. The classic phrase was "For every mouth there is a pair of hands to feed it." No notion came through of a limiting environment. But now we are coming to concede the earth to be finite. The debate has been going on for the quarter of a century since World War II and has had, rather curiously at first sight, strong protagonists and antagonists. This is because the issue has been rather more than the acres of earth; it has also included the question of how much of the future concerns us, and [whether] technology [is] a multiplying factor without limit. Regardless, we have lined ourselves up as either pessimists or optimists, into believers in "our plundered planet" [see Osborn, 1948] versus believers in a world of "enough and to spare" [see Mather, 1944]. While, in my observation, the optimists have usually won in face-to-face arguments, they are nonetheless wrong.

Quite recently, I believe, [the optimists] have come to concede that they have been wrong. But they have not been defeated by intellect. If you should ask me, the clinching argument has been the vision of that beautiful, blue-green planet, so little and so lonely, presented in literal photographs taken by the astronauts. So much for the power of the intellect.

Be that as it may, the pessimists have seen, for quite some time now, that population growth must end. And they, the pessimists at least, have agreed that we would prefer population growth to end on our terms, with long life expectancy and small families, rather than under the alternative of short lives and large families.

An inescapable consequence of the conclusion that population growth must end is the corollary that economic growth must end. For many of us, this is a far more terrifying and unwelcome proposition than any vision of the end of population growth. Perhaps, in fact, it is economic growth we are hooked on, and population growth as an attractive proposition is entirely subordinate to it.

This aspect struck me hard only in the summer of 1969, on an evening when I had been talking to graduate students in economics at Berkeley on the subject of population. They, all of them interested in environmental issues, asked what they as economists could do about the problems. I suggested to them that the most important problem they could attack was to identify the terms and conditions under which a static economy could operate to our satisfaction. With that, it seemed to me, they all dropped out, lost interest, changed the subject. My feeling is that they had such an emotional involvement in growth that they were unable to question it. A month previous to [that] evening, a forester had criticized some folks for having a "hang-up on trees" and I had replied that other folks have a "hang-up on dollars." I will generalize, in fact, and say that I don't object to arguing conservation issues with economists, foresters, and engineers, if they wouldn't get so emotional.

So much for preliminaries.

David Brower first suggested that I inquire into these matters in 1963. But he also suggested that Galbraith and others of far greater competence than I do so, and I have waited patiently for them to come up with the answers. They have—Galbraith, Boulding, and other economists—said repeatedly that there is no reason to need growth. But this is not enough. Recently, though, Abbah Lerner at the University of California has observed that economists have repeatedly proved propositions of great public interest but have given them little publicity. Only, he [has] said, when outsiders have used poor logic to reach rather obvious but important conclusions, have the economists become interested and worked to provide substantiating detail and proof.

Accordingly, I view my role here as [that of] a fool rushing in where angels hesitate to tread, and I have the express object of fumbling with the issue as a bull, a foolish bull in a china shop, a china shop feared by angels. Perhaps by so doing we can precipitate definitive action by the economists; perhaps we can force them to abandon their emotional hang-up on growth.

Let me observe then, as aggravatively as possible, that if ecology, from *oikos*, the household, and *logos*, the word, is the study of the household, then economics, from *oikos*, again, and *nemein*, to manage, to administer, is applied ecology, the subdivision of the study of the household which concerns itself with making decisions on how to manage the household. While many economists will bridle at the notion of being applied ecologists, some of them, God bless them, insist [that] this, in fact, is the task. They say economics must deal with not merely money and banking, but with how to decide on environmental quality, too. The only problem, again, is that they have not brought their achievements to our attention. Accordingly, it is geographers who worry about how to make decisions on environmental quality—on aesthetics in contrast to usefulness, in the landscape.

As the next observation, please recall that our economic system was not given to us by God, completed and ready to handle any problems which might arise. Rather, it has evolved, beginning with the earliest specialization of human activity; with communication of wants; and with trading among specialists, whether tools for food, arrow flints for salt, aesthetics for subsistence. What it has done for us is to ease enormously the task of deciding what to buy and how much. But it does this better for us with small than with large purchases; it did better when we were poor than [it does] now when we are rich. Today, the obsession with growth which has developed suggests strongly that the economy is in charge of us, not we in charge of the economy.

Well, if we are to talk about a macrostatic economy, what shall be the measure of it? Shall we demand that the gross national product [GNP] cease to grow? I think not, for two reasons.

First, the GNP is no measure of what concerns us; in some respects, it is quite unrelated to the finiteness of the world. GNP is a summing up of transactions. Many of these reflect extractions from and impingements on the environment, but many do not. As a trivial example, the gambling enterprises of Reno take money to the bank every evening, and this, I suppose, contributes to the GNP. If the legislature were to require that every nickel into a slot machine must go to the bank, and [that] every jackpot, or less, must be paid by check, then the contribution of legalized gambling to the GNP would surely be increased many-fold. Again, the costs of communication—tele-phoning, for instance—contribute to GNP, but they can increase with very little obvious limit and do not appear to be restricted in any substantial way by the finiteness of the earth. [As a third example,] Sylvia Porter (1970) reported that auto thefts come to one million a year, at an average loss of $300 each, and that the number grows 16% per year. If such growth were to continue, the time for a ten-fold increase is 15.5 years and in 50 years the number of thefts would be one billion; say, one theft per month per car. The contribution of such thefts would be $300 billion, a decidedly handsome and, I suppose, admirable contribution to the GNP. In [a] similar vein, a number of people have noted that a growing portion of GNP is for mitigation of malefits. Thus, if I buy gasoline for my car, that purchase is part of the GNP. If, then, to mitigate my share of the smog, I must buy a smog control device, that also adds to GNP. It has been suggested [that] the GNP may end up composed half of things we did because we liked them and half of measures to counteract the problems created by the first half. That is the first reason for rejecting GNP as a measure of a macrostatic economy.

The second reason is that GNP is an index of the happiness of the corporate individual and not of the real individual. The corporate individual, and we must never forget it, has a much simpler purpose than the real individual. It has no legitimate purpose other than to maximize dividends to its stockholders. It has intellectual problems: How much [in] dividends this year? How much in a decade? And how much effort spent on environmental quality or on public relations will pay off in dividends, now or later? Again, the corporation may be subverted by its managers. They, being real people, may have purposes other than maximization of dividends, and included among these purposes may be the improvement of personal image and the quite unselfish optimization of community amenities. But these, it must be emphasized, are subversions and cannot be the corporate purpose.

GNP, probably being closely related to corporate dividends, is a plausible index of corporate welfare. It is not of great merit as an index of the general welfare, of public good. Accordingly, let the GNP rise as it may wish; this is not our test of the macrostatic economy.

If GNP is not a satisfactory criterion, what is? Perhaps we are in real trouble if we try to define any optimum in this area. In the case of population, we can easily satisfy ourselves that the earth is finite [and] that a limit must exist, but if we try to estimate an optimum population, we don't get far. Whelpton, over 20 years ago [cited in Thompson & Whelpton, 1969], thought 90 million people might be optimum for the United States. Currently, estimates for an optimum world population seem to hover around 500 million, about a seventh of the current actual population. But the circumstances which dictate the optimum change by the year. For each who says the optimum is diminishing because of what we have pulled out of place and strewn around the world, there is an antagonist who says it is increasing because of the increasing competence of our technology.

We have worse difficulties with economic activity. It would be easy to accept 500 million people as an optimum population and then to proceed to the requirements for an optimum diet, housing, transportation, [and] cultural and environmental amenities, and let it go at that. But the whole thing smacks of an authoritarian management which seems more likely to take the diversity and richness of living out of our lives than to do anything else. Optimum living is not apt to be determined by any authority.

Still, while I do not know how to set optima, this does not mean they do not exist. In the case of population, it is generally easy to secure assent to the proposition that a world in which population growth is let go until it is curbed by short life expectancy is a far-from-optimum world. In similar fashion, if economic activity expands until it is curbed by the rising cost of mitigation of nuisance and destruction, we will be unhappy. . . . and any optimum will be utterly missed.

Coming to the issue, if I cannot set an optimum, I can still express the suspicion that we are beyond it, and argue that what we are concerned with is the impact of economic activity on natural resources, including the economic externalities of the environment, what may be called the quality of the environment, but not the aesthetic quality of the landscape. This last exclusion I have tried to justify elsewhere [see the first paper in Part Seven] on the score of the incommensurability of aesthetic values with economic values.

The nature of our difficulty is that our economic processes give little concern to the condition of our natural resources. These processes do promote efficiency, but they do not submit to Garrett Hardin's theorem that in any system you cannot maximize both efficiency and stability. They do provide an allocation of scarce resources, but only of immediately scarce natural resources. We have established institutions essentially on the premise that natural resources are infinite.

Garrett Hardin (1968), who comes on strong in this field, has written on this problem in "The Tragedy of the Commons," published in *Science* a little over a year ago. His parable speaks of the commons where any villager may graze his cattle without charge. But when the commons is grazed to capacity, additional cattle will damage it, will lower its productive capacity. Each of them will add less production than its diminution of the collective production of prior cattle. From the collective viewpoint, such additional cattle are a disaster. Nonetheless, an individual villager may find it to his advantage to put an additional cow on the commons. Even though the production of the entire herd is diminished, the return to our individual villager may be increased.

We have left a great deal of our environment in the commons. Examples could range widely, from individual determination of family size to ownership of pelagic fisheries to acquiescence in an extraordinary diversity of pollution. It is hard to escape the conviction that this pattern reflects anything but belief in the infinity of the natural resource base, the infinity of the earth.

In passing, an astonishing and delightful record of early conservation measures in the New England colonies has come to my attention. Within 50 years after arrival on this continent, these people were having to restrain their members from taking advantage of the commons in a great many ways: literally pasturing too many cows on the village commons, cutting oak and walnut for inferior uses, overusing fish as fertilizer, fishing out of season, and so on. One wonders if the colonists, freed of the confines and repressions of a crowded England, had felt initially that here no restraints would ever be needed [and] that here in the New World was an infinitely abundant environment, and [if] they learned better within their first century here.

The general response to the tragedy of the commons was to accord private ownership of resources. Thus, if the villager owned only his proportionate share of the commons—no longer a commons—the folly of overpasturing should bear in on him. And if not, it was his funeral (or was it only his?).

We did, [at an] early [stage], grant ownership in land, but this was probably more a matter of strategic location and of the impossibility of several men cropping the same piece of land simultaneously than of any recognition of limits.

While we have virtually given away almost any of our natural resources that anyone asked for, we have not often granted full ownership of a resource except under the guise of land ownership. You may own a mining claim, but this is only a right to recover minerals. You may have mineral rights on petroleum-rich land, but if someone drains away your oil before you get to it, [your chance of] recourse is slim. You may have rights to use water, but you don't own it. We seem to have felt ownership to be unimportant; enterprise to develop was the important contribution to the society.

This was a land which was empty and abundantly capable of meeting the resource needs of its scarce inhabitants. They were at the same time poor and with limited wants and limited capabilities for exploiting their resource base. In that situation, we developed a set of resource policies and institutions germane to the time and the place and the people.

Now, we are many and our wants are immense, and we are stuck with an outworn tradition. We are plagued on every front with tragedies of the commons, and perhaps this is more our problem than any absolute ceiling on some index of the economy.

The answer, it seems to me, is fairly straightforward and simple. It is to put a price on those of our natural resources which lead to economic goods, and [to make this] a price sufficient to bring demand for them down to a level which can be sustained. Six categories can be mentioned:

1. Pelagic marine resources. By and large, these have no owners. By treaties, we have partitioned up fishing rights to some of the harder pressed of these resources. Again, we have decidedly failed on others by related but less coercive means. The case of the International Whaling Convention and the blue whale is spectacular and dismal. The United Nations would like to claim ownership of resources not already claimed. It would satisfy my criterion if the United Nations succeeded, and if they then licensed harvest of those resources which are pressed beyond sustainable yields and exacted fees sufficiently large to reduce harvests to sustainable yields. This is hardly an answer to the world's shortage of animal protein, but overuse of the resources is not an answer, either.

2. The vast resources in the United States which remain in the public domain.

a. Timber. We sell cutting rights in the national forests, usually at auction. Demand, then, not cost of production, determines price. The volume is large enough to be a substantial factor in determining timber values on private lands as well. A probable result is that the return from timber sales from private lands is insufficient to permit good management. Recently, Congress was debating a National Timber Supply Act, which seemed to view forest productivity in the same light as the productivity of a factory. It provided for more intensive management and increased cutting rates at the expense of other components of the multiple uses of the national forests. But, in fact, the productivity of a forest differs from that of a factory and depends on the inventory of growing trees as much or more than on the application of management capital and labor. . . .

Let us increase the charges for cutting rights in the national forests until we diminish the demand so that forests will grow at least to the neighborhood of the maximum yield before being cut [the point that will allow maximum production of wood]. Doing this will also provide incentive for constructive management of privately owned forests. It will also bring our use of the forest resource down to a sustainable level and thereby approach the macrostatic condition.

b. Grazing leases on the public domain have been a wonderful prerequisite. They do not dominate the grazing picture to the degree [that] timber for the national forests does [the logging picture]. The Bureau of Land Management has been trying to raise grazing fees, but the grazing lobbies are still ahead. Give these fees the same treatment as cutting prices.

c. Minerals have been so much in the public eye on issues of royalties for fuels, but also depletion allowances, that it is hard to ask for much other than pinching down depletion allowances and exacting severance taxes . . . which is perhaps what each of these items comes to.

d. Water. No one pays for water; we pay only for its management. If we viewed the resource itself as being as valuable as we say it is, we should not be reluctant to pay for it. So, again, I propose exacting a considerable price for the use of water; let me suggest $25 per acre-foot, just to indicate the ball park.

e. National commercial fisheries. Exact a severance tax and license rights to harvest so as to do away with the destructive inefficiencies we now impose.

3. Privately owned productive land. Exact a land tax—based on its productivity or its production, I'm not sure which, but not on its locational value. The latter is not a resource value.

4. The fourth category is the right to pollute the environment. We took this for granted when the land was empty. Now it becomes intolerable. Some success has been had in charging polluters for the costs of cleaning up their effluents. The classical case is in the Ruhr River watershed in Germany. My proposal goes further and suggests charging more than the cost of managing effluents. The matter, of course, goes far beyond water pollution. Tax cars, too, for their pollution. Tax durable containers. Tax noisy motorcycle exhausts.

Please note, in passing, that it is not my purpose in this discussion to abate such nuisances; that is another matter. My purpose here is to limit the impact of the economy on the resource, to direct economic activity away from resource deterioration.

5. The fifth category that comes to mind (you will think of more) is to provide incentive for recycling of durable unrenewable resources—most conspicuously to get automobile hulks back to the steel mills, with, perhaps, diversions to the copper refineries and aluminum smelters. "No-deposit-no-return" bottles may be even more conspicuous.

6. The sixth and last category, one which perhaps is only on the

margin of the resources picture, is to price services provided by the public sector of the economy so as to limit use to the capacity of the facility. As an example, the two major bridges in the San Francisco Bay Area were built at Depression prices. They are essentially paid for, and the public has been accustomed to 25¢ tolls. It is claimed [that] new bridges are needed, but new bridges would cost so much that saturation traffic on them would not pay the interest on construction costs. Despite the traffic burden on the existing bridges, we still grant bargain rates to commuters who largely use the bridges at the most crowded hours. This is manifest nonsense; it stems from archaic customs developed in an economy of scarcity, when it seemed good business to accord diminished prices to large customers. That situation is gone. The land is not empty; it is full. Use of such facilities should be discouraged, not encouraged. Curiously, with that activity cited earlier as having little impact on the resource base, the telephone, we do encourage off-peak use by everyone. With electricity, halfway between, we encourage only the big customers in this fashion. None of this seems paradoxical.

But when we propose similar pricing policy on family size, it is attacked as an outrageous invasion of the sanctity of the family. (It does disturb me, but for another reason: I don't like the vision of children being restricted to the economically acquisitive. The trait might be inheritable. If children are to be taxed, be sure the surtaxes escalate dramatically.) It takes James Reston to reflect that if the state must not constrain the number of children, then surely it must similarly not constrain the number of wives—or husbands.

Revenue from all of these fees might come to a considerable sum. If we may accept a view of the social contract which says that the natural resources of a society are inherently the common wealth of the members of the society, and if we can accept the view that the society cannot permanently alienate its rights to these resources, then we can argue that this is the revenue which appropriately can go to provide GAI, the guaranteed annual income. If we proposed to provide everyone over, say, 21 (this is not a measure to alleviate poverty) with $1000 per year, the price exacted for natural resources would have to be much higher, perhaps ten times more than now.

I do not dare suggest that the aggregate of fees, severance taxes, and penalties imposed on the extraction of economic goods from the environment be balanced against the needed GAI, but it does seem a matter worth exploring.

Nothing has been said about the microdynamic aspect of this economy. I see nothing in these proposals to inhibit innovation, and a good deal of stimulus for it.

Brief mention only has been given to those resources which are not economic: to aesthetic resources, wild game, outdoor recreational opportunity, wilderness. These matters are too important to be allowed into the economy.

Finally, in conclusion, perhaps I have vandalized the economic premises enough. Perhaps the economic bosses are [on] horseback and will eject me, and the clean-up crews will come along and give us a proper account of teloeconomics and how to achieve a microdynamic, macrostatic economy.

THE LIMITS-TO-GROWTH CONTROVERSY

By the middle and late 1970s, Luten's writing on the future had become increasingly sophisticated. No longer saying simply that the environment acts as a constraint on human activities or suggesting that the economy be molded to suit human purposes, he was drawn into wondering about the history of attitudes toward growth and questioning why people see the possibilities for continued growth so differently. The catalyst for these more involved matters was the publication in 1972 of The Limits to Growth (Meadows et al., 1972) and the debate that it generated. The argument was, put simply, whether or not the world's resources were infinite and thus able to support endless growth, or finite and thus able to sustain growth only until

Reprinted by permission from K. A. Hammond, G. Macinko, and W. Fairchild (eds.), *Sourcebook on the Environment* (pp. 163–180). Chicago: University of Chicago Press, 1978. Copyright © 1978 by The University of Chicago Press.

"the end of the tether" is reached (the latter is the viewpoint expressed in *The Limits to Growth*). Referring to a *New York Times* book review, Luten commented, "It comes as a shock to one who has been immersed in this literature for years . . . to read, 'If this [book] doesn't blow everybody's mind who can read without moving his lips, then the earth is kaput.'" Indeed, *The Limits to Growth* reached "a much larger, more worldly, and less idealistic audience" than that involved with Earth Day of 1970, and "more than any other contemporary work, [this book] has drawn attention to the problems posed by growth." Still, as Luten pointed out, the argument is not new. It is easily identifiable over the last several centuries, with threads extending back much farther. No earlier pronouncement resolved the debate, nor did *The Limits to Growth*; the controversy continues unabated. Thus, regardless of the time, Luten's historical account and analytical reflections prod us to think.

THE PROBLEM IN PERSPECTIVE

"No wonder they disagreed so endlessly; they were talking about different things." With these words Robert L. Heilbroner (1953, p. 82), though referring to differences between [Thomas] Robert Malthus and David Ricardo, cautions all participants in the limits-to-growth debate. Seeing all of the problem may, in fact, be the major part of the problem.

Millennia ago at least some of our forebears could see virtually all of the problem simply by scanning the reaches of the single valley that comprised their own territory. What went on outside their own small watershed was beyond concern, had no influence on them, and was not influenced by them. But as men have become progressively more and more involved with mankind, the task of keeping one's eye on all of the problems has increased at an accelerating rate.

Malthus, with whom this discussion begins, had an easier time of it than we do. By means of a few great simplifications of diverse merit, he managed to assemble most of the problem. Thus:

1. *Unrestrained populations tend to grow geometrically.* This is close enough to reality.

2. *Food production tends to grow arithmetically.* This has less merit; we will examine in the next section the way in which he phrased

his statement. Moreover, much of the criticism and controversy subsequently surrounding Malthus stems from his decision to let "food" stand for *all* natural resources.

3. Malthus has much to say on human welfare, but he has been read variously and this has led to conflicting evaluations. Part of this conflict stems from disagreements on whether man is to be considered subject to the harsh laws of nature or whether man is perfectible, is "master of his own destiny," and is ascending to Utopia. On the issue of human purpose, Malthus comes through even less clearly than on the matter of food.

Whether any writer, in today's far more complex, more closely woven, more communicative world can do better in explaining the problems posed by growth remains doubtful. Surely it is a severe test of genius. We must be warned at every step along the way that any appearance of simplicity is deceptive. The problem *does* appear simple to some of us; the answer fairly shouts at one. And yet others utterly disagree. Are some among us irrational and unwilling to adhere to the rules of human reasoning, or are we "talking about different things"?

With this warning out of the way, we can phrase the basic question: Is this world, for practical human purposes, infinite, or is it finite? It is easily said that of course it is finite, but almost a dozen elements obscuring the answer and largely supporting the opposite view can be identified. These, grouped in five categories, are listed in the following paragraphs.

First, the consequences of growth and interspersal: To primitive men, circumscribed by their valley walls and the unfriendly men beyond, it may well have seemed finite. Many such groups established stable, enduring relationships with those limited environments. I have commented on this sparingly elsewhere. . . . As such groups came to be assembled into larger societies with a substantial measure of intercommunication, it is easy to say their world was still finite, with just a larger numerator over a larger denominator. But, in fact, new elements were added:

1. In the primitive, isolated society, innovation diffused slowly to neighboring groups and may often have been abandoned on the way. In the larger, intercommunicating society, innovation diffused faster and with fewer losses.

2. In the larger society, a buffering capacity existed whereby one region could lend support to another during a local spell of ill fortune.

3. Larger societies, if imperialistic, could force a flow of goods from the rim to the heartland—flows that could persist as long as expansion lasted, but not much longer.

Second, the biases of history:

4. Paradoxically, when Magellan circled the earth, he proved it to be physically finite, but also, by hinting at its magnitude and diversity, he may well have lent force to the idea of infinity. Later explorers may have strengthened rather than weakened the conviction of infinity. Because we have never encountered the limits of the earth, we have come to believe there are none. More hubris, even arrogance, has resulted from successful expansion. Is this warranted, or is it simply more people whistling in the dark (Leopold, 1966, p. 110)?

5. Our economic theory began during a period (the 18th and early 19th centuries) when the world, practically viewed, seemed too large and too rich ever to be seriously impaired by human exploitiveness. The idea of an infinite world is built into economics.

Third, the problem of concern for the future:

6. We cannot possibly be as much concerned for the remote as for the near future, but we differ in the patterns of the decline of our concern with increasing remoteness. Biologists, almost certainly, have a longer vision of the future than social scientists. Economists, among the latter, quantify their declining concern by "discounting the future": the compounded decrement of annual interest subtracted from something of value in the future. Thus, the present value of a resource that will be used in a century may be quite small: something worth $1000 in the year 2075 discounted at the rate of 5% per year, modest by today's standards, is worth only six dollars today ($1000 \times 0.95^{100} = \$6$). Accordingly, economically, one can hardly concern himself with shortages a century from now, and a world with enough for a century is, practically speaking, infinite. Biologists, in asking for a longer concern, are "low-discount" people; economists, commonly "high-discount" people, are, by that token, concerned only for the near future. Each finds his position so rational as to feel that it requires no defense.

7. Curiously, and again paradoxically, as our economy becomes more hard pressed, interest (discount) rates increase and the period into the future with which economists are concerned shrinks. If such a shrinkage should outrun resource depletion (and this may be the case

in the middle 1970s), our economic guides might even be construed as teaching us that the world is becoming more infinite than in the past.

Fourth, the issues of purpose, while not clearly supporting one side or the other, have certainly obscured the debate.

8. Should we seek the welfare of the individual, the society, the nation–state, all of mankind, or all of life? If our concern is for the individual, we must proceed cautiously in exploitation of the planet's sources in order to retain a diversity on this earth to match the diversity of individual needs. If concern is for all of life, extraction of the planet's resources must be restrained. In between these extremes, constraints may be less.

9. Ideas of "optimum" come up and with them the issue of "quality of life." Shall we try for an economic optimum, if we can identify one, or for an even more elusive economic–aesthetic optimum?

10. If we use the criterion of full employment to define the optimum, Keynesian economics suggest that a capitalistic society finds it much easier to achieve happiness while growing (Petersen, 1961, pp. 531–533). That is, the optimum is not definable as a level of activity but rather as a rate of growth of activity.

Fifth, a matter of the philosophy of science:

11. People assess evidence differently. Some are persuaded more by the plausibility of a principle than by the weight of empirical data; others are not. Preparatory to a later section, I suggest that biologists tend to fall in the former category, social scientists in the latter.

Summing all of this up, like it or not, belief in an infinite world has become an institution. We are concerned in the latter half of the 20th century with assessing this institution; with luck we shall make up our minds before the century is out—for institutions do not die easily. When they do die, equity is transferred: One man's gored ox is another's prime roast! Insofar as they can see the consequences, the first resists change, the other demands it.

MALTHUS AND HIS TORMENTORS

"Every year Malthus is proven wrong and is buried—only to spring to life again before the year is out. If he is so wrong, why can't we forget him? If he is right, how does he happen to be so fertile a subject for criticism?" (Hardin, 1964, p. 3).

Thomas Robert Malthus (1766–1834) did not initiate concern for the adequacy of the world to meet human needs; he was not the first pessimist. Nonetheless, we can begin with him. Earlier writers have contributed little to the modern debate. Those who wish to attain more background might profitably begin with the excellent work by Glacken (1967) and proceed to the account by Hutchinson (1967).

The first edition of the *Essay on the Principle of Population* by Malthus was published in 1798. A facsimile edition was published in 1926. The first edition is described by Petersen (1961, p. 509) as having been "written with an aggressive confidence, a dashing style that passed over exceptions, anomalies and minor points, and swept on to the main conclusion with youthful confidence." Later editions, to a total of seven (the last published posthumously in 1872), were more sober and more intricately documented. Perhaps more useful for our present purpose is a condensation that was prepared for the 1824 "Supplement" to the *Encylopaedia Britannica* and then was revised and shortened for publication in 1830 (Malthus, 1830 [/1960]).

Although the so-called "Malthusian principle" can be phrased in several ways, the approach and simplifications listed in the initial paragraphs of this chapter are as straightforward as any. The geometric increase of an unrestrained population we would identify as exponential growth or, occasionally but incorrectly, as logarithmic growth. Exponential growth is not just any rapid growth, but growth according to a pattern in which population increases by a given factor—say, a factor of two—in a constant interval of time. That is, the time for doubling remains the same, no matter how many doublings have occurred. Such growth, if plotted on semilogarithmic graph paper, will appear as a straight line (whence the term *logarithmic growth*). And the numbers, taken at equal time intervals, form a geometric progression: 2, 4, 8, 16, 32, 64, . . .

Malthus was basically right: A population with a constant birth rate in excess of a constant death rate will increase exponentially. Additionally, he thought, from examining the new republic across the Atlantic, that the doubling time for unrestrained human population growth must be about 25 years.

Next, the arithmetic increase of food. Here he was cautious, and said only (Malthus, 1830[/1960, p. 29]):

If, setting out from a tolerably well-peopled country such as England . . . we were to suppose that by great attention to agriculture, its produce could be permanently increased every twenty-five years by a quantity equal to that which it at present produces, it would be allowing a rate of increase decidedly beyond any probability of realization. . . . Yet this would be an arithmetic progression.

Facing the dilemma of geometric versus arithmetic increase, he postulated that two sorts of checks, *positive* and *preventive*, ensure that the population cannot exceed the food supply. (Let us remember this and try to avoid saying, "and so the population increases beyond the food supply." No human society, excepting a lifeboat under severe discipline, shares food equally during famine. When food is less than nutritional requirements, starvation occurs; the weak and the poor die first.) Broadly speaking, *positive* checks are those that shorten life and *preventive* checks are those that diminish births. Some checks may be classed as misery (for example, famine); some as vice (for example, wars); and others as moral restraint (for example, postponed marriage with premarital continence). Mention of contraception turns up first in the 1817 edition; Malthus opposed it, largely on the score that its use would magnify the natural indolence of people (Petersen, 1961, pp. 516–517).

Malthus is commonly damned by social scientists for his opposition to the "poor laws"—laws to provide assistance to the poor. Petersen insists that Malthus has been misread; he was merely trying to point out the adverse consequences of attempts to mitigate poverty by measures so remote from the real causes as the poor laws. But Frank Notestein (1960, p. x) says flatly, "Malthus is important today as the father of the most regressive social doctrine of our time." At any rate, a great quarrel has ensued, and much has been written on the subject. The citations already given will provide ready access to the views of many others, including those of two great social philosophers, Godwin and Condorcet.

Bogue (1969, p. 17) has tried to end the debate: "Demographers of the world unite—in burying the population theories both of Malthus and of Marx." But the debate cannot be ended so easily. Perhaps, following Hardin (1964, p. 3), it is the social scientists who bury Malthus in odd-numbered years, only to have the biologists resurrect him in even-numbered years. In the end, Malthus may be deemed important primarily for having catalyzed (one can hardly say "crystallized," since the waters are still so murky!) the distinction between two schools of thought that we may term *optimism* and *pessimism*. It is worth noting that the optimists have commonly been social scientists allied with technologists; the pessimists have commonly been biologists.

Social scientists and biologists may differ in respects other than their attitudes toward Malthus. A biologist is apt to take a simpler view of "law" and, with the physical scientists, to accept it as a generalization of observation. "Law" and "theory" become more complex in the social sciences. Hauser and Duncan (1959, p. 82) suggest some of the complexity and specifically cite Kingsley Davis on confusions on the part of Malthus—for example, "failure to distinguish scientific from moral ideas" (p. 90). These differences between social and natural scientists may be growing; for instance, a geographer recently said, "We formulate theories for a social purpose. If they serve that purpose, we validate them; if not, we reject them" (Blaut, 1975). What matter, then, if Malthus might have said, "They were painting a world of roses and sunshine, but when I looked out the window it was dour, grim, and raining. I remarked on the reality and am damned for it." His critics might have rejoined, "If only he had kept his eyes on the painting until it were done, we might all believe the world to be rosy; think how happy we could be!"

Biologists, less empirical and more concerned with law as generalization, know little directly of Malthus. What they do know is that Malthus focused Darwin's attention on the severity of the struggle for existence and led him to understand that the potential for geometrical growth of the populations of organisms means that very few individuals survive long enough to reproduce. Left out of the discussion is any mention of "vice," "misery," or "moral restraint." Few biologists have heard of the poor laws. What remains is simply an idea, a principle, an axiom: "Populations tend to grow geometrically; food arithmetically. Populations press hard against the means of survival."

There are, then, two Malthuses: first, the "disproven" author of "regressive social doctrine," unappealing to empiricists and to the utopian believers in the perfectibility of man; second, the enunciator of an idea that stimulated Darwin, himself the keystone of modern biology.

THE 19TH-CENTURY SEQUELS

Of five philosophic threads running through the 19th century that affect this discussion, four can be traced back to the beginning of the century and to Malthus. One of these, social science and its optimism, perhaps most active early in the century, we have already mentioned. The second, biological science and its pessimism, latent until long after Darwin, has also been mentioned. A third, neo-Malthusianism, was an immediate response to Malthus. Its proponents were his supporters, and they gave rise in due course to philosophies and programs in support of birth control. Although it has become common to refer to all of the pessimists as *neo-Malthusians*, the term is probably best restricted to describe solely those of the 19th century. The fourth thread is Marxism; Marx's views on population were sharply antagonistic to those of Malthus. The fifth is the American conservation movement, which, although it has no clear origins until the 1850s and in its early phase has no clearly discernible relations to the population issue, does become involved with it in the middle of the 20th century.

Supporters of Malthus were soon busy with activities that he would have deplored. By 1822, in a book supplemented by widely circulated handbills, Francis Place recommended contraceptives as a population control measure rather than Malthus' moral restraints. Other books on Malthusianism were soon published on both sides of the Atlantic. Jeremy Bentham and John Stuart Mill became interested. But it all remained rather obscure until 1877, when Annie Besant and Charles Bradlaugh tested a court decision banning *Fruits of Philosophy* (Knowlton, 1833), one of the best books, and thereby generated greatly increased publicity (and book sales!). A summary of the incident appears in Hardin (1964, pp. 198–203). A Malthusian League was founded and spread. In the United States, a generation later, Margaret Sanger led a similar crusade. The best source of information for this period is Himes ([1936/]1970). Petersen (1961, pp. 549–555) gives a good abstract, and I have condensed his material further here because this focus on family planning is a deviant thread that wanders away from the limits-to-growth issue and back toward utopianism. Thus, Petersen (p. 555) says that "the early emphasis on the economic effects of population growth gave way to a narrower concentration on family budgets or the health of the mother." That is, emphasis shifted from the national (or world) economic dilemma to the family economic dilemma. Margaret Sanger's Planned Parenthood League and its affiliates became enormously successful, promoted improved contraception techniques, and fought laws that restricted contraceptive information and abortion. Not until the 1960s did the League become allied with William Draper's World Population. Thereby, at least nominally, it returned to the mainstream of the argument with its emphasis on the national and worldwide effects of population growth.

Marxist doctrine, in contrast, has had a lot to do with the issue. Societies under Marxist influence have evidenced complex policies on populations, at once utterly liberal on abortion, but denying that anything such as overpopulation could occur in a "properly organized society." Marx refers to the "contemptible Malthus" and argues that "every special historic mode of production has its own special laws of population" (Petersen, 1961, p. 560). In short, he argues that no overriding principle is common to all societal organizations. By and large, it seems that Marx, in common with so many economists, subscribed to the vision of an infinite world. The tradition persists: Socialists, including Russian writers on such matters, usually line up on the side of the optimists in the great debate.

The fifth thread, conservation, beginning in the mid-19th century with George Perkins Marsh (1864[/1964]) became well developed before taking any position on the limits to growth. The history of the conservation movement has been recounted too many times and in too much detail in the geographical literature to be reconsidered here. The post-World War II resurgence of the limits-to-growth issue can be attributed to writers who were as much conservationists as they were biologists. However, they were mostly from the utilitarian side of the movement. The majority of the active preservationists came along a little later, in the mid-1960s.

By the end of the 19th century, the birth control movement, though still small, was healthy and growing. The other threads, particularly those with English or European origins, seem to have been relatively subdued, and the writers were still primarily English. Carr-Saunders (1922, 1925, 1936) is a major figure who explored the idea of economically optimum populations, took a broadly Malthusian view of the limits to growth, and (1936, esp. pp. 17–45) consolidated the earlier work of Beloch and Willcox on populations since A.D. 1650. An additional reference is Marshall, Carr-Saunders, and others (1938). Of course, at the same time, as already noted, Keynes was examining other aspects of this problem.

Little attention was paid to population pressure in the United States. Did our resources still seem infinite? Strengthening this lack of concern, Raymond Pearl (1925) made elaborate statistical projections on logistic assumptions and concluded that the American population might well stabilize at 200 million and the world's at two billion "in the present cycle of growth" and "if the conditions of the nineteenth century were to remain permanently unaltered." They have not, of course, but Pearl may have helped to reassure us that the problem was not one of continuing growth, but rather of termination of growth.

One American book in this period by a sociologist, Edward Alsworth Ross (1927), is decidedly Malthusian ("who takes mankind to board needs an India-rubber globe!"; p. 118) and in places sounds amazingly like some of the abundant literature in this country a generation later. Ross concludes (p. 355) with the proposition that the regions of the earth with high living standards and stable populations must, in their own defense, erect an immigration barrier until the remainder of the world should have achieved:

> no subjection of women, no prepuberty marriages, . . . no infanticide or abortion, no high infant mortality, no unschooled ignorant masses, . . . no degrading mass poverty, no famine in the train of crop failures, no multitudes hanging on to life by their fingertips and dropping into the abyss at a gossamer touch. When it [the barrier] has served its purpose let it be removed.

THE POST-WORLD WAR II FLOOD

For whatever reason, the literature on the subject became largely American after World War II. Perhaps it was an idea whose time had come; perhaps it reflected a realization of the enormous toll the war had taken of American resources; perhaps the ending of the Western frontier was sinking in. Europe, overwhelmed by the problems of reconstruction, was preoccupied. British writing by no means disappeared, but it was a trickle compared with the stream of American books.

William Vogt gave wings to the controversy with his *Road to Survival* (1948), one of the very few books of this kind (*Silent Spring*

[Carson, 1962] is another) to benefit from being a Book-of-the-Month Club selection. Fairfield Osborn followed with *Our Plundered Planet* (1948) and *The Limits of the Earth* (1953). There were rebuttals, among them Josué de Castro's *The Geography of Hunger* (1952), and counterrebuttals, such as Karl Sax's *Standing Room Only* (1955). There were affirmations of plenty, such as Kirtley Mather's *Enough and to Spare* (1944). Harrison Brown's *The Challenge of Man's Future* (1954) stands out as probably technically the most competent writing of the period. There were great tomes by Zimmerman (1951) and by Woytinsky and Woytinsky (1953), and surveys by Dewhurst and his associates (1947) and by the President's Materials Policy Commission (1952), commonly referred to as the "Paley Commission." The statistical abstracts steadily gave more and more detail on both population and production.

The bulk of the concern in this expanding stream of literature was for the nightmare of unending growth generated by a decline in the world's death rate and compounded in this country by an enduring surge in the birth rate, which had seemed, during the Depression of less than a generation earlier, to be settling down close to the death rate.

The stream of books became a flood during the 1960s. Even to list them becomes impractical. What is truly astonishing is the diversity of arguments they presented. One would think that ultimately the extraneous elements would thin out and the core of the controversy become apparent. That it hardly does so testifies to the complexity of the matter. However, as one examines the record over the past 25 years, one reassurance does appear; the earlier books were factually thin and dilute in content, whereas the more recent ones are packed full of information. The debate has certainly stimulated the compilation and increased the availability of pertinent information. Yet even now we know so little! Only a few of the elements can be examined.

Biologists had noted the rarity of famine in an animal world presumed to be Malthusian (after all, it was the Malthusian image that had stimulated Darwin). Marston Bates ([1955/]1962) and later, others, suggested that pervasive *territoriality*, whether instinctive or cultural, must be a strong deterrent to reproduction in excess of dependable food supply. Individuals unable to claim a territory do not become part of the breeding population; whether in a strictly topographic sense or in some other way, they are forced to the margin of the habitat

of the species, the margin where conditions are unsuitable for reproduction. Wynne-Edwards (1965) made a related point concerning the
colonial nesting of sea birds and hypothesized (1962) that the phenomenon might be well-nigh universal. Calhoun (1962) strengthened the
case by demonstrating in rats the collapse of stable reproductive patterns under conditions of extreme crowding. Ever since, we have been
wondering just how ratlike we may turn out to be! Should we, then,
consider famine to stem largely from the failure of institutions of
territoriality?

In contrast, de Castro (1952) argued that it is starvation that leads
to excess reproduction. Few scholars agree, and Bates ([1955/]1962,
pp. 150–153) and Sax (1955, especially pp. 162–167) have replied explicitly and, I think, conclusively.

Garrett Hardin, an unwavering advocate of the earth's finiteness,
elucidated (1968) the antithesis of territory, namely, the *commons*, a
pervasive complication of resource management. Allegorically, the
villagers who pasture their cattle on the commons have strong individual incentives for each to increase the number of his cattle while
hoping that his neighbors will not. For even when the extramarginal
cow that lowers the total productivity of the herd is led onto the
commons, the aggressive owner of that last cow stands to gain at the
expense of his neighbors. The right to have as many children as one
chooses was probably the "commons" uppermost in Hardin's mind.
But pelagic fisheries are also a most conspicuous commons, and the
predicament of the great whales bears witness to the tragedy of the
commons. Despite such tragedies, if we sought to abolish all commons, we might find ourselves in some new and unwelcome predicaments.

Many demographers have argued that, if we could only accelerate
the development of the poor societies, we would catalyze the *demographic transition* and quickly bring them into the condition of Western societies, with low birth and death rates, low growth, and good
living conditions and education. Virtually all texts on demography
discuss the transition, but Petersen (1961, pp. 11–14) almost alone has
questioned it as a predictive law.

Paddock and Paddock (1967), convinced that pandemic famine is
imminent, have argued that some societies cannot be saved and that
aid from the developed world should be reserved for those poor lands
that can be helped through the demographic transition only with

outside aid. The analogy is to triage in military medicine: When disastrously overburdened with wounded, ignore those who will recover without medical aid and those who will die even if they are given help, and concentrate the limited facilities on those who can be saved only if helped.

The economists still spoke up for effective infinity. Barnett and Morse (1963), writing with support from Resources for the Future, make the strongest case. They focus on "Ricardian scarcity" (pp. 101–125), which is the hypothesis that the richest of natural resources are the first to be harvested and that continued increase in demand requires exploitation of less and less rewarding resources. Next (pp. 237–251), they hypothesize that today's technological society generates technological advance at least as fast as Ricardian scarcity develops. They conclude that costs of raw materials in such a society should not be expected to increase (p. 246): "Output per capita, as measured by any suitable indexes at our disposal, may conceivably increase into the indefinite future, and our eventual overcrowding is by no means a foregone conclusion."

Barnett and Morse do foresee a possible need for the limitation of population growth, but they regard this as not critical and as a matter that will be manageable through institutional change in due course. Pessimists see the same need but with greater urgency, and they are less assured that control will be easy.

The book by Barnett and Morse is the most carefully written defense of economic cornucopianism. It has been enormously influential. It is in large measure an empirical defense based on extrapolation of existing trends. Schematically, we may express it in these terms: If availability of resources declines exponentially under mounting pressures of population and affluence, still an exponentially increasing technology applied to those waning resources may lead to a slower but still exponentially increasing productivity, plausibly in excess of population growth, and therefore may also lead to exponentially increasing affluence.

Several demurrals may be voiced. Extrapolation of dominant trends will not forecast revolutions, and yet we have revolutions. In the decade since the book was written, some trends have broken sharply with tradition. In particular, "energy . . . in unlimited quantities at constant cost" (p. 239) seems more, not less, remote.

Again, technological growth must be a function of the number of scientists and technologists. During the last 50 years, pretty much the base period for extrapolation of technological growth, the number of scientists and engineers has also grown exponentially and at such a rate that by early in the next century its continuation would require that all of our children become scientists and technologists. Disagreeing with Barnett and Morse, I suspect that technology is becoming an activity of diminishing return. Consider for a moment the fruitfulness for human welfare of the basic scientific principles discovered since Copernicus lived. Does anyone care to speculate whether as many more, equally fruitful, will be discovered during the next 500 years? The question is unanswerable, but human destiny demands an affirmative answer if we are to follow the optimists' path.

Finally, Barnett and Morse argue (p. 249) against the conservationists' concern for the limits of the earth: "By devoting itself to improve the lot of the living, . . . each generation, whether recognizing a future-oriented obligation to do so or not, transmits a more productive world to those who follow."

Colin Clark (1970), an incredibly optimistic Australian economist, thinks the world can readily supply food for 80 billion. Ester Boserup (1965), in a wonderfully terse little book, argues that it is population growth that has forced agricultural progress. This may well be, provided that populations grow slowly enough for adaptive responses. That this has frequently been true in the past does not assure that it will continue to be true. Neither does past experience warrant extrapolation into a quite unknown future for technological agriculture.

But another sort of economist has taken up the cudgels in support of the no-growth economy—for example, Mishan (1967), Johnson and Hardesty (1971), and Daly (1973). The fall 1973 issue of *Daedalus* (Graubard, ed., 1973) examines both sides. The no-growth position differs sharply from that of the optimists by rejecting hopes of ever-expanding production. The penalties of growth, avoided in a steady-state economy, are carefully detailed. No convincing answer is given on how to achieve such a no-growth state and how to distribute the claims on production. That is, no answer to the Keynesian argument in favor of growth to provide jobs is forthcoming.

I have merely hinted at the participation of the conservation movement. The Sierra Club, driven by its executive director, David Brower, and stimulated by contributions from Cowles (1960), Luten

(1963, 1964a), Day (1966), and Ehrlich (1970), came in on the side of the pessimists in the late 1960s. Most major conservation organizations have since concurred.

The conservation movement, as another oppressed minority, was at least a lesser darling of the supporters of liberal issues until 1970 when, with Earth Day, conservation or "ecology" took center stage away from civil liberties and the Third World. It thereby engendered substantial resentment and has been under intermittent attack from the Left ever since. Barry Commoner (1971) and Paul Ehrlich have engaged in a major dispute over whether the problem is, broadly, population growth or overconsumption by the affluent (Ehrlich, Holdren, & Commoner, 1972). The issue is, really, for how much of the future are we concerned? If for the short term, Commoner has a good point; if for the long run, Ehrlich wins. In the long run, in the race for consumption, individual affluence will always contribute less than unrestrained reproduction. Hardin (1972a) chides and praises both opponents for their argument and for their efforts in the "unending work of public education."

Climaxing and in a sense terminating the debate of the 1950s and 1960s was Ehrlich's *The Population Bomb* (1968). Immensely popular, selling more than a million copies, the book was a call to action. It makes little difference that, written in a great hurry, it is unscholarly and occasionally in error. What makes it significant is that it came at a time when an expanding audience was ready for it. It is dramatically written. Right or wrong, it has probably awakened more people to this issue than have any of its predecessors; perhaps more than all—such is the nature of exponential growth.

THE LIMITS TO GROWTH

In 1972, hard on the heels of the subsidence from the environmental excitement of 1970 and at a time when an optimistic counterattack might have been in order, another pessimistic book appeared. *The Limits to Growth*, by Donella and Dennis Meadows and their colleagues (1972), was carefully framed and phrased. But it was terse and necessarily depended on bold assumptions and sweeping abstractions. It seemed to excite more adverse reviews than any earlier book. Economists clearly disliked it. Conservationists adored it. If Ehrlich reached a naive youthful audience, the Meadows got to the intelligentsia—perhaps for the first time. It comes as a shock to one who has been immersed in this literature for years and who thinks everyone must be familiar with it to read, "If this [book] doesn't blow everybody's mind who can read without moving his lips, then the earth is kaput" (Passell, [Roberts, & Ross,] 1972). In fact, the audience for conservation literature has been small, specialized, and uninfluential. The events immediately before and after 1970 prepared the field for a much larger, more worldly, and less idealistic audience—and *Limits* seems to have found that audience. Because this book, more than any other contemporary work, has drawn attention to the problems posed by growth, the reader may find it instructive to sample at least some of the voluminous commentary it has generated. . . . Gillette (1972), in a review published in *Science*, treats *Limits* as a frivolous effort, while Ophuls and Wilson (1972) provide rebuttals in later issues of the same journal. Another comparison is that between the critical review by Kneese and Ridker (1972) and the rebuttal by Hardin (1972b), who sees the Kneese–Ridker review as an example of sophistry and shortsightedness. In a slightly different vein, one might compare the scathing denunciation of *Limits* by Passell, Roberts, and Ross (1972) with [A.] King's (1972) analysis that emphasizes the preliminary, but nonetheless systematic, nature of *Limits* and points out that the study is manifestly projective rather than predictive in its intent.

The authors identified five major variables important in human subsistence: population, industrial equipment, agriculture, mineral resources, and pollution. They lumped ("aggregated") highly diverse, highly dispersed components, and they postulated functional relationships, including inventories and delays in interactions, both reinforcing and regulatory. Many of the functions are nonlinear. Some of them are very shaky, and the authors admit this. The worst may be the relationship between pollution and life expectancy. No one knows what it is. In one sense, the authors' assumption seems conservative, in another unrealistic. Thus, it almost has to be conservative to imagine that 100 times more pollution than today's world diminish life expectancy by only 50%. But it is also unrealistic, for a 100-fold more carbon monoxide on a Los Angeles freeway might well kill its users before they reached an exit.

All of these relationships were assembled as sets of rate equations amenable to computer processing. The authors ran a set through, then changed the assumptions and ran it through again to see what happened. They admitted throughout how uncertain some of the assumptions were, but they thought, and I concur, that the results had meaning nonetheless.

Opponents, including as a class those who would have us take their extrapolations of tradition seriously in this world of revolution, wish also to take *Limits* narrowly and precisely, despite contrary protestations by the authors. Opponents have protested that *Limits* uses a Malthusian model and so of course gets a Malthusian answer. If they had used a non-Malthusian model—for instance, one like that of Barnett and Morse—they would have gotten a non-Malthusian result. Granted, but what if it *is* a Malthusian world? Faced with such a choice—even if the arguments in favor of limits were not persuasive—the rational course to follow is to look at the probable results from acting as though we believe the one when the other is actually true (Ehrlich, 1968). If we act as though we believe in infinite expansion, and this turns out to be impossible, we risk an ultimate disaster for humankind. We may well destroy most of the biosphere in our desperate attempts to survive. Indeed, we may well eliminate much of the planet as a suitable place for human habitation. Man-induced expansion of deserts, areas of exhausted and eroded soils, and denuded hill slopes testify to this possibility. Ultimately it may prove impossible to reverse such a trend, for the resources needed to accomplish such a reversal would be unavailable.

If we believe in nonexistent limits and voluntarily restrict our growth—possibly even reduce total population—what losses do we risk? Some geniuses (and some scoundrels) who might have been born will not be born so soon. Perhaps, to compensate, we can better afford to develop the talents of those now neglected. We will have slowed down exploitation of the planet for the benefit of man. We will be faced with serious problems of the equitable distribution of existing goods and services, but at least more could be available per capita, however unevenly distributed. If growth and expansion later prove to be both possible and desirable, it would appear absurdly easy to set the process in motion once again. The resources would still be here. One can do little better here than quote Ehrlich (1968, p. 198), who strongly urges that we act as though there are limits. "If I'm right, we will save the world. If I'm wrong, people will still be better fed, better housed, and happier, thanks to our efforts."

Limits makes telling use of what we have come to call the "Malthusian corollary" in dealing with nonrenewable resources (the minerals). This is the proposition that if use of such a fixed-stock resource increases exponentially, then the amount used in each doubling interval equals the amount used in past history. Schematically, the amount used in the past, $1 + 2 + 4 + 8 + 16$ equals 31; the amount used in the next doubling period is 32. (Actually, the amount used in a doubling period is the amount used in the first year of the doubling interval times the length of the interval times 1.445.) The book's estimates of mineral resource magnitudes may be in error—for example, one wonders whether any estimate can be made for the aluminum resource when most of the earth's crust is quite rich in aluminum. But the authors note, correctly, that so long as you postulate exponential growth—and the optimists are stuck with that—it makes little difference how accurate your estimates of resource magnitudes are; the end is never remote and it comes most abruptly.

The authors' unfamiliarity with the resources field (and probably with the population field) shows up in the persistence for two years, until the 13th printing (December 1973), of a startling error (p. 57)—namely, that the United States produces 13% of the world's coal and consumes 44%. But, don't we export coal? Yes, and more than anyone else. It is noteworthy, too, that not one of the great gaggle of economists baying at the authors' heels, some of them manifestly nitpicking and eager to find errors, spotted this one. It may be worth a moment's reflection that our destiny is being plotted and is being criticized by persons who seem to have less factual background than do graduate students in geography.

The computer results indicated catastrophe, unless we change our ways: a catastrophe that is not imminent, but not remote either—just far enough away so that it cannot be dismissed as preposterous, but close enough to be unsettling: the middle of the next century.

SOME CONCLUDING THOUGHTS

On the limits-to-growth issue there is no place for fence sitters. The world is infinite or it is finite. This time it is wrong for scholars to see "merit on both sides." If my position on the matter has not been clearly revealed, one more citation (Luten, 1971) should do it. Convictions outlined there are: (1) The earth is finite; (2) the population growth of the past few generations was rare through most of man's history; (3) the present rate of growth cannot continue for long into the future; (4) at some point there must be no growth at all, for a slower rate, however desirable, merely postpones the day limits are reached; and (5) choosing to limit births to match low death rates is preferable to increasing deaths to match births.

Obviously, however, humanity is not ready to come to a decision. The debate will continue. It is moving now from scholars' desks to national commissions and international conferences; presently the chancelleries will scrutinize it.

The poor nations are castigating the rich nations with charges of resource exploitation; at the same time, the poor lands see population growth as a new bargaining lever. Logic, presumably, has no place in this setting. If the world is infinite, resources are worthless; if it is finite, population growth is a burden. In a related vein, the Arabs are proving to the world that natural resources may be of great value, but they are having doubts on the morality of contraception; perhaps they think the oil resource will never run out. The Russians argue for an infinite world and they can hardly lose, whether it proves infinite or finite, since so much of it is Russian. When the rest of the world goes dry and has to turn to Russia for raw materials, will they be priced as from an infinite stock or from a finite one?

The consequences of the wrong answer to the great question of the world's finiteness may be of grievous magnitude to humanity, and even more so to the rest of the biota that are our fellow travelers on this planet. Still, we should escape absolute disaster—unless the optimists are almost right. Our best chance, our greatest luck, may be to have the limits of the earth close at hand, perhaps even before we reach a population of five billion. Giddings (1973) has argued persuasively that the chances of nuclear war go up as the cube of population, and he guesses, as have several others, that the chance is only one in a thousand per year with today's four billion people. If, however, we should reach 40 billion, then nuclear war would become an even chance each year. How long will biocosmologists persist in their current search for evidence of galactic life outside the solar system (Sagan [& Drake], 1975) before concluding that all intelligent societies destroy themselves at about the time they become interested in galactic life (MacIntyre, 1970)?

The swords of debate will become tougher and sharper; the debate will grow in complexity, but some issues will be winnowed out. Even if we believe that the earth has limits, we know better than to say we have reached those limits. The world's production of wheat, of maize, and probably of rice has roughly tripled in the last 50 years; who is to say it can't triple again? No one. All that can be said is that it can't triple many more times.

The heraldry of the debate will continue, too—all of the magnificent catch phrases: "geometric versus arithmetic growth"; "standing room only"; "enough and to spare"; "the squeeze"; "the doomsayers"; "for every mouth a pair of hands to feed it"; "for every pair of hands a mouth to be fed"; and so on and on.

Part of the problem in the debate is the intellectual need on the one side to postulate a world that won't happen. The pessimist hopes he is making a self-defeating forecast. Institutions will bend; adjustments will be made. No one will ever know whether the changes were as fast as they could be, or whether faster change would have helped or hindered. But you cannot argue for a changed course by admitting that you will probably change course. Rather, you must cry, "Rocks ahead; change course!"

The literature will continue to grow ([Barney, 1977; Cole, Freeman, Jahoda, & Pavitt, 1973; Goldsmith, Allen, Allaby, Davoli, & Lawrence, 1972;] Ophuls, 1973, 1977) seemingly without limit, but is anything really new added?

I suspect that we witness a quarrel between two faiths: The one is of biologists believing in the reality of constraining principles; seeing mankind at one extreme of a great continuum of life, partaking to some degree of all of its attributes for better or worse, and subject to the environment of this world. The other faith is of social scientists, empiricists and skeptical of principle; seeing man as a thing apart and human society as perfectible, given enough study; and seeing man as superior to and capable of controlling the environment of this world.

Finally, a curious and disquieting matter: How large is the earth? Here is an issue profoundly geographical, but to which geographers have made no great contributions. Have they feared to cross swords with those from harder disciplines? Or have they seen all too clearly the size and diversity of the earth and are they appalled at efforts to summarize it in the scope of a single book? One is tempted to cry out, "Only geographers can know the earth is finite. Economists must ask them, 'How big?'; demographers must ask, 'How much room, and where?'"

But if the authors of *The Limits to Growth* are generally right, all this won't make much difference. If the data become firmer, the optimists will have another field day of refined extrapolation. But is it our purpose, anyway, to fill the earth with people? If not, why bother to learn how many it will hold? The critical question is, Do more people today, or in the next generation, or in the next, make a better earth? Both those who feel that the answer is "yes," and those who feel that the answer is "no" will continue to seek supporters.

And so we end up almost where we began: No wonder they disagreed so endlessly; conflicting faiths hid different premises—they were talking about different things!

ECOLOGICAL OPTIMISM IN THE SOCIAL SCIENCES

In this paper, Luten continued his thinking on why people hold conflicting viewpoints on the question of whether or not the earth can sustain growth. He expanded a matter raised in the preceding selection—the differences between social scientists and biologists in the debate over the finiteness of the earth. Moreover, he searched for the reasons that may help explain why the controversy so often seems to polarize along disciplinary boundaries. He suggested that "pessimists and optimists assume very different 'models of man,'" thus making their "ever obtaining agreement on the issue of limits to growth for human societies" unlikely.

Luten wrote in the preceding selection that on "the limits-to-growth issue there is no place for fence sitters." Although the approach he took here was mainly a scholarly analysis of the dichotomy of the controversy, his bias against the side of the optimists was even more in evidence than in previous papers. For example, in contrast to his stance in the paper about

Reprinted by permission from *American Behavioral Scientist*, 24(1), September/October 1980, pp. 125–151. Copyright © 1980 by Sage Publications, Inc.

teloeconomics, Luten's attitude here was more chiding than playful: He repeatedly cited the optimists as exhibiting emotionalism in their arguments, in one case referring to an "emotional diatribe." There was no trace now of his once-voiced optimism that growth will voluntarily decline during the next bicentennial; instead he contemplated disaster on "the 30th day"—in a more believable way than most doomsayers, perhaps because that image of the decision makers' "prepar[ing] new grant proposals" on the evening of the 29th day is so in keeping with the irony of human nature. But remember Luten's warning that a pessimistic forecaster neither believes his forecast nor wishes it to come true, but rather intends to raise concern and cause a public "to change its conduct so as to avoid a bleak future."

For a good 200 years now, the question of limits to growth and optimism and pessimism regarding the human prospect has been debated without consensus. Interest has waxed and waned more times than can be counted. First one side, then the other has seemed to be succeeding. But still in 1980, a century plus four score and two years after Malthus's (1798[/1926]) *Essay on the Principle of Population* first appeared, we have no agreement.

This seems a negation of Thomas Kuhn's (1970[, p.] 178) proposition that "before the transition from the pre- to the post-paradigm period . . . a number of schools compete for the domination of a given field. Afterwards, in the wake of some notable scientific achievement, the number of schools is greatly reduced, ordinarily to one." The issue in this article is less to ask why we have not been led by some "notable scientific achievement" into a postparadigm period of consensus than to examine a lesser question—namely, the nature, and reasons for the persistence, of differences in the limits-to-growth debate.

After a brief overview of the recent history of the limits-to-growth debate, we will present a tentative description of the opposing sides— the "optimists" and the "pessimists." We will note that social scientists tend to be optimists; biologists tend to predominate among the pessimists. Next we will suggest some reasons for this disciplinary alignment on the issue of limits. Then we will review in some detail two particularly important and opposing books on limits, and illus-

Author's Note: I am indebted to Riley E. Dunlap for bringing to my attention many of the items from the literature of the social sciences that have been discussed in this article, for careful review and discussion of its earlier drafts, and for help in sharpening its focus.

trate the ecological optimism of social scientists by examining their strong negative reaction to the pessimistic book. We will suggest that pessimists and optimists assume very different "models of man," and end by describing the difficulty of ever obtaining agreement on the issue of limits to growth for human societies.

THE "LIMITS" DEBATE: RECENT HISTORY

Whether the world is ample to support mankind was not a new issue even with Malthus. Yet, while the quarrel has waxed and waned repeatedly since his time, it has grown conspicuously since World War II, has involved more people, has had more ramifications, and has perhaps become more bitter.

RECENT RECRUITMENT

New entries enliven the jousting from time to time. Each envisions the issue as having originated immediately before he or she became aware of it. Thus, an engineer of my acquaintance saw it beginning with publication of *The Limits to Growth* (Meadows *et al.*, 1972; hereinafter referred to as "Meadows"). Many believe "Earth Day" begat it in 1970. Many, many more became aware of it with *The Population Bomb* (Ehrlich, 1968). An editor of *Nature* saw it stemming from the policy concerns of the nuclear scientists after World War II (Maddox, 1972). The conservation movement's chroniclers may find roots back to Theodore Roosevelt. More thorough scholars will cite *Man and Nature* (Marsh, 1864[/1964]) or *Walden* (Thoreau, 1854[/1964]) or, as Glacken (1967) has done, look much further back. Biologists and demographers will cite Malthus [see the preceding selection].

Certainly, as each of us became aware of the issue, he felt himself a discoverer. Only later do we learn that little is new. And yet, if a question has roots going back to the first person to argue it, surely it also acquires structure, branches, foliage, so to speak, as its concerned public grows. Each time these numbers double, the new participants gain a proprietorship in the issue comparable to the vested interests of all their predecessors. And each of these recruits, I suspect, joins with a vision of the problem as transparently simple. However, it is unlikely that this is so. If it were, we should have come to agreement long ago.

Not having done so, each recruit may bring new elements, perhaps constructive, perhaps only confusing. One wonders if problems that endure as long as this ever come to an intellectual solution or if they finally just run down and end with a policy determination, good, bad, wise, stupid, whatever, but at last ended.

Oscillations in Aggression

Beginning after World War II, with two notable titles, an impressive series of books and innumerable journal articles have taken opposing sides, optimistic and pessimistic, on the issue of limits to growth. Some of the more challenging books include:

Optimistic	Pessimistic
Enough and To Spare (Mather, 1944)	
	Road to Survival (Vogt, 1948)
	Our Plundered Planet (Osborn, 1948)
The Geography of Hunger (de Castro, 1952)	
	The Limits of the Earth (Osborn, 1953)
	The Challenge of Man's Future (Brown, 1954)
	Standing Room Only (Sax, 1955)
	Silent Spring (Carson, 1962)
Scarcity and Growth (Barnett & Morse, 1963)	
No Need for Hunger (Garst, 1963)	
Natural Resources for U.S. Growth (Landsberg, 1964)	
	Famine, 1975 (Paddock & Paddock, 1967)
	The Population Bomb (Ehrlich, 1968)
The Doomsday Syndrome (Maddox, 1972)	
	The Limits to Growth (Meadows *et al.*, 1972)
Models of Doom (Cole *et al.*, 1973)	
The Next Two Hundred Years (Kahn, Brown, & Martel, 1976)	
(and innumerable reviews of Meadows)	

The pattern of statement and counterstatement, of assertion and rebuttal represented by the above tabulation may be strained; still this is the image in my mind. Although about the same number of books is listed on each side, in fact, the number of pessimistic books must by now have far outrun the optimistic. No response after 1972 is listed against the optimistic rebuttals to Meadows, but this reflects the lack of challenging titles, not the lack of busyness of writers.

Public interest in these matters is hard to assess in retrospect. It may have been aroused by pessimistic books, then lulled rather than additionally stimulated by optimistic ones. In contrast, authors lull authors who agree, and stimulate those with opposing views. Post-World War II periods of notable stimulation of attack followed by counterattack began with Vogt (1948) and Osborn (1948) emphasizing the population issue. The response was by de Castro (1952). The second spate was on resources (Brown, 1954); a response came much later from Barnett and Morse (1963). The third spate (Carson, 1962) was narrowly on pesticides, more broadly on pollution; it provoked bitter reaction in technical journals but no books that caught our attention. The fourth one (Ehrlich, 1968) was back to population and to Malthus. Ehrlich's book may have been viewed as material for popular consumption and not worth serious counterattack. But it helped marshall the audience that was later to support Meadows. Finally, in 1972, Meadows, despite such support, provoked a storm of antagonism from another quarter.

For those who feel this is only a see-saw, first one side aggressive, then the other, an examination of the literature will show quickly that we do progress. A comparison of *The Limits of the Earth*, published in 1953, with *The Limits to Growth*, published in 1972, shows the older book to be thin, light, low in content; our sophistication has grown enormously in this last quarter century. Earlier writers might have produced bulk (consider Malthus and the eight editions of his *Essay*), but in much of that bulk they were grasping at and trying to build solid structures from straws of information. For all but the most dedicated or wrangling of scholars, Malthus' last version (1830[/ 1960]), perhaps 60 pages, tells adequately what he has to say.

ATTRIBUTES OF PARTISANS

Optimists and pessimists seem to have consistently different affiliations, but ones that often do not mesh easily with conventional sociopolitical polarizations. Thus:

Optimists include:	Pessimists include:
Gifford Pinchot conservationists dedicated to "wise use" of natural resources	John Muir conservationists dedicated to landscape preservation
Those whose focus is on quantity (the economy)	Those whose focus is on quality (the environment)
Those who believe new technologies can be created to solve any problem	Those who believe technological innovation has limits and that the side effects of technological solutions are often worse than the original problems
Economists, engineers, physicists, and Europeans	Biologists, especially field biologists and Americans
Social scientists having a heritage of rejection of Malthus and dedication to Keynesian growth	Biologists having a heritage of adherence to a broad Malthusianism via Darwin
Political liberals, Marxists, but also conservative businessmen	Arrant reactionaries but also liberal biologists
Those who place hopes in the classical demographic transition	Those who place hopes in explicit pressure to reduce birth rates and who have never heard of the demographic transition or are skeptical of its inevitability

The attributes listed above cannot be rigorous. The principal issue, let it be emphasized again, is that this division is not along conventional political axes, from conservative to liberal. The authors of the several optimistic books can be grouped as follows: Barnett and Morse and Landsberg are economists; nearly all of Cole's group are social or physical scientists; de Castro was a geographer; Mather a geologist; Garst an agriculturist; Kahn and Maddox are physicists. On the other side we find mostly biologists: Vogt, Osborn, Sax, Carson, and Ehrlich; Brown is a geochemist; one Paddock is an agronomist, the other a diplomat; the meadows group are primarily computer scientists or engineers. Evidence of a pattern among the debaters is substantial: While biologists predominate among the pessimists, the optimists are composed largely of social scientists, especially economists, and physical scientists. (I must confess to speculation whether some of the vitriolic response to Meadows [see in particular Golub & Townsend, 1977] stems from their role as scientist–engineers deserting the "good ship optimism" and its complement of economists, engineers, and physicists for the demeaning company of biologists.) Curiously, conservationists (excepting Osborn), demographers, and geographers (excepting de Castro), even though partisans in the quarrel, do not appear among the book authors; is it because they are not given to phrasing challenging book titles?

Documentation of the above classification scheme is not easy; by and large it stems from my own observations and contacts (and I admit to having argued it in class meetings years before the Meadows book appeared). However, the polarization has been recognized even longer. Kenneth Boulding (1956[, p.] 1087) voiced, in famous doggerel, the dichotomy (excerpted below):

A conservationist's lament:	The technologist's reply:
The world is finite, resources are scarce,	Knowledge is power, and the sky's the
Things are bad and will be worse . . .	limit.
Fire will rage with man to fan it,	Every mouth has hands to feed it . . .
Soon we'll have a plundered planet.	All we need is found in granite
People breed like fertile rabbits,	Once we have the men to plan it.
People have disgusting habits.	Yeast and algae give us meat,
Moral:	Soil is almost obsolete.
The evolutionary plan	Moral:
Went astray by evolving Man.	Man's a nuisance, Man's a crackpot,
	But only Man can hit the jackpot.

THE SEEDS OF DICHOTOMY

Before moving to a more detailed look at two major works in the limits-to-growth debate, three distinctions in ways of thinking that contribute to the optimist–pessimist dichotomy are worth examining. Additional items are mentioned at the end of this section.

FORECASTS: GOSPEL OR FABLE?

The focus of the quarrel is always on the nature of the future. Both optimists and pessimists estimate the future. The optimists see it bright, the pessimists see it bleak. In fact, both seek the same future— one of progress, whether or not of growth. The optimists hope their forecasts are self-fulfilling. The pessimists hope their forecasts are self-defeating.

Perhaps here is one element of the durability of the quarrel: Optimists believe in their forecasts and wish them to come true and, perhaps without thinking, assume that all forecasters, including pessimists, believe and wish similarly. In fact, though, I have no knowledge of a pessimistic forecast made with the wish that it come true; all of those I have encountered, scores perhaps hundreds, were made with the opposite intent: to cause a public to become concerned and to persuade it to change its conduct so as to avoid a bleak future. What hope is there of a meeting of minds when one side, the optimists, sees its opponents as wrong and at best as insincere and the other, the pessimists, sees its opponents as wrong and as shallow and complacent?

MODEL OR DATA?

It is a current jargon to describe much, perhaps all, of scientific hypothesizing as "model building." Malthus proposed a model; Meadows is a refinement of it. Models are used to persuade as much as to explore. And yet, persuasion also depends on information, on the data supporting the model. We all know that correlation does not prove cause; but we know just as well that a hypothesis by itself proves nothing. What is persuasive is a plausible hypothesis well supported by data.

If I should present you with four situations, namely, the combinations of good and bad data with good and bad models, two of the combinations are trivial. [That of] good data and good model is persuasive; [that of] bad data and bad model is not. But which is the more persuasive: good model and bad data, or bad model and good data? Those who find the former more persuasive, I suspect of being natural scientists; those who find the latter—good data and bad model—the more persuasive, I suspect of being social scientists.

The difference is plausible: Natural scientists have had considerable success with the proposition that their universe is basically simple; bold hypotheses have, on occasion, been brilliantly confirmed when pertinent data became available. In contrast, in the social sciences, bold hypotheses have led as often to protracted controversy as to success. The result has been a commendable caution, an insistence on waiting until the data come in.

The matter is less simple than presented above. Thus, we must quickly agree that it is difficult beyond measure to quantify the "goodness" of a model. Nonetheless, all of us can recall examples of which we could only say, "That is not plausible; that's a bad model," and conversely, "What an elegant model; so plausible, surely it must be right!"

Another difficulty is that models are not universal. Some very persuasive laws, gravity is an example, are without models in the minds of most of us. Whether this is a historical pattern, whether an equation is the model, or whether the data are persuasive beyond rebuttal (planets more than apples), I cannot say.

Elsewhere I have suggested [see the preceding selection] that this difference between natural and social scientists sheds light on the roots of the limits debate. Thus a biologist may well say that unending exponential growth in a finite world is, in principle, impossible; in contrast, a social scientist might wish to reserve judgment until more data are in! This difference is perhaps best regarded as a difference in scientific faiths.[1]

Environment or Culture?

Third in this listing of differences between optimists and pessimists is perception of the role of the environment relative to culture. The range in attitudes of different scientific fields is too great for examination here . . . Catton and Dunlap (1978a, 1978b) and Dunlap and Catton (1979a, 1979b) have begun an examination that will not be quickly or easily ended. With it is a long overdue taxonomy of environment (Dunlap & Catton, 1979b[, pp.] 74–79). Just as one example of the difficulties, consider the experience in the field of geography with the issue that was called "environmental determinism."

As something of an outsider, I found this a puzzling issue; surely one can observe that Eskimos eat few coconuts and surely this is environmentally determined. But the environmental determinists had rather different matters in mind. They argued that temperate climates lead to advanced civilizations, the tropics to sloth (Huntington, 1915). Such extremes were voiced as, "The inhabitants of basaltic regions are difficult to govern" (G. Soulavie, in Burton, Kates, & Kirkby, 1974[, p.] 102).

Platt (1948) criticized such thought on the score that it could not "explain Argentine" and, seeking an alternative, he took refuge in "free will." I, counting myself a determinist, would not dream of trying to identify the myriad of causes needed to "explain Argentine" and suggest that David Hume might have responded to Platt's espousal of free will with, "It is not that he may do as he wishes but rather that he must do as he wishes."

Much controversy followed; it has led to well-nigh universal rejection of the idea and it is a rare geographer who, even today, will not bridle a bit if charged with a tendency to environmental determinism. And yet, Rostlund (1956), summing up, had to say, "Geographers have not disproved environmental determinism, they have disapproved it."

The quarrel is relevant to the present issue, although less clearly than one might wish. Environmental determinism had an interesting positivism; that is, the environment was seen more as a positive directing force, whether benign or malign, than as a constraint. Contemporary pessimists clearly see the environment as a constraint. In contrast to both those outlooks, however, optimists see environment as unimportant, quite subordinate to culture, or at most as a force influencing the direction of but not constraining human potential.

OTHER SEEDS

The three preceding sections do not even begin a catalog of the differences in perceptions, attitudes, beliefs, or scientific faith between social and biological scientists, between optimists and pessimists. Space permits only mention of others (some of these are considered in other contributions to this volume): view of world as infinite versus finite; man as dominant over his environment versus man as subject to his environment (see Luten, ["Resource Quality and Value of the Landscape" and "The Ethics of Biotic Diversity and Extinctions: From Pleistocene to Aldo Leopold and a Step Beyond," elsewhere in this book,] for an examination of the hypothesis of short-term dominance but long-term subservience); man as separate from and superior to the animate world (White, 1967) versus man as part of the living world; man as master of his destiny versus man as victim of circumstance; growth and development versus stasis and preservation; man as perfectible (see Glacken, 1967; also Bury, 1955) versus man as essentially biological. . . . Social scientists tend to choose the first alternative of each dichotomy, which no doubt contributes to their ecological optimism.

THE FLOWERING OF DICHOTOMY:
TWO RECENT MILESTONES IN
THE LIMITS DEBATE

In this section, two relatively recent and particularly influential books in the ongoing debate are examined: *Scarcity and Growth* by Barnett and Morse (1963) and *The Limits to Growth* by Meadows *et al.* (1972). Barnett and Morse's "optimistic" analysis has been accepted rather uncritically, but the pessimistic analysis of Meadows has been subjected to intense criticism. I suggest that this difference in reaction cannot be attributed to differences in the merits of the two analyses.

SCARCITY AND GROWTH

This book by Barnett and Morse (1963) precedes Meadows by nearly a decade and was written with the support of Resources for the Future, a foundation so perennially optimistic that it has been referred to as the "Pollyanna Institute." Because it is cited so often in support of technological optimism, the authors' model that technology can more than compensate for increasing Ricardian scarcity (Chapter 11) is worth examination. Barnett and Morse cite trends from the past without disasters of the sort projected by pessimists and, not surprisingly, extrapolate into the future without foreseeing disasters. However, their familiarity with this entire field is limited. They are excellent economists but know nothing of technology directly and little even at second hand.

Specifically, they have already been proven terribly wrong in assuming that energy at 1960 costs will be available in unlimited supply (p. 239). Since they wrote, costs (corrected for inflation) of fuels in the United States have doubled, with more increases to come. The bright hope of nuclear power is fading for technical and political reasons. During the three centuries since invention of the steam engine, its efficiency has doubled eight times. Each doubling effectively doubled the fuel resource insofar as it was used to provide work.[2] Such increase is at an end; no more doublings will occur.[3] Extrapolation from the past will not reveal this; instead it requires elementary understanding of the science of heat engines, and *faith* that the Second Law of Thermodynamics will not be revoked, neither by technology nor by legislation. Faith in the Second Law is a cornerstone in the scientific faith of natural scientists; it is a faith in a *principle*, and a "good scientist" will hold fast to it in the face of innumerable allegations of its fallibility (e.g., certain sorts of perpetual motion schemes). Turning to a final energy item, it is at last being conceded that U.S. petroleum production is turning downward, as is the world's, presently. Hubbert (1949) told us this a generation ago. It was folly to extrapolate upward.

Barnett and Morse cite numerous "technological breakthroughs," but some of them are simply misapprehensions. Thus, the notion of "iron in taconite once held there inseparably" (p. 10) but now available because of technology was largely without foundation. Taconite just could not compete with better ores. Now, with technological improvement (not "breakthrough") *and* depletion of better ores, it can compete. They say, "aluminum yields its secrets to technology" (p. 10). Aluminum yielded its secret to Hall in 1886 and nothing that has happened since equals that one step.

They argue that "[o]nce energy becomes available in unlimited quantities at constant cost, the processing of large quantities of low-grade resource material presumably can be undertaken at constant cost" (p. 239). In fact, several remorseless realities argue against such a Utopian view: (1) As already noted, the vision of such energy is waning. (2) The statement suggests a constant cost for the target material in the ore but it only says a constant cost per ton of progressively leaner ore. Leaner ores mean more ore broken, removed, hauled, and crushed per pound of target material. Each of these means more energy and, in all likelihood, at high unit costs. (3) Also, the economies of scale in the immense overburden shovels used to reach such lean ores are close to the limit imposed by the strength of steel with which the shovels are made. At most, one more doubling in size can be managed (Jackim, 1974). (4) Leaner ores must be crushed finer to recover the minute crystals of target material with, again, a higher energy cost. Energy and chemical costs to extract the target material will increase per pound of target material, if not per ton of ore, as ores become leaner.

Lovering (1969), a geologist, flatly contradicts Barnett and Morse on these points, and more detailed studies (National Academy of Sciences, 1975; see also Cook, 1976) support him.

Barnett and Morse can also be faulted for their belief in a technology that can grow forever. They wrote at the end of an era of extraordinary growth in the number of scientists, at a time when one could say such things as "90% of all scientists who have ever lived are still alive." But the numbers, if extrapolated at the rates prevailing before 1960, would lead early in the next century to values for recruitment of scientists and engineers that exceeded probable recruitment to the entire labor force. Or, as Derek Price (quoted by Jahoda, 1973[, p.] 211) said, "two scientists for every man, woman, child and dog in the population." Such growth has well nigh ended, at least in the United States, and a couple of generations before the relentlessness of sheer numbers would have forced it to end. The number of scientists and engineers in the United States appears to have increased at only 1.9% per year from 1960 to 1978 (calculated from U.S. Bureau of the Census, 1979[, p.] xxvii). With this slowing, projections of an ever-growing technology have become much less plausible.

One could challenge Barnett and Morse repeatedly, but one could also find a host of ways in which they are right. The central difficulty may be that no one knows enough of all the fields involved to summarize them honestly, constructively, and concisely. And yet policy, if it is to be made democratically at all, depends on just such summaries. While [one does not wish] to question Barnett and Morse's competence in economics, it is easy to challenge the book on scientific and technological grounds. In fact, the authors know far too little to have become involved in these fields.

The central issue for this article is that despite its shortcomings and errors, Barnett and Morse's *Scarcity and Growth* has been widely and uncritically accepted, especially by economists. There can be little doubt that this is largely because their optimistic conclusions are so widely shared.

THE LIMITS TO GROWTH

In contrast, *The Limits to Growth* by Meadows *et al.* (1972), has met with widespread and adverse critical analyses. The argument of the

Meadows book has been summarized repeatedly [see the preceding selection, pp. 293–314. . . .

Because the authors postulate limits to arable land, to investment in capital equipment, [and] to stock (mineral) resources, and because they accept the optimists' implicit requirements of continuing growth at roughly constant rates both of population and of per capita consumption, they come out with quantitatively calamitous conclusions. Malthus, with much simpler postulates, came out with qualitatively similar conclusions.

Both Meadows and Malthus have, in fact, followed similar logic: population does grow exponentially if life expectancy and completed family size are held constant. Arithmetic growth, whether explicit or as carefully postulated by Malthus (1830[/1960]), will, ultimately, fail to keep pace. Parenthetically and curiously, although critics damn Malthus for his failure to envision the enormous growth in production of the 19th and 20th centuries, his words taken literally concede the possibility of a growth in food by now of almost seven times that of 1800.[4] Today's population is only 4.5 times that of 1800. An estimate of food per capita today of 7/4.5 times that of 1800 may be pretty close to reality.

Meadows has also used with great effectiveness what we have come to call the "Malthusian corollary." This is the proposition that, in an exponentially growing series, say, of copper consumption, the amount consumed in each doubling period equals the total of previous consumption: $1 + 2 + 4 + 8 = 15$; the next doubling is 16 (for details, see [the preceding selection, p. 311]). The implication of this corollary is that under conditions of exponential growth assumed possible by the optimists, it makes little difference how accurate the estimates of resource magnitude are; scarcity is rarely remote and it comes most abruptly (see Ophuls, 1977[, pp.] 62–66, and the "Epilog" to this article).

Meadows is, of course, vulnerable to criticism. The assumed relation between pollution and lifespan, identified as unsubstantiated by many critics, is, it is true, almost without foundation. Meadows admits this but still must use some relationship even though speculative. They have also been heavily criticized for "aggregating"—for lumping the entire world together; for recognizing no differences of region, development, resource attribute, social structure, demographic evolution. But the critics do not seem to realize that all such information is aggregated; no one talks about the corn crop, ear by ear. No one has suggested what an optimum level of aggregation might be. Nonetheless, aggregation does lead to problems in many areas, and as much in the diverse sphere of pollution as anywhere.

Perhaps a fundamental weakness in Meadows is that the authors have not been able to introduce into their functional relations a distinction between what we are already doing to resolve these problems and what we still must do. The authors, it seems to me, have better access to the literature of physical science than of biology. They have paid little attention to preservation issues; they show little knowledge of quite stable biological systems. But they also fail to distinguish between mineral resources, such as iron and aluminum, that are hardly exhaustible and those that probably are exhaustible. On this one point the economists may be on better ground than Meadows.

Although the critics engaged in a great deal of nitpicking over the model and data used by Meadows (and exposed their fallibility by their universal oversight of a transparent error),[5] perhaps the most popular theme of the numerous critiques was "Malthus in, Malthus out"—that is, since Meadows uses a Malthusian model it naturally gets a Malthusian answer (Boyd, 1972; Kneese & Ridker, 1972; Passell et al., 1972). But if Meadows had used a non-Malthusian model like that of Barnett and Morse, would they not have gotten a non-Malthusian result just as surely? Accordingly, might not one charge Barnett and Morse with "optimism in, optimism out"!

SOCIAL SCIENCE CRITIQUES OF MEADOWS

Given the tendency noted earlier of social scientists to reject the notion of "limits" for human societies, it is not surprising that many of the critiques of *The Limits to Growth* have come from social scientists. Economists, of course, have been conspicuous among the critics. For example, Passell et al. (1972), who describe Meadows as "an empty and misleading work," are as optimistic as Barnett and Morse about technological growth, quick to see that Meadows uses a Malthusian model, dogmatic about Malthus being wrong, and annoyed that the program dice were loaded in a Malthusian pattern. Kneese and Ridker (1972) are equally critical of Meadows and display the technological optimism one expects from Resources for the Future economists (the intellectual heirs to Barnett and Morse), leading the biologist Hardin (1972[b]) to stigmatize their review as sophistry and an example of shortsightedness.

Kaysen (1972) goes to the economic extreme in his review:

> The notion that such limits must exist gains plausibility from the use of physical terms to indicate the relevant quantities—acres of arable land, tons of chrome ore reserves—implicitly invoking the physical finiteness of the earth as the ultimate bound. But this is fundamentally misleading. Resources are properly measured in economic, not physical, terms.

That is to say, if we could only get over our illogical language habits, we could live happily in economic space and get along entirely without this physical world! Macinko (1974) discloses a 100-fold error by Kaysen in estimated maximum world population, apparently a consequence of a discussion with a physical scientist that lasted but two minutes. Macinko, noting that Meadows says "nothing not said many times over the past twenty years," goes on to say in his exhaustive review of the situation that he suspects economists are reacting emotionally because the computer message is less easily rejected than the same message presented in qualitative terms.

The economists do not have a corner on emotionalism. Thus, Bell (1977), a sociologist, flippantly dismisses *The Limits to Growth* and ascribes its impact to its presentation as a "media event," aided immeasurably by having been published "fortuitously close in time with a worldwide Arab oil embargo" (p. 13). He goes on to observe that "[u]nder severe criticism from the academic community, most of the assumptions and the logic of analysis of the Club of Rome study was found to be faulty" (p. 14). Finally, with a degree of technological optimism rivaling that of the economists, Bell rejects the idea of "physical limits" and argues that if limits to growth exist they will be "social limits." In a similar vein, another sociologist, Sandbach (1978), attributes the attention given to Meadows as mainly due to the attractiveness of its message of "limits" to the environmentalist movement which was near its peak of strength in 1972, rather than to the basic soundness of its message.

Not all social science reviewers are so united in antagonism toward Meadows. For example, the economist Heilbroner (1972) looks beyond the computer details, as all readers should have done, and is most concerned about whether we can change our ways fast enough when the crunch comes. Surely, this is the essential issue. And a political scientist, Ophuls (1973, 1977), rebutted a critical review and subsequently published an enormous literature on the subject of ecological limits which should be consulted by anyone wanting to study the issue in great detail and depth. (Ophuls, in passing, comes closest to my assessment; namely, that it is a quarrel between social and natural scientists.) But is anything to be gained by more detailed inquiry; isn't the issue really how it has affected our thinking?

CONFLICTING "MODELS OF MAN"

The most extreme antagonism I have found is by Jahoda (1973), a social psychologist and chairman of the Sussex Group which published *Models of Doom* (Cole *et al.*, 1973) as a direct response to and intended refutation of Meadows. One can only regard her words as an emotional diatribe and speculate on the reasons. Thus: "Men's values are . . . partly . . . the major source of interference with the exponential growth of the physical properties of the world." (p. 211) What on earth can she mean? The earth's physical properties hardly change. Does "physical properties of the world" mean natural resources?

Again, Jahoda (1973[, p.] 211) says:

> Meadows explains the nature of exponential growth by a beautifully simple child's guide to compound interest. Yet there must be many people who can testify that their assumption of turning $100 in 40 years into $800 has not come true. The mathematics is correct but currencies change.

This is close to saying two plus two is not always four because sometimes two is only one!

Next, she quotes Derek Price, as noted earlier, on the rapid growth in the number of scientists, and goes on to say, "this particular disaster of exponential growth is already in the process of being averted" by young people choosing not to become scientists (p. 212). It is as if she thought the disaster would, in fact, occur were it not for such decisions by people. The social solution carries more weight than the physical impossibility!

The importance of these excerpts is not, I think, in their overt illogic. Instead, it is in the frustration that is revealed, a frustration apparently stemming from Jahoda's focus on the social environment, not the physical environment, as the ultimate constraint on human potential. To support this image, the antithesis of Meadows' image, Jahoda must destroy the idea that mankind's ability to adapt the physical world to its needs has limits.[6] Having done this to *her* satisfaction, she writes in her conclusion:

> It is in the nature of purposeful (human) adaptation that the course of events can be changed dramatically if social constraints are experienced as intolerable. . . . It makes no sense in this context to talk of exponential growth in a finite world. Man's inventiveness in changing social arrangements is without limits, even if not without hazards. (p. 215)

In other words, the "world model" of Meadows conflicts with Jahoda's optimistic "model of man"; therefore, Meadows' model must go.

The four authors of Meadows, in their "Response to Sussex" (1973[, p.] 239), pinpoint the importance of the difference in the "concept of man" held by them and by the Sussex Group. They begin by noting:

> One possible concept of man, the one that is held by the Sussex Group, is that *Homo sapiens* is a very special creature whose unique brain gives him not only the capability but the right to exploit for his own short-term purposes all other creatures and all resources the world has to offer. This is an age-old concept of man, one firmly rooted in Judeo-Christian tradition and newly strengthened by stunning technical achievements in the last few centuries.

After a paragraph of elaboration, they look at the other side:

> The opposite concept of man is also an ancient one but it is more closely related to the Eastern religions than to the Western ones.[7] It assumes that man is one species with all other species embedded in the intricate web of natural processes that sustains and constrains all forms of life. It acknowledges that man is one of the more successful species, in terms of competitiveness, but that this very success is leading him to destroy and simplify the natural surrounding web, about which he understands very little. Subscribers to this view feel that human institutions are ponderous

and short-sighted, adaptive only after very long delays, and likely to attack complex issues with simplistic and self-centered solutions, [and they] also question strongly whether technology and material growth, which seem to have caused many problems, should be looked to as the sources of solution to these same problems in the future.

Meadows *et al.* (1973[, p.] 240) conclude, somberly enough, with:

> We see no objective way of resolving these very different views of man and his role in the world. It seems to be possible for either side to look at the same world and find support for its view. Technological optimists see only rising life expectancies, more comfortable lives, the advance of human knowledge, and improved wheat strains. Malthusians see only rising populations, destruction of the land, extinct species, urban deterioration, and increasing gaps between the rich and the poor.

DISCUSSION: THE BITTER FRUIT

One can understand, therefore, the reasons for the persistent dichotomy in thought on the issue of limits—that is, between optimists and pessimists. One wonders, though, whether much can be done about it. I have no evidence that anyone has been won over from the one side to the other, whether by reason, by weight of numbers, or by volumes in print. Perhaps it *is* important, as has been argued traditionally in matters of faith, to turn to the young for recruits. Whether this is because the young are malleable or because the human mind works better at six than at 60, I cannot say.

American scientific thought is not about to give up its intense specialization in favor of transdisciplinary approaches, especially over such a broad spectral range as that which would combine social science and biology. Wilson (1975[, p.] 4) has doubts: "Whether the social sciences can be truly biologicized in this fashion remains to be seen." On top of this educational predicament, as we become more urbanized, our contact with the physical world well-nigh vanishes.

Nonetheless, we do learn. While we cannot distinguish between kilowatts and kilowatt-hours, only a few of the press still confuse gallons and barrels of oil, and some of us know that a barrel of oil is 42 gallons. But are we overtaking the quarry? On the record (Bartlett,

1978), the nature of exponential growth is widely, even deliberately misunderstood; few have any comprehension of the Malthusian corollary; and the record of public statements on energy is atrociously bad.

I can only suggest three alternate ways out of the predicament:

1. An intellectual solution by a priesthood, namely, "technocracy." I must admit to sensing, occasionally, in Meadows a penumbra of such attitudes. I doubt whether the authors of Meadows would concur and believe they would retort that it is my bad reading or, at worst, unintended.

2. If no other intellectual solution is possible, we can only expect a policy decision stemming from power, from whatever leverage one side or the other can muster; or perhaps we shall oscillate from one policy to the other, from optimism to pessimism; or perhaps we shall simply wallow in between.

3. But perhaps we can reach an intellectual solution and one reached by some semblance of democratic procedure, not handed down by a priesthood. Because no possibility exists of the American, or any other, public digesting an infinity of detail, the argument will have to be about a model and one that is plausible and persuasive enough to gain the rank of a principle.

And yet were I to suggest that the Malthusian doctrine of limits is simple, is comprehensible, and has merit if not taken too literally, I would simply be issuing invitations to another inning. That inning would begin with a rhetorical question: Is Malthus a phoenix destined to rise eternally from his ashes? It would proceed to remind me that social science continues to believe in the ecologically optimistic doctrine of man as master of his destiny. In their turn at bat, the biologists, recalling Rostlund (1956), might say that Malthus has been disapproved, not disproved. Disproof, they might add, is not possible, Malthusian doctrine being of the nature of an axiom, and to be taken as a parable. Malthus' warning is simply that growth must end some day, and he asks whether it would not be prudent to modify our conduct while time remains to maneuver.

It is a curious paradox that the deterministic biologists commend this route while the social scientists espousing man as master of his destiny argue that economic forces will see us safely through. Who then is the master: man or economic law? Does the society exist to serve its economy?

Yes, we do need a great new paradigm, but there's not a glimmer of light from anything on the horizon that might bridge this gap and reduce the number of schools to one.

EPILOG

Meadows, as has many another, tells the "riddle of the lily pond" in an effort to impress the reader with the way exponential growth sneaks up quietly and then suddenly becomes catastrophic. It goes like this: A water lily in a pond doubles each day; if unchecked it would cover the pond in 30 days, choking out all other life. But it won't be a problem until it covers half the pond. When will that be? On the 29th day. You then have but one day to save the pond (Meadows et al. 1972[, p.] 29).

It seems to me [that] the essence, the relevance that would make a proper parable of it is overlooked. Grant the facts, but focus attention on the open water remaining. This, the open water, is the symbol for remaining natural resources. Concede, too, that one can estimate its magnitude only to within 10%; this is a most generous estimate of precision in that very difficult field.

Now, let us watch the pond as the lily grows. For 25 days the judgment is easy: Open water has not diminished within our ability to measure it; its value remains at 100%.[8] Surely, after 25 estimates of remaining resources, we have assurance by repeated confirmation of careful evaluation that the resources are in fact infinite. Why continue the experiment? But if you insist (perhaps our contract still has unspent funds!), let us look at the 26th day: strangely the reading is uncertain; perhaps we should say only nine-tenths remain (the exact value is 93.75%). What do we find on the 27th day? Yes, only 90% remains (the exact value is 87.5%); but only a tenth or so is gone and this is after 27 days. If you are worried, please look at our extrapolation: at use rates averaged over all of our experience (that is, 27 days), it will last 270 days. But, while no need to worry exists, we will monitor the pond closely. What does the 28th day reveal? The value is 80 or perhaps 70% (it is exactly 75%); curious that it should have shrunk so much in a single day; is this a bad reading? We shall do a very careful evaluation tomorrow: Heavens! it's half gone; something beyond the ability of man to forecast is taking place. Call the committees together! Tonight we will prepare new grant proposals; by morning we will have careful plans and will invoke policies for conservation for the remaining resources with rationing to ensure availability and equitable distribution for all of us throughout the foreseeable future. Do not panic; after all, we still have half of all the open water we ever had (see Luten, 1964a, for similar parables).[9]

Comes the 30th day, gray, cold, bleak . . .

NOTES

1. While I believe that natural scientists as a group tend to differ from social scientists by their greater faith in models relative to data, biologists seem much more likely to be pessimists, while physicists (perhaps because of their ties to technologists such as engineers) tend to join social scientists as optimists.

2. "Work" in the physical sense as distinguished from "heat." See Luten ["United States Requirements," elsewhere in this book] for clarification.

3. The consensus of heat engine technologists is that efficiencies in excess of 40% are unlikely. The extrapolation of heat engine efficiency by Resources for the Future economists (Landsberg[, Fischman, & Fisher,] 1963[, pp.] 264, 825) from implied levels for the U.S. national average of 32% in 1960 to 38% in 1980 and 45% in 2000 has not come to pass. It remains at 33% (U.S. Bureau of the Census, 1978[b, p.] 592; 1979[, p.] 599).

4. The so-called arithmetic progression in food production was stated quite carefully by Malthus. In his last revision (Malthus, 1830[/1960, p. 30]), he phrases it several times; the most general version follows: "[if] we refer to . . . the whole earth—the supposition of a future capacity in the soil to increase the necessaries of life every twenty-five years by a quantity equal to that which is at present produced must be decidedly beyond the truth." With seven periods of 25 years since 1800, all that he claimed was that food production in 1975 must be "decidedly" less than seven times what it was in 1800. The sense of "decidedly" and the facts of food production are hardly well enough established to support a categorical verdict of "wrong."

5. [See the preceding selection, p. 311, for details on this error.]

6. Jahoda's statements epitomize social scientists' adherence to the "Human Exemptionalism Paradigm" (Dunlap & Catton, 1979a[, p.] 250; see also Catton & Dunlap, 1978a, 1978b).

7. Meadows's choice of "Eastern religions" for contrast suggests its authors are more aware of countercultural affinity for Zen Buddhism than of the roots of American conservation thought. Huth (1957) and Leopold (1966) have provided insights into occidental origins of the ecological model of man.

8. Given the assumption that the water lily grows exponentially and covers the entire pond in 30 days, we can, by working backward, calculate the fraction covered and from that the fraction uncovered, as follows: day 30: $1 - 1 = 0\%$ uncovered; day 29: $1 - 0.5 = 50\%$ uncovered; 28: $1 - 0.25 = 75\%$; 27: $1 - 0.125 = 87.5\%$; 26: $1 - 0.0625 = 93.75\%$; 25: $1 - 0.03125 = 96.875\%$; day 24: $1 - 0.015625 = 98.4375\%$ uncovered. Given imprecise measurement, it is unlikely that we will notice the lily, and thus the shrinkage in the open pond, until day 26.

9. If my own position in this debate remains obscure, my preference for parables over citations should shed light.

AIR POLLUTION'S IMPACT ON GROWTH IN SOCIETY

In the early 1980s, society was increasingly worried about environmental contaminations. Appropriately, this paper was one of a group of papers that were to examine a theme involving air pollution: "Air Pollution's Impact on Growth." The other papers focused on one interpretation of the theme, the effects of pollution control on growth of industry; Luten, in contrast, addressed a second interpretation, pollution as a constraint on growth in society.

The apparently iconoclastic spirit of the paper is only one feature that makes it classic Luten. He spoke here of human purpose, of Malthus, of systems; he discussed boundaries between "goods" and "bads," wondered about the formulation of environmental policy, and suggested that the educational system has failed to educate the American population adequately to deal with environmental problems; he took a historical perspective but looked to the future; and, most of all, he provoked his hearers to think by questioning their assumptions: "The task [of controlling air pollution] is enormously complicated by the fact that we really don't dare say explicitly what it is that we are trying to accomplish. . . . I suspect that efforts to 'optimize the quality of life' are quite beyond assessment and, practically, not worth undertaking . . . "

Andy Rooney [1983], in a recent Sunday column worrying about pollution, recalled T. S. Eliot's "This is the way the world ends/ Not with a bang but a whimper." A few days later, I, reading of another record-breaking court judgment in an environmental pollution personal injury case, recalled an earlier phrasing of my own: "Until finally nothing can grow but litigation." Then I tried a new combination: "This is the way the world ends/ Not with a bang, *not* with a

Paper presented at the annual meeting of the Association of American Geographers, Denver, CO, April 1983.

whimper/ But in litigation;/ Complaint, crosscomplaint, denial, demurrer."

In contrast, the Meadows and their associates, in *The Limits to Growth* [1972], found they could only make qualitative guesses as to the effects of pollution on life expectancy, and, via that route, on growth. But their guesses suggested that this was not a likely pathway for regulation of the size of human populations. That is, they found [that] other pathways would limit human populations before bad air, bad water, bad dirt, and so on.

Many would disagree, but you should keep in mind that even in our dire world of smog, [of] polluted groundwater, of dioxin and PCB, of rampant radioactivity, in this nation's environment of new and terrifying hazards, life expectancy at birth was only this month reported at a new high, perhaps an average for both sexes of 75 years at birth. But, on the other side, you must also keep in mind just how a life expectancy at birth is derived and recognize that it, too, has failings as a keen-edged discriminator between good and bad. And, of course, since it sums up gains and losses, one can hardly know how [many] of each [are included]. Note, too, that in the most careful study of environmental carcinogenesis I know of, virtually no consequences are found, except for cigarettes and asbestos.

Then I went back 30 years, to a time when I was chairman of the Safety Committee at Shell Development Company's laboratories in Emeryville, California. There, one day when we were faced with problems of disposing of some strange new and most unpleasant substances, I suggested the time would come when we would spend as much money [in] getting rid of chemicals from those laboratories as in buying them. I have—many times, I must admit—wished that I had put that down on paper then.

Going back a bit further than my youth, Thomas Malthus [1830/ 1960, pp. 38–39] included among his "positive checks" on population growth

> all the causes which tend in any way prematurely to shorten the duration of human life, such as unwholesome occupations, severe labour and exposure to the seasons, bad and insufficient food and clothing arising from poverty, bad nursing of children, excesses of all kinds, *great towns and manufactories* [my emphasis], the whole train of common diseases and epidemics, wars, infanticide, plague and famine. Of these positive checks, those which appear to arise from the laws of nature may be called

exclusively misery; and those which we bring on ourselves, such as wars, excesses of all kinds and many others which it would be in our power to avoid are of a mixed nature. They are brought upon us by vice, and their consequences are misery.

Finally, to complete the nostalgic trip, Samuel Taylor Coleridge (of Malthus's generation), in writing upon Cologne [1834/1924], said,

> I counted two and seventy stenches
> All well defined, and several stinks! . . .
> The river Rhine, it is well known,
> doth wash your city of Cologne;
> But tell me, Nymphs, what power divine
> Shall henceforth wash the river Rhine?

But we [here] are [not] dealing with all of pollution, neither with all of air pollution, but only with air pollution's effect on growth. A narrower question is not an easier one. As I studied the title, it grew tougher and I tauter. Did he mean to ask: Can air quality become so bad it will end growth? By what means? By killing everyone? The Meadows say no; Malthus suggests yes. [Will it] stimulat[e] policies for abatement of increments to pollution stemming from the industry that is requisite to growth?

Three paths to control come to mind; the audience today will suggest more.

1. Let pollution control growth directly, whether by shortening lives and thereby limiting population, or by rendering a region so unattractive that people stay away from it.

2. A system, perhaps more social than physical, of sensing pollution [and] amplifying the conclusions until action occurs at a policy level to control pollution in some specific fashion, whether by limitation of each source or by setting ceilings in a region and denying right to pollute to new sources.

3. A system, as above, for sensing and amplifying conclusions, but proceeding in a different policy direction—namely, of denying permits to build residences or to drive automobiles so that the control is directly on population rather than on its direct and indirect activities.

4. Surely, some will think of additional paths, general ones.

The life expectancy results already mentioned suggest that we have not tried the first method. Legislative history tells us that we have employed the second method. The history goes back, in fact, hundreds of years, but it has only become a part of everyday living within the last 15 years with passage of the Clean Air Act and its amendments. The third method has been used in a few local cases (Boulder, Colorado, and Petaluma, California, notably), but while the objective has been environmental, air pollution has been a minor component.

So the focus of attention is on the second method—the way in which we learn that air pollution is bad for us; the way we decide how much we should permit; the way we move toward legislated policy' and, finally, to[ward] enforcement [of that policy].

Perhaps I should ask now whether we really care to examine these questions. My own impression is that almost no element of rationality can be found in the process from beginning to end.

In the first place, we are concerned with boundaries, boundaries between goods and bads, between good air and bad air. We preach that there is a categorical difference. [However,] a few minutes' thought would persuade almost anyone that the boundaries are fuzzy; that there is no sharp line between good and bad; that the very distinction between good and bad derives not from experience in this field, but from moralistic traditions, from an age of "thou shalt not kill," [a] field in which distinction is sharp. But if 0.1 parts per million (ppm) of SO_2 is set as the maximum allowable concentration (MAC), are we to conclude that 0.09 ppm is benign and 0.11 ppm lethal? Of course not; their effects are well-nigh indistinguishable. But we dare not admit it.

The task is enormously complicated by the fact that we really don't dare say explicitly what it is that we are trying to accomplish. If one were to propose that we seek to optimize the quality of life and that duration of life is only one component, the political backwash would be destructive. As a rather different target, [if] one were to propose that we seek to minimize the years of life sacrificed to pollution, one would find little support—but is it just as important to "save" the life of a person who is going to die next week as the life of a child with 60 more years of life expectancy? I think not, but I think I know better than to advocate such a matter politically. What do we mean by "save a life," anyway? If there is one thing we can be sure of, it is that very few of us will get out of this world alive.

I suspect that efforts to "optimize the quality of life" are quite beyond assessment and, practically, not worth undertaking, but that efforts to add years of life are worth undertaking.

Have we, then, set MAC so as to add the maximum number of years of life? Or the maximum number at some tolerable cost? I rather doubt whether anyone has bothered to answer such a question. In the light of our procedures, it is irrelevant. Certainly, what we have done has ignored the answer to such a question, if known, if it could be known. Instead, we set up an amplifying adversarial system of white hats against black hats—both are essential to its operation. An MAC is proposed, then others, and bargaining for them continues on and off stage; the senior proposal seems always to have a considerable advantage. At first the information flow is limited to a few people; presently it is amplified to an environmental organization, then a group of them. Then as it becomes a legislative issue, the pros and cons both generate increased interest, and the matter becomes a public controversy. Thence it proceeds to a legislative decision, based on whatever bargaining positions have been generated—whether stemming from information, lobbying pressures, political coalitions, or contributions.

Does the result depend on what we learned from animal studies, from epidemiology—medical geography, if you please—from careful statistical analysis of clinical pathology? It seems unlikely.

One might say that we are attacking problems that our society is poorly prepared to deal with. One might say, in fact, that we are witness to the failure of an educational system. The American people, it can be strongly argued, are quite unable to assess the merits of the arguments pro and con; the decisions are as apt to stem from the level of hysteria that can be generated as from any substance. One might ask, too, whence comes environmental policy? How do the environmental organizations decide on environmental policy? I think an examination of this question might shock a lot of us. Boards of directors, I suspect, at best merely ratify policies already being pushed by activists, whether hired staffs or the volunteers of these organizations. In some instances, I am quite sure the boards have virtually nothing to do with setting environmental policies. Who, then sets the policies? Perhaps it is the person who wrote that letter asking you to join and promising to rectify so many wrongs that you finally did join. But isn't that the essence of democracy? The organization does what its members want.

And yet, irrational as it may be, our air is better than it was at Denora in 1948, at London in 1952. And we are better off and a touch happier because of it. Whether we are optimally better may some day be determinable, but not yet.

Now, to [the] question asked of this panel. With the Clean Air Act and its amendments, the Meadowses become right: Air pollution need not limit growth—we must find other ways to limit growth.

REFERENCES CITED

Barnett, H. J., & C. Morse. 1963. *Scarcity and Growth*. Baltimore: Johns Hopkins University Press.

Barney, G. O. 1977. *The Unfinished Agenda*. New York: Thomas Y. Crowell.

Bartlett, A. A. 1978. "Forgotten Fundamentals of the Energy Crisis." *American Journal of Physics*, 46: 876–888.

Bates, M. 1962. *The Prevalence of People*. New York: Scribner's. (First published in 1955.)

Bell, D. 1977. "Are There 'Social Limits' to Growth?" In K. D. Wilson (ed.), *Prospects for Growth* (pp. 13–26). New York: Praeger.

Blaut, J. 1975. Verbal statement at meetings of the Association of American Geographers, Milwaukee, WI, April 21, 1975.

Bogue, D. J. 1969. *Principles of Demography*. New York: Wiley.

Boserup, E. 1965. *The Conditions of Economic Growth*. Chicago: Aldine.

Boulding, K. 1956. "A Conservationist's Lament—The Technologist's Reply." In W. L. Thomas, Jr. (ed.), *Man's Role in Changing the Face of the Earth* (p. 1087). Chicago: University of Chicago Press.

Boulding, K. 1968. *Beyond Economics: Essays on Society, Religion, and Ethics*. Ann Arbor: University of Michigan Press.

Boyd, B. 1963. "Deer Hunting on 'Bikes.'" *San Francisco Chronicle*, October 19.

Boyd, B. 1964. "A Pox on Water Skiers." *San Francisco Chronicle*, January 9.

Boyd, R. 1972. "World Dynamics: A Note." *Science*, 177: 516–519.

Broad, C. D. 1930. *Five Types of Ethical Theory*. London: Routledge & Kegan Paul.

Brown, H. 1954. *The Challenge of Man's Future*. New York: Viking.

Burns, R. 1979. "To a Mouse." In M. H. Abrams (general ed.), *The Norton Anthology of English Literature*, 4th ed., Vol. 2 (pp. 92–93). New York: Norton. (First published in 1786.)

Burton, I., & R. Kates. 1964. "Slaying the Malthusian Dragon: A Review." *Economic Geography*, 40: 82–89.

Burton, I., R. Kates, & A. Kirkby. 1974. "Geography." In A. E. Utton & D. H. Henning (eds.), *Interdisciplinary Environmental Approaches* (pp. 100–126). Costa Mesa, CA: Educational Media Press.

Bury, J. B. 1955. *The Idea of Progress*. New York: Dover Press. (First published in 1932.)

Calhoun, J. B. 1962. "Population Density and Social Pathology." *Scientific American*, 206(2): 139–148.

Carr-Saunders, A. M. 1922. *The Population Problem: A Study in Human Evolution.* London: Oxford University Press.

Carr-Saunders, A. M. 1925. *Population.* London: Oxford University Press.

Carr-Saunders, A. M. 1936. *World Population: Past Growth and Present Trends.* London: Oxford University Press.

Carson, R. 1962. *Silent Spring.* Boston: Houghton Mifflin.

Carter, L. 1973. "Earl Butz, Counselor for Natural Resources: President's Choice a Surprise for Environmentalists." *Science*, 179: 358–359.

Catton, W. R., Jr., & R. E. Dunlap. 1978a. "Environmental Sociology: A New Paradigm." *American Sociologist*, 13: 41–49.

Catton, W. R., Jr., & R. E. Dunlap. 1978b. "Paradigms, Theories, and the Primacy of the HEP-NEP Distinction." *American Sociologist*, 13: 256–259.

Chase, S. 1936. *Rich Land, Poor Land.* New York: McGraw-Hill.

Clark, C. 1970. *Starvation or Plenty?* New York: Taplinger.

Cole, H. S. D., C. Freeman, M. Jahoda, & K. L. R. Pavitt (eds.). 1973. *Models of Doom: A Critique of the Limits to Growth.* New York: Universe Books.

Coleridge, S. T. 1924. "Cologne." In E. H. Coleridge (ed.), *The Poems of Samuel Taylor Coleridge* (p. 477). London: Oxford University Press. (First published in 1834.)

Commoner, B. 1971. *The Closing Circle.* New York: Knopf.

Conrad, J. 1960. *The End of the Tether.* In *The Nigger of the Narcissus and The End of the Tether* (pp. 173–320). New York: Dell. (First published in 1903.)

Cook, E. 1976. "Limits to Exploitation of Nonrenewable Resources." *Science*, 191: 677–682.

Cowles, R. B. 1960. "Population Pressure and Natural Resources." In D. Brower (ed.), *The Meaning of Wilderness to Science: Proceedings of the Sixth Biennial Wilderness Conference* (pp. 79–94). San Francisco: Sierra Club.

Daly, H. E. 1973. *Toward a Steady-State Economy.* San Francisco: W. H. Freeman.

Daly, H. E. (ed.). 1980. *Economics, Ecology, Ethics: Essays toward a Steady-State Economy.* San Francisco: W. H. Freeman.

Day, L. H. 1966. "The Pressure of People." In B. M. Kilgore (ed.), *Wilderness in a Changing World: Proceedings of the Ninth Biennial Wilderness Conference* (pp. 32–39). San Francisco: Sierra Club.

de Castro, J. 1952. *The Geography of Hunger.* Boston: Little, Brown.

Dewhurst, J. R., & Associates. 1947. *America's Need and Resources.* New York: Twentieth Century Fund.

Dickens, C. 1954. *A Christmas Carol.* In *Christmas Books* (pp. 1–76). London: Oxford University Press. (First published in 1843.)

Dunlap, R. E., & W. R. Catton, Jr. 1979a. "Environmental Sociology." *Annual Review of Sociology*, 5: 243–273.

Dunlap, R. E., & W. R. Catton, Jr. 1979b. "Environmental Sociology: A Framework for Analysis." In T. O'Riordan & R. C. d'Arge (eds.), *Progress in Resource Management and Environmental Planning*, Vol. 1 (pp. 57–85). Chichester, England: Wiley.

Ehrlich, P. 1968. *The Population Bomb*. New York: Ballantine Books.

Ehrlich, P. 1970. "Population and Conservation: Two Sides of a Coin." In M. E. McCloskey (ed.), *Wilderness, the Edge of Knowlege: Proceedings of the Eleventh Biennial Wilderness Conference* (pp. 3–10). San Francisco: Sierra Club.

Ehrlich, P., J. P. Holdren, & B. Commoner. 1972. "A Bulletin Dialogue on *The Closing Circle*." *Science and Public Affairs: Bulletin of the Atomic Scientists*, 28(5): 16–27; 28(6): 42–45.

Emerson, R. W. 1957. *Nature*. In S. E. Whicher (ed.), *Selections from Ralph Waldo Emerson* (pp. 21–56). Boston: Houghton Mifflin. (First published in 1836.)

Empey, A. G. 1917. *Over the Top*. New York: G. P. Putnam's Sons.

"Engineers Project Heat Rejection Requirements." 1970. (News report of a paper by R. T. Jaske, J. F. Fletcher, & K. R. Wise.) *Chemical and Engineering News*, March 2, pp. 34–35.

Federal Power Commission. 1964. *National Power Survey, Part 1*. Washington, DC: U.S. Government Printing Office.

Firey, W. 1960. *Man, Mind, and Land*. Glencoe, IL: Free Press.

Fremlin, J. H. 1964. "How Many People Can the World Support?" *New Scientist*, 26: 285–287.

"Fusion Power—Future Necessity." 1956. *Chemical and Engineering News*, December 24, p. 6290.

Gaffney, M. (ed.). 1967. *Extractive Resources and Taxation*. Madison: University of Wisconsin Press.

Galbraith, J. K. 1965. "Economics versus the Quality of Life." *Encounter Magazine*, January, pp. 31–39.

Gardner, E. S. 1962. "Some Rights Should Be Left." *Sports Afield*, September, pp. 48–49; 85–86.

Garst, J. 1963. *No Need for Hunger*. New York: Random House.

Gates, P. 1968. *History of Public Land Law Development*. Washington, DC: U.S. Government Printing Office.

Gibbon, E. 1932. *The Decline and Fall of the Roman Empire*. New York: Modern Library. (First published in 1776.)

Giddings, J. C. 1973. "World Population, Human Disaster and Nuclear Holocaust." *Science and Public Affairs: Bulletin of the Atomic Scientists*, 29(7): 21–24, 45–50.

Gillette, R. 1972. "The Limits to Growth: Hard Sell for a Computer View of Doomsday." *Science*, 175:1088–1092.

Glacken, C. J. 1967. *Traces on the Rhodian Shore*. Berkeley: University of California Press.

Goldsmith, E., R. Allen, M. Allaby, J. Davoli, & S. Lawrence. 1972. "A

Blueprint for Survival." *The Ecologist*, 2(1): 1–43. (Commentary is found in the same journal: 3: 20–22; 4: 23–25; 5: 27–29; 7: 22–25.)

Golub, R., & J. Townsend. 1977. "Malthus, Multinationals, and the Club of Rome." *Social Studies of Science*, 7:201–222.

Graubard, S. R. (ed.). 1973. "The No-Growth Society." *Daedalus*, 102(4): 1–253.

Gregg, A. 1955. "A Medical Aspect of the Population Problem." *Science*, 121: 681–682.

Gunter, E. 1673. *Works*, 5th ed. London: AC.

Guyton, A. C. 1956. *Textbook of Medical Physiology*. Philadelphia: W. B. Saunders.

Hardin, G. 1959. *Nature and Man's Fate*. New York: Holt, Rinehart & Winston.

Hardin, G. 1963. "A Second Sermon on the Mount." *Perspectives in Biology and Medicine*, 6: 366–371.

Hardin, G. 1964. *Population, Evolution, and Birth Control*. San Francisco: W. H. Freeman.

Hardin, G. 1966. "Abortion and Human Dignity." *Per/Se*, 1: 16. (See also G. Hardin, 1973, *Stalking the Wild Taboo*. Los Altos, CA: W. Kaufmann.)

Hardin, G. 1968. "The Tragedy of the Commons." *Science*, 162: 1243–1248.

Hardin, G. 1972a. *Exploring New Ethics for Survival*. New York: Viking Press.

Hardin, G. 1972b. "Population Skeletons in the Environmental Closet." *Science and Public Affairs: Bulletin of the Atomic Scientists*, 28(6): 37–41.

Hauser, P. M., & O. D. Duncan. 1959. *The Study of Population*. Chicago: University of Chicago Press.

Hawkes, H. B. 1960. "The Paradoxes of the Conservation Movement." *Bulletin of the University of Utah*, 51: 11.

Hays, S. P. 1959. *Conservation and the Gospel of Efficiency*. Cambridge, MA: Harvard University Press.

Heilbroner, R. L. 1961. *The Worldly Philosophers*. New York: Simon & Schuster. (First published in 1953.)

Heilbroner, R. L. 1972. "Growth and Survival." *Foreign Affairs*, 51: 139–153.

Hibbard, B. H. 1924. *A History of the Public Land Policies*. New York: Macmillan.

Himes, N. E. 1970. *Medical History of Contraception*. New York: Schocken. (First published in 1936.)

Holmes, O. W. 1889. "The Deacon's Masterpiece: Or the Wonderful 'One-Hoss Shay.'" In *The Autocrat of the Breakfast-Table* (pp. 350–353). Boston: Houghton Mifflin. (First published in 1858.)

Housman, A. E. 1924. "Shropshire Lad." In *The Collected Poems of A. E. Housman* (p. 88). New York: Holt.

Hubbert, M. K. 1949. "Energy from Fossil Fuels." *Science*, 109: 103–109.

Hubbert, M. K. 1969. "Energy Resources." In Committee on Resources and Man (eds.), *Resources and Man* (pp. 157–242). San Francisco: W. H. Freeman.

Huntington, E. 1915. *Civilization and Climate.* New Haven, CT: Yale University Press.

Hutchinson, E. P. 1967. *The Population Debate.* Boston: Houghton Mifflin.

Huth, H. 1957. *Nature and the American: Three Centuries of Changing Attitudes.* Berkeley: University of California Press.

Huxley, A. 1932. *Brave New World.* Garden City, NY: Doubleday, Doran.

Jackim, B. 1974. "The Land Movers: Megalomachine Excavators." Unpublished manuscript, Berkeley, CA.

Jahoda, M. 1973. "Postscript on Social Change." In H. S. D. Cole, C. Freeman, M. Jahoda, & K. L. R. Pavitt (eds.), *Models of Doom: A Critique of the Limits to Growth* (pp. 209–215). New York: Universe Books.

Johnson, W. A., & J. Hardesty (eds.). 1971. *Economic Growth versus the Environment.* Belmont, CA: Wadsworth.

Jones, H. 1965. *John Muir and the Sierra Club.* San Francisco: Sierra Club.

Kahn, H., W. Brown, & L. Martel. 1976. *The Next Two Hundred Years.* New York: William Morrow.

Kaysen, C. 1972. "The Computer That Printed Out W*O*L*F." *Foreign Affairs,* 50: 660–668.

King, A. 1972. "The Totality of the World Problematique Must Now Be Addressed." *Center Report,* 5(4): 26–29.

King, J. 1959. *The Conservation Fight.* Washington, DC: Public Affairs Press.

King, P. B. 1959. *The Evolution of North America.* Princeton: Princeton University Press.

Kneese, A., & R. Ridker. 1972. "Predicament of Mankind." *Washington Post,* March 2, pp. 81–89.

Knowlton, C. 1833. *Fruits of Philosophy, or the Private Companion of Young Married People.* Boston: Publisher not available.

Kuhn, T. S. 1970. *The Structure of Scientific Revolutions.* 2nd ed. Chicago: University of Chicago Press.

Landsberg, H. H. 1964. *Natural Resources for U.S. Growth.* Baltimore: Johns Hopkins University Press.

Landsberg, H. H., L. L. Fischman, & J. L. Fisher. 1963. *Resources in America's Future.* Baltimore: Johns Hopkins University Press.

Langbein, W. B. 1959. "Water Yield and Reservoir Storage in United States." *U.S. Geological Survey Circular 409.*

Lawrence, T. E. 1935. *The Seven Pillars of Wisdom.* London: Jonathan Cape.

Leopold, A. 1966. *A Sand County Almanac.* 2nd ed. New York: Oxford University Press.

Leopold, L. B. 1959. "Probability Analysis Applied to Water-Supply Problem." *U.S. Geological Survey Circular 410.*

Lotka, A. J. 1925. *Elements of Physical Biology.* Baltimore: Williams & Wilkins.

Lovering, T. S. 1969. "Mineral Resources from the Land." In Committee on Resources and Man (eds.), *Resources and Man* (pp. 109–134). San Francisco: W. H. Freeman.

Luten, D. B. 1961. "Metropolis in Flood." In *Proceedings of the Twelfth Annual Conference, California Society of the American Institute of Park Executives.*

Luten, D. B. 1963. "How Dense Can People Be?" *Sierra Club Bulletin,* 48(9): 80–93.

Luten, D. B. 1964a. "Numbers Against Wilderness." *Sierra Club Bulletin,* 49(9): 43–48.

Luten, D. B. 1964b. "On Chemistry and Taxonomy—Both Biological and Chemical." *Lloydia,* 27: 135–137.

Luten, D. B. 1971. "Population Growth." In M. Brown (ed.), *The Social Responsibility of the Scientist* (pp. 184–197). New York: Free Press.

Macinko, G. 1968. "Conservation Trends and the Future American Environment." *The Biologist,* 50(1–2): 1–19.

Macinko, G. 1974. "World System Models: A Critical Commentary on their Assessment." Paper presented at meeting of the Commission on Quantitative Methods, International Geographic Union, Palmerston North, New Zealand, December 4–7.

MacIntyre, F. 1970. Discussion. In M. E. McCloskey (ed.), *Wilderness, the Edge of Knowledge: Proceedings of the Eleventh Biennial Wilderness Conference* (pp. 250–254). San Francisco: Sierra Club.

Maddox, J. 1972. *The Doomsday Syndrome.* New York: McGraw-Hill.

Malthus, T. R. 1926. *An Essay on the Principle of Population.* London: Macmillan. (First published in 1798.)

Malthus, T. R. 1960. "A Summary View of Population." In F. Notestein (ed.), *On Population: Three Essays* (pp. 13–59). New York: Mentor Books. (First published in 1830.)

Marsh, G. P. 1964. *Man and Nature; or, Physical Geography as Modified by Human Action* (with editorial comments and introduction by D. Lowenthal). Cambridge, MA: Harvard University Press. (First published in 1864.)

Marshall, T. H., A. M. Carr-Saunders, H. D. Henderson, R. R. Kuczynski, & A. Plant. 1938. *The Population Problem.* London: George Allen & Unwin.

Marx, L. 1964. *The Machine in the Garden.* New York: Oxford University Press.

Mason, P. 1971. "Some Geographical Considerations of Siting Nuclear Power Reactors Along the California Coast." *The California Geographer,* 12: 21–29.

Mather, K. 1944. *Enough and to Spare.* New York: Harper & Brothers.

McConnell, G. 1954. "The Conservation Movement—Past and Present." *Western Political Quarterly*, 7: 463–478.

McElyea, J. R., & J. W. Cone. 1960. *Potential Uses of Watershed Lands of the East Bay Municipal Utility District.* Menlo Park, CA: Stanford Research Institute.

Meadows, D. H., D. L. Meadows, J. Randers, & W. Behrens III. 1972. *The Limits to Growth.* New York: Universe Books.

Meadows, D. H., D. L. Meadows, J. Randers, & W. Behrens III. 1973. "Response to Sussex." In H. S. D. Cole, C. Freeman, M. Jahoda, & K. L. R. Pavitt (eds.), *Models of Doom: A Critique of the Limits to Growth* (pp. 209–240). New York: Universe Books.

Mishan, E. T. 1967. *The Costs of Economic Growth.* New York: Praeger.

Mumford, L. 1962. "The Human Prospect." In *The Role of the Region* (pp. 29–39). Davis: University of California (An Institute on Planning for the North Central Valley).

Nash, R. 1967. *Wilderness and the American Mind.* New Haven, CT: Yale University Press.

National Academy of Sciences, Committee on Mineral Resources and the Environment. 1975. *Mineral Resources and the Environment.* Washington, DC: National Academy of Sciences.

National Agricultural Land Study. 1980. "Where Have the Farmlands Gone?" (brochure). Washington, DC: National Agricultural Land Study.

Notestein, F. 1960. "Introduction." In F. Notestein (ed.), *On Population: Three Essays* (pp. vii–x). New York: Mentor Books.

Ophuls, W. 1973. *Prologue to a Political Theory of the Steady State: An Investigation of the Political and Philosophical Implications of the Environmental Crisis.* Ph.D. dissertation, Yale University. Available from University Microfilms, Ann Arbor.

Ophuls, W. 1977. *Ecology and the Politics of Scarcity.* San Francisco: W. H. Freeman.

Ophuls, W., & C. Wilson. 1972. "Understanding Growth." *Science*, 176: 1287.

Osborn, F. 1948. *Our Plundered Planet.* Boston: Little, Brown.

Osborn, F. 1953. *The Limits of the Earth.* Boston: Little, Brown.

Paddock, W., & P. Paddock. 1967. *Famine, 1975.* Boston: Little, Brown.

Passell, P., M. Roberts, & L. Ross. 1972. "The Limits to Growth, World Dynamics, and Urban Dynamics." *New York Times Book Review*, April 2, pp. 1, 10–13.

Pearl, R. 1925. *The Biology of Population Growth.* New York: Knopf.

Petersen, W. 1961. *Population.* New York: Macmillan.

Platt, R. S. 1948. "Determinism in Geography." *Annals of the Association of American Geographers*, 38: 126–132.

Porter, E. 1963. *Glen Canyon: The Place No One Knew.* San Francisco: Sierra Club.

Porter, S. 1970. "The Race against Stolen Cars." *San Francisco Chronicle*, February 6.

Potter, V. R. 1971. *Bioethics.* Englewood Cliffs, NJ: Prentice-Hall.

President's Materials Policy Commission. 1952. *Resources for Freedom.* 5 volumes. Washington, DC: U.S. Government Printing Office.

Putnam, P. C. 1953. *Energy in the Future.* New York: Van Nostrand.

Rooney, A. 1983. "This Is the Way the World Ends." *San Francisco Examiner and Chronicle,* March 27.

Roper, L. W. 1952. "A Preliminary Report (1865) by Frederick Law Olmsted on the Yosemite Valley and the Mariposa Big Trees." *Landscape Architecture,* 43: 12–25.

Ross, E. A. 1927. *Standing Room Only?* New York: Century.

Rostlund, E. 1956. "Twentieth Century Magic." *Landscape,* 5(3): 23–26.

Sagan, C., & F. Drake. 1975. "The Search for Extraterrestrial Intelligence." *Scientific American,* 232(5): 80–89.

Sandbach, F. 1978. "The Rise and Fall of the Limits to Growth Debate." *Social Studies of Science,* 8: 495–520.

Sax, K. 1955. *Standing Room Only.* Boston: Beacon Press.

Seebohn, F. 1914. *Customary Acres.* London: Longmans, Green.

Seton, E. T. 1923. *The Arctic Prairies.* New York: Charles Scribner's Sons.

Shakespeare, W. 1969. *Macbeth.* In A. Harbage (ed.), *William Shakespeare: The Complete Works* (pp. 1110–1140). Baltimore: Pelican Books. (First published in 1623.)

Shaler, N. 1895. *Domesticated Animals.* New York: Charles Scribner's Sons.

Shaler, N. 1905. *Man and the Earth.* New York: Duffield.

Slovic, P., B. Fischhoff, & S. Lichtenstein. 1979. "Rating the Risks." *Environment,* 21(3): 14–20; 36–39.

Steffenson, D. (ed.). 1973. "Ethics for Environment: Three Religious Strategies." *Proceedings of a National Conference on Ethics and the Environment.* Green Bay: University of Wisconsin, Green Bay.

Stone, C. 1974. *Should Trees Have Standing?* Los Altos, CA: W. Kaufmann.

Stone, M. 1949. *Japanese Economic Statistics.* Bulletin 34, Section III, June, pp. 2–42.

Summers, C. 1971. "The Conversion of Energy." *Scientific American,* 224(3): 149–160.

Thompson, W., & P. K. Whelpton. 1969. *Population Trends in the United States.* New York: Gordon & Breach Science Publishers.

Thomson, J. 1895. *City of Dreadful Night and Other Poems,* Vol. 1. London: Reeves & Turner.

Thoreau, H. D. 1964. *Walden.* In C. Bode (ed.), *The Portable Thoreau,* rev. ed. (pp. 258–572). New York: Viking Press. (First published in 1854.)

U.S. Bureau of the Census. 1977. *U.S. Census of Agriculture, 1974: State and County Data.* 50 vols. Washington, DC: U.S. Government Printing Office.

U.S. Bureau of the Census. 1978a. "Residential Energy Uses" (pamphlet). Washington, DC: U.S. Government Printing Office.

U.S. Bureau of the Census. 1978b. *Statistical Abstract of the United States.* Washington, DC: U.S. Government Printing Office.

U.S. Bureau of the Census. 1979. *Statistical Abstract of the United States.* Washington, DC: U.S. Government Printing Office.

U.S. Department of Agriculture. 1979. *Agricultural Statistics.* Washington, DC: U.S. Government Printing Office.

U.S. Department of Commerce. 1960. *Historical Statistics of the United States.* Washington, DC: U.S. Government Printing Office.

Vale, T. R. 1979. "Use of Public Rangelands in the American West." *Environmental Conservation,* 6: 53–62.

Vogt, W. 1948. *Road to Survival.* New York: William Sloane Associates.

von Foerster, H., P. M. Mora, & L. W. Amiot. 1960. "Doomsday: Friday, 13 November, A.D. 2026." *Science,* 132: 1291.

Waddington, C. H. 1960. *The Ethical Animal.* London: G. Allen & Unwin.

White, L. 1967. "The Historical Roots of Our Ecologic Crisis." *Science,* 155: 1203–1207.

Wilson, E. O. 1975. *Sociobiology.* Cambridge, MA: Harvard University Press.

Wolf, A. 1947. "Ethics." *Encyclopedia Britannica,* 14th ed., Vol. 8, pp. 757–761.

Wood, R. W. 1907. *How to Tell the Birds from the Flowers.* San Francisco: P. Elder & Co.

Woytinsky, W. S., & E. S. Woytinsky. 1953. *World Population and Production.* New York: Twentieth Century Fund.

Wynne-Edwards, V. C. 1962. *Animal Dispersion in Relation to Social Behavior.* New York: Hafner.

Wynne-Edwards, V. C. 1965. "Self-Regulating Systems in Populations of Animals." *Science,* 147: 1543–1548.

Zelinsky, W. 1967. "Future Environments of North America" (book review). *Landscape,* 17(2): 38–39.

Zimmerman, E. W. 1951. *World Resources and Industries.* 2nd ed., rev. New York: Harper & Brothers.

INDEX

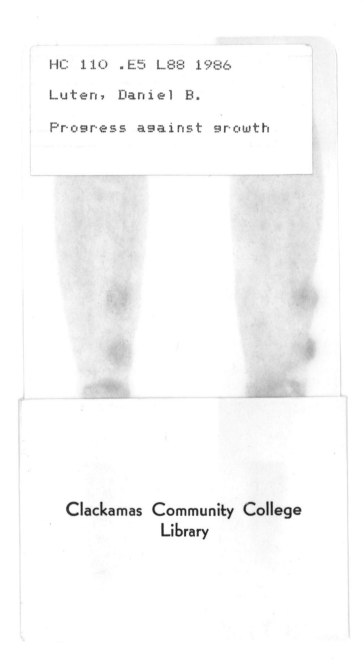